Y0-CHN-819

MINORITY RIGHTS PROTECTION IN INTERNATIONAL LAW

Research in Migration and Ethnic Relations Series

Series Editor:
Maykel Verkuyten, ERCOMER
Utrecht University

The Research in Migration and Ethnic Relations series has been at the forefront of research in the field for ten years. The series has built an international reputation for cutting edge theoretical work, for comparative research especially on Europe and for nationally-based studies with broader relevance to international issues. Published in association with the European Research Centre on Migration and Ethnic Relations (ERCOMER), Utrecht University, it draws contributions from the best international scholars in the field, offering an interdisciplinary perspective on some of the key issues of the contemporary world.

Other titles in the series

Immigrant Women and Feminism in Italy
Wendy Pojmann
ISBN 978-0-7546-4674-7

Cities and Labour Immigration
Comparing Policy Responses in Amsterdam, Paris, Rome and Tel Aviv
Michael Alexander
ISBN 978-0-7546-4722-5

Diversity Management and Discrimination
Immigrants and Ethnic Minorities in the EU
John Wrench
ISBN 978-0-7546-4890-1

**EUROPEAN RESEARCH CENTRE
ON MIGRATION & ETHNIC RELATIONS**

Minority Rights Protection in International Law
The Roma of Europe

HELEN O'NIONS
University of Lincoln, UK

ASHGATE

Published by
Ashgate Publishing Limited
Gower House
Croft Road
Aldershot
Hampshire GU11 3HR
England

Ashgate Publishing Company
Suite 420
101 Cherry Street
Burlington, VT 05401-4405
USA

Ashgate website: http://www.ashgate.com

British Library Cataloguing in Publication Data
O'Nions, Helen
  Minority rights protection in international law : the Roma
  of Europe. - (Research in migration and ethnic relations
  series)
  1. Romanies - Civil rights - Europe 2. Romanies - Legal
  status, laws, etc. - Europe 3. Europe - Ethnic relations
  I. Title
  305.8'91497'04

Library of Congress Cataloging-in-Publication Data
O'Nions, Helen, 1971-
  Minority rights protection in international law : the Roma of Europe / by Helen
O'Nions.
      p. cm. -- (Research in migration and ethnic relations series)
  Includes bibliographical references and index.
  ISBN 978-0-7546-0921-6
  1. Romanies--Civil rights--Europe, Eastern. 2. Romanies--Legal status, laws, etc.--
Europe, Eastern. 3. Europe, Eastern--Ethnic relations. 4. Romanies--Civil rights--
European Union countries. 5. Romanies--Legal status, laws, etc.--European Union
countries. 6. European Union countries--Ethnic relations. I. Title.

  DX210.O55 2007
  323.1191'49704--dc22

ISBN-13: 978-0-7546-0921-6

2007002017

Printed and bound in Great Britain by Antony Rowe Ltd, Chippenham, Wiltshire.

Contents

Acknowledgements

This book represents the culmination of 12 years of research on human rights law and the Roma in Europe. I owe particular gratitude to my mentor, Professor Fiona Cownie, who has provided critical insights, advice and encouragement throughout my research. Without Fiona's continued support and faith it is doubtful this book would have been completed. I hope it does not disappoint.

I am also grateful to those who have taken time in their busy schedules to read and criticise various chapters – notably Philip Leach of London Metropolitan University, Professor Bill Bowring of Birkbeck College, London and Ceri Baldwin.

Over the years, there are a number of individuals who have inspired and encouraged me. This list is not exhaustive but thanks are due to Colin Clark, Luke Clements, Hester Hedges, Will Guy, Rachel Morris and Phil Thomas. Particular thanks are due to Professor Thomas Acton who, during a meeting at the University of Greenwich in 1995, impressed me with his intellect and his determination to make a difference.

Finally, I need to thank Darren for his humour and love, and my parents for everything.

For Luca – although you certainly would prefer a funnier book

Chapter 1

The Treatment of Roma in Europe:
A 'Litmus Test for Civil Society'[1]

Introduction

While the statement above is concerned predominately with the former Communist states of Europe, it also reflects the difficulties in accommodating this diverse diaspora of people within the new European order that prides itself on showing respect for human rights and democratic values in a secular, individualist paradigm. As a result of the entrenched social, economic and political exclusion, Anna Meijknecht describes the Roma as a people without a future.[2] Prejudice is exhibited by the non-Roma (Gadjo[3]) citizens, media, government officials and law enforcers alike. The Roma activist, Rudko Kawczynski, makes reference to President Havel's statement in these terms:

> We Roma have in the last few years become the measure for the newly created democracies in Europe: so long as those countries are not ready to let go of their anti-Roma policies, they are as far from democratic development as they ever were under their communist regimes. So long as in those countries human rights violations against Roma are a normal occurrence, the resistance to their policies will remain a duty. Without respect for Roma, there can be no democracy in those countries and certainly no open society.[4]

The problem of anti-Roma prejudice and discrimination while more acutely felt in Central and Eastern Europe, is by no means confined to this region. Indeed, recent inflammatory reports in the British press demonstrate the deep-seated hostility towards Gypsies, particularly those who continue to adopt a nomadic way of life in the face of great adversity. A MORI poll examining patterns of prejudice found that dislike of Gypsies was more common than for any other ethnic group.[5] A survey of 1521 eight

---

1   *New York Times* 'Havel calls Gypsies "Litmus test"' 10 December 1993 pA11. See also Nieuwsma, Greg 'A depressing decade: Czech-Roma relations after the Velvet Revolution' (1999) *Central Europe Online* Vol 1, 18; Fawn, Rick 'Czech Attitudes towards the Roma: "Expecting More of Havel's Country"?' (2001) *Europe-Asia Studies*, Vol. 53, 8, pp 1,193–1,219.

2   Meijknecht, Anna *Minority Protection. Standards and Reality* (2004) TMC Asser Press at 67.

3   Gadjo (Gadje – plural) is the word used by the Roma to describe those not of Romani ancestry and will be used hereafter in this book for the same purpose.

4   Kawczynski, Rudko 'The politics of Romani politics' *Transitions* (1997) Vol. 4, No. 4 September.

5   Thirty-five per cent of the respondents admitted to disliking Gypsies (interestingly this was roughly the same proportion of people expressing a dislike for the other great Outsider

and nine-year-old Italian children found that of the 60% who expressed fear of crossing open spaces, 32% attributed that to 'Gypsies, drug addicts and Moroccans'.[6]

Recent estimates place the Romany/Gypsy population of Europe at around ten million people, making them Europe's largest minority group.[7] Due to their comparatively high birth rate the proportion of Roma in Europe is likely to increase.[8] These figures are only estimates and the difficulties of collecting reliable data are immense: particular factors include a reluctance to admit to Roma identity, the disparate nature of Roma communities, fears of discrimination and ghettoisation and the absence of reliable census data in some countries.[9] The result is that reliable statistics on the number of Rom and other travelling peoples in Europe are notoriously illusive. In the 1991 Czechoslovak census only 80,000 Slovak people declared themselves to be of Roma origin, the true figure being estimated at 500,000.[10] Kertzer and Arel have noted that while census data is seldom reliable it does play a key role in the construction of reality, reflecting minority-majority relations and providing a context for policy.[11] In a country with a population of over one million Roma, former President Ceausescu was able to comment: 'Don't talk to me about Gypsies, there are no Gypsies in Romania'[12] What is clear is that most Roma are living in conditions of poverty and deprivation in some of the richest countries in the world. Ironically, these are countries with multi-ethnic societies that have embraced the principles of democracy and the fundamental importance of human rights for all.

This book aims to examine this level of exclusion in the light of the principal human rights standards and their implementation. Considering TH Marshall's three concepts of modern citizenship and applying it to three specific situations it becomes apparent that the Roma are denied active 'citizenship' at all levels.[13] Marshall's civil dimension focuses on individual freedoms, which are examined in the context of

– the asylum seeker) MORI poll commissioned by Stonewall 'Citizenship 21: Briefing Notes on Profiles of Prejudice' (2001) Available at: http://www.mori.com/polls/2001/stonewall-b2.shtml.

6   Survey by Instituto Recerche Economico-Sociali del Piemonti as cited in European Roma Rights Centre Campland. *Racial Segregation in Italy* March (2000) ERRC.

7   European Commission, Employment and Social Affairs *The situation of Roma in and Enlarged European Union* (2004).

8   Kawczynski, R suggests 12 million in 'Europe's Roma demand Recognition as a Minority' 19 November (1998) *Agence France Presse*.

9   Council of Europe Roundtable 'Roma and Statistics' MG-S-ROM (2000) 13. UN Development Program Avoiding the Dependency Trap Bratislava (2002) pp 24–25.

10   Radio Prague 'Ever less citizens consider themselves members of a Roma community' 5 July 2001 found that only 11,716 Roma identified themselves as such in the 2001 Czech census (less than 5% of the actual Romani population).

11   Kertzer, David and Arel, Dominique *Census and Identity. The politics of race, ethnicity and language in national censuses* (2002) Cambridge Univ. Press.

12   Tanja, Jaap 'More than a million Gypsies in Romania' (1990) *O'Drom* p14-16 at 15. The same article notes that estimates as to the number of Roma in Romania vary from 650,000 to over two million, at 14.

13   Marshall, T.H. and Bottomore, Tom *Citizenship and Social Class* (1992) Pluto Press. Malloy, Tove notes that modern citizenship is now considerably more complicated than Marshalls's original analysis in *National Minorities in Europe* (2005) OUP at 45.

the Czech Republic in Chapter 4. The social dimension is examined in Chapter 5 looking at education policies across Europe and the political dimension of public participation and representation is examined in Chapter 7 with reference to the Hungarian self-government experiment.

The individualistic focus of these standards will be shown as limited in addressing the level of exclusion. An alternative focus recognising group rights of the Roma as a 'national' or 'ethnic' minority will be critically addressed, as will demands for recognition as a transnational minority group.

Following on from increased international awareness at the plight of the Roma, in 2005 the governments of eight CEE countries launched the 'Decade for Roma Inclusion', a 10-year initiative to redress some of these deep-seated problems.[14] This development is to be welcomed and it is sincerely hoped that pilot projects will be established, monitored and, where desirable, expanded to real effect. An essential part of the decade is the Roma Education Fund which will provide additional funding for positive education programmes.[15]

However, this will not mark the end of marginalisation, exclusion and discrimination. As will become very apparent, international and national policies are one aspect of a complex interaction of relationships. All too often initiatives are not pursued at a local level and a concerted, high-profile effort is needed to demonstrate that discrimination against the Roma is neither legitimate nor tolerable in a democratic, civil society.

Origins of Roma in Europe: What's in a name?

The Roma are one of the oldest surviving minorities in Europe. Linguists[16] have demonstrated that the Rom descended from North Indian castes that left to migrate across Europe between 500 and AD 1000.[17] The migration across Europe saw their arrival in small groups in Turkey in the eleventh century and by the fifteenth century in Sweden, Germany and Belgium. The first record of their arrival in England is dated 1514, with further movements into Scandinavia in the sixteenth century.[18]

The name 'Gypsy' is derived from the term 'Egyptian'.[19] When Gypsies began to arrive in England from Egypt they were identified as different by the colour of

---

14   'Overcoming Exclusion: The Roma decade' 29 August 2005, *Journal of the Open Society Institute.* eumap.org.

15   'Roma Education Fund; a Concept note' in *Roma in an Expanding Europe*: *Challenges for the Future* World Bank and SOROS Foundation Conference, Budapest July 2003.

16   For discussion see Kenrick, D *Gypsies: From India to the Mediterranean* (1994) Gypsy Research Centre-CRDP Midi-Pyrenees Interface Collection Toulouse.

17   Fraser, Angus *The Gypsies* (1992) Blackwell: Oxford, Chapter 1; Brearley, Margaret (1996) 'The Roma/Gypsies of Europe: A persecuted people' *Jewish Policy Research Paper No 3* December 1996, p5.

18   Liégeois and Gheorghe *Roma/Gypsies: a European Minority* (1995) Minority Rights Group, London at 7.

19   Fraser *supra* n17 at 46–8.

their skin and dress and these were attributed to their Egyptian origins. The term 'Gypsy' and associated labels such as 'Cygani' and the Spanish 'Gitano' can thus be seen as inaccurate and pejorative descriptions.[20] The term 'Rom' or 'Roma' (in the plural) is generally preferred,[21] although in British travelling communities 'Gypsy' and 'traveller' is still the most common form of self-identification.

The European Roma are today a heterogeneous community with many different cultural values as well as linguistic and religious diversity.[22] Nevertheless, the common ancestry of the Rom can be used to provide evidence of an underlying core of values and traditions, some of which have since been eroded or altered on account of the need to adapt to the conditions of the host state. Europe's High Commissioner on National Minorities noted:

> ... there are significant commonalities perceived as binding the Roma together: commonalities in origin, language, culture, historical experience and present-day problems in the region. In addition to a Romani cultural heritage, including a strongly itinerant tradition that is both the cause and effect of their history, the Roma also share the use (or remembrance) of a common, though highly variant language, also known as Romani or Romanes.[23]

Furthermore, as Bancroft notes, there is one experience common to almost all Roma and travellers in Europe, namely the degree of discrimination and hostility they face from the rest of society.[24] This is possibly the biggest factor in the identification of Roma as a 'transnational minority'.

Finding an appropriate terminology

Overshadowing much of the debate about the rights of Roma and travelling people is the issue of appropriate terminology. If one is to consider extending human rights protection to those designated Roma or *travellers* as a minority, a suitable label must be identified. However, it is difficult to find a label which neither depends on the exclusion of certain sub-units nor encompasses a variety of geographically dispersed groups with no common ancestry or traditions. Even amongst English Gypsies, as Thomas Acton has shown, there is considerable ethnic diversity attributed to different historical experiences.[25]

---

20   See the discussion in Guy, Will *Between Past and Future. The Roma of Central and Eastern Europe* (2001) Univ. of Hertfordshire Press at 19.

21   The First World Romani Congress of 1971 rejected the terms 'Tsiganes', 'Zigeuner', 'Gitano', 'Gypsies', opting for the preferred term 'Rom': Liégeois, J.P *Roma, Gypsies, Travellers* (1994) C/E: Strasbourg, p258.

22   Fraser *supra* n17; Pogány, István 'Minority rights and the Roma of Central and Eastern Europe' (2006) 6 *Hum Rts L Rev*.1 p 1 pp 17–18.

23   Report of the High Commissioner on National Minorities *Roma* (Gypsies) *in the CSCE Region* CSCE (1993) at 3.

24   Bancroft, A *Roma and Gypsy Travellers in Europe* (2005) Ashgate at 47.

25   Acton, Thomas *Gypsy Politics and Social* Change 1974 Routledge, Kegan and Paul: London p 18.

The ideal situation would be of course to ask each individual whether they would prefer the label Gypsy/Rom/traveller or 'traditional traveller' and this would be likely to yield every combination of response. Each of the terms may be seen as problematic for different reasons and the absence of a core group in a geographically defined territory means that such responses will vary depending on the particular host state. Furthermore, the practice of nomadism, by which many Gadje characterise the Gypsies of England, is no longer a characteristic of Roma in other European states.[26]

Beverly Nagel Lauwagie has examined the ethnic classifications of travelling peoples and was able to identify several main groups with different historical origins.[27] Yet her examination of the circumstances of the groups in question reveals striking similarities:

> All are engaged in occupations which are irregular and unpredictable and often marginal to the economy in which they reside. In all cases there is a strong sense of territoriality. All the groups, including the non-Rom, have their own language or dialect different from that of the host society. All are organised into a larger extended family of lineage group, with smaller groups acting as economic units. All groups seem to be extraordinarily prolific …. Most important, in each case a distinct ethnic boundary is maintained. The major difference between the groups appears to be in the extent to which they observe cleanliness rituals and taboos.[28]

Ideologies of assimilation demand categorisations which enable the exclusion of those defined as undeserving 'Outsiders'. Acton notes that the 'true-Gypsy' stereotype provides a useful avenue for discrimination by officials which can be directed at social deviants rather than members of a racial group.[29] Similarly, Liégeois observes that when the goal is assimilation, Gypsies are stripped of racial or ethnic identity and become defined as 'persons of nomadic origin':

---

26   See for example, Chapter 5 on the experiences of the Czech Roma. Liégeois, J.P. *Gypsies. An Illustrated History* (1986) Al Saqi, London at 50–57 notes that 'Not all Gypsies are nomads, and not all nomads are Gypsies'. However, he goes on to stress that nomadism is still an important factor underscoring the identity of the 'Gypsy': 'Nomadism is a state of mind more than a state of fact. Its existence and importance are pyschological more than geographical'. Liégeois could be accused himself of romanticism in this respect, but it is apparent that many aspects of the culture still found in sedentary Romani and Gypsy communities indicate the pyschological significance of movement. The recent migrations to Canada and the West of apparently sedentarised Roma from the Czech and Slovak Republics give credence to this argument.

27   Lauwagie, Beverly Nagel 'Ethnic boundaries in modern states: *Romano Lavo-lil* Revisited' (1979) *AJS* Vol. 85, 2, pp 310–337 at p318 the author notes that the major groups which condiser themselves as Rom are Kalderash, the Lowara, the Tshurara and the Macvaya. Under the heading 'Gypsies and travellers' she places a number of closely related groups such as the Yenische in Germany and the Scottish travellers as well as the Irish travellers.

28   *Ibid.* at 331.

29   Acton, T. 'The social construction of the ethnic identity of commercial nomadic groups' in Grumet, J. (ed) *Papers from the 4th and 5th Annual Meetings of the Gypsy Lore Society National Annual Conference* (1985) pp 1–20 Gypsy Lore Society, Maryland at 5.

These Gypsies – now deprived, by this description, of roots and identity – then represent a 'social problem' of 're-adaptation' that must be solved in order to absorb them into the rest of society .... Gypsies are not defined as they really are, but as socio-political requirements say they have to be.[30]

The pressures of assimilation and integration have been remarkably unsuccessful in destroying the identity of the Roma and other travellers in almost every country. Yet cultural distinctions have emerged between members of different groups and between different borders. In Eastern Europe the term Rom is clearly preferred to the term 'Gypsy' which is regarded as pejorative.[31] Many British Gypsies prefer to use the description 'traditional travellers' to distinguish themselves from newer groups of travellers and Irish travellers. It should also be noted that the protection of the Race Relations Act 1976 will only apply to Irish travellers[32] or those identified as Gypsies.[33]

As this book adopts a European perspective on the treatment of travelling people, it is appropriate to adopt the term which is commonly used in Europe, while noting that it may still include those who do not identify specifically with this term but share similar cultural values. Thus, the label Roma will generally be used when referring to the group across Europe, to include those commonly classified as Gypsies and traditional travellers.[34] It is noted by Liégeois that this corresponds to the socio-cultural reality and political will of the groups in Central and Eastern Europe which amount to 70% of those identified as Gypsies in Europe.[35]

Acton prefers to describe the English Gypsies as a continuity of culture rather than a community of culture. Furthermore, he argues that myths of racial purity are as much a fiction for the Gypsies as they are with any other people of the world.[36] There are plenty of sociologists, anthropologists and linguists who may be able to provide interesting insights on this topic.[37] For the purpose of this work however, I am keen to include those people commonly considered, and considering themselves to be, of Gypsy or Romani origin.

A history of prejudice

The adaptation of the Roma and the survival of much of their cultural identity can be regarded as an amazing feat given the climate of prejudice in which they often live.[38] In

---

30   Liégeois *supra* n26 at 139.
31   See Hancock, I. *The Pariah Syndrome* (1987) Ann Arbor, Michigan.
32   *O'Leary* vs. *Allied Domecq* 29/8/2000 CL 950275.
33   *CRE* vs. *Dutton* [1989] QB 7 [1989] 1 ALL ER 306.
34   When referring to Roma in spepcific regions where the term is not well-used I shall use the more accepted term.
35   Liégeois (1994) *supra* n21.
36   Acton, T (1974) *supra* n25 at 19.
37   See for example the contrasting approaches of Acton *supra* n25 and Okely *The Traveller-Gypsies* (1983) Cambridge University Press *passim*.
38   For example, Hawes and Perez comment that Gypsies 'Accommodate each new threat be it extermination or assimilation, with a degree of equanimity to be envied,' in *The Gypsy and the State* SAUS, Bristol (1995) at 126.

the introduction to his historical account, Angus Fraser reflects: 'When one considers the vicissitudes they have encountered – one has to conclude that their main achievement is to have survived at all'.[39]

Such adaptation has inevitably led to the diversification that we see today and the inability of traditional constructs of 'minority' and 'community' to accurately describe the current situation of the group. Nomadism provides the clearest example of this diversity. In Britain the Gypsy community is often described as a mobile group, moving for economic and social reasons to find new work and make contact with other family members.[40] For centuries legislation has sought to eradicate this aspect of their culture as it is seen to pose a direct challenge to the glue that holds the sedentary society together, namely home ownership and wage labour. The Caravan Sites Act introduced in the UK in 1968 sought to provide authorised campsites for Gypsies and in so doing created a partly sedentarised community. Subsequent legislation, the Criminal Justice and Public Order Act 1994, added to the pressure to settle, imposing criminal penalties on those travelling people who occupy unauthorised encampments.[41] Nevertheless, a substantial number of travelling families do continue to exist,[42] albeit on the edge of society, dodging the sanctions of the criminal law. Events such as the Stow and Appleby fares still command impressive turnouts. Similarly in France the Sarkozy law criminalises illegal camping, while only one in four municipalities has complied with their statutory duty to provide a stopping place.[43] The Council of Europe has issued two recommendations in recent years which guarantee the right of encampment for travellers and the right to pursue a nomadic or sedentary lifestyle.[44] Member states have an obligation to create the conditions necessary for these rights to be exercised.[45]

In Eastern and Central Europe the situation is very different. Largely, as a result of economic coercion and the Communist industrial drives, the overwhelming majority of the Roma now live on the fringes of the cities and towns, usually in concentrated groups. Pogany notes that the condition of the Roma has worsened dramatically since the collapse of Communism where a right to work was enshrined in the political ethos:

---

39 Fraser *supra* n17 at p1.

40 Okely, J (1993) *supra* n37 Chapter 8.

41 s77 Criminal Justice and Public Order Act (1994).

42 In 1994 when the Criminal Justice and Public Order Act (1994) was introduced, 32% of Gypsies did not have an authorised caravan site (D/E *Count of Gypsy* Caravans 1994). In July 2004 the number of Gypsy caravans counted by the Office of the Deputy Prime Minister was 15,009 which represented a slight, steady increase over the previous two years. The number in unauthorised encampments remains at around one-third: ODPM 'Gypsy and traveller site data and statistics' 2004 Office of Deputy Prime Minister, HMSO.

43 Canal Plus Documentary 'Genes du voyage: la repression et l'absurde' aired 10 May 2004. The statutory duty is found in Law 2000-614 of 5 July 2000.

44 C/E Committee of Ministers Recommendation (2005) 4 on Improving the Housing Conditions of Roma and Travellers in Europe and Rec (2004) 14 on the Movement and Encampment of Travellers in Europe

45 Rec (2005) 4 para 3.

Since 1990, in the transition from command to market economies, Roma poverty and social exclusion have worsened dramatically, swiftly reversing the painstaking socio-economic gains experienced by most Gypsies during the socialist era.[46]

Their housing conditions are generally extremely poor and the implementation of a free market economy has enabled employers to reject Roma applicants on nebulous grounds, creating a high level of unemployment and poverty reinforced by a climate of discrimination and hostility.[47]

The situation of the Roma in Europe today

Josephine Verspaget, a Rapporteur for the Council of Europe, highlighted the position of disadvantage common to most Roma:

> The position of many groups of Gypsies can be compared to the situation in the third world: little education, bad housing, bad hygienic situation, high birth rate, high infant mortality, no knowledge or means to improve the situation, low life expectancy .... If nothing is done, the situation for most Gypsies will only worsen in the next generation.[48]

In 1994, the Organisation for Security and Co-operation in Europe (hereafter OSCE) and the Council of Europe held the first international seminar on the situation of the Roma in Europe. In his opening speech, the Deputy Secretary of the Council of Europe noted several factors which gave rise to the current level of concern. He described a community of people who were victims of economic insecurity; who often found themselves to be stateless because of the division of certain multi-national states; and who were victims of institutionalised prejudice and widespread intolerance. Furthermore, in the former Yugoslavia, as under the Nazi regime in the Second World War, he noted that the Roma were victims of ethnic cleansing policies, their lack of territory making their negotiating position in the peace talks that followed untenable.[49]

Despite the increasing international awareness over the past decade, there has little tangible difference in this situation. The plight of the Roma in the former Yugoslavia and Kosovo remains particularly dire.[50] The former Yugoslavia had one

---

46   Pogany, I. 'Refashioning rights in Central and Eastern Europe' (2004) *EPL* Vol 10, 1 at 87. See also Barany, Z. *The East European Gypsies* (2002) Cambridge University Press.

47   United Nations Development Programme found that unemployment averaged 40% in the five CEE countries surveyed. Report *Avoiding the Dependency Trap* (2003) UNDP, Bratislava.

48   Parliamentary Assembly of the Council of Europe Report on Gypsies in Europe 11 January 1993 Doc 6733 at para. 29.

49   Peter Leuprecht in CSCE *Human Dimension Seminar on Roma in the CSCE Region* (1994) CSCE.

50   European Roma Rights Centre Notebook 'Expelled Roma in Former Yugoslavia Testify' in *Roma Rights Quarterly*; Minorities at Risk *Assessment on Roma in Croatia* Dec 31st 2003 University of Maryland; European Roma Rights Centre *A pleasant fiction: the Human rights situation of Roma in Macedonia* July 1998 ERRC.

of the largest Roma communities in Europe, numbering 850,000 in 1981. They had been formally recognised as a minority under the Yugoslav Constitution of 1974.[51] However, a significant non-territorial minority does not fit neatly into any of the new states created by the Dayton Peace Accord and consequently they are subjected to violence and discrimination as 'outsiders' wherever they live. In Kosovo they are regarded by many as Serb collaborators and have been subjected to violence and forced from their homes by ethnic Albanians.[52] Yet, despite the extent of documentary evidence, the issue is largely invisible to the international media.

The expansion of the EU into Eastern and Central Europe has led to increased political recognition of the problems experienced by Roma across Europe. In the wake of two Directives on Racial Equality and Employment Equality the European Commission's Directorate-General for Employment and Social affairs commissioned a detailed study on Europe's Roma.[53] The report demonstrates that despite increasing political awareness, very little has changed in the last 10 years – with Roma still significantly disadvantaged in the fields of education, employment and healthcare.[54] The report called for more positive measures and the adoption of a Roma Integration Directive under Article 13 Treaty of Amsterdam 1997. Such moves have been echoed internationally. For example, the International Committee against the Elimination of All Forms of Racial Discrimination adopted a specific recommendation on discrimination against Roma in 2000.[55] Such developments suggest that existing laws of human rights, emphasising on non-discrimination and individualism, are unable to respond adequately to these challenges.

Violence and discrimination

The history of the Rom in Europe has been a story of oppression, violence and discrimination culminating in the Nazi holocaust or 'porajmos' where between 200,000 and 500,000 Roma were executed.[56] In recent times, state policies of sterilisation, compulsory name-changing and forced adoption have been highlighted in several European countries, with an aim of restricting the birth rate and eliminating

---

51   Edwards, A. 'New Roma Rights Legislation in Bosnia and Herzegovina: Positive, negative or indifferent' (2005) *International Journal of Human Rights* Vol.9 No 4.

52   Human Rights Watch, *Abuses against Serbs and Roma in the New Kosovo* August 1999, Vol 11 No 10. Available at: http://www.hrw.org/reports/1999/kosov2/.

53   European Commission *supra* n7.

54   These findings are supported by the UNDP report *supra* n47 at 4.

55   ICERD *General Recommendation on Discrimination against Roma* XXVll, 57th session 2000.

56   Brearley *supra* n17 at 21. For more detailed account see Hanocock, I. 'Gypsy history in Germany and neighboring lands: A chronology leading to the Holocaust and beyond,' in David Crowe and John Kolsti, eds, *The Gypsies of Eastern Europe* (1989) Armonk: E.C. Sharpe, pp. 11–30; Kenrick, D. and Puxon, G. *The Destiny of Europe's Gypsies* (1972) London: Sussex University Press *passim*, Milton, S. 'The context of the Holocaust' *German Studies Review* (1990) Vol XIII No 2 pp. 269–284.

the reproduction of those considered 'social undesirables'.[57] In December 2005, a report by the Czech ombudsman found:

> The problem of sexual sterilization – carried out either with unacceptable motivation or illegally – exists, and that Czech society stands before the task of coming to grips with this reality.[58]

In November 2005, in the first court case of its kind, the Ostrava District Court found that a Romani woman coercively sterilised in 2001 had been unlawfully deprived of her dignity.[59] Research by the Centre for Reproductive Rights suggests that Slovak doctors continue to coerce Romani women into sterilisation.[60]

The collapse of Communism, and consequent economic instability, appeared to awaken fears amongst the people of Eastern Europe. The level of violence towards 'foreigners', specifically Roma, increased dramatically with widespread, group attacks which were tolerated by the police and local communities. Twenty-six Roma were murdered in racially motivated attacks in Czechoslovakia alone in 1992 and throughout the region there have been attacks on Roma communities by fellow villagers.[61] Evidence of continued violence towards Czech Roma and police unwillingness to pursue the racially motivated nature of many attacks persists.[62]

In the Burgenland region of Austria in 1995 four Roma were murdered by a bomb which had been attached to a sign outside a Roma settlement. The sign read 'Roma zuruck nach Indien' (translated as 'Roma back to India'). Initial reports in the Austrian press suggested that the deaths were attributable to an internal Roma feud and the police searched the settlement for evidence of arms and drugs smuggling.[63] The Austrian police arrested one Gadjo man in connection with the incident in October

---

57   A report by the Centre for Reproductive Rights found that Slovakian Roma continue to be subjected to this procedure which potentially contravenes the 1948 Genocide Convention: 'Forced sterilisation and other assaults on Roma reproductive freedom' January 2003, Ro19. In 1992 Human Rights Watch reported the sterilisation of Czech Roma women, often without full consent, HRW *Struggling For Ethnic Identity: Czechoslovakia's Endangered Gypsies* (1992) HRW, NY at 19. This practice has also been identified in Norway by International Helsinki Federation Annual Report (1997) at 194. The seizure and forced adoption of Roma children in Italy and Switzerland has also been recorded, Puxon, *Roma: Europe's Gypsies* 1987 Minority Rights Group, London at 6 and 8.

58   As reported by European Roma Rights Centre 'Coercive Sterilisation of Romani Women: organisations welcome Ombudsmans report' 10 January 2006.

59   ERRC 'First Court victory in Central Europe on Coercive Sterilisation of Romani Women' 11 November 2005 ERRC.

60   Centre for Reproductive Rights Body and Soul, *Forced Sterilisation and Other Assaults on Roma Reproductive Freedom in Slovakia* (2003) p119 Centre for Reproductive Rights.

61   Crowe, D *A History of the Gypsies of Eastern Europe and Russia* (1995) St Martins Press, New York at 64.

62   See for example the reports from the Independent Race and Refugee Network: www.irr.org.uk and the report of the All Parliamentary Group on Roma Affairs in Stage One Accession Countries (2003) European Dialogue.

63   ERRC *Divide and Deport: Roma and Sinti in Austria* (ERRC, Budapest September 1996).

1997. Press reports suggest that the police believe that this man may have had funding and support from a larger cell.[64] In 1998, a bomb was thrown into a Roma house in Fechenheim, Germany. The Christian Democratic Union's district leader was quick in attributing involvement to the Roma occupants.[65] These problems persist despite greater publicity and awareness. Racist violence towards Roma in Poland coupled with police complicity attracted high profile criticism from the UNHCR in 2004.[66] Similarly, in Russia there have been recent examples of orchestrated campaigns of violence against Roma,[67] and in Bacu, Romania in January 1995, the church bell signalled the villagers to raze all Romani houses to the ground after a local argument.[68] Amnesty International documented a similar incident in Poprad, Slovakia which, like many other incidents was characterised by police indifference.[69]

The most recent information available on the level of right-wing extremist attacks on people identified as being of Romany origin suggests that the violence is increasing. One Slovak police officer suggested that overall racially motivated attacks had doubled in 2002.[70] In the 1990s the European Roma Rights Centre documented an alarming number of serious attacks on school children and families. Police records indicate that the perpetrators were rarely detained.[71]

The Roma of Eastern and Central Europe are not alone in experiencing such hostility and it is clear that the breakdown of the highly regulated Communist state is not the sole causative factor. The situation of the Roma in France is particularly interesting as French national identity is built on a concept of a Republican citizenship that promotes equality and does not allow for the existence of minorities. A recent comprehensive report by the European Roma Rights Centre reveals that this individualised approach has not prevented the Roma from being stigmatised in all aspects of society.[72] 'Neutral laws' can be used to chip away at aspects of minority

---

64   Hall, William 'International: Austria police arrest suspect' *Financial Times*, 6 October 1997.

65   Romnews Correspondent 'The atmosphere in the district of Fechenheim has been strained for a long time' 27 November 1998 Roma National Congress, Hamburg.

66   UNHCR 'Poland: Incidence of violence against Roma, particularly by skinheads or racist groups; police response to violence against Roma (January 2000–October 2004)' October 2004.

67   Dzeno Association 'Anti-Roma violence in Pskov' 27 September 2005; Union of Council of Jews in the former Soviet Union 'Arrests made in connection with mass attack on Gypsies in Iskitim' June 2005; 'More Anti-Roma violence in Iskitim; girl burned in her own bed' November 2005.

68   Romania has seen some thirty similar incidents since December 1989. In the Giurgiu District alone four such incidents occurred between April and May 1991. The perpetrators of the violence have not been bought to justice; Liégeois and Gheorghe *supra* n12 at 14. See also UNHCR *Background paper on Romania refugees and asylum seekers* Geneva November 1994.

69   Human Rights Watch Lynch Law: *Violence Against Roma in Romania*, Vol 6 No 17 (November 1994); Amnesty International Annual Report (2003) documented by RFE/RL *Newsline* Vol 7 No 100, Part II 29 May 2003; ERRC *State of Impunity* (2001) ERRC.

70   *Supra* n2 at 54.

71   See for example the ERRC Newsletters Spring, Summer and Winter 1998 – particularly the sections entitled 'Snapshots from around Europe'.

72   ERRC *Always Somewhere Else: Anti-Gypsyism in France* 2005 ERRC, Budapest.

identity such as nomadism to the extent that an entire way of life can be marginalised and, in some cases, criminalised. The ERRC report concluded:

> Paradoxically, it is France's very attachment to a restrictive concept of equality that acts as a significant barrier to remedying the existing inequality of a segment of its population. If France is to live up to its constitutional guarantee of equality in practice, the dramatic human rights situation of Travellers and Gypsies needs to be immediately recognised and remedied.[73]

In Germany, reunification bought with it a ten-fold increase in racist attacks particularly directed towards immigrants and refugees.[74] The German authorities were clearly concerned about the number of migrants attempting to enter Germany[75] and in 1992 a bilateral treaty was signed with Romania in order to repatriate those immigrants, mostly Roma, assumed to be of Romanian origin.[76] In return for their co-operation the Romanian Government were offered a favourable loan of 1000 million DM.[77] Anti-Roma prejudice remains rife in Germany[78] and racist attacks remain a significant problem. Recently, a former government spokesperson advised black visitors to avoid the eastern district of Brandenburg because racism and violence was rife.[79] Two days later, a German politician of Turkish origin was violently attacked after being identified as a 'dirty foreigner'.[80]

Police complicity in the anti-Roma violence sweeping Eastern Europe is a common allegation. The European Roma Rights Centre have revealed particularly disturbing cases of raids without warrants on Roma settlements[81] and police violence in Austria[82] and Hungary where the power of arrest has been used to abuse and racially taunt Roma.[83] Similar issues were raised by the Human Rights Watch World report on the Czech Republic and Slovakia in 2002.[84]

---

73   *Ibid.* at 305.

74   Hockenos, P *Free to Hate* (1993) Routledge, NY at 28–9 and 39.

75   For details on the extent of problems facing the Roma generally in Germany see Roma National Congress Report On *the situation of the Roma in Europe* RNC, Hamburg.

76   Reported in Open Media Research Institute Daily Digest, 3 November 1992.

77   The European Parliament have expressed disapproval at the treaty in European Parliament. Session Documents 'Agreement between Germany and Romania on the Forced Repatriation of Romanian Gypsies,' Doc B3-1503/92, Doc EN/RR/247/247/101, PE 206.967/fin, 3 November 1992.

78   Joint EU Monitoring and Advocacy Programme/ERRC Shadow report *Commenting on the Fifth Periodic report of the the Federal the Republic of Germany submitted under Article 18 of the UN Convention on the Elimination of All Forms of Discrimination Against Women* 9 January 2004.

79   Interview with Uwe Karsten-Heye reported in der Spiegel Online 18 May 2006.

80   'Turkish politician injured in racist attack' reported in *Deutsche Welle* 2 June 2006.

81   ERRC (1996) *Sudden Rage at Dawn: Violence against Roma in Romania* (Budapest September 1996); ERRC (1996) Newsbrief *Police in Slovakia Use Electric Cattle-prods during Raids on Romani Community.*

82   ERRC (1996) *supra* n63.

83   ERRC Press Release *Police Brutality in Hungary* 26 March 1997 (ERRC, Budapest).

84   Human Rights Watch *World Report 2002* HRW, New York.

An aspect of police complicity is also the problem of inadequate investigations by the police and prosecuting authorities, with the majority of cases failing to result in prosecution. Recently, the European Court of Human Rights found several violations of the Convention resulting from incidents which occurred in 1993 in the village of Haradeni, Romania.[85] These events are worth summarising as they demonstrate both police complicity and judicial acquiescence in anti-Roma violence.

Following the death of a Gadjo man in an argument, the three Roma suspects were attacked and killed by an angry mob. Many Roma houses were then burned to the ground. Those responsible for the murders were quickly identified and it was apparent that several police officers had been involved in the mob violence. Senior police officials advised local residents not to comply with the criminal investigation and the original suspects were quickly released. When a trial did take place, the Târgu-Mureş County Court convicted five civilians of 'extremely serious murder' and 12 civilians, including the deputy mayor, of destroying property, outraging public decency and disturbing public order. The court ruling did however suggest that some of the blame may lie at the door of the Roma inhabitants:

> Due to their lifestyle and their rejection of the moral values accepted by the rest of the population, the Roma community has marginalised itself, shown aggressive behaviour and deliberately denied and violated the legal norms acknowledged by society.[86]

The sentences of between one and seven years were subsequently reduced by the Court of Appeal and the convictions were again diluted on appeal to the Supreme Court where they were reclassified as 'murder with extenuation'. In 2000, the Romanian president pardoned two of the defendants. While some funds had been made available to rebuild homes, several Roma remained homeless a decade later. The European Court of Human Rights was unable to apply the convention to the initial events in 1993 as Romania was not at that time, a signatory to the Convention. However they ruled unanimously that the subsequent behaviour of the authorities, including some discriminatory judicial pronouncements and police complicity amounted to a serious violation of Articles 3, 6(1), 8 and Article 14 of the Convention.

Anti-Gypsy or anti-Roma rhetoric often plays an intrinsic part in electoral success. In 1993, the Slovak Prime Minister was understood to be referring to the Roma when he stated that his country was under threat from the 'extended reproduction of the socially unadaptable population' of whom he had earlier publicly stated 'if we don't deal with them now, then they will deal with us in time …'.[87] It thus comes as no surprise that in a recent opinion poll, 94% of Slovaks said that they would not wish to have Roma as their neighbours.[88] In the United Kingdom, anti-Gypsy sentiment was frequently expressed by politicians during the passage of the Criminal Justice and Public Order Act 1994, one MP describing them as 'mobile spivs'.[89] More recently, complaints

---

85   *Moldovan and Others v Romania.* Applications No 41138/98 and 64320/01. 2 July 2005.

86   Para 40.

87   *Associated Press* 8 September 1993.

88   1999 poll cited in Barany *supra* n46 at 193.

89   O'Nions, 'The Marginalisation of Gypsies' 1995 3 *WebJCLI.*

were made to the Campaign for Racial Equality against the Welsh Labour Party after the publication of leaflets condemning the opposition for supporting a local traveller encampment.[90] The right-wing Italian party, Lega Nord, and the Austrian Freedom Party use openly anti-Roma sentiment and policies to gain electoral success.[91]

It can also be argued that anti-Roma prejudice is increasing as a direct consequence of anti-asylum initiatives in the West which seek to prevent unauthorised travel and demonise the 'Outsider'. Wootliff-Bitusikova argues that the Slovak visa restrictions introduced by the UK and other Western states in 2000 led to increased hostility towards the Roma at home:

> Building new borders, enforcing new rules and erecting a new Iron Curtain may help the Western countries keep out refugees, but it leads to an increase of hatred and violence against Roma in their home countries.[92]

Economic insecurity

Housing and employment conditions indicate the extent of Roma poverty across Europe. In Eastern and Central Europe, Roma tend to occupy settlements on the outskirts of cities and towns. They are commonly over-crowded, with poor facilities, in 'temporary' accommodation. In the Czech Republic this meant that many were unable to establish permanent residence in order to satisfy citizenship criteria.[93]

Homelessness and unemployment are common problems among the 350,000 Greek Roma.[94] Forced removal and homelessness remains a common problem with an estimated 100,000 Roma living in sub-standard housing.[95] The Committee on Economic, Social and Cultural Rights have expressed grave concern 'about numerous reports on the extrajudicial demolition of dwellings and forced evictions of Roma from their settlements by municipal authorities … frequently without payment of adequate compensation or provision of alternative housing'.[96] The European Committee on Social Rights also upheld a complaint by the European Roma Rights Centre that Greece had breached Article 16 of the European Social Charter.[97]

---

90   Buchanan 'Race body probes anti-Gypsy leaflet' *Western Mail* 28 June 2004.

91   The success of the Lega Nord is documented by ERRC Campland. *Racial Segregation in Italy* March 2000 ERRC. The success of the Freedom Party was highlighted as a matter of concern by ERRC in 'Letter Concerning Situation of Roma in Austria' 28 August 2000.

92   Wootliff-Bitusikova, A 'The EU's Red Card. Roma in Slovakia' 2000 *Central Europe Review* Vol 2 No 41.

93   See Chapter Four at 172.

94   International Helsinki Federation for Human Rights *Annual Report* (1997) pp 129–30.

95   Minority Rights Group 'Open letter to Greek Prime Minister on forced evictions of Roma communities in Patras' 2005. Available at: http://www.minorityrights.org/International/int_stat_detail.asp?ID=97. See also Council of Europe Committee of Minister Resolution ResChS(2005)11 which followed the decision in *ERRC* vs. *Greece* complaint No. 15/2003. Decision of 8 December 2004.

96   *Ibid.*

97   *ERRC* vs. *Greece* Collective complaint No. 15/2003. Decision of 8 December 2004.

In Spain there have been violent outbursts following the government's attempts to provide housing for the Roma[98] and in Italy, discrimination and violence remain big obstacles to the realisation of secure encampments.[99] The 80% of travelling Roma and 30% of Gypsy families who do not have a legal place of abode in France and the United Kingdom respectively face similar difficulties. Struggles such as inadequate sanitation, no running water, limited health care and education as well as daily intolerance, are commonplace.[100]

Statelessness

Statistics on the number of Roma who have migrated to Western Europe are unavailable. Many are afraid to reveal their Romani identity for fear of discrimination and identity papers are often surrendered as a condition of transit.[101] However, selective country data are available which paints a picture of widespread emigration coupled with increasing entry restrictions in the West. Bosnian, ex-Yugoslavian, Romanian, Macedonian and Turkish asylum seekers entering Austria are considered to include a significant number of Roma. The 1993 Asylum Law tightened entry control and human rights observers estimate that between 90 and 95% of those seeking asylum in Austria are declared illegal.[102] Many of these people will be deported to Hungary, others may spend up to six months in Schubhaft, a prison aimed at preventing illegal residence. In the United Kingdom and Finland visa restrictions were briefly introduced against Slovakia to deter Roma from seeking asylum with laws and policies hastily changed to reflect the perception of Roma as economic migrants.[103] Three years later the tabloid media expressed concern over the impact of European enlargement, specifically 'The coming hordes'[104] of asylum seekers from Slovakia, most considered to be of Romani origin.[105] Indeed, there was a well-documented, unsubstantiated, fear that European enlargement would result in millions of Roma coming to the UK to claim benefits and work.[106]

The collective expulsion of 74 Slovak Roma seeking asylum in Belgium led the European Court of Human Rights to find a violation of the right to liberty under Articles 5(1) and 5(4); the prohibition on the collective expulsion of aliens under Protocol 4, Article 4 and the right to an effective remedy under Article 13 of the European Convention on Human Rights.[107]

---

98   Hernandez (member of the Spanish secretariard) p4 in Puxon *supra* n57.

99   Gypsy Council for Education, Culture, Welfare and Civil Rights (1994) *The first Romani Congress of the European Union* Seville 18–21 May 1994.

100   O'Nions *supra* n89.

101   For example, in certain areas of the former Yugoslavia there appears to have been clear persecution on account of Romani identity ERRC (1996) *supra* n63.

102   Katharina Ammann, Amnesty International in ERRC 1996 *supra* n63.

103   Meijknecht *supra* n2 at 68.

104   *The Economist*, 15 January 2004.

105   See for example the front cover of the *Daily Express*, 20 January 2004.

106   Documented by Waringo, K 'Who is Afraid of Migrating Roma?' (2004) *EUMAP*. http://www.eumap.org/journal/features/2004/migration/pt2/whoafraid.

107   *Conka v Belgium* (no. 51564/99). [2002] ECHR 14 (5 February 2002).

The plight of stateless Roma was raised by the Czech Citizenship Law, discussed in Chapter 4. Roma who forfeited their Slovak identity in order to unsuccessfully obtain Czech identity found themselves stateless with neither Czech nor Slovak identity papers. Many Czech Roma emigrated to Canada and the West following a television programme depicting a haven where Roma would be guaranteed financial and personal security.[108] In the Ostrava district, the authorities were even offering to pay two-thirds of the travel costs for prospective émigrés.[109] The Czech premier, mindful of the international attention associated with EU membership, called press conferences urging that the 'thousands' of Roma preparing to emigrate to reconsider their decision.[110] Nevertheless, the number of those fleeing continued to rise. In 2002, officials from the United Kingdom Home Office were stationed at Prague airport to prevent those suspected to be of Romani origin from departing for the UK. This practice was condemned by the House of Lords as subjective and discriminatory in a landmark court ruling.[111]

According to recent estimates from the European Commission, an estimated four-fifths of the Romani population of Kosovo (around 120,000 persons) is displaced within the region. The Commission's report described the events following the withdrawal of peace-keeping forces as 'the worst catastrophe it [the Romani community] has endured since World War II'.[112] In the United Kingdom, as in several other European countries, the former Yugoslav states and Albania appear on a 'white-list' of supposedly safe countries which generate no serious risk of persecution. Consequently any applications for asylum will be fast tracked for removal.

Why human rights? The language of empowerment and equality

The use of human rights language to improve the treatment of minority and disadvantaged groups became increasingly popular in the latter half of the twentieth century.[113] At the same time, there was a rapid growth in the number of Romani non-governmental organisations, particularly since the collapse of Communism in Eastern Europe,[114] and the 'Romani issue' has now been firmly placed on the agenda at both regional and international levels.[115]

Roma activists are comparatively new to politics and international human rights language. Initial reluctance to formulate such demands probably stemmed from the

---

108   ERRC Press Statement 15 August 1997.

109   Sliva, Jan 'Gypsies Seek Good Life in Canada' *Associated Press*, 13 August 1997.

110   RFE/RL 'Czech Premier Meets with Roma' 1997 *Newsline* Vol 1 No 96, part 2, 15 August.

111   *R v IO at Prague Airport and Another exp ERRC* [2004] UKHL 55.

112   European Commission (2004) *supra* n7 at para 10.

113   The first international World Romani Congress was held in 1971 and was attended by delegates from 14 countries. For details on this growth see Liégeois (1994) *supra* n21 pp 249–266.

114   Trehan, Nidhi 'In the name of the Roma? The role of private foundations and NGO's' in Guy *supra* n20 pp 134–149.

115   Mirga, Gheorghe *The Roma in the Twenty-first Century: A Policy paper*, Project on Ethnic Relations, Princeton, US (May 1997) at 5.

absence of formal political organisation, formal education and a certain amount of mistrust for Gadje channels of communication. Industrialisation, the development of modern technology and the rising tide of ethnic violence across Europe has forced the Roma, along with other traditionally-inclined groups, to define a 'political space' and familiarise themselves with international discourse that could serve to improve their situation.[116]

New as they are to the international political arena, the Roma elite have suffered criticism for the absence of a unified stance. The language of human rights appears to have been embraced, however, as a real opportunity to improve the situation of their people throughout the world. There have been several international conferences and seminars which have helped to forge bonds between the components of the mosaic. Following extensive lobbying by academics and activists, particularly over the last decade,[117] the Council of Europe[118] and the Organisation on Security and Co-operation in Europe have funded numerous initiatives and have established mechanisms to increase awareness of the problems faced by the Roma community. A contact point has been established in Warsaw to provide information and debate and within the community itself there have been efforts to standardise the Romani language and to create a definitive Romani dictionary. Such recognition has been mirrored in the United Nations. In 1992, the Commission on Human Rights accepted the Sub-Commission's Resolution 65/1992 *on the Protection of Roma and Gypsies.*[119] Perhaps the greatest recognition of the development of international Roma political organisation came in 1993 when the Economic and Social Council of the United Nations upgraded the status of the *International Romani Union* to Category II Observer status.[120]

Increasingly, the use of the law to empower the Roma at a grass roots level can also be seen, although there are often considerable obstacles, such as police reticence, to contend with. In the first case of its kind in the Hungarian courts, the victim, Mr Gorman − a 31 year-old Rom, was awarded damages from a bar owner who had refused to serve him on account of his race. Following the verdict, Mr Gorman commented '… if I were the president now of a Gypsy organisation I would know how to help other Gypsies …. Maybe now, with this penalty, people will think twice'.[121] In this respect the work of the *European Roma Rights Centre* has been particularly significant, with the use of expert lawyers to advise and represent clients in the region, many of whom would otherwise have been deterred from taking such action.

---

116   *Supra* n115.

117   See Gheorghe, N 'The social construction of Romani identity' in Acton (ed) *Gypsy Politics and Traveller Identity* (1997) Univ. of Hertfordshire Press at 153−7.

118   The Council of Europe publishes a regular newsletter *Activities on Roma/Gypsies* which details and reports on recent C/E events in the field.

119   Germany has refused to accept that Roma are a national minority in Germany as they are not confined to a specific area as they claim not to be affected by the resolution, Jansen, M 'Sinti and Roma: An ethnic Minoirty in Germany' in Packer and Myntti (eds) *The Protection of Ethnic and Linguistic Minorities in Europe* (1993) Abo Akademi University at 199.

120   Liégeois *supra* n21 at 260.

121   Roddy, M 'Hungarian Gypsy's Court Victory Hailed' *The Globe and Mail, Canada* pA9 27 August 1997.

The over-riding theme of exclusion

Exclusion is the common theme behind the prejudice exhibited towards the Roma. The feeling that Roma exist outside of society and do not deserve to be included is illustrated aptly by the debate about Czech citizenship and segregated schooling policies as well as in the rising tide of violence. Recent reports indicate the prevalence of exclusionary policies, with up to 75% of Roma in some regions being educated in segregated schools and a significant number of Czech Roma still without Czech citizenship.[122]

Often the Roma are blamed for the disadvantage they experience. The responses of the Czech Government representative to the Committee on the Elimination of All Forms of Racial Discrimination are noteworthy in this respect. For example:

> Certain negative socio-pathological phenomena within the gypsy population have resulted in the fact that the percentage of children who are placed in children's homes … is higher among gypsy children ….[123]

Bulgarian and Romanian representatives have similarly attributed discrimination in their education systems to the attitudes of the Roma themselves.[124]

For centuries the Roma have suffered from the introduction of unsuccessful assimilationist policies. Integrationism and pluralism are now the buzz words in international politics. Pluralism involves recognition of group difference; its most extreme form demands a level of spatial separation and independence which is unlikely to commend it to human rights advocates or politicians, such a method for example could justify a policy of separate schooling.[125] When coupled with an integrationist stance which seeks to include the Roma as active citizens in the wider society, pluralism can enable choice and identity to develop freely.[126] The identity of the group is protected while the individual is also a full member of the wider society. The first Romani congress of the European Union in 1994 resolved:

> We are European citizens, and as such we must have free access in Europe. There must be integration of the minorities into Europe, yet still maintaining their individual cultures. Europe is multi-cultural, multi-language, multi nationality, etc., and the Gypsy peoples are members of the rich tapestry of this European Community, our culture, language, music and art, form part of the rich tapestry of this European heritage.[127]

---

122   Prior to the amendment in 1999 the OSCE estimated that 15,000 Czech Roma were stateless: *Romani Human Rights in Europe* of 21 July 21 1998. European Commission (2004) *supra* n7.

123   UN Doc CERD/C/172/Add.5 1988 at para 15 cited in Rooker, Marcia *The International Supervision of Protection of Romany People in Europe* (2004) University of Nijmegen at 106.

124   *Ibid.* at Chapter VII.

125   See the discussion in Chapter 5.

126   For different interpretations of pluralism see Gordon, Milton. M *Human Nature, Class and Ethnicity* (1978) Oxford Univ. Press Chapter 5 passim.

127   GCEWCR *supra* n99.

Integration of course depends on a commitment to its aims by both Roma and Gadje alike. Rudko Kawczynski, a Romani and representative of the Roma National Congress, argues that majority acceptance is crucial in the equation:

> Integration can take place only if the majority population accepts and tolerates the minority in its midst. A minority can strive to become integrated, but if the majority is unwilling to let them integrate, to acknowledge the minority and accept them as having equal rights, then all the minority's efforts have been in vain no matter how hard it has tried to win recognition.[128]

The level of violence and discrimination directed at the Roma indicate that bona fide integration will not be easy to achieve. A pluralist approach which respects the rights of cultures as distinct units of society may thus be a more desirable strategy for human rights protection. Group-based rights theorists and Communitarians advocate pluralist politics which support cultural differences. However, there is concern over the potential to artificially maintain and strengthen group boundaries which may provide justification for separate but equal policies such as segregated schooling. It could also be argued that the creation of a separate Roma polity could be highly divisive and would further increase marginalisation.[129] As Kovats argues, the most effective way of improving the situation of the Roma may be through equality of opportunity rather than through the creation of a distinct Roma/Gypsy polity. Effective pluralism is also limited in practice in that it would seem to demand greater group autonomy (both titular and cultural) and would thus depend on the equal allocation of resources and information.

Minority vs individual rights

While the Romani elite have embraced human rights discourse, debate over the best strategy for securing rights for the Roma people of Europe has often been fractious and fragmented. As a result several strains of debate have emerged as the most effective ways of improving human rights protection and none command unilateral support. The first part of the debate centres on the realisation of group versus individual rights. In Chapters 4 and 5 it will be argued that the individual emphasis on human rights advocated by international law fails to meet the needs of the most disadvantaged communities by underplaying the importance of communal values to the individual rights-bearer.

It can be seen that much of the concern about increasing the rights of groups per se centres on the perceived threat to state security that this would entail. There has clearly been an increased recognition of the Roma as a minority group and there has been no threat to state stability posed by such recognition. Demands for territorial independence are obviously at odds with the geographical and cultural diversity of many Roma communities. Thus, there is in principle no political reason why a state should be unwilling to recognise the Roma as a minority group.

---

128 Kawczynski, Rudko. J 'Roma' *ROMNEWS Network* (1998) Online Service of the Roma National Congress, Hamburg.

129 Kovats, Martin 'The European Roma Question' (2002) The Royal Institute of International Affairs, Briefing Paper No 31.

While the need for a collective dimension to human rights protection is gradually being recognised particularly in the European arena,[130] the extent to which collective rights are, or could be, justiciable is problematic. Acknowledging the ineffective, relativist stance of individual human rights does not necessarily entail support for justiciable group rights. Chapter 7 will discuss possible ways of developing minority-based rights as complimentary rather than alternatives to individual rights.

Support for collective rights is seen by many as the only viable solution to problems of minority conflict and discrimination. Minority rights can thus be viewed as one part of the commitment to democracy and the rule of law. As Andre Erdos argues:

> The progress of democracy must be accompanied in every country by the implementation of a sound, sensible and generous national minorities policy which excludes all kinds of nationalism and chauvinism either on the part of the majority or the minorities.[131]

Methods of collective rights recognition

Recognition of a collective identity is necessary for the protection of the Roma as a national minority. However, it must be acknowledged that the diversity of the Roma, Gypsies and traveller people poses significant problems. Any notion of group-based rights necessitates the drawing of ethnic boundaries in a manner which cannot precisely mirror the reality of the groups concerned. There is no doubt that the diverse 'multicultural' mosaic of people poses difficulty for the group rights theorist and contradicts the need felt amongst the Roma elite to define themselves as a unified, particular ethnic group.[132] The Roma ethnic identity is arguably weak, indeed Michael Stewart has argued that it does not exist.[133] Acton and Gheorghe note that such historic diversity creates a serious constraint on the formalisation and codification of Romani culture and such issues will need to be adequately resolved if there can be any effective minority rights protection.[134]

Furthermore, the designation 'national minority', preferred by the Council of Europe and the OSCE, poses particular challenges.[135] In the UN the focus is on 'ethnic, religious or linguistic' minorities – such a focus widens the net to non-territorial groups and may be preferable for accessing international protection.

---

130   The OSCE although only a politically rather than legally binding document, has clearly progressed into the realm of collective rights, see for example The Document of the Copenhagen Meeting of the Conference on the Human Dimension of the CSCE, June 29th 1990 reprinted in (1990) *HRLJ* 232, Part IV deals specifically with minority rights. Recognising them as 'an essential factor for peace, justice, stability and democracy in the participating State'.

131   Erdos, Andre 'Minority Rights' *New Hungarian Quarterly* (1987) Vol. 28, 106 p 131–135 at 132.

132   Acton and Gheorghe 'Dealing with Multiculturality: Minority, Ethnic, National and Human Rights' in *ODIHR Bulletin* Spring (1995) Vol 3, 2 at 29.

133   Stewart, Michael *The Time of the Gypsies* (1997) Boulder CO, Westview at 28. This view is criticised by Barany, Zoltan *supra* n46 at 77.

134   *Supra* n132.

135   See Chapter 6 at 301.

The emphasis on the individual 'in community with other members of the group' in both regional and international documents is addressed in Chapter 2. It will be seen that international law at present ascribes rights to members of minority groups rather than the group per se and as a result it appears to be unclear whether a group could demand the necessary resources to improve the situation of their people.

The need to fit within the construct of a national minority has led some of the Roma elite to strive to present a unified homogeneous community with a common cultural identity. This process of 'ethnogenesis' has led to a growth in Romani ethnonationalism.[136] The very words 'national minority', although not specifically defined in international documents, presuppose the existence of a national identity and perhaps even a homeland, forcing the construction of a separate nationality.[137] It has further been argued that an emphasis on ethnic distinction and separatism enables states to evade responsibility to minority groups by reinforcing the validity of the nation-state. In a powerful critique, Nicolae Gheorghe contends:

> The discourse of national minorities is another way to reproduce and to reinforce the nation-state. The fact that the nation-states are so generous now to these 'minorities' is just one device to reinforce the legitimacy of these states as ethnic states, states which actually belong to an ethnic 'majority'.[138]

A growth of nationalism of any size is at odds with the fundamental importance of human rights for all and such a consequence will need to be seriously considered in an account advocating group minority rights. The emphasis on 'ethnic, religious and linguistic minorities' in Article 27 of the ICCPR may avoid this difficulty, but the language increasingly being favoured in European documents such as the *Framework Convention on the Rights of Persons Belonging to National Minorities*, shows a clear preference for 'national' rather than 'ethnic' minorities. This has prompted some Romani intellectuals and activists to call for a new status as a legally recognised transnational minority. A status that would be afforded irrespective of citizenship and residence.[139] As Marushiakova and Popov note, 'Gypsies form a specific ethnic community that has no parallel among other European nations'.[140] The Roma National Congress draw attention to their unique history as a non-territorial minority confronted with racism and persecution, and advocate a 'European Charter on Romani Rights' to provide a firm legal status for Roma throughout Europe.[141] The Charter envisaged by the RNC would include: the right to political representation as an ethnic minority and the right to operate an autonomous education system as well

---

136   For further discussion see Gheorghe *supra* n117 at 160.

137   Acton and Gheorghe *supra* n132 at 32–40.

138   Gheorghe *supra* n117 at 160.

139   Roma National Congress *supra* n75 at 1.

140   Marushiakova, Elena and Popov, Vesselin 'Historical and ethnographic background: Gypsies, Roma, Sinti' in Guy, Will *supra* n20 at 33.

141   Roma National Congress 'Roma in Europe: Status Regulation through self-determination' Statement prepared for the *CSCE Seminar on Roma in the CSCE Region*, Warsaw 20–23 September 1994.

as more traditionally inclined rights to protect against discrimination and violence.[142]
The advocates of a transnational approach suggest the need for the deconstruction of
a human rights system based on national self-determination in favour of individual
self-determination allowing all people to partake in active citizenship.[143] This
proposition is discussed further in Chapter 7 and may provide a way forward in the
murky water of group and collective rights recognition. However, caution should
be exercised as the label 'transnational minority' lacks clarity with some writers
grounding it in equality and non-discrimination and others apparently affording it a
supra-national minority rights status.[144]

The general principles of the 'Roma Participation Program' of the Open Society
Institute, Budapest echoes the need to draw on transnational perspectives:

> As a de facto non-territorial minority in Europe, the Roma occupy a unique position,
> both historically and politically. Their situation is analogous with that of European
> Jewry, except that the Roma do not have the option of claiming political sovereignty as
> an independent state. Efforts to improve the situation of Roma must acknowledge this
> unique position.[145]

While this may be an appropriate description of the Roma today, it sits uneasily with
the individual emphasis of human rights standards as well as with the primacy of
the state as evidenced through the importance of territorial integrity, characteristic
of international legal documents. Newly emerging concepts of national minority
intrinsically favour loyalty to the state over any minority identity. Thus, such a claim
will be unlikely to receive support from the major players, the member states, who
may regard their territorial integrity as under threat.

Concluding remarks

The Roma voice, stifled for centuries, is getting louder. Demands for increased
political representation accompany the wider debate on the Charter for Romani
Rights. To be effective, such demands must involve some sort of affirmative action
strategy or group rights recognition. If a strategy based on the recognition of the
collective nature of rights is deemed inappropriate it remains to be seen how far
the rights of Roma can be redressed in the individualist emphasis. A challenge is
clearly presented for the human rights theorist: what use are such rights if they
cannot protect the most vulnerable and weakest members of civil society? In a
statement to the OSCE, the Legal Director of the European Roma Rights Centre

---

142   RNC 'Why a European Charter on Romani Rights?' *Romnews Network Online*
1998.

143   Gheorghe, N and Acton, T 'Citizens of the world and nowhere: minority ethnic
and human rights for Roma during the last hurrah of the nation-state' in Guy, Will *supra* n20
54–70 at 67.

144   Gheorghe and Acton *ibid.* adopt the equality and non-discrimination perspective
whereas the Roma National Congress appear to be seeking a degree of ethnic homogenisation
when they advocate a European Romani Charter.

145   Roma Participation Program 'About the RPP' *Reporter*.

presented data on the systematic abuse of human rights across Europe. This abuse is demonstrated by police, officials, politicians, social workers, educationalists and the neo-Nazi movement in Europe, it derives credibility from public acquiescence and, in many cases, public participation. The evidence of the ERRC, supported by the other delegates, was presented with the statement:

> I hope I do not overstate matters when I tell you that the ill-treatment of Roma is perhaps the most important human rights concern in Europe today, and the problem is getting worse.[146]

As a litmus test, the present treatment of Roma in Europe indicates societies far from civil. The ideals of tolerance and equality lying behind the movement for universal human rights protection, now in place for half a century, are not protecting the most vulnerable citizens of Europe. Having examined the experiences of the East European Gypsy peoples, Zoltan Barany describes them as a marginal group *extraordinaire* who can 'scarcely be considered "dominant" in any context'.[147]

Nevertheless, societies respectful of the rule of law and democracy must be seen to promote respect, through education and tolerance. Such respect must start from the top and work down. When it comes to treatment of the Roma however, it would not be an exaggeration to suggest that such respect is absent at all levels. The civil society, to which Havel alludes, appears to be a distant vision for Europe's fastest growing minority.

---

146 Goldston, James speaking at OSCE (1998) *supra* n122 at 12.
147 Barany *supra* n46 at 63.

Chapter 2

The Protection of Groups in International Human Rights Discourse

Introduction

This chapter focuses on the theoretical arguments underpinning the debate on the most effective ways of improving access to justice for the Romani communities of Europe. In assessing the value of affirmative action strategies and special group-based rights, the discussion necessarily entails an analysis of the individual versus collective rights debate. It will become clear that the individualist emphasis, still predominant in international human rights law, cannot meet the demands of this universally marginalised group. In recent times ethnic mobilisation has led to calls for recognition of the Roma as a transnational minority group.[1] Such a proposition, while alien to the language of international human rights law at present, is regarded by some as essential to redress entrenched prejudices and empower the Roma as a community. It is unclear how such an identity could be defined. It runs the risk of promoting enforced homogeneity through the exclusion of sub-groups such as settled Roma from a newly construed ethnic identity. Alternatively, a broader conception of Roma identity could make it difficult to identify common cultural factors.[2] Perpetuating the myth of the 'true-blooded' Romany, such a prescribed, static label has the potential to increase exclusion and marginalisation.

This chapter will endeavour to find a way around this disruptive, antagonistic dichotomy. To meet this objective, the theoretical approaches to minority protection are evaluated and applied to the Roma. The impact of the different approaches will then be given a practical dimension in the following chapters.

The language of liberalism and human rights

An examination of the individual emphasis of human rights law in Chapter 3 will reveal the paradox of limited group rights recognition within the individualist framework. The drafters of the United Nations Charter and Declaration were proud to leave behind the language of minority rights endorsed by the League of Nations regime.[3] Nevertheless, it is apparent that many of the positive rights in the International Covenants of 1966 have collective dimensions; without acknowledgement of the

---

1   Mirga, A and Gheorghe, N *The Roma in the Twenty-first Century: A Policy Paper* (May 1997) PER, Princeton NJ at 21–2.

2   Barany, Zoltan *The East European Gypsies* (2002) Cambridge Univ. Press at 203.

3   See Chapter 6 at 267.

group these rights become redundant. Such is the case with freedom of religion and association, both of which entail a collective element. However, the way that these rights are framed in both the United Nations Covenants and in the European Convention on Human Rights and Fundamental Freedoms (hereafter ECHR) is abstract, applying only to the individuals who comprise the groups in question. This abstraction is also applicable to the minority rights provision in Article 27 of the International Covenant on Civil and Political Rights (hereafter ICCPR) which vests in 'members of minorities'.[4]

In keeping with this abstraction there has been an unwillingness to define a minority in international human rights law, discussed further in Chapter 6. Even the Council of Europe's Framework Convention on the Protection of National Minorities avoided the difficulty of arriving at a definition.[5] The recognition of collective rights is further complicated by the recognition of different types of minorities in various international documents. Article 27 of the *ICCPR* refers to 'ethnic, religious or linguistic minorities' whereas the regional provisions such as the Helsinki Final Act and the Framework Convention prefer instead the term 'national minority', as discussed further in Chapter 6. It is not only international law that suffers from this imprecision. Academics have afforded group rights recognition to a variety of specific beneficiaries, including 'co-nations' and 'homogenous, constitutive communities'.[6] Many of these special status labels exclude non-territorial minorities, explicitly or impliedly excluding the Roma.

Academic debate on the nature of group rights

The discussion on group based rights is a relatively modern phenomena. Its popularity can be traced back to the writings of the German legal theorist, Otto von Gierke (1841–1921) who challenged the Roman theory which defined group interests as the aggregate of individual constituent interests.[7] Gierke's work was translated into English by F. W Maitland (1850–1906) and thus the tradition of English Pluralism developed.[8] Writers such as R.M MacIver[9] and J.N Figgis[10] argued that citizenship does not reflect all the societal interests of individuals. The state was considered to represent one of many claims on an individuals' loyalty. G.H. Cole developed this approach, arguing that groups could be sovereign within the functional sphere which concerns them. Cole's discussion regards the state as sovereign only in areas of national concern, such as national security; with no jurisdiction over the interests of groups.[11]

---

4   Macdonald, Ian 'Group rights' *Philosophical Papers* Vol. XVIII (1989) No 2 pp 117–136 at 121.

5   C/E H (1995) 10, Strasbourg February 1995.

6   Malloy, Tove *National Minority Rights in Europe* 2005 OUP and Galenkamp, Marlies 'Collective Rights: Much Ado about Nothing?' *Neth HRQ* 3 1991 at 297.

7   Maitland, F.W. 'Introduction to his translation of O.Gierke' *Natural Law and the Theory of Society, 1500–1800* (1934) Cambridge passim.

8   Stapleton, Julia *Group Rights* (1995) Thoemmes Press, Bristol.

9   MacIver, R.M., 'Society and State' *The Philosophical Review*, XX (1911) at 41.

10   Figgis J.N.,'Respublica Christiana' (1910) reprinted in Stapleton *supra* n8 at 38.

11   Cole, G.D.H., 'Conflicting social obligations' (1915) rep. in Stapleton *supra* n8 at 94.

English pluralists focused on the group rights of voluntary associations, formed for a variety of purposes, including leisure and work.[12] The relevance of the debate to specific ethnic or national minorities had been touched upon by thinkers such as J.S Mill, who advocated national self-determination as a prerequisite to the realisation of political freedom.[13] However, it appears to have received little theoretical development until the post-war emphasis on the internationalisation of political theory.

Any conception of international minority rights was to be dealt a blow by the collapse of the League of Nations regime, discussed in Chapter 6, and the rise of National Socialism in Germany. The Nazis systematically abused the (group rights based) minorities protection mechanisms of the League of Nations in order to provide pretexts of aggression.[14] The protection of groups was seen by many as synonymous with a violation of individual rights with the Marxist critique of human rights receiving little credibility during the post-war years.[15] In recent times however, as discussed in Chapter 6, there has been increasing international recognition that the traditional liberal focus on the individual is failing to protect the liberty of members of groups, particularly ethnic minorities.[16]

Within the academic community a debate has emerged over the most effective way of protecting the individual rights of members of minorities. Vernon Van Dyke is critical of Rawls' *Theory of Justice* as it fails to consider the representation of groups in the original position.[17] Blindness to group difference, once viewed as essential to respect the sanctity of the individual, promotes the false assumption that societies are homogeneous,[18] glossing over serious ethnic inequalities that permeate many Western nations, serving to promote lack of understanding and intolerance.[19] This debate is best viewed as a continuum. There are those who contend that some form of collective rights are necessary for the full realisation of human rights (such as Margalit and Raz, Kymlicka, Van der Wal and Young[20]) and there are those who

---

12   Stapleton *supra* n6 at xxiii.

13   Mill, J.S., *Considerations on Representative Government* 1861 (1958) Liberal Arts Press, New York Chapter XVI.

14   See Chapter 6 at 267.

15   Dembour, Marie-Benedicte *Who Believes in Human Rights? Reflections on the European Convention* Cambridge Univ. Press (2006) Chapter 5.

16   In Rawls's *Theory of Justice*, widely regarded as the cornerstone of liberal political theory, the focus is purely on justice for individuals – Rawls, John *A Theory Of Justice* (1973) OUP, Oxford.

17   Van Dyke, Vernon (1975) 'Justice as Fairness for Groups?' *American Political Science Review* Vol. 69 at 614.

18   Van Dyke, Vernon (1995a) 'Ethnic Communities in Political Theory' in Kymlicka (ed.) *The Rights of Minority Cultures* OUP at 48.

19   *Ibid.* at 50 argues 'Individualism, combined with the usual stress on personal merit, is destructive of cultures other than the majority or dominant culture'.

20   Margalit, A and Raz, J 'National Self Determination' in Kymlicka (ed.) *The Rights of Minority Cultures* (1995a) OUP; Kymlicka, W *Multicultural Citizenship* (1995b); Vander Wal, K 'Collective Human Rights: A Western View' in Berting *Human Rights in a Pluralist World* (1990) Meckers, The Netherlands; Young Iris M 'Together in Difference' in Kymlicka (1995a) at 155–176.

argue by contrast that only individual rights should be recognised by international law (such as Waldron and Donnelly).[21] Yet much of this ostensibly necessary dichotomy between the two perspectives is misleading and has probably contributed to the reluctance, evidenced in international treaties, to recognise group-based claims.[22]

The value of community

A confusion in terms has contributed to this uneasy dichotomy, particularly the terms 'group rights' and 'collective rights' which are often used interchangeably. Collective rights, as properly understood, are derivative in that they vest in the individual members of groups, with group, or corporate rights, vesting in the group as a moral entity. The starting point with both the collective and group rights schools is a belief in the value of cultural membership to the individual. Avishai Margalit and Joseph Raz state:

> It may be no more that a brute fact that our world is organised in a large measure around groups with pervasive cultures. But it is a fact with far-reaching consequences. It means, in the first place, that membership of such groups is of great importance to individual well-being, for it greatly affects one's opportunities, one's ability to engage in the relationships and pursuits marked by the culture. Secondly, it means that the prosperity of the culture is important to the well-being of its members. If the culture is decaying, or it is persecuted or discriminated against, the options and opportunities open to its members will shrink, become less attractive, and their pursuit less likely to be successful.[23]

It is argued that liberalism with its dual emphasis on autonomy and freedom cannot ignore the inherent value of culture as a precondition to individual freedom.[24] Thus, the recognition of cultural communities is essential and minority rights (whether collective or group based) must be recognised so that the culture can flourish.

The value of cultural identity is also stressed by others concerned with group rights, such as Darlene Johnston,[25] Iris Marion Young,[26] Michael Hartney[27] Yoram Dinstein,[28] Johan Degenaar,[29] Vernon Van Dyke[30] and Charles

---

21   Waldron, Jeremy 'The Cosmopolitan Alternative' in Kymlicka (1995a) *supra* n16 at 93–119; Donnelly, J 'Human Rights, Individual Rights and Collective Rights' in Berting (ed.) *supra* n20 at 39–62.

22   Caney, Simon Liberalism and Communitarianism: A misconceived debate' *Political Studies* 1992 Vol 40 273–289 at 273–4.

23   *Supra* n20 at 87.

24   See Kymlicka *Liberalism, Community and Culture* OUP 1989 Chapter 8.

25   *Ibid.* at 13.

26   Young *supra* n20 at 166; 'Towards a Critical Theory of Justice' Social Theory and Practice Vol.7 No. 3 (Fall 1981) pp 280-302.

27   Hartney, M 'Some Confusions Concerning Collective Rights' in Kymlicka (1995a) *supra* n20.

28   Dinstein, Y 'Collective Human Rights of Peoples and Minorities' (1976) *ICLQ* at 117.

29   Degenaar, Johan 'Nationalism, Liberalism and Pluralism' in Butler, Elphick and Welsh (eds.) *Democratic Liberalism in South Africa* (1987) Wesleyan Univ. Press, Connecticut at 247.

30   Van Dyke, Vernon 'Justice as Fairness: For groups?' American Political Science Review Vol. 69 (1975) p607–614; *Human Rights, Ethnicity and Discrimination* (1985)

Taylor[31] to name but a few. Membership and allegiance to a particular group is not simply a significant element of a person's life, but is considered by some writers to frame individual personality.[32] The demand for *recognition*, Taylor argues is fundamental to our understanding of ourselves.[33] The attitude of the enveloping society towards our culture has profound effects on our identity:

> The thesis is that our identity is partly shaped by recognition or its absence, often by misrecognition of others, and so a person or group of people can suffer real damage, real distortion, if the people or society around them mirror back to them a confining or demeaning or contemptible picture of themselves.[34]

Minorities that have suffered misrecognition will have a depreciatory image of themselves and will have internalised their inferiority. This echoes Frantz Fanon's argument that dominant class will crystallise its hegemonic superiority by subjugating those deemed 'inferior' or 'different'[35]. This demand for recognition, according to Gutmann, necessitates both the protection of individual rights and the recognition of particular needs of members of cultural groups.[36] The method of achieving the latter is the point of departure between traditional liberals, constructive liberals and communitarians.

One of the fundamental questions here is whether cultural membership can be construed as a good in itself, as communitarians argue, or whether it is deemed to be a value in its facilitative capacity as constructive liberals have argued. The consequences of these approaches become particularly apparent when one addresses the issue of illiberal cultural practices. However, both constructive liberals and communitarians agree that the state cannot remain indifferent to the plight of these cultural groups.

The importance of cultural identity

The cultural dimension of identity, even if constructed in a multi-layered, cosmopolitan framework, is very important to individual notions of self. This is perhaps most apparent in the case of disenfranchised minority groups such as the Roma. The

---

Greenwood Press, Connecticut; 'Ethnic communities in political theory' in Kymlicka (1995a) *supra* n18 pp 30–56.

31   Taylor, Charles *Philosophical Arguments* (1995) Harvard University Press, Cambridge, Mass; 'Atomism' in Avineri, S and De Shalit, A (eds.) *Communitarianism and Individualism* (1992) Oxford Univ. Press, Oxford pp 29–50; 'The modern identity' in Daly, M (ed.) *Communitarianism − A New Public Ethics* (1994) California: Wadsworth pp 55–71; 'Cross-purposes: the liberal-communitarian debate' in Rosenblum, N.L. (ed.) *Liberalism and the Moral Life* (1989) Harvard University Press, Cambridge, Mass.

32   McDonald, Michael 'Should communities have rights? Reflections on liberal Individualism' *4 Canadian Journal of Law and Jurisprudence* (1991) 217 at 219.

33   Taylor, C 'The Politics of Recognition' in Gutmann (ed.) *Multiculturalism* (1994) Princeton Univ. Press, NJ pp 25–73.

34   *Ibid.* 25.

35   Fanon, Frantz *Les Damnés de la Terre* 1961 Maspero, Paris.

36   Gutmann in *supra* n33 at 8.

question remains as to how far cultural identity should be actively protected rather than simply respected. According to Liégeois, the identity of the individual Roma is enmeshed in the group:

> The individual is that which his belonging to a given group makes him. He is neither known nor recognised as an individual, but by the situation within the group, which determines his identity both for himself – his self-designation – and for others: the ways in which he will be seen by them, and see them in turn. Hence the significance, when people meet, of employing linguistic and cultural elements and designations, enabling the individuals in question to defines themselves and each other, to differentiate themselves and yet feel a common bond.[37]

Positive recognition and protection of identity is advocated by Michael Sandel, who espouses the view that hatred is flourished by an anomic, mass society that does not support cultural identity and group rights: 'Intolerance flourishes most where forms of life are dislocated, roots unsettled, traditions undone'.[38] Sandel's 'communitarian' perspective is the extreme point of recognition of the importance of the collectivity; rejecting the political discourse of rights altogether and demanding that the State actively promote the identity of groups.

Yet the importance of cultural identity is not lost on most individualist theorists.[39] Macdonald is critical of the view of the group as merely an aggregate of individuals but argues that notions of group rights are unnecessary to enable groups to develop and flourish.[40] Similarly, Jeremy Waldron argues against the notion that liberals necessarily reject all social dimensions of a person's identity.[41] While not denying the value of cultural membership, Hartney stresses that such value is individualist in nature, in that the value of the group is based on its value to the lives of individual members. The group has no value over and above the interests of its constituent members.[42] The consequence of this approach is that groups cannot claim rights as legal entities against the state. Individual members could have a collective interest in the preservation of the group but this will be realised through individual rights rather than the rights of the collectivity which could essentially undermine individual rights. Theorists such as Jack Donnelly and Michael Walzer offer very different theoretical

---

37   Liégeois, J. P *Roma, Gypsies, Travellers* (1994) C/E at 63.

38   Sandel, M 'Morality and the Liberal Ideal' in J.P. Sterba (ed.) *Justice: Alternative Political Perspectives* (1992) Belmont, California at 224.

39   There are some notable exceptions, particularly the Cosmopolitan Alternative advocated by Jeremy Waldron. He criticises Kymlicka and other theorists who treat cultural membership as necessary to the individuals well-being, arguing that such cultural identity is not necessary for rational meaning and choice: 'In general there is something artificial about a commitment to preserve minority cultures. Cultures live and grow, change and sometimes wither away; they amalgamate with other cultures, or they adapt themselves to geographical or demographic necessity' (Waldron, J *supra* n21 at 109).

40   *Supra* n4.

41   Waldron, Jeremy 'Values and Critical Morality' in *Liberal Rights* (1993) Cambridge Univ. Press pp 168–202.

42   Hartney, M 'Some Confusions Concerning Collective Rights' in Kymlicka (1995a) *supra* n20 at 205–7.

perspectives which recognise the importance of culture yet they conclude that the state should not interfere with the private sphere of personal life, which includes cultural membership:

> For support and comfort and a sense of belonging, men and women look to their groups; for freedom and mobility, they look to the State.[43]

The recognition of groups is clearly at odds with the view that liberalism enables the divorce of ethnicity from the civic/political community and offers neutrality in terms of the good life. In Donnelly's defence of the Universal Declaration model he envisages equal access to essential goods, services and opportunities through an individualist paradigm. He argues that the liberal state can protect difference while favouring a particular liberal vision based on equal concern and respect. Therefore, the strength of the liberal state is its neutrality regarding particular conceptions of the good life but correspondingly 'it is required *not* to be neutral towards activities that infringe or violate human rights'.[44] Brian Barry similarly offers a persuasive 'difference–blind' model of liberalism which does not privilege any particular minority interests.[45]

Chandran Kukathas also emphasises the importance of group membership to the individual but believes that the liberal language of individualism is the only way that such competing group claims can be treated fairly.[46] This can clearly be seen in his elevation of the individual right to exit the group over the interests of the group to self-preservation.[47]

Indeed, even individualist, anti-liberalist thinkers such as Frederick Nietzsche[48] and Martin Heidegger[49] recognised the significance of group membership in the formation of the person. The implications of such theories is far from an endorsement of collective rights but serves to caution against the notion of the Self as purely atomised.

It is thus apparent that modern political theorists do not ignore the value of cultural identity but this does not necessitate an inevitable recognition of particular minority rights. The individualist will argue that cultural identity can be respected and secured through the application of non-discrimination. In some cases this has been extended to support for very narrowly defined collective rights in the form of

---

43   Walzer, M 'Pluralism: A Political Perspective' in Kymlicka (1995a.) *supra* n20 at p139–154 at 148.

44   Donnelly, Jack 'In defense of the Universal Declaration Model' in Lyons and Mayall (eds) *International Human Rights in the Twenty-first Century*. (2003) Rowman and Littlefield at 31.

45   Barry, Brian *Culture and Equality* (2001) Polity, passim.

46   Kukathas, C 'Are there any group rights?' in Kymlicka (1995a) *supra* n21 at 230.

47   *Ibid.* at 238.

48   Nietzsche, F 'Homer's Contest' in Levy, O (ed.) *The Complete Works of Frederick Nietzsche* (1911) London, T.A. Foulis at 59 and 'The natural value of egoism' in *Twilight of the Idols* Middlesex Penguin (1968).

49   Heidegger, Martin *Being and Time* (1962) Blackwell, Oxford; *Existence and Being* (1968) 3rd ed. Vision Press, London.

affirmative action. Those in favour of active protection for groups argue by contrast that a rethink of traditional liberalism is required beyond affirmative action in the form of special minority rights.

The importance of the group to the individual

The key distinction between the individual and group rights approaches lies in the extent to which group membership is considered important to the individual and the most effective way to recognise this importance. There is a strong argument that universal human rights as typically understood are afforded to individuals and that any group rights would conflict and potentially undermine individual human rights. Jack Donnelly contends that unless human rights rest solely in individuals they are meaningless:

> If we are serious about the idea of human rights, there is no alternative to holding firm on the principle that they are the rights of individuals, and of individuals only.[50]

It is considered that the application of rights based on group status will inevitably threaten individual rights by promoting 'a separatist mentality that elevates ethnic identity over universal human identity'.[51] An enlightened interpretation of the non-discrimination standards codified in international documents; coupled with the recognition of other substantive rights such as freedom of association and expression is regarded as sufficient to protect the cultural elements of personal identity.[52] Such an argument receives support from the absence of international recognition of group rights discussed in Chapter 6.[53]

In my view, such an ethnocentric perspective fails to recognise the intricate link between group identity and individual rights which makes individual rights without a collective dimension meaningless for many people.[54] The primacy of the individual

---

50   Donnelly, J *supra* n21 at 45.

51   Rockefeller 'Comment' in Gutmann (ed.) *supra* n33 at 89. See also Packer, John 'Problems in defining Minorities' in Fottrell and Bowring (eds) *Minority and Group Rights in the new Millennium* (1999) Kluwer: The Hague, Chapter 10.

52   Rodley, Nigel. S 'Conceptual Problems in the Protection of Minorities: International Legal Developments' *HRQ* (1995) Vol.17 at 64–5; Packer, John 'On the definition of minorities' in Packer and Myntti *The Protection of Ethnic and Linguistic Minorities in Europe* (1993) Abo Akademie Univ., Finland pp 23–65, argues that the basic error of post-War minority protection has been to depart from the general premise of equality and emphasise difference.

53   Rodley *ibid.*

54   Such criticisms have been levied at the individualistic interpretations of Western thinkers in the context group rights in Developing World nations. See Zvobgo, Eddison Jonas Mudadirwa 'A Third World View' in Kommers and Loescher (eds) *Human Rights and American Foreign Policy* (1979) at 95; Panikaar, R 'Is the notion of human rights a Western concept?' (1982) Diogenes 120 p75–102. Donnelly recognises that the values of Aboriginal communities are at odds with the individualist tradition. He advocates individual human rights even though at odds with their traditions as providing a powerful weapon against the destruction of their land and values: Donnelly, J *supra* n17 at 52–3. However, it is apparent

over their community can be seen as an attractive approach where all people are given equal opportunities and have equal access to education. However, for many people born into unequal, disadvantaged situations, the primacy of individual rights does not represent their reality. J Herman Burges concurs with Donnelly[55] that the purpose of human rights should be in securing the indispensable conditions necessary for existence as a human being, yet also regards the realisation of group rights as compatible with, and often essential to meet this objective.[56] A broad interpretation of equal dignity incorporating recognition of individual difference, as advocated by Taylor and Rockefeller, necessitates support for the survival of cultural groups.[57]

Indeed, individual rights violations often arise from the denial of collective rights.[58] For example, when the cultural values of a minority group are tolerated but not protected by the state, individual members may find that their rights of expression and association are restricted.[59] In such a case it would appear fallacious to draw a sharp distinction between individual and collective rights.

The distinction may also appear absurd when one considers the option of leaving the group, especially when the particular group is a visible cultural minority. The issue of choice is a key point of debate within liberal theory. Liberals place a great emphasis on the capacity to make choices and many argue that membership of cultural groups is a choice, even if it is not acknowledged as such by the individual.[60] John Packer stresses the importance of choice and criticises attempts to show that a theory of justice is wrong if it fails to recognise group rights. He argues against the perception of culture as a static commodity, perceiving group membership as 'established by free association in relation to a specific issue' rather than by birth or particular features.[61] However, in considering groups with a high social profile, Margalit and Raz observe that there is no question of choice being involved in membership of a particular cultural group.[62] Self-identification is only one of a number of ways in which minority status is afforded and maintained. Indeed, many Roma are reluctant to identify themselves as such in official surveys yet this does not mean they have rejected their cultural identity. Boundary maintenance between groups is maintained through interaction with the dominant ethno-civic group.[63] It is not an easy process

---

that in defending their land rights Aboriginal communities have had most success in working as a group to secure reserves for their people.

55   Donnelly, J *The Concept of Human Rights* (1985) Routledge.

56   Herman Burgers, J 'The Function of Human Rights as Collective and Individual Rights' in Berting *supra* n20 at 73.

57   *Supra* n33 Taylor at 39–42 and Rockefeller at 87.

58   Baehr, Peter. R and Vander Wal, Koo 'Human Rights as Individual and Collective Rights' in Berting *supra* n20 at 37.

59   The cultural insensitivity of Part V of the Criminal Justice and Public Order Act 1994 which criminalises unauthorised camping-rights to non-interference with family life and freedom of association are seriously undermined as a result.

60   Tamir, Yael Liberal *Nationalism* (1993) Princeton Univ Press at 21–5.

61   Packer *supra* n52 at 43.

62   Margalit and Raz 'National self-determination' in Kymlicka (1995a) *supra* n20 at 84.

63   Bancroft, Angus *Roma and Gypsy-travellers in Europe* (2005) Ashgate.

for a member of a high-profile minority group such as the Roma, to assume the values of the dominant group and be accepted as a member of that group. Entrenched prejudice and a relational conception of ourselves complicate this movement. This is one of the reasons why denying group rights to immigrant communities, often defined by political theorists to include the Roma, appears simplistic.

Integration into an alternative or dominant culture is likely to be a very slow process. With this in mind it is difficult to see how any theory of justice can treat the application of group and individual rights as anything other than interdependent.

The Cosmopolitan Alternative

Advocated by Jeremy Waldron, who refers to the writing of Salman Rushdie, the 'cosmopolitan alternative' acknowledges the importance of culture to our individual identities, but also emphasises the variety of cultural sources to which we are exposed.

> From the fact that each option must have a cultural meaning, it does not follow that there must be one cultural framework in which each available option is assigned a meaning. Meaningful options may come to us as items or fragments from a variety of cultural sources.[64]

Waldron argues that it would be unwise to promote certain ethnic cultures simply because they are singularly fundamental to individual well-being. Indeed, he goes so far as to assert that there are no such things as distinct cultures and certainly no need to protect particular cultural values.[65] Such a claim receives support if one looks strictly at the overlaps between different groups, for example those occasioned by inter-marriage. In this sense cosmopolitanism is compatible with traditional liberalism as the state is perceived to be neutral among many competing claims and values. To Waldron we are 'cultural borrowers' capable of choosing a variety of allegiances, views and practices. Thus, he defines the modern person as a 'creature of modernity, conscious of living in a mixed-up world and having a mixed-up self'.[66]

It is evident that Waldron has a particular type of 'modern' person in mind, presumably those people who do not feel bonds with numerous cultural sources are regarded as 'primitive' and undeveloped. Borrowing from a variety of cultural stimuli may be an increasing occurrence, even a desirable ideal if we seek to escape fundamentalism and extremism, but one could argue that it is unrealistic when applied to disadvantaged and long-term marginalised communities. Waldron's own culture may allow him the choice to 'dip' into alternative cultural sources but it would seem profoundly unjust if people immersed into a particular cultural group, spatially or culturally removed from surrounding influences, were to have their identity undermined because they have not 'developed' to partake in the cultural exchange. Margaret Moore argues that cosmopolitanism may simply be a mask for Western individualism in that it promotes a global culture centred on secularism, consumerism and individualism:

---

64   Waldron *supra* n21 at 106.
65   A view supported by Kateb, George 'Notes on Pluralism' Social Research 61/3 (1994) pp 512-37.
66   Waldron *supra* n21 at 95.

Global capitalism tends to favour those cultures that operate in technologically advanced economies; and some languages and cultural narratives and practices will be disadvantaged in relation to other cultures .... Because the various cultures of the world do not compete on a level playing field, state action in support of minority cultures can be justified in terms of an appeal to equality and fairness.[67]

Furthermore, it is difficult to accept the glory of borrowing from a variety of cultural perspectives when the particular culture one wishes to borrow from is constantly threatened by hegemonic forces. In this respect there is limited recognition amongst cosmopolitans of the necessity for strong alternative cultures. Ross Poole notes that for the 'rooted cosmopolitan' the individual's commitment to their own culture will be tempered by the recognition that others have precisely the same commitment to theirs.[68] I would argue that Waldron's desire for alternative stimuli would not be adversely affected by a greater recognition of the rights of groups. On the contrary, cultural borrowing may be facilitated by such recognition. The lack of recognition of the travelling needs of many Gypsy families in the United Kingdom led to the Criminal Justice and Public Order Act 1994. The decision by many 'new age travellers' to adopt a nomadic lifestyle was frustrated by the legislation which sought to protect the dominant cultural values of stringent planning controls and sedentarism.

Waldron fears the artificial maintenance of group boundaries, the dangers of which are exposed in the writings of Iris Marion Young. For Young the self is constituted in the community.[69] However, concerned with the use and exclusion of the 'other' in the formation of identity, she argues:

The ideology of group difference in this logic attempts to make clear borders between groups, and to identify the characteristics that mark the purity of one group off from the characteristics of the Others.[70]

As an alternative Young advocates a relational conception of difference in which groups must be seen as overlapping, as constituted in relation to each other. Addis similarly argues that ethnic groups do not have strict boundaries and are constituted relationally and that this is also the case for individuals thus it cannot be a reason for denying groups rights.[71] This is in keeping with Taylor's need for recognition which he frames in a dialogical context: 'my own identity crucially depends on my dialogical relations with others'.[72] This dialogue has not worked well for the Roma whose ethnic identity has been formed in part by their position in or, more often outside, society. This argument is developed by Angus Bancroft who defines the Roma as a

---

67   Moore, Margaret 'Globalization, Cosmopolitanism and Minority Nationalism' in Keating and McGarry (eds) *Minority Nationalism and the changing International Order* (2001) OUP at 54.

68   Poole, Ross *Nation and Identity* (1999) Routledge at 162.

69   Young, Iris Marion 'Polity and group difference: A critique of the ideal of universal citizenship' (1989) *Ethics* 99 at 260.

70   Young *supra* n20 at 158–9

71   Addis, Adeno 'Individualism, Communitarianism and the rights of ethnic minorities' *notre Dame Law Review* (1991–92) Vol 67 pp 615–676 at 655.

72   Taylor *supra* n33 at 34.

status group whose ethnicity has been partly constituted by their economic activity.[73] As this economic activity has traditionally existed at the periphery of the majority society it has become easy for them to be excluded and defined as the Other.

Any decision to exit the group, even if possible, must be based on informed choice. If a person chooses to remain within their particular ethnic community then the practice of undermining that community in order to promote greater awareness of 'alternatives' amounts to nothing more than imperialist rhetoric. For those who are fortunate enough to be exposed to and enjoy a variety of cultural influences throughout their lives, choice is essential. This choice is evidently not facilitated by the false maintenance of ethnic boundaries but neither is it assisted by the erosion of minority identities.

The Communitarian critique

Communitarianism was popularised by, but is by no means confined to, the American sociologist Amitai Etzioni in his work *The Spirit of Community*.[74] According to Elizabeth Frazer and Nicola Lacey the basic message of a communitarian philosophy is clear:

> ... unless we can revive the idea of a substantial common life, unless we can design political (state and non-State) institutions which enable each of us to feel empowered and involved as citizens, our society may disintegrate, either literally or in the sense that it will be governable only by authoritarian means.[75]

Plagued by his perception of teenage American apathy, Etzioni is concerned to stress the responsibilities and duties of the citizen to their community in an attempt to recreate the sense of belonging through reaffirming a set of shared moral values:[76]

> We suggest that free individuals require a community which backs them up against encroachment by the state and sustains morality by drawing on the gentle prodding of kin, friends, neighbours and other community members ....[77]

Etzioni is offering a critique of individualism coupled with a prescription to make society 'better' by prioritising communal values. However, this should not be used to detract from some of the more interesting communitarian arguments as to the boundaries of group identity.

The Communitarian philosophy rejects the notion of the atomistic individual and with it the contractarian vision of the individual existing before society.[78] Thomas Moody explains the deficiency of liberal theory:

---

73   Bancroft, Angus *Roma and Gypsy-travellers in Europe* (2005) Ashgate at 43–45.

74   Etzioni, Amitai the Spirit of Community (1993) Fontana, London.

75   Frazer, Elizabeth and Lacey, Nicola *The Politics of Community. A Feminist Critique of the Liberal-communitarian Debate* (1993) Harvester Wheatsheaf, NY at 104.

76   Etzioni *supra* n74 at 15 and 18)

77   *Ibid.* at 15.

78   For a readable overview of this debate see Bell, Daniel *Communitarianism and its Critics* (1993) Oxford University Press and Mulhall, Stephen and Swift, Adam *Liberals and Communitarians* (1996) Blackwell.

... Communitarians attempt to reconstruct important liberal ideals such as respect for persons, liberty and justice on a more acceptable metaphysical basis, i.e., based on a relational self and a non-foundationalist epistemology.[79]

The communitarian theorist, Daniel Bell argues that the enlightenment ideal of an autonomous subject divorced from surroundings and entanglements of history is one of the deepest problems of liberal theory.[80] The importance of the community to individual development can be seen at its strongest point in Sandel's brand of 'constitutive communitarianism' in which the community constitutes the person.[81] The nationalist theorist Johann Gottlieb Herder argued that language and culture were not merely aspects of the external world that frame our identity, rather they are constitutive of ourselves.[82] Zelim Sukabrty explains the importance of collective identity thus:

> ... the 'profane' dimension of collectivity is not something counterpoised to the 'sacredness' of an individual, but represents one of the vital ingredients of the individual's self, the psyche (self-consciousness, self-image, self esteem, etc.) as well as the most important vehicle through which it experiences, actualizes and objectivates itself. From this point of view, the preferred ways of dichotomization of these inseparable facets of the same integral phenomenon seem unwarranted and artificial.[83]

The language of individualism, which seeks to isolate the self from its surroundings, appears deficient in that it does not attach sufficient importance to the cultural aspect of identity. According to Taylor our identity is forged through a dialogue with those people that share our values and culture.[84] It could be argued that identity is also forged through the attitudes, including misrecognition, of others.

Furthermore, it is regarded as a myth that individualism, where the right is prior to the good, does not promote a particular vision of the good life. In *On Liberty*, J.S Mill defends the liberal proximation of the priority of right:

> The only freedom which deserves the name, is that of pursuing our own goods in our own way, so long as we do not attempt to deprive others of theirs, or impede their efforts to obtain it.[85]

Sandel's communitarian critique supports Kymlicka's analysis of the liberal state's 'benign neglect' by which the state is supposedly neutral and not linked to any

---

79   Moody, Thomas 'Some Comparisons between Liberalism and an Eccentric Communitarianism' in Peder and Hudson (eds.) *Communitarianism, Liberalism and Social Responsibility* 187–197 Studies in Social and Political Theory Vol. 14, Edwin Mellen Press, Lewiston at 188.

80   Bell, Daniel *Communitarianism and its Critics* (1993) OUP at 29.

81   Sandel, M *Liberalism and the Limits of Justice* (1982) Cambridge Univ. Press: Cambridge at 147–155.

82   Herder, J.G. *J.G. Herder on Social and Political Culture* (1969) Cambridge Univ. Press.

83   Skubarty, Zelim *as if Peoples Mattered* (2000) Kluwer at 278.

84   Taylor, Charles *Multiculturalism and the Politics of Recognition* (1992) Princeton Univ Press at 32–3.

85   Mill, J S. 'On Liberty' in Daly, M (ed.) *supra* n31 p11–21 at 17.

aspiration of the good life.[86] Dworkin contends that a liberal state will not promote a particular substantive view of the good life, promoting instead the universal notion of equal respect.[87] In a similar vein, Kukathas recognises the disadvantage experienced by many minorities but argues that the state must not be seen to favour or promote such private interests.[88] However, this is itself a particularist, albeit broadly constructed, version of the good life which promotes autonomy as the greatest good and is thus little more than an example of liberal hegemonic cultural supremacy. Such a view with its emphasis on formal equality does not recognise the inevitability of the pervasive dominance of the majority culture in modern states.[89]

Charles Taylor argues that the affirmation of certain rights ties us to the affirmation of particular capacities and thus defines certain standards by which a life may be judged full or truncated.[90] Furthermore, the conception of ourselves as autonomous individuals could not have been sustained alone or in a different type of society.[91] Consider, for example, members of a geographically isolated community that has been marginalised and excluded from the larger society – they do not exhibit any desire to choose between different conceptions of the good life. A common criticism directed towards the Roma is their lack of active interest in formal education and unwillingness to engage in wage-labour. Both make possible the liberal view of the good life, enabling the individual to maximise potential for choice in life by promoting personal autonomy and self-development. The conception of the good life is likely to be very different for members of a culture which values family relations and group networks over the individual. Taylor wonders how long we could continue understanding autonomous choices without public debate concerning moral and political questions.[92] Thus, in the absence of a particular liberal cultural framework the concepts of individualism and autonomy may find no place.

To maximise human potential, the political system must, Sandel argues, be based on collective interests:

> To imagine a person incapable of constitutive attachments such as these is not to conceive an ideally free and rational agent, but to imagine a person wholly without character, without moral depth. For to have character is to know that I move in a history I neither summon nor command, which carries consequences nonetheless for my choices and conduct.[93]

---

86   See below at 71.

87   Dworkin, R 'Liberalism' in Hampshire, Stuart *Public and Private Morality* (1978) Cambridge Univ. Press, passim. and *A Matter of Principle* Clarendon, Oxford at 191.

88   Kukathas 'Are there any cultural rights?' *Political Theory* Vol. 20 (1992) pp 105–139 at 234–7.

89   Poole *supra* n68 at 121.

90   Taylor 'Atomism' in Avineri, S and De Shalit, A (eds.) *supra* n31 p 29–50 at 43; and *supra* n33 at 43.

91   Taylor, Charles 'The Modern Identity' in Daly, M (ed.) *supra* n31 p55–71 at 59.

92   *Ibid.*

93   Sandel, M 'The Procedural Republic and the Unencumbered Self' in Avineri and De Shalit (eds.) *supra* n31 p12–28 at 23.

One of the greatest difficulties presented by the communitarian approach is how to calculate these collective interests. Indeed, Frazer argues that the whole concept of 'community' is complex and encompasses several contradictions.[94] For John Packer, communitarian assertions are 'illiberal in nature' as the fundamental significance attached to groups contradicts the premises of equality and autonomy.[95] Kukathas accepts that there are criticisms of liberalism's priority of the individual but also rejects the priority, advocated by communitarians, of political community.[96] Individuals may 'belong' to a variety of different communities which constitute their identity and communitarianism fails to address the complexity of relationships when it focuses on the one political community.[97] Furthermore, Kukathas argues that the need to prioritise the political may in fact weaken other allegiances and communal ties.[98]

A powerful critique of communitarianism has been offered by feminist writers such as Elizabeth Kingdom[99] and Marilyn Friedman[100] who are concerned that the attractive discourse of community spirit and togetherness can mask and legitimise oppressive practices and attitudes towards women. Traditional liberal individualism has also been criticised for ignoring the experience of women and allowing the public/private dichotomy to operate through the undermining of women's experiences.[101] Feminists find an appealing aspect in a political theory which is keen to advocate the collective experience rather than simply the white, male, dominant experience.[102] On closer inspection though, the gender issue appears undeveloped in much of communitarian thinking. Frazer and Lacey observe that:

> It hardly begins to address the political problem of overcoming the domination and inequalities which deprive certain groups of a voice, or give their voices systematically lower status.[103]

The promotion of a particular public good in the communitarian agenda may exclude 'different' groups and alternative moralities. The issue of who has the power not just to speak but to be heard is undeveloped. Addis argues that communitarianism

---

94   Frazer, Elizabeth *The Problems of Communitarian Politics* (1999) OUP.

95   Packer, John in Räikkä (ed) *do we need Minority Rights?* (1996) Kluwer, Martinus-Nijhoff at 132.

96   Kukathas, Chandran 'Liberalism, Communitarianism and Political Community' in Paul, Miller and Paul *The Communitarian Challenge to Liberalism* (1996) Cambridge Univ. Press pp 80–104 passim.

97   *Ibid.*

98   *Ibid.* at 92.

99   Kingdom, Elizabeth 'Gender and citizenship rights' in Dermaine and Entwistle (eds) *Beyond Communitarianism. Citizenship, Politics and Education* (1996) St Martins Press, NY pp 30–41; Friedman, Marilyn in May, Friedman, Clark (eds) *Mind and Morals: Essays on Cognitive Science and Ethics* (1996) MIT Press Cambridge (Massachusetts), passim.

100   Friedman, M *Capitalism and Freedom* (1964) Chicago: Univ. of Chicago Press.

101   See for example Frazer and Lacey *supra* n75 Chapters 2 and 3.

102   Phillips, Anne 'Democracy and Difference' in Kymlicka (1995a) *supra* n20 pp 288–299 at 293 comments that 'abstract individualism imposes a unitary conception of human needs and concerns, and this serves to marginalise those groups who differ from the dominant norm'.

103   Fraser and Lacy *supra* n75 at 145.

is assimilationist at a national level with its emphasis on the common good and exclusionist at a local level whereby people are isolated on account of their difference.[104]

As a political theory, communitarianism has many critics but it does provide a powerful ontological critique as to the isolation of the Self from its surroundings.[105] Furthermore, as Taylor argues, the position of liberal neutrality is exposed as a myth. The liberal state with its emphasis on equality and non-discrimination is seen as "inhospitable to difference because it can't accommodate what the members of distinct societies really aspire to, which is survival'.[106]

Situating group rights in the political space

Assimilation, integration and pluralism in practice

The United Nations 'Study on Racial Discrimination in the Political, Economic Social and Cultural Spheres' considered the different approaches a State may adopt when dealing with minorities.[107]

Assimilation is a strategy based on the 'superiority of the dominant cultural group;' minority groups will be accepted in society so long as they abandon their distinct culture.[108] Such a policy has been used continuously with respect to Roma in most states. Some of the more obvious recent examples which will illustrate this point include the forcible name changing policy of the Bulgarian Government which ended in 1989,[109] the forcible sterilisation of Roma in Czechoslovakia and the Czech Republic,[110] and the prohibition of unauthorised camping in the UK.[111] Douglas Sanders notes that assimilationist strategies are not the exclusive property of Western democratic states having been equally evident in the socialist tradition.[112] This is evidenced in Zoltan Barany's authoritative account of the history of East European Gypsies and can be seen in the context of Hungarian politics in Chapter 7.[113]

For those who choose to resist assimilation, the strategy may involve exclusion or containment. Liégeois notes that the unintegrated Gypsy or traveller is perceived as physically threatening and ideologically disruptive, particularly through their

---

104   Addis, Adeno *supra* n71 at 647.

105   Taylor, Charles 'Cross-purposes: The liberal-communitarian debate' in Rosenblum (ed.) *supra* n31.

106   Taylor *supra* n84 at 61.

107   UN Sales No 71.X IV.2.

108   *Ibid.* para. 370.

109   Human Rights Watch *Destroying Ethnic Identity – The Gypsies of Bulgaria* (1991) HRW, NY at 11. It is estimated that some 400,000 Gypsies were forced to change their names and by 1985 virtually all Bulgarian Gypsies had received Bulgarian names.

110   Human Rights Watch *Struggling for Ethnic Identity: Czechoslovakia's Endangered Gypsies* (1992) HRW, NY at 50–51. see also Chapter 1 *supra* n45.

111   See O'Nions "The Marginalisation of Gypsies [1995] 3 *WebJCLI* no pagination.

112   Sanders, Douglas 'Collective Rights' (1991) *HRLQ* Vol. 13 pp 368–386 at 371.

113   Barany *supra* n2 passim.

laziness and asocial behaviour.[114] It is the nomadism of the traveller that has generated a particular fear. The traveller is defined as an asocial marginal with no fixed abode – the traveller is not born Gypsy, but becomes so.[115]

Integration is a less hostile objective, aiming to combine diverse cultural groups in unity while retaining their distinct cultures. Such a strategy according to Special Rapporteur Capotorti, would seek to:

> (i) eliminate all purely ethnic lines of cleavage; ii) to guarantee the same rights, opportunities and responsibilities to all citizens, whatever their group membership.[116]

While this may appear to be a desirable objective, it gives rise to one serious question namely how is transcultural unity to be achieved without damaging the cultures of the constituent units? Furthermore, it will be shown that serious human rights issues are raised when the dominant culture attempts to impose any sort of unity on minority cultures. It is easy to envisage how the integration objective may mean that a state is hostile towards special minority rights which aim to improve the situation of particular groups as such measures may also promote heterogeneity.

An alternative approach, recognising this deficiency, is offered by pluralism which regards cultural diversity as inherently valuable to the whole of society. It attempts to enable groups to maintain and develop their identity while uniting different ethnic groups within a framework of mutual independence, respect and equality.[117] A pluralist policy should promote diversity at the grass roots level within a framework of unity and co-operation. This approach is compatible with the recognition of special minority rights and tries to avoid creating a cultural hierarchy. In his recommendations to the Sub-commission on the Protection of Minorities, Special rapporteur Eide endorsed a pluralist approach:

> The state should be the common home for all parts of its resident population under conditions of equality, with separate group identities preserved for those who want it under conditions making it possible to develop those identities. Neither majorities nor minorities should be entitled to assert their identity in ways that deny the possibility for others to do the same, or that lead to discrimination against others in the common domain …. Priority in minority protection should be given to members of groups that are truly vulnerable and subject to discrimination and marginalisation by the majority.[118]

Although Eide refers to 'members of groups,' he evidently perceives minorities as having their own particular identity and the vision he advocates for minority rights protection is manifestly pluralist in nature.

---

114   Liégeois *supra* n37 at 145–6.

115   *Ibid.* This is evidenced by the UK's legislative approach to nomadism which defined gipsies [sic] as 'persons of nomadic habit of life whatever their race or origin' Caravan Sites Act 1968 s16.

116   Capotorti, F *Study on the Rights of Persons Belonging to Ethnic, Religious and Linguistic Minorities* UN Study Series 5, (1991) paras 373–377.

117   *Supra* n116 paras 366–7.

118   Eide, A 'Protection of Minorities: Recommendations to the UN Sub-Commission' *Profile in Minority Rights Group Minorities in Central and Eastern Europe* (1993) MRG, London.

Pluralists argue that accommodation of group difference can serve to promote confidence and allegiance to the larger polity, as members of minorities will see that their identity is nurtured and not threatened.[119] It is submitted that a pluralist vision is the only approach which does not threaten the individual human rights of members of minorities. Furthermore, there is an emerging Western consensus that the denial of pluralism and forced homogeneity can lead to ethnic conflict thus the recognition of specific minority rights may be necessary to level the playing field.[120]

Implications of pluralism for the group/individual rights debate
There are few, if any, ethnically homogenous societies in existence today.[121] Pluralist societies are a matter of fact, but questions remain as to whether ethnic pluralism should be promoted or discouraged and whether the liberal state can genuinely accommodate this plurality. Does ethnic diversity have anything positive to offer society, as suggested by Lord Scarman,[122] or is it divisive and potentially detrimental to national unity?

Liberalism would aim to stay neutral on this question, viewing ethnic affiliation as essentially a matter of personal choice. Advocates of group rights, however, challenge traditional liberal norms and seek to promote a vision of a pluralist society where the ethnic diversity of the populace is not simply a private matter but is reflected in public policy. Indeed, Rolf Darendorf argues that heterogeneity in a climate of peace and security is preferable to homogeneity 'as a test of human tolerance but also as a source of human creativity'.[123]

Walzer outlines three functions of pluralism as the defence of ethnicity against cultural naturalisation; the celebration of an ethnic identity (involving both celebration of diversity itself and more specifically, of the historical and cultural development of the group); and finally, ethnic assertiveness which may serve to promote institutions and provide specific educational and welfare services.[124] Adeno Addis has differentiated between two kinds of pluralism – 'paternalistic pluralism,' which aims to 'protect' and isolate the minority as the Other; and 'critical pluralism', which is committed to a relational dialogue between minorities and the majority.[125] This critical pluralism which Addis advocates depends on the allocation of resources and institutional structures for minorities.[126]

---

119   Kymlicka *supra* n20 (1995b) at 191.

120   Jackson-Preece, Jennifer in Lyons and Mayall (eds) *supra* n44 at 60; Räikkä, observes this consensus amongst writers in *supra* n95 at 6.

121   Walzer, M 'The politics of difference' *Ratio Juris* (1997) Vol 10, 2, pp 165–176 at 169. Kymlicka observes that less than 10% of countries are culturally homogenous in *supra* n24 at 222.

122   Scarman 'Minority Rights in Plural Society' in Whitaker, B (ed.) *Minorities A Question of Human Rights* (1984) Pergamon Press, Oxford pp 63–68.

123   Darendorf, R 'Minority Rights and Minority Rules' in Whitaker *supra* n122 p79–92 at 81.

124   Walzer *supra* n43 at 146–7.

125   Addis *supra* n71 at 621.

126   *Supra* n104 at 650.

The pluralist approach while desirable is not generally reflected in the language of international human rights law which views ethnic membership as a private matter and aims to promote equality and non-discrimination in an integrative framework which sometimes looks uncomfortably akin to assimilation. Young argues:

> The tradition of liberal individualism promotes an assimilationist ideal. It condemns group based exclusions and discriminations, along with the essentialist ideologies of group superiority and objectification that legitimate these oppressions. Liberal individualism not only rightly calls these conceptions of group identity and difference into question, it also claims that social group categorisations are invidious fictions whose sole function is to justify privilege .... The liberal individualist position associates group based oppression with assertions of group differences as such; eliminating group oppression such as racism, then, implies eliminating group differences.[127]

She is critical of this approach as it fails to reflect the actual experience of many people and presumes a conception of the self which transcends social context. This voluntarist conception of the self is unrealistic, undesirable and unnecessary and, furthermore, it will not be likely to succeed as a strategy where some groups are more privileged than others – the cultural assumptions of the dominant cultural group evolve to become the oppressive norm.[128]

As we have seen, the liberal tradition prioritises autonomy and individual choice over diversity and cultural security. According to Crowder it offers 'approximate neutrality' but remains the best possible method of securing diversity as it allows many competing claims to 'exist'.[129] My emphasis on 'exist' is relevant here as what minorities often need and seek is a thriving cultural life rather than marginal existence.[130] As Gray argues:

> Liberal societies tend to drive out non-Liberal forms of life, to ghettoize or marginalize them, or to trivialize them.[131]

Rights attributed on the basis of group membership are perceived as essential to prevent the imposition of the cultural hegemony on members of more economically and socially marginalised groups.

It is immediately obvious that the state cannot in reality be neutral to the interests of ethnic minorities if we consider the foundation of the individual self to be rooted in the culture to which they belong. Governments tend to represent the dominant cultural group in society and policies introduced by a dominant culture are unlikely to have the same blanket effect on all members of the populace.[132] This is most visible in the imposition of a common language for public affairs and education in

---

127   Young in Kymlicka (1995a) *supra* n20 at 162.

128   *Ibid.*

129   Crowder, George *Liberalism and Value Pluralism* (2002) Continuum at Chapter 6.

130   See Taylor *supra* n84 at 61.

131   Gray, J *Berlin* (1995) Harper Collins, New York at 154.

132   Clear examples can be seen with respect to education policy. Walzer, *supra* n43 at 149 gives the interesting example of public welfare provision which undermines the strength of cultural institutions.

most liberal states. Rodolfo Stavenhagen is one of several writers who dismiss the argument that the realisation of individual rights can adequately protect members of minorities who find their cultures undermined by social and economic environments outside their control.[133] Guaranteed political participation for minority groups may be an effective way for government policies to be adequately monitored so that their effects are not disproportionate. Such a proposition is discussed further in Chapter 7.

Inherent in the pluralist approach is the belief that cultural minorities should be supported and are thus relatively stable units. This does not mean however, that the members of the particular group do not have a right to choose to question collective decisions or pursue an alternative way of life, although in practice this choice could be complicated as boundaries may be more defined. For example, segregated schooling may be compatible with the pluralist vision but the divisive potential of strengthening ethnic boundaries through the education system is obvious.[134] Considering Gray's criticism of a pluralist conception of liberalism, Crowder argues that giving equal value to all conceptions of the good life will violate the primacy of the individual and may lead to some people being treated as 'mere instruments for the well-being of others'.[135] Nevertheless, it could be argued that a society which reflects diversity will facilitate plurality of opinion and will 'ensure reflection about one's own culture within a genuine context' and thus may ultimately secure a greater respect for human rights including the promotion of autonomy.[136] In this respect, Tamir advocates strengthening civic society to promote a nationalist framework while allowing and enabling genuine plurality of cultural views.[137]

The bearer of group rights

The extent to which individual rights are bound up in the realisation of group rights is essentially a subjective issue that depends on the nature of the group boundaries as well as the extent of ostracism from the dominant culture. In explaining the needs of certain groups for collective rights recognition, Sanders contrasts the needs of cultural minorities with other discriminated groups where there is no cohesive group identity:

> In contrast, cultural minorities seek more than the right of their individual members to equality and participation within the larger society. They also seek distinct group survival. Because economic and social forces, as well as state policies, tend to promote assimilation, the leaders of cultural minorities often look to the state for support. They seek either

133   Stavenhagen, Rodolfo 'Indigenous peoples and other ethnic groups' in Eide, *A Human Rights in Perspective* (1992) Nobel symposium 74: Blackwell, Oxford pp 135–151 at 142. See also Sanders, Douglas 'Collective Rights' (1991)*HRLQ* Vol. 13 pp 368–386 at 373; Van Dyke, V (1995) *supra* n18 p 30–56 at 50.
134   Discussed further in Chapter 5 passim.
135   Crowder *supra* n129 at 152.
136   Tamir *supra* n60 at 30.
137   *Ibid.* passim.

protection or autonomy as the means to ensure that their collectivities can survive and develop.[138]

Galenkamp argues that in order to provide a strong case for collective rights, such rights must themselves be understood as non-reducible. Such an understanding would presuppose 'the existence of de facto, pre-legally existing non-reducible collectivities, having collective interests'.[139] Therefore, she argues that collective rights should be restricted to relatively homogeneous communities where the identity of individual members is clearly framed by their membership in that community.[140] In communities where the individual well-being is not so bound up with the collective identity, the individual rights of non-discrimination and compensatory affirmative action measures may be sufficient to remedy any disadvantage suffered on account of group membership.

In arguing for the protection of the individuals' societal culture,[141] Will Kymlicka distinguishes between immigrant groups which are 'not "nations" and do not occupy homelands' and 'national minorities'.[142] It is the latter to which he extends his concept of group based rights, arguing that immigrant groups seek to maintain their ethnic differences within a general policy of integration as determined by the host State.[143] He then distinguishes both of these groups from 'new movements', i.e., associations of marginalised people such as women and the disabled who often comprise sub-cultures within the various groups.[144]

It is evident that the Roma do not fit neatly into such categories by political theorists who tend to afford minority rights to those groups considered to constitute involuntary minorities.[145] This hierarchical approach is in my view, highly problematic in that it perpetuates a false division between deserving and undeserving minorities and obscures the reality of disadvantage faced by a variety of minority groups. It is not my intention to argue that all minorities should be given special rights but merely to point out the danger of picking out special 'favoured' minorities for special treatment. Indeed, it is precisely because the Roma cannot rely on a specific homeland state to argue their corner that they have such a strong need for additional protection. It has been too

---

138   Sanders *supra* n133 at 370.

139   Galenkamp, Marlies 'Collective Rights: Much Ado about Nothing?' (1991) *Neth HRQ* Vol 3 at 297. See also Vander Wal, K *supra* n20.

140   *Ibid.* at 299.

141   Kymlicka rejects the category of collective rights as misleading, preferring to refer to group-differentiated citizenship which encompasses a variety of group rights as well as rights vesting in the group itself such as rights to self-government.

142   A distinction is made between Old World countries of 'intact rooted communities' and New world countries of immigration and ethnic diversity in the works of Walzer, M *The Politics of Ethnicity* (1982) Harvard University Press at 6–11 and Glazer, N *Ethnic Dilemmas* (1983) Harvard Univ. Press at 76–83.

143   Kymlicka, Will (1995b) *supra* n20 at 14–5.

144   *Ibid.* at 19.

145   Kallen, Evelyn 'Ethnicity and self-determination: a paradigm' in Clark and Williamson (eds) *Self-Determination. International perspectives* (1996) Macmillan pp 113–124 at 121 discusses Mede's distinction between voluntary and involuntary migrants.

easy for theorists to fuel the marginalisation of Roma by defining them as economic minorities whose problems could somehow be solved by a large injection of cash. Tove Malloy's recent work *National Minorities in Europe* provides an illuminating theoretical argument for the protection of certain group rights in international human rights law. However, she too distinguishes voluntary and involuntary minorities and ascribes minority rights to co-nations defined as 'autochthonous national minorities'.[146] She expressly excludes the Roma considering them to be, in the absence of evidence, primarily nomads.[147] Typically the Roma are placed in a miscellaneous category along with refugee communities in that they are neither voluntary migrants nor involuntary minorities. Rather than scrapping this false dichotomy the debate simply neglects these groups altogether, a rather unfortunate consequence for a discourse aimed at securing better human rights protection for all. It also conforms to the views of many Europeans who see Roma as Outsiders in every society.

Will Kymlicka's distinction between immigrant groups and national minorities interprets 'national minority' as requiring a common homeland and historical language, in much the same way as the definition of a 'people' as discussed in Chapter 7.[148] This approach perpetuates the myth of the genuine Romani-Gypsy whose ancestors left India in the eleventh century to migrate across Europe and into the Americas.[149] It is no coincidence that there have been recent efforts to mobilise support for a Romani nation[150] and demands for a European Charter on Romani rights.[151] Such an approach is considered further in Chapter 7 but inevitably, it sees us engaging in descent-based arguments that Kymlicka himself seeks to avoid.[152]

While he recognises that certain groups, particularly African-Americans, fall between the two categories, he tends to gloss over the consequential injustice such categorisations could promote.[153] Again, the relevant question for Kymlicka is whether the group in question arrived voluntarily in the particular country or whether they were forced to come.[154] Although he does acknowledge that an immigrant group may evolve into a national minority over time,[155] the implication of this aspect to his theory is that minority rights are a gift or privilege granted by the State to compensate for previous mistreatment.

In order for collective rights to be realistically addressed there are other questions that need to be considered, particularly as to the way in which the interests of a group are to be ascertained. As we have seen, many writers argue that group rights are meaningless and alien to the language of international human rights. To some extent

---

146   Malloy *supra* n6 at 40.

147   *Ibid.* pp 23–24.

148   Liégeois, J.P., observes that 'Gypsies do not fall into the usual categories' *A History of the Gypsies* (1986) Al Saqi at 180.

149   Discussed in Chapter 1.

150   Mirga and Gheorghe *supra* n1.

151   Romani National Congress Report on the Situation of the Roma in Europe (RNC Hamburg) pp 7–19.

152   Kymlicka (1995b) *supra* n20 at 23.

153   *Ibid.* at 25.

154   *Ibid.* at 24–25.

155   *Ibid.* at 25.

this criticism is misguided as international law already recognises the rights of certain groups, notably peoples and states. Furthermore, the specific rights of members of minorities are dependent on the group itself having a certain status. However, there is a notable reluctance among commentators to accept any expansion of the current position. Alexander Ossipov argues that the word 'right' is misused in this context:

> Strongly worded universal declarations of group rights in the cultural area, which actually define obligations of the state, are unlikely to offer suitable solutions. They would be more likely to lead to the artificial creation of groups of persons who did not previously consider their rights to be violated. This process would risk bringing nothing more that increased tensions and intolerance.[156]

Similarly, there are questions about group representation and the domination of inner minority elites. A minority that wishes to claim group rights would need to provide guarantees as to the individual rights of its members. These are serious questions which if left unanswered pose serious problems for the realisation of group rights.

The Individualist approach

Non-discrimination and affirmative action

For many human rights theorists, minority rights are regarded as essentially disruptive and separatist,[157] thus the only way to protect cultural interests is through the application of non-discrimination and equality. In his criticism of Rawls, Walzer argues that there are no common goods and that all goods are socially constructed.[158] Yet he is keen to confine rights to the spheres of non-discrimination and equality in order to avoid differentiated citizenship which would privilege particular cultural groups.[159]

In some cases non-discrimination measures will suffice in protecting the interests of the group but in many cases where there is existing inequality of opportunity, equal rights cannot provide equal outcomes.[160] Thus, a purposive conception of non-discrimination, to include affirmative action measures, may be useful to enable an enhanced conception of equality which can address the structural, social and factual disadvantages of the group through differentiating rules.[161]

A recognition of collective rights is important here whereby the rights of the individual group members are not simply aggregated but become more than the sum of

---

156   Ossipov, Alexander "Some doubts about 'ethnocultural justice' in Kymlica and Opalski (eds) *Can Liberalism be Exported?* (2001) OUP at 175.

157   See Waldron *supra* n21 at 113.

158   Walzer, Michael *Spheres of Justice: A Defence of Pluralism and Equality* (1983) Martin Robertson, Oxford at 7.

159   Kymlicka (1995b) *supra* n20 at 10.

160   Malloy, Tove *supra* n6 at 36.

161   Palermo and Woelk 'From Minority protection to a law of diversity? Reflections on the evolution of minority rights' *European Yearbook of Minority Issues* (2003–04) Vol 3 pp 5–13 at 8.

their parts. Affirmative action amounts to the recognition of collective rights and several liberal theorists have accepted this as compatible with a liberal egalitarian agenda.[162]

Affirmative action strategies

Some of the harshness of the individualist approach was recognised during the drafting of Article 26 of the *ICCPR* which prohibits discrimination on the basis of natural or social categories. It is now understood that 'discrimination' is used in a 'negative sense only, to mean a distinction of an unfavourable kind'.[163] Affirmative action aimed at redressing the inequalities experienced by particularly disadvantaged groups appears to be acknowledged as a necessary, although temporary, measure which does not constitute 'discrimination' in international and regional human rights provisions.[164] The content and scope of these provisions is discussed further in Chapter 3.

In practice, special measures have been used in a variety of situations to remedy a disadvantage suffered by a community, examples include special land rights for particular groups;[165] quotas of seats in the legislature and specific language rights.[166]

In the USA the issue of affirmative action has been the subject of considerable debate.[167] The Civil Rights Act of 1964 prohibiting all distinctions on the grounds of colour was soon accompanied by a quota system. Dworkin's examination of two US cases concerning individuals claiming to be victims of discrimination reveals the difficulties of a blanket non-discrimination approach.[168] In the Sweatt case, a black applicant was refused admission to law school because Texas federal law provided that only whites could attend. The Supreme Court held that this violated his rights under the 14th amendment to the Constitution, which provides that no state shall deny a man the protection of its laws.[169] This can be contrasted with the DeFunis case of 1974 in which a Jewish applicant was refused admission on account of his grade scores which, despite being lower than the cut off admission rate, where higher than many of the successful black applicants.[170] The policy of reverse discrimination introduced to remedy the disproportionately low number of black lawyers, clearly posed a difficulty for many Americans raised in the liberal tradition. If justice should be colour-blind, then the colour of applicants should be irrelevant, despite

---

162   Barry *supra* n45 at 114.

163   Ramcharan, B G 'Equality and non-discrimination' in Henkin, L *The International Bill of Rights* (1981) Columbia Univ. Press, New York observes that the necessity of differential measures was noted by the representatives of Chile, The Netherlands, and Uruguay.

164   *Supra* n163 at 261; see also Roth, Stephen 'Toward a Minority Convention: Its need and content' *Israel YBHR* Vol.20 pp 93–126 at 104.

165   See, e.g., *Gerhardy* v *Brown* (1985) Australian Law Reports 472, Lovelace and Canada (1981) (1997) Vol 2 *HRLJ* 158.

166   Van Dyke (1975) *supra* n30 at 611.

167   Discussed in Glazer, N. *Affirmative Discrimination* (1975) New York: Basic and Van Dyke (1985) *supra* n30 at Chapter 6.

168   Dworkin, Ronald *Taking Rights Seriously* (1977) Duckworth, London Chapter 9.

169   Sweatt v Painter, 399 US 629, 70 S. Ct. 848; discussed in Dworkin *ibid.*

170   DeFunis v Odegaard, 94 S. Ct. 1704 (1974); discussed in Dworkin *ibid.*

the evidence that blacks had been and were still regularly discriminated against on account of their colour and were thus at an extreme disadvantage.[171] In the event, the University of Washington agreed to allow Mr Defunis to graduate regardless of the outcome and the Supreme Court thus declined to give judgement on the constitutional aspects of the case.

Dworkin presents his view that the cases should be regarded as distinct and that 'reverse discrimination' is not at odds with the individualist tradition. The Equal Protection Clause did not define the nature of equality and thus DeFunis was relying not on a fundamentally asserted right that justice be colour blind but rather on a particular assertion of the interpretation of equality. Thus, in a simplified version of Dworkin's argument: because this was not a strong right but rather a derivative right, it could be trumped by other claims, particularly in the interests of the wider society.[172]

Nevertheless, the subtlety of Dworkin's distinction between a strong (or fundamental) right and a derivative right, seems to elude many writers and members of the legal profession as well as the American public. In 1978, the US Supreme Court ruled by a narrow margin, in favour of a white medical student who had been denied admission to the University of California Medical School. The University operated a quota system, whereby 16% of places were reserved, in order to increase the number of black doctors.[173] The belief that justice should be colour-blind and thereby indifferent to the racial disadvantage suffered by members of some groups prevailed against any notion of group rights.[174] Such a view appears to have support from all sections of American society, with a recent Gallup poll suggesting that approximately half the population remain opposed to the practice.[175]

The unpopularity of affirmative action strategies may be simply attributed to the prevalence of the approved language of individualism. In an ideal world, justice should be colour-blind but in the real world difference-blind policies will produce unequal consequences. An alternative explanation, concerned with the unpopularity of reverse discrimination among members of minorities, could lie in the stigmatisation of disadvantaged groups and their members which may result. A black doctor for example may feel that she is regarded by non-black staff as being the token black person regardless of her performance and ability.

Affirmative action strategies still have many obstacles to overcome if they are going to be accepted by individualist writers and the public at large as just responses to an unjust situation. Nevertheless, many states have found a need to introduce these policies. In the Czech Republic, a special initiative was introduced to increase the

---

171   Glazer, Nathan 'Individual rights against Group rights' in Tay and Kamenka *Human Rights* (1978) Edward Arnold, London Chapter 7 at 89.

172   Dworkin *supra* n168 at 225–228.

173   A discussion of the Bakke case and its implications can be found in Glazer, Nathan 'Why Bakke won't end reverse discrimination' *Commentary* September 1978 pp 36–41.

174   Glazer, N 'Individual rights against group rights' in Kymlicka (1995a) *supra* n20 at 132.

175   Gallup Poll of 8–25 June 2006 available at www.pollingreport.com. This is an improvement on the *New York Times* poll of 1 May 1977 in which 83% of whites and 64% of non-Whites were opposed to affirmative action strategies.

number of Romany police officers.[176] Due to their lack of formal secondary education, many Roma could not comply with the education criteria necessary to train as an officer. These standards were relaxed so that more Roma would be able to train, the justification being that the police needed to be made more aware of Romani issues and that the Romani community itself may be more likely to put trust into the police force. Thus, the interests of the wider society are promoted by relaxing the application criteria.

Affirmative action may go some way to remedying the defects of past inequalities, but significant doubts remain as to whether it can really succeed in securing a remedy for entrenched inequalities that serve as a barrier to the effective realisation of human rights. Most of the Czech Roma who took up the opportunity of police training left within the first few years of the programme, unimpressed by the latent racism and insurmountable obstacles they faced in being treated as equals. The fact that they were recruited through preferential criteria may have contributed to these problems.

Problems with the individualist perspective

(i) Equal treatment: unequal consequences It is apparent to me that a purely individualistic approach to human rights is theoretically flawed. Treating people equally without regard to their cultural specificity and positions of inequality can lead to gross injustices and there are many examples of people coerced into accepting the dominant cultural values. Examples include the recognition of one official state language and the imposition of the national curriculum on all state schools irrespective of religious and ethnic denomination.[177] Individual autonomy may thus enable people to enjoy their cultural identity, but only up to a point and only so long as it does not interfere with the values of the majority culture.

(ii) The principle of liberal neutrality Liberal writers often argue that state must not favour a particularist conception of the good life and should remain neutral in the different choices which individuals seek. Dworkin explains the rationale of the doctrine:

> Since the citizens of a society differ in their conceptions [of what is the good life], the government does not treat them as equal if it prefers one conception to another, either because the officials believe that one is intrinsically superior, or because it is held by the more numerous or powerful group.[178]

It may seem an obvious point, that a liberal state in a modern, heterogeneous society should not impose one particular version of the good life onto its citizens. Nevertheless, the vision of neutrality is contradicted by reality. Furthermore, Waldron argues that the justification for neutrality should be in the aims it seeks to serve (i.e., that of promoting a more tolerant and liberal society).[179] He argues that liberal neutrality is not a self-justifying policy: 'one is always neutral for a particular reason, and it is obvious that

---

176   Radio Prague e-mail service 'Romanies invited to join police force' 7 March 1998.
177   See Bradney, A *Religion, Rights and Law* (1993) Leicester Univ. Press.
178   Dworkin, Ronald 'Liberalism' *A Matter of Principle* (1985) Cambridge, Mass. at 191.
179   Waldron, Jeremy 'Legislation and Moral Neutrality' *supra* n41.

one cannot be neutral about the force of that reason'.[180] Thus, liberalism promotes a paradox of neutrality; it is neutral only regarding liberal conceptions of the good life.

In his liberal critique of the individualist approach to human rights, Will Kymlicka argues:

> It is not enough to simply assert that a liberal state should respond to ethnic and national difference with benign neglect. That is an incoherent position that avoids addressing the inevitable connections between state and culture.[181]

Positing a more relational account of the self, Thomas Moody also argues against a belief in liberal neutrality − 'any social order will favour some forms of life over others'.[182] Addis observes that dominant cultural understandings tend to become universalised, marking out marginal groups as the 'Other' which should either be excluded or 'normalized'.[183] He further argues that it is meaningless to argue that 'Aboriginal people enjoy the same rights as European Australians for their culture to compete in the market-place of cultural values'.[184]

The liberal state will always privilege certain values and interests as this is part of the task of nation building based on a common civic identity. This leads us, as Kymlicka argues, to a different question:

> The question is no longer how to justify departure from a norm of neutrality, but rather do majority efforts at nation-building create injustices for minorities? And do minority rights help protect against these injustices?

The burden of proof now falls on defenders of the neutrality approach to show that injustice to minorities is not perpetuated by the status quo.[185]

Kymlicka contends that the domination of the majority culture in liberal societies leaves four choices for minorities: emigration to a friendly state, integration into the dominant culture, self-governance or permanent marginalisation.[186] In reality these are not 'choices' as Kymlicka labels them, rather the strategy is typically determined by the actions or indifference of the majority.

(iii) Affirmative action in the absence of special measures protecting identity   Affirmative action measures, such as the American quota system,[187] tend themselves to conflict with individual rights and are dependent on the individuals

---

180   *Ibid.* at 165.

181   Kymlicka (1995a) *supra* n20 at 127.

182   Moody *supra* n53 at 192. Van Dyke concurs, arguing: 'Even if the members of the majority are committed to upholding the dignity and equality of all and justice for all, somehow it usually works out that what dignity and equality and justice require is also compatible with their own interests. They can champion democracy, knowing that democracy assures and sanctions their dominance' at 220 in *Human Rights, Ethnicity and Discrimination* (1985) Greenwood, CT.

183   Addis *supra* n71 at 619.

184   *Ibid.* at 644.

185   Kymlicka, W *Politics in the Vernacular* (2001) OUP at 33.

186   Kymlicka and Opalski (eds) *supra* n156 at 22.

187   Discussed at length in Glazer (1984) *supra* n142.

desire to redress the grievances of her group. They may also entrench ethnic hostility rather than respect for minority cultures as the dominant group in society may perceive the beneficiaries of such programmes as 'privileged' and thus, undeserving.[188]

Many minority groups require specific measures, which are actively supported and funded by the state, so that their culture can survive constrictive pressures. The temporary nature of affirmative action measures and the control exercised over the provisions of such measures by the dominant group, mean that many groups will not benefit unless they have a strong political voice and internal unity. The difficulty here is that inequality defines the relationship between minority and majority and therefore temporary measures cannot be sufficient to redistribute this imbalance of power.[189] Unpopular, marginalised groups are unlikely to be in a position to request affirmative action unless their identity is first protected and allowed to flourish. The aggregate will of the individual members cannot compete with the power of the state-reinforced dominant cultural values.

A further problem with non-discrimination provisions is their inherent dependence on individual action to correct injustices. A major weakness of the non-discrimination provisions in the ICCPR is the denial of any group right to petition the Human Rights Committee. Article 1 of the Optional Protocol states:

> A State Party to the covenant that becomes a party to the present Protocol recognises the competence of the Committee to receive and consider communications from individuals subject to its jurisdiction who claim to be victims of a violation by that State party of any of the rights set forth in the Covenant.[190]

The absence of a group right to petition, discussed in Chapter 3, is bound to deter many victims from considering such a challenge. The ICERD does recognise a group right to petition the Committee on the Elimination of Racial Discrimination but few states have recognised the competence of the Committee to hear individual complaints and as a result there have been no minority cases heard by the Committee to date.[191]

While for some minority groups the non-discrimination provisions have proved to be beneficial in redressing prejudices as well as empowering members of the minority group, for many other groups that are not so well organised and focused, a great deal of work still needs to be done. International awareness of the plight of particularly disadvantaged communities is unlikely to be sufficiently promoted via the present focus on individual action.[192]

---

188   Means, Gordon. P 'Human Rights and the Rights of Ethnic Groups – A Commentary' (1974) *International Studies Notes* at 17: Describes affirmative action measures as 'special' and 'preferential privileges'. This definition tends to lead to a conclusion that such measures are undeserved, rather than emphasising the unequal position that the measures aim to redress.

189   Kymlicka *supra* n24 at 190.

190   (First) Optional Protocol to the International Covenant on Civil and Political Rights (1966).

191   Alfredsson and de Zayas 'Minority rights: Protection by the United Nations' (1993) *HRLJ* 14 No 1–2 at 7–8.

192   Henkin *supra* n163 at 113 notes that while there has been much interest in racial discrimination perpetrated by white people against black people, there is less concern where

The special minority rights approach

Special minority rights can be distinguished from the types of affirmative action which fall within the substantive equality approach discussed above. Affirmative action is based on recognition of the disadvantage suffered by individuals as a result of their involuntary membership in specific groups. It enables members of systemically disadvantaged groups to access the 'good' life as defined by the majority. It is thus a 'collective right' in that it pertains to individuals as members of a particular group. Special minority rights in contradistinction may be termed 'group rights' in that they are derivative of the groups per se rather than individuals.

Special group rights are necessary to support the cultures of many minority groups in order to prevent enforced integration and assimilation. Such measures may be of a temporary nature so that members of particular groups can be placed on an equal footing with those of the majority or may extend at the fullest point to self-determination and self-government. Jackson-Preece argues that the declarative universal module favoured by Donnelly is not undermined by recognition of minorities if we see that recognition as furtherance of the self-determination principle.[193] Either way it must be clear that non-discrimination provisions alone cannot prevent the erosion of minority cultures. Ramaga argues that culture and group consciousness are mutually supportive and collective rights are thus the only way that minority cultures can survive the implicit contrary pressure exerted by the dominant groups in society. To focus on the individual enjoyment of culture would be to ignore the group dimension by which that culture is nurtured.[194]

One of the key aspects to this approach is the perception that many groups do not have fluid boundaries and that their members lack a real opportunity to engage in cultural borrowing. For many liberal thinkers this is highly problematic angle as it suggests that minority rights will entrench ethnic boundaries and therefore decrease individual autonomy.[195]

Yet, many states have rejected the simple individualist emphasis and have engaged in actively promoting the interests of specific minority groups. For example, in Canada the law grants a right to French and English speaking communities the right to education in their own language.[196] In Quebec Province, the French speaking community form a majority of the population and thus are a powerful lobbying force. In some cases minority self-government is possible whereby the minority may be given power to manage its own distinctiveness. For example, the Hungarian minority government system, discussed in Chapter 7, enables increased representation of minority interests at a national level while providing local government that reflects the cultural values of the region. A degree of autonomy for certain minorities is also adopted in the Spanish Constitution which allows autonomous regional parliaments

---

Africans discriminate against Asians; and 'virtual indifference' where the victims are other groups such as tribes or ethnic and religious communities.

193   Jackson-Preece, Jennifer *supra* n44 at 68.

194   Ramaga, Phillip V 'The Group Concept in Minority Protection' (1993) *HRQ* Vol. 15 at 583.

195   Glazer, Nathan *supra* n171 at 98 and *supra* n142 at 268; Packer, J *supra* n138.

196   Constitution Act 1982 Charter of Rights and Freedoms s23.

for cultural and linguistic minorities.[197] Such initiatives suggest that many states are beginning to see minority rights as part of the solution rather than the cause of ethnic tension.

Problems with the group rights approach

Peter Jones argues that it is impossible to allocate human rights to any entity other than individuals as human rights must vest in all people equally and therefore they must be conceived of individually.[198] This is indeed a theoretical dilemma but perhaps it is possible to solve it practically with a flexible and localised conception of group rights that supplements individual human rights and indeed provides them with meaning. This is why group rights theorists have limited the application of such rights to particular groups such as Kymlicka's 'national minorities' and Galenkamp's 'homogeneous constitutive communities'.

Alternatively, one could argue that collective rights that are viewed as more than the sum of individual interests could provide the answer. This is certainly less alien to the language of liberalism and universal individualism and is compatible with international human rights provisions and affirmative action programmes. For Jones this would be sufficient:

> If we adopt the collective theory, the claims of the few may have to yield to those of the many, but at least the claims of the few will be counted.[199]

However, I doubt that such counting is really going to redress persistent discrimination and disadvantage. The disadvantage and marginalisation of the Roma has been acknowledged by every international human rights institution but this has not resulted in any substantial change to their position.

A more practical problem arising from measures protecting particular minority groups is that they may codify and entrench difference. This may in turn erode individual rights to criticise the culture and to move between cultures. It does seem inevitable that a degree of cultural entrenchment may occur but it has already been argued that the degree of cultural choice exercised by members of disadvantaged minorities is at present, severely limited. Membership of a minority rarely results from the exercise of individual autonomy rather it is a product of a whole combination of cultural and societal pressures over which the individual has very little actual control. If anything, an emphasis on individual rights, non-discrimination and equality perpetuates this lack of individual control as there is no element of cultural security – already acknowledged as fundamental to the wellbeing of individuals. An individual will be reluctant to question the culture and traditions of their group if in so doing they will be threatening the existence of the group and security of other members.[200]

---

197   Simons 'Catalan is Spoken Here (Do you hear Madrid?)' *New York Times* 19 April 1991 A9.

198   Jones *supra* n221.

199   *Ibid.* at 93.

200   Malloy *supra* n6 at 159.

Furthermore, it seems clear that rather than enforced pluralism the danger which threatens the existence of minorities is assimilation.[201] To give minorities the tools necessary to survive such pressures there will inevitably be a certain amount of artificial boundary construction between groups, and some groups may be artificially maintained as a result. However, the liberal critique of collective rights also identifies a more worrying threat to individual rights, namely the problem of the illiberal minority.

(i) The illiberal minority
Support and resources given to minorities may lead to the entrenchment of cultural values, some of which may be less than liberal. Theorists who place a high emphasis on autonomy and choice but who value group rights are faced with the dilemma of an illiberal minority that restricts the choices of its members in the interests of group preservation. This is particularly the case when territorial separation is an issue. For example, in the former Yugoslavia, individuals from mixed marriages had to choose their ethnic allegiance in societies composed of many different ethnic groups.[202] Michael Walzer responds to this problem by requiring equal respect for all people as 'culture-producing creatures'.[203] In endorsing the inherent value in diversity there can be no legitimate external infringement with the culture of others. Walzer presents a direct challenge to traditional liberalism with its priority on autonomy and freedom. For Stephen Macedo the eradication of certain forms of diversity can be justified by the promotion of tolerance and peace offered by a liberal society.[204] This is a contentious point given recent history and the realisation amongst human rights activists and theorists that peace is unlikely to be fostered in a climate that does not recognise and support minorities.

William Galston argues that occasional illiberal practices must be accepted if liberty is not to be narrowed dramatically.[205] He criticises Kymlicka's prioritisation of autonomy and free choice as it may undermine the lives of people that have alternative priorities. When properly understood, Galston argues, liberalism is 'about the protection of legitimate diversity'.[206] Any intrusion with the cultural practices and beliefs of other groups will undermine diversity and therefore the liberal pluralist agenda. In some extreme cases, for example human sacrifice or withholding medical treatment to children, such interference may be justified but in general the state power should not encroach on the interests and values of cultural groups.[207] Yet Barry, citing JS Mill, contends that liberalism is neither justified solely by reference to autonomy or diversity and that the central role of the liberal state is not focused on the prioritisation of any one good.[208] The legitimacy of diversity causes problems

---

201   Sanders *supra* n133 at 373.
202   Young, Iris M *supra* n20 at 168.
203   Walzer *supra* n158 at 314.
204   Macedo, Stephen *Liberal Virtues: Citizenship, Virtue and Community in Liberal Constitutionalism* (1990) OUP at 278–9.
205   Galston, William *Liberal Pluralism* (2002) Cambridge Univ. Press 20–21.
206   *Ibid.* at 23.
207   *Ibid.* at 114.
208   Barry *supra* n45 at 119.

for both Barry and John Packer who observe that an emphasis on 'cultural equality' can justify illiberal practices such as female genital mutilation:

> Morally, can we sustain the positive value of female genital mutilation as a cultural practice? To the extent that such a practice violates an individual right, and so would not form part of a valid contract, contractarians would hold the morally sustainable position of rejection female genital mutilation as a cultural practice. If this is to say that 'liberal culture' is superior to 'illiberal culture' then the moral conclusion would be 'Yes'.[209]

Tamir also cautions against laws and policies emphasising 'survival' of minorities as they may be used to justify illiberal and inhuman practices.[210]

These arguments certainly have some credibility when we observe Taylor's reluctance to criticise the practices of alternative cultures for fear of hegemonic supremacy.

Kukathas contends that the problem of illiberal minorities can only be avoided through an individualist perspective, as a union of individuals, any one of whom can decide to leave the group if their interests are not respected.[211] The extent of injustice within the minority, he argues, is tempered by two factors: the degree of integration with the wider society − communities more integrated will find it more difficult to infringe rights, and, the principle upholding freedom of association and dissociation.[212] However, this view while attractive in principle, is obviously limited. Kukathas recognises that the freedom to exit requires a wider society that is happy to accept the cultural dissident, in many cases this is an idealistic vision.[213] Immigrants who have chosen to enter a new country with different cultural values are rarely accepted by the new society − they tend to be perceived as Outsiders, particularly if they have distinguishing physical characteristics.[214] Pogány goes further in arguing that the right not to be treated as a member of a minority[215] is paradoxically complicated by the widespread emphasis on minority rights which informs the responses of politicians, educators, the media and NGO's.[216]

Furthermore, the elevation of the individual right to leave the group which, Kukathas contends will prevent a minority from undermining individual rights,

---

209   Packer *supra* n95 at 134.

210   Tamir *supra* n60 at xi.

211   Kukathas, C in Kymlicka (1995a) *supra* n20 at 252.

212   *Ibid.* at 251–2.

213   See for example Oestreich, Joel 'Liberal theory and minority group rights' (1999) *HRQ* Vol 21 pp 108–132 at 119.

214   Van Dyke *supra* n30 at 157 argues on the issue of school segregation in the U.S. that whites always regarded blacks as a race apart. The group is kept subordinate by discriminating against individual members − 'To lynch one black was to intimidate them all, and to educate one was to encourage them all'. Consider for example the case of the Pike family who wished to move into a house in the Somerset village of Middlezoy were greeted by a petition of ninety objecting villagers. None of the villagers had ever met the family in question, their objections were based solely on the Gypsy origins of the family. The *Independent* 16.5.92.

215   Article 3 (1) C/E *Framework Convention on National Minorities* H(1995)010.

216   Pogány, István 'Minority rights and the Roma of Central and Eastern Europe' (2006) *HR L* Vol 6, 1 at 16.

ignores the depth of the cultural bonds which are so fundamental to the individuals wellbeing. Leslie Green is similarly sceptical:

> The argument is sound only if members of minority groups do in fact have a fair chance to leave if mistreated. To see how rarely that is the case, one must assess the real prospects for exit.[217]

Nevertheless, the individual right of exit is viewed by many as essential if groups are to be afforded rights. Essentially, the right of exit is a safety net which aims to keep group rights within the framework of individual rights. Although in practice deep-rooted ties linking individuals to their community may make it an unlikely resort, it would appear to constitute a necessary limit on the abuse of power by an undemocratic minority.

It is easy to conceive of a situation where the pressure to assimilate leads a minority to restrict the expression of its members – internal minorities may thus be silenced and disempowered.[218] Mill called the tendency to compel social conformity 'one of the most universal of all human propensities'.[219] However, the extent of this threat to the individual rights of internal minority members is largely contingent upon the perceived need to keep the minority 'pure' and unified in order to prevent assimilation.[220] Thus, this perceived need is dependent on the attitude of the dominant forces in society; if the majority seek to assimilate the minority they will look for evidence of disunity and division. So it may well be the case that if special minority rights were recognised in a society, the rights of internal minorities would also be less vulnerable.[221]

Those liberals and communitarians that regard culture as constitutive of self and identity argue that it should therefore be protected as an end in itself. Whereas liberals, such as Kymlicka who see culture as important to enable freedom and autonomy are only willing to view its protection if it is compatible with those overriding objectives. He argues that the liberal pluralist approach aims to eliminate such inequality and injustice between ethnocultural groups and therefore cannot remain indifferent to such practices within the groups.[222] George Crowder argues that the liberal state should be pluralist in that it can accommodate many forms of the good life but should not be wholly neutral when it comes to conceptions of the

---

217   Green, L 'Internal Minorities and Their Rights' in Kymlicka (1995a) *supra* n20 at 264.

218   *Supra* n217 at 268.

219   Mill *supra* n85.

220   Hannum argues that the increase in nationalistic tendencies among groups is a response to a state which does not recognise their needs: Hannum, Hurst 'The Limits of Sovereignty and Majority Rule: Minorities, Indigenous Peoples, and the Right to Autonomy' in Lutz, Hannum and Burke *New Directions in Human Rights* (1989) Univ. of Pennsylvania Press, Philadelphia pp 6, 18.

221   Sanders *supra* n133 at 375 makes the point that tolerance of minorities will facilitate adaptation and evolution within the minority. Interestingly, he goes on to point out that tolerance may thus be a 'sophisticated route to minority assimilation'.

222   Kymlicka *supra* n156 at 352.

good.[223] The marginalisation of minority communities and interests is seen as a fair price to pay for a liberal society based on equality and dignity of all.

However, Kymlicka also points out that most nations and dominant groups in society have illiberal pasts – a fact all too easily forgotten when it comes to questions of minority autonomy:

> ... It seems hypocritical to insist that minorities prove their liberal credentials before acquiring self-government rights when the majority doesn't face the same test.[224]

Liberalisation of minority cultures must be left to the minority itself in a climate of tolerance and respect. The possibility of illiberal practices are best addressed within the secure cultural framework of the minority, they should not be used as a reason for denying rights to all minorities.

Although there may be conflict between the individual and interests of the collective this is neither an unavoidable certainty nor a fatal flaw. Although, the restriction of individual rights may be part of a transitional stage in the development of most minority identities, this should not preclude recognition of group rights. However, individuals within collectivities may not be the only people at risk of having individual rights threatened in the name of the collective good. Special minority rights for particular groups will necessarily involve the restriction of the majority's individual rights. This is an inevitable consequence of group – based rights, whether they have their basis in the collective rights school or the individualist tradition.

(ii) The inevitable conflict with individual rights

For many writers the concept of differentiated citizenship itself is meaningless and there will inevitably be a conflict between individual rights and the recognition of groups.[225] Barry argues that if cultural survival is considered an end in itself, as communitarian's desire, the inevitable result will be the devaluing of individual human rights and a 'perversion of common sense'.[226]

The 'politicisation of ethnicity' is clearly a concern which may threaten the concept of universal citizenship especially if the minority is given self-government rights. Territorial autonomy arrangements may have seriously detrimental consequences for smaller minorities. If the criticisms of Barry, Donnelly and others are well-founded, the Roma may experience even greater hostility and discrimination under an expanded conception of human rights. Such a possibility is certainly borne out by evidence from the former Yugoslavia where the Roma have suffered significantly as the 'Other' in all newly defined territorial regions.[227] If one wants to avoid increasing the misrecognition of the Roma, the option of group rights, including self-government must be handled with extreme caution.

---

223   Crowder *supra* n129 passim.

224   *Supra* n156 at 353.

225   Jones, Peter 'Human rights, group rights, peoples' rights' (1999) *HRQ* Vol. 21 pp 80–107 at 88.

226   Barry *supra* n45 at 67.

227   See Edwards, Alice 'New Roma Rights legislation in Bosnia and Herzegovina: positive, neutral of indifferent?' 2005 *IJHR* Vol. 9, 4 pp 465–478.

This matter has already received some coverage in international human rights jurisprudence. In Quebec a measure aimed at promoting the Francophone community prohibited the use of any language other than French on commercial signs. The English speaking community of Quebec challenged the law, alleging an infringement of the right to free expression under the Constitution and the Canadian Supreme Court had to consider where the balance of collective vs. individual rights should lie.[228] Although the Supreme Court ruled against a total ban on the use of other languages finding that such a ban was disproportionate to the collective needs of the Francophone community, they also held that other measures which potentially restricted individual expression could be justified in the interests of protecting the Francophone community in Quebec.[229] Similarly, in *Kitok* vs. *Sweden*, the Human Rights Committee were asked to consider whether reindeer husbandry, a traditional occupation of the Sami minority, should be confined to the Sami community.[230] The Human Rights Committee found that such a right could be protected by Article 27 of the *ICCPR* and thus, a non-Sami could be legitimately restricted from such an occupation.

The conflict between individual and group rights is nothing new however. The liberal state already recognises and promotes one particularist vision which has marginalised and excluded certain groups of people. Indeed, as Parekh and Kymlicka recognise, citizenship is much more differentiated than many political theorists recognise.[231] Furthermore, the disruption to individual rights, which may occur with misrecognition and the denial of group rights, may have far wider ramifications for civil society. The denial of recognition can be linked to a loss of self-esteem which in turn promotes disengagement from the political process possibly culminating in ethnic violence and separatism.[232]

There are few human rights that can be regarded as absolute and universal.[233] The matter is essentially one of balance: between the interests of one or a community of individuals and the rights of another. Freedom of expression is necessarily limited by the potential harm caused by racist sentiments and by public order and national security considerations.[234] Even the rights of freedom of thought, conscience and religion can be limited in the interests of public safety, order, health, or morals or the fundamental rights and freedoms of others.[235] The implementation of international human rights standards is thus dependent on balancing and limiting the human rights listed. Gillian Triggs argues for a wide interpretation of equality to encompass group rights:

---

228 *Ford* vs. *Quebec*, 2 S.C.R 712 (Canada, 1988) cited in Sanders *supra* n133 at 378.

229 *Ibid.*

230 HRC no 197/1985 (1988) UN Doc A/43/40 Annex VII.G.

231 Parekh, Bhikhu 'The Rushdie Affair: research agenda for political philosophy' (1990) Political Studies Vol 38 pp 659–709 at 702.

232 Malloy, Tove *supra* n6 at 155 notes that without self-esteem it is difficult to function fully in society.

233 Only Article 7 of the ICCPR which concerns torture or inhuman and degrading treatment is absolute. Even the right to life may be taken away as a sentence for serious crimes where the death penalty has not been abolished (Article 6(2)).

234 See *J.T. v Canada* (1983) 4 *HRLJ* p 193.

235 Article 18(3) *ICCPR* (1966).

The salient point is, that if special rights are not granted to such groups to defend their cultures, the practice of their religion, and the use of their languages, they will be treated unequally and unjustly. Minority rights thus have the purpose of ensuring the effective implementation of fundamental individual human rights.[236]

The issue concerning those advocating a greater recognition of group or collective rights is that the present focus on the individual is insufficient. Vernon Van Dyke describes the liberal focus as 'unduly limited':

> It is not enough to think in terms of two-level relationships, with the individual at one level and the state at another; nor is it enough if the nation is added. Considering the heterogeneity of mankind and of the population of virtually every existing state, it is also necessary to think of ethnic communities and certain other kinds of groups.[237]

If we accept, contrary to Waldron, that some cultural groups are sufficiently distinct so as to form separate focus groups, Van Dyke's reference to 'ethnic communities and other kinds of groups' raises the next important issue in this debate. The question of which cultural groups should be protected by group-based or collective rights is fraught with difficulties. It may be helpful here to briefly consider the approach taken by international law where a limited recognition of group identity can be observed.

(iii) Defining a minority

Juhn Räikkä expresses this problem succinctly: 'it is unclear what "minorities" are'.[238] He highlights the disagreements over immigrant minorities and the practical problems of defining linguistic minorities and goes on to pose several related questions, namely who belongs to these minorities and what kind of obligations are envisaged by minority protection.[239] Indeed, many theorists recognising the inherent value of culture and community have stopped short of advocating collective rights for precisely this reason. As Tamir argues in the context of national groups:

> Unlike commercial companies or other formal organisations, national groups lack clear criteria of membership, and the idea of granting them rights is fraught with theoretical and moral difficulties.[240]

Van Dyke's ethnic community comprises a group of people primarily of common descent 'who think of themselves as possessing a separate identity based on race or on shared cultural characteristics, usually language or religion'.[241] This self-affirmation of cultural membership is crucial. A group whose members do not wish to be defined as such would not be regarded as deserving such protection; to enforce

236 Triggs, Gillian 'The Rights of "Peoples" and Individual Rights: Conflict or Harmony?' (1988) in Crawford (ed.) *The Rights of Peoples* (1988) Clarendon: Oxford pp 141–157 at 145.
237 Van Dyke (1995) *supra* n18 at 31.
238 Räikkä, Juhn (ed) *Do We Need Minority Rights?* (1996) Kluwer, Martinus-Nijhoff.
239 *Supra* n17 at 9–10.
240 *Supra* n60 at 47.
241 *Supra* n17 at 32.

protection would be a violation of the individual rights of its members to express themselves how they choose and to associate freely.

The problem of defining a minority for the purposes of international law has troubled international lawyers and academics since the League of Nations first became concerned with minority protection. Fifty years later and there is still no accepted definition as to what constitutes a minority in international law.[242] Furthermore, the types of minority protected by international documents vary from 'ethnic, linguistic and religious' minorities (in the ICCPR) to 'national' minorities (in the CSCE and Council of Europe documents). This lack of definition is generally blamed on the complexity of the subject. However, other commentators have also pointed to the traditional antipathy and 'fear' that talk of minority rights invokes in national governments.[243] These difficulties are discussed in more detail in Chapter 6.[244]

It has been argued that the definitional difficulties should not be considered fatal to affording special minority protection. It would appear that in most cases recognising a group as a minority does not present a particular difficulty and it is clear that international law will not treat as conclusive the status ascribed to groups by the particular state in which they live.[245] It is submitted that there is nevertheless a need for some international codification in this area.

States at present can easily evade protection for unpopular or small minorities and if necessary can invoke the lack of international clarification to support their domestic policies. It does seem clear that the Roma are recognised as both an ethnic and a national minority in the regional instruments. The High Commissioner on National Minorities clearly considers the Roma to fall within his remit following the 2000 'Report on the Roma and Sinti in the OSCE Area'. Peter Leuprecht, former Deputy Secretary General of the Council of Europe, avoiding the technicality of providing a definition and noted:

> Let us not hide behind legal hair-splitting as to whether this or that definition of minorities applies to the Roma. Let us be honest. We all know that the Roma are a minority and a particularly vulnerable one.[246]

Yet, while this may be an accurate representation of the international legal position, Francesco Capotorti has found that the Roma are rarely recognised by states as being a legal minority targeted with special measures aimed at equality and non-discrimination:

> It is important to remember that in most cases the groups recognised as 'minorities' or as communities which are to benefit from special treatment are well-defined groups. Certain groups, including those which are scattered throughout the territory of a country, seldom appear among those forming the subject of recognition by the State with legal effect. Such

---

242   UN Declaration on the rights of Persons Belonging to National or Ethnic, Religious or Linguistic Minorities UN Res 47/135 of 18 December 1992.

243   Packer *supra* n61 at 25–6.

244   See Chapter 6 pp 259–264.

245   Capotorti *supra* n116 para. 570.

246   CSCE *Roma in the CSCE Region* (1994) Warsaw at p7 para. 7.

is the situation, for instance, of the groups described as 'Gypsies' in a large number of European countries.[247]

This situation is gradually improving thanks to the work of the Advisory Committee on the Framework Convention on the Protection of National Minorities which has sought assurances from states that the Roma are recognised as a minority. The EU has also focused increasingly on the protection of the Roma as a specific non-territorial, European minority.[248] While it is apparent that they do not fit neatly into the theoretical paradigm for group rights recognition, the Roma are a European minority comprising approximately eight million people. In *Can Liberalism be Exported*, Kymlicka finds that they do not fit neatly into any of his categories of minority groups and defines them along with Crimean Tartars, Cossacks and Russian settlers in the Baltics as 'hard cases'.[249] While recognising that they may require some additional protection he rather disappointingly concludes: 'There are no Western models for this complicated process'.[250] This tendency exhibited by governments and academics to exclude them from consideration for special measures is misguided and unfortunate.

(iv) Identifying minority rights
Given the difficulties of squaring special minority rights with the individual rights of group members and others, Stephen Roach seeks to avoid the multiculturalist exclusion trap through his emphasis on cultural autonomy rather than group-specific entitlements.[251] An analysis of the Hungarian minority self-government system, discussed in Chapter 7, considers whether such a strategy may present a possible solution.

Addressing the situation in the Czech Republic, Pavel Barša compares the situation of the Roma to indigenous peoples in North America and Australia although he accepts that there are significant differences, most notably the absence of a specific territory.[252] He avoids advocating full cultural autonomy but is concerned to see a new inclusive civic identity. He concludes, rather optimistically given the problems in civic states, that Roma disadvantage can be addressed through genuine multiculturalism with improved political representation and education.[253] This climate of improved dialogue and minority interaction informs Jurgen Habermas's deliberative democracy. Habermas argues that law can provide the procedural rules to facilitate communicative action, enabling minority and interests groups to participate and debate their particular perspectives in a universalist framework.[254] The theory

---

247   Capotorti *supra* n116 at para. 77.
248   EU Network of Experts on Fundamental Rights the Situation of Roma *in an Enlarged European Union* 2004 European Commission.
249   *Supra* n186 at 73.
250   *Ibid.* at 76.
251   *Ibid.* at 43.
252   Barša, Pavel 'Ethno-cultural justice in East European states' in Kymlicka and Opalski (eds) *supra* n156 at 253–4.
253   *Ibid.* at 254–6.
254   Habermas, J *The Theory of Communicative Action* (1984) London Heinemann.

offers a middle-way approach which recognises collective interests yet aims to avoid a separatist dimension. However, the requirement for minorities to engage in rational dialogue may be problematic for those not familiar with political organisation and debate and, as Malloy argues, there is a risk of strategic bargaining.[255] Indeed, it is difficult to conceive of a perfect speech situation which is not open to abuse from dominant interests or unrepresentative elites.[256]

Recently, some Roma advocates have been considering a different tactic for securing representation based on the recognition of the Roma as a transnational minority. Such a process would seek to emphasise the homogeneity of the geographically dispersed Roma/Gypsy community.[257] Habermas describes this process as a 'thoroughly modern movement of renewal'[258] which reinvents aspects of a diminishing cultural identity. The dangers are all too apparent with the potential for further ostracism of those that do not conform to the traditional stereotype. Citing Todd Gitlin, Barry warns that such cultural reinvention and traditionalist defence can be used to justify essentially racist practices and biological determinism.[259]

While some authors romanticise the ideological desire to travel shared by all Roma, Gypsies and other travelling people,[260] it is unlikely that the majority of Roma have entertained the idea of taking to the road for generations. The issue is not whether they would have continued travelling if the pressures to assimilate had not been so severe, but rather whether as a collective they wish to travel now. Clearly, it becomes impossible to impose the concept of a collective will onto Roma and travellers throughout the world as a homogenous group. Communities with a common origin and, undoubtedly, some common values and beliefs, must not be forced to meet standards of homogeneity in order to qualify for recognition as a minority group with specific and distinct needs. This would have the effect of imposing a new kind of assimilation.

One final approach from Barry deserves mention. He argues that multiculturalists overplay the significance of culture in as much as discrimination may not be attributable to cultural difference but just difference per se.[261] Indeed, when one considers the disadvantage experienced by the Roma who are a heterogeneous community, this argument carries some weight. It could indeed be argued that the settled majority in the UK do not have a specific problem with cultural practices such as nomadism and cleansing rituals, rather their problem is with 'Gypsies'. This is the 'Gypsy' as defined by the majority – an image that may be romanticised, as fortune-teller, or may be denigrated as 'dirty' and 'thieving'. It is unclear where this argument leads us – if these false images are to be challenged, which they must surely be, some form of multicultural strategy is surely the only way forward. Recognising the unique

---

255 Malloy *supra* n6 at 197.

256 Young *Justice and the Politics of Difference* (1990) Princeton Univ Press.

257 See below at 385.

258 Habermas, J 'The struggle for recognition' in Gutmann (ed.) *supra* n33 pp 107–148 at 132.

259 Barry *supra* n45 at 261.

260 Liégeois (1986) comments that 'Nomadism is still a state of mind' *supra* n148 at 57.

261 Barry *supra* n45 at 306.

cultural perspectives of the Roma is a way of meeting and challenging these false images from a position of equality and strength. If we accept (which I do not) that assimilation or integration should be the preferred alternative to multiculturalism and pluralism, as Barry appears to advocate, these images surely prevent such a process. The majority Gadje population in many states with large Roma populations simply do not want the Roma to integrate, hence the separate education programmes and housing initiatives. Given this barrier to further integration which is maintained not just by the minority but more apparently by the majority it is unclear how disadvantage and discrimination can be challenged.

Equal treatment cannot offer a simple solution – equal treatment in the context of such unequal circumstances can only perpetuate the problem. For example, the UK's planning laws have a disproportionate affect on nomadic Gypsies. The solution often offered by local authorities is conventional housing which is entirely unsuitable to the lifestyle of most Gypsies and will further promote discrimination and disadvantage. Barry may argue that this is an acceptable outcome and that the majority should not have to support such alternative cultural practices. Even if we accept this argument the problem of discrimination and disadvantage will not disappear. As I have argued, the barriers between the sedentary and Gypsy communities are not solely the construct of the minority and they cannot simply be deconstructed on the terms of the majority.

Group rights as supplemental

It has been argued that the emphasis on individual rights in most international human rights treaties cannot by itself redress the rights grievances of many minority groups.[262] While the individual rights approach does allow for affirmative action measures to ensure de facto equality of opportunity, it is submitted that many smaller and unpopular groups will be unable to access such measures. The emphasis on individual action to redress wrongs makes the realisation of full human rights protection a distant dream for many minorities. In a critique levied at both the traditional liberal interpretation of rights and the radical collectivist stance, Jurgen Habermas argues:

> A correctly understood theory of rights requires a politics of recognition that protects the integrity of the individual in the life contexts in which his or her identity is formed .... All that is required is the consistent actualisation of the system of rights.[263]

The community was and still is a vital unit of Gypsy/Romani organisation and group rights recognition may be essential if the community interests are to be preserved and developed.[264] An individual rights emphasis fails to meet many of the challenges presented by this minority, and in some of the new Eastern European regimes this

---

262   The exception to the individual emphasis is the International Labour Orgamnisation Indigenous and Tribal Peoples Convention No 169 (1989) adopted by the General Conference of the ILO at its 76th session.

263   Habermas *supra* n258 at 113.

264   Any serious account listed in the bibliography to this book will demonstrate the significance of the community to Romani/Gypsy identity.

problem is already being addressed. In Hungary, the minority government system aims to increase the participation of specific minorities from a collective dimension. This can be contrasted with the situation of the Roma in the Czech Republic where the absence of internal autonomy and collective constitutional guarantees left many thousands of Roma without citizenship.

Group rights should not be regarded as an alternative but as a supplement to individual rights where it is clear that the latter cannot be adequately protected without some collective protection.[265] An enhanced conception of self-determination may be the answer whereby, as Gábor Kardos argues, individual rights are accompanied by the strengthening of the constitutional status of the communities themselves.[266] McGarry and O'Leary have explored possibilities for greater minority representation at a constitutional level. They advocate dramatic changes to the typical undifferentiated civic system to incorporate proportional representation, a guaranteed veto for minorities, improved institutions and community autonomy.[267]

Greater European representation for the Roma, discussed in Chapter 8, may also help to achieve this end. Common issues such as the violence and intolerance faced by the Roma and other travellers can be internationally addressed, but local issues require flexible solutions. A framework of cultural autonomy may help to achieve this end and promote interest in politics so that active citizenship is encouraged.

Much of the theory on group rights offers nothing to the Roma. Kymlicka's notion of group rights only extends to national minorities which specifically excludes the Roma. He recognises this omission but is unable to offer any theoretical alternative. Marginalised and excluded from society the Roma are also marginalised and excluded by political theory. As Europe's largest minority they receive barely a paragraph in Kymlicka's extensive works. Is this respect it is interesting to note Kymlicka's own criticism of Nathan Glazer who regards the American-Indian situation as an anomaly, of no real interest when considering American colour-blind policies.[268] The Roma lack the territorial and political cohesion of national minorities and they do not fit the definition of immigrant minorities. Nevertheless, they experience the same kind of personal harm as members of indigenous communities, including school failure, alcoholism and mental illness.[269] Yet whether this harm arises from forcible cultural transplantation or from exclusion from civic society is a debatable. Indeed, it would appear that an extensive policy of multiculturalism could address many of the Roma's problems. Yet it is difficult to see where the impetus for such policies will come from. Karl-Otto Apel opines that there is no functioning civil society

---

265   Geroe, Michael. R and Gump, Thomas. K 'Hungary and a New Paradigm for the Protection of Ethnic Minorities in Central and Eastern Europe' *Columbia Journal of Transnational Law* (1995) Vol. 32, No 3 at 679.

266   Kardos, Gábor 'Human rights: A matter of individual or collective concerns?' pp 169–183 in Pogany, I (ed.) *Human Rights in Eastern Europe* (1995) Edward Elgar, Hants UK at 183.

267   McGarry and O'Leary *The Politics of Ethnic Conflict* (1993) Routledge London pp 35–6.

268   Kymlicka *supra* n24 at 257 criticising Glazer *Affirmative Discrimination: Ethnic inequality and Public Policy* (1975) Basic Books, New York.

269   Kymlicka *supra* n24 at 176.

or constitutional state where multiculturalism is 'more than at best a compromise between assimilation to the dominant value tradition'.[270] Most Western European states already consider themselves as multicultural and offer a range of policies and laws aimed at improving access to education and civil society for ethnic minority groups. In some states, particularly Hungary and the Czech Republic multiculturalism has been used to defend practices of separate schooling and this has led to further exclusion and denial of Roma as equal citizens.

Often genuine multicultural policies result from well-orchestrated lobbying from minority representatives or external pressure from the European Union. It is far too easy for a dispersed minority such as the Roma, lacking a significant political voice, to be regarded as a national problem to be solved by assimilation. In this respect there are obvious similarities with indigenous peoples.

There are clearly theoretical problems with both individualist and group rights approaches to the protection of minorities. However, these difficulties should not be used to prevent practical solutions and constructive proposals. Richard Rorty argues that human rights need passion and courage rather than theoretical justifications and reason. He suggests that the search for philosophical foundations is doomed to failure and offers nothing. Rights are certainly secured by practical battles rather than theories.[271] Oestreich also advocates a pragmatic approach cautioning against the use of semantics regarding the terms group and collective rights.[272]

Active promotion and support for minority cultures is certainly needed if we are to avoid the injustice perpetuated by the guise of liberal neutrality. Judge Lohmus, of the European Court of Human Rights, recognised 'living in a caravan and travelling are vital parts of gypsies' cultural heritage and traditional lifestyle' yet when balanced against the state's interest in strong planning laws that promote the vision of a sedentary society, this identity could be denied.[273] A supplemental approach would thus weigh the interests of the local community with the applicant's right to respect for home and family life. Additionally, it must then aim to protect the rights of British travelling people to live in a caravan as an essential aspect of their heritage and travelling identity.

---

270 Apel, Karl-Otto 'Plurality of the Good? The problem of affirmative tolerance in a multicultural society from an ethical point of view' (1997) *Ratio Juris* Vol 10, 2 pp 199–212 at 201.

271 Rorty, Richard 'Human rights, rationality and sentimentality' in Shute and Hurley *On Human Rights* (1993) Basic Books, Harper Collins, 112–130.

272 *Supra* n213 at 132.

273 *Buckley v UK* App 20348/92; European Court of Human Rights, Strasbourg, Judgement of 25 September 1996 para. 426.

Chapter 3

The Protection of Minorities through Individual Rights

Introduction

Following the collapse of the League of Nations regime,[1] the concept of a general, universal protection of human rights evolved.[2] The United Nations Charter was proclaimed by the General Assembly as 'a common standard of achievement for all peoples and all nations' which 'seeks to enlist every individual and every organ of society in a universal human rights movement'.[3]

A brief overview of the various human rights instruments reveals a clear focus on the rights of the individual, although there is a limited recognition that the individual personality can only fully develop within the context of community.[4] The individual is viewed within a variety of social relationships which are protected under the instruments, such as family and religious groupings. Yet the rights to petition the Human Rights Committee in the UN are available to the individual rights holder only. There is no inherent concept of justiciable group-orientated rights.

This chapter will examine the position of the group within this individualist perspective and identify the limitations of this approach. The following two chapters will examine, in detail, areas where the individualist focus is clearly seen to be inadequate to protect the human rights of Roma − education and citizenship. The question is how far, if at all, individual rights can effectively protect the cultural identity of the Roma.

The two tenets of international law: Equality and non-discrimination

The principles of equality and non-discrimination are essential pre-requisites to the realisation of human rights. They support the understanding of human rights

---

1   See Chapter 6 at 267.

2   Ramcharan, BG *The Concept and Present Status of the International Protection of Human Rights: 40 years after the Universal Declaration* (1989) M.Nijhoff, Dordrecht at 200. It was generally believed that the interests of minority groups would be protected by the observance of the non-discrimination principle − McKean 'The Meaning of Discrimination in International and Municipal Law' (1970) *BYIL* Vol. 44 pp 177–192 at 178.

3   Van Boven, Theo 'UN and human rights: A critical appraisal' in Casesse UN Law/ Fundamental Rights: *Two Topics in International Law* (1979) Sijthoff and Noordhoff, The Netherlands at 121.

4   E.g., Article 29(1) UDHR.

as universally applicable; no personal characteristic can entitle a person to greater human rights than another.[5]

Equality and non-discrimination are often viewed as synonymous terms. More accurately, it can be said that non-discrimination is the negative formulation of the equality principle.[6] It has been argued that the prevalence of non-discrimination provisions in international law is indicative of their status as part of customary international law.[7] Together proclaimed as official policy in virtually every state,[8] both equality and non-discrimination are essential to any recognition of minority based rights.[9] Indeed, it is often argued that the full realisation of non-discrimination provisions would make the need for minority – based rights protection redundant.[10] This view must regard non-discrimination as encompassing substantive or real equality, which would include 'special' measures for minorities when required.

The advantages of an individual approach to human rights

It has already been noted that those involved in establishing a new human rights order after the collapse of the League of Nations regime were concerned to prevent the re-growth of nationalist tendencies. Drawing attention away from group affiliations enables a policy of blanket equality for all citizens to be adopted, irrespective of any specific group disadvantage. On the surface this is an attractive argument. Biological racial differences are no longer regarded by social scientists as legitimate reasons for denying or ascribing rights to particular groups.[11] Most societies are multicultural and there is no such thing today as a pure race.[12] Furthermore, the very notion of giving extra rights to members of a particular group will invariably diminish the rights of

---

5   Sieghart, Paul *The International Law of Human Rights* (1983) Clarendon at 75.

6   Lerner, Natan *Group Rights and Discrimination in International Law* (1991) Martinus-Nijhoff, Dordrecht at 25; Partsch 'Fundamental principles of human rights: self-determination, equality and non-discrimination' (1976) in Vasak *The International Dimensions of Human Rights* (1982) Vol. 2 UNESCO, Paris notes the various interpretations given to the term 'equality', which has led to the negative formulation of 'non-discrimination' order to achieve clarity and certainty.

7   See Judge Tanaka's dissenting Opinion in the South-West Africa Case *ICJ Reports* (1996), pp 3, 293. Shaw substantiates this argument by reference to Articles 55 and 56 UN Charter, Articles 2 and 7 UDHR and the provisions in the international covenants; regional documents and state practice – *International Law* (1997) Cambridge Univ. Press at 213.

8   Sigler, Jay *Minority Rights. A Comparative Analysis* (1983) Greenwood Press, CT at 178–9 notes that in reality, enforcement of the non-discrimination provisions varies greatly from nation to nation.

9   *Ibid.* at 149.

10   For example: Packer, J 'On the Definition of Minorities' in Packer and Mynti *The Protection of Ethnic, and Linguistic Minorities in Europe* (1992) Abo Akademie, Finland at 44.

11   For further discussion see Kohn, Marek *The Race Gallery* (1996) Vintage, London especially Chapter 9.

12   Mack, Raymond W and Duster, Troy S *Patterns of Minority Relations* (1964) Anti-Defamation League of B'Nai B'rith, US at 25.

other individuals and cause resentment. Such resentment may be incompatible with the ultimate goal of preventing discrimination. Indeed, if we accept that most people hold prejudiced attitudes in at least one respect, it has been argued that there are only two ways of preventing people actively discriminating. The first is to remove the opportunity to discriminate; the second is to show that discriminatory behaviour is socially unacceptable (usually through punishment).[13] The recognition of the rights of minorities is unlikely by itself to stop active discrimination in society.

Related to this point is the concern, discussed in Chapter 2, adopted by writers such as Nathan Glazer, that group rights may be seen to exaggerate and promote group difference.[14] Artificial boundaries are thus retained and become entrenched, with the possibility of deepening ethnic conflict.

In addition, there is of course the massive practical problem of determining which groups deserve additional rights and how these rights are to be distributed within the group itself. An emphasis on the rights of the individual arguably avoids these complications in favour of a simple, egalitarian approach.

The approach of international law

McKean defines discrimination as 'any act or conduct which denies to individuals equality of treatment with other individuals because they belong to particular groups in society'.[15] Not all forms of discrimination are prohibited in international law. The crucial grounds are factors over which the individual has no control.[16] The Charter of the UN mentions the four criteria for non-discrimination of sex, race, religion and language. This list has been considerably enlarged since the Universal Declaration of Human Rights which included 'political or other opinion, national or social origin, property, birth or other status'.[17]

Discrimination is prohibited in the International Covenants, the Universal Declaration of Human Rights and the European Convention on Human Rights and Fundamental Freedoms. It is necessary however, to examine the scope of these provisions in order to understand the limitations of these instruments in the absence of further guarantees of group protection.

Non-discrimination in the UN Covenants

The International Covenant on Civil and Political Rights (hereafter ICCPR) attends to the principle of non-discrimination in three separate provisions. Article 2(1) is

---

13   *Ibid.* pp 39–41.

14   See Chapter 2 Glazer, Nathan 'Individual Rights against Group rights' (1978) in Kamenka, E and Tay, E (eds.) *Human Rights* (1978) Edward Arnold, London at 98 and *Ethnic Dilemmas* (1983) Harvard Univ. Press.

15   McKean, W *Equality and Discrimination under International Law* (1983) OUP at 10–11.

16   *Study of Discrimination in Political, Economic, Social and Cultural Spheres*, UN Doc E/CN.4/Sub.2/288, paras 46–8.

17   Article 2(1) UDHR.

the general comprehensive non-discrimination and equality clause, absent from the European Convention. Article 26 provides for equal protection before the law and Article 3, of limited purpose in this context, provides for equality between the sexes.

The variety of terms used including equality before the law, equal protection of the law, non-discrimination and non-distinction is illustrative of the inconsistency of the provisions but can also be seen as encompassing an extensive range of situations.[18] In all three provisions, the positive obligation to promote equality rests alongside its negative corollary of non-discrimination. Ramcharan argues that the objective of genuine equality may, as discussed below, necessitate some differential treatment. The non-discrimination elements exist to limit the areas where differential treatment is acceptable.[19]

Article 2 is comparable in scope to Article 14 of the ECHR in that it requires state parties to respect and ensure 'the rights recognised in the present Covenant, without distinction of any kind'. Therefore, it does not prohibit discrimination outside the boundaries of substantive Covenant rights. However, when read in conjunction with Article 26 it can be seen that the potential of Article 2 is far greater than that offered in the regional instrument. Article 26 provides equal treatment before the law and could cover a vast range of situations where discriminatory treatment has occurred as a result of unequal application of the law.

The Human Rights Committee and the Roma

The issue of minority protection is dealt with in Chapter 6. However, in those states where Roma are not officially recognised as falling within the definition of minority, the non-discrimination provisions become of paramount importance. In its General Comment on Article 2, the Committee clearly establishes that distinctions and exclusions based on matters including national or social origin as well as 'birth or other status' will contravene the non-discrimination provisions.[20] It is confirmed that identical treatment is not appropriate in every instance and that affirmative action may be necessary to diminish or eliminate conditions which perpetuate discrimination.[21]

It may then come as some surprise that the Human Rights Committee itself has said surprisingly little on the subject of Roma and other travellers. The formal absence of non-governmental organisations in the reporting process necessarily means that much of the evidence of discriminatory practices is not available to the Committee. When the Roma are listed as a subject of concern the state party can evade criticism by highlighting examples of economic initiatives designed to improve the situation of Roma communities.[22]

---

18   Ramcharan, B.G 'Equality and non-discrimination' in Henkin *The International Bill of Rights* (1981) Columbia Univ. Press, NY at 251.

19   *Ibid.* at 252.

20   CCPR *Non-discrimination: 10/11/89 General Comment 18* para. 7

21   *Ibid.* paras 8 and 10.

22   See for example *Concluding Observations of the Human Rights Committee: Hungary 3/08/93* CCPR/C/79/Add. 22 para. 10.

The International Convention on the Elimination of All Forms of Racial Discrimination

Since 1969, The International Convention on the Elimination of All Forms of Racial Discrimination (hereafter ICERD) has operated as the one universal human rights instrument dealing specifically with the right of non-discrimination. The large number of ratifications is indicative of a broad support for the principles it endorses across a wide range of political cultures.[23] The Preamble emphasises the equality and dignity 'inherent in all human beings' and states that 'the existence of racial barriers is repugnant to the ideals of any human society'. Certain distinctions are permitted under the ICERD, such as those between citizen and non-citizens or nationals and aliens 'provided they do not discriminate against any particular nationality'.[24] There is no special reference to minorities, the main objective being to promote conditions of equality both de jure and de facto.[25]

'Race' is defined by Article 1(1) to incorporate national or ethnic origin. Partsch contends that the important question is whether a person is deemed to be socially, physically or culturally distinct by others, whether this is in fact true or not.[26] This construction would favour the inclusion of Roma/Gypsies without requiring an examination of their distinct ethnic origins.

S2(1) imposes a negative obligation on state parties to pursue without delay a policy to eliminate racial discrimination; measures to be undertaken include effective provisions to review Government policies and to nullify/rescind/amend laws of a discriminatory nature and to encourage integrationist, multiracial movements and ways of eliminating barriers between races.

ICERD and the Roma

The Committee on the Elimination of Racial Discrimination, charged with overseeing the implementation of the provisions in the Convention, has received evidence on the treatment of the Roma on several occasions. Following the Hungarian Report of March 1996, the Committee expressed approval at the new policy regarding the treatment of minorities.[27] However, the report is critical of the racism experienced by several minorities including the Roma and, in recommending increased attention to their needs, goes on to state that:[28]

> The persistent marginalisation of the large Gypsy population, in spite of continuing efforts by the Government, is a matter of serious concern. It is noted that the de facto discrimination Gypsies face in the enjoyment of their economic, social and cultural rights

---

23   As of 1 January 1993 the Convention had 132 state parties: *HRLJ* 14 No 1–2 at 69.

24   ICERD Article 1 (3); Lerner *supra* n6 at 49.

25   Pejic, J 'Minority Rights in International Law' (1997) *HRQ* 666–685 at 676.

26   Partsch *supra* n6 at 72.

27   CERD *Concluding Observations: Hungary.* 03/28/96 CERD/C/304/Add. 4 at para. 11.

28   *Ibid.* at para. 21.

increases their vulnerability in a context of economic crisis. Concern is expressed that three quarters of the Gypsies are unemployed with no prospect of entering the labour market.[29]

Following submission of follow up reports, the Hungarian Helsinki Committee and the Roma Press Centre made written representations to the Committee in 2002. It is clear from the reports that the marginalisation of the Roma continued and in some cases intensified. In particular, attention was drawn to the continued use of hate speech in the public arena and the failure of the authorities to pursue prosecutions.[30] The Committee's report found that discrimination towards Roma was widespread and highlighted a number of particular problems including police complicity, forced evictions and educational segregation.[31]

It is obvious that the Roma are considered to fall within the ambit of the Convention, with the Committee criticising the treatment of Roma in a variety of countries including Spain[32] and Czechoslovakia.[33] The recent report by the Committee on Ukraine raised issues of forced eviction and discrimination.[34] It is clear from many of the reports that while non-discrimination and equality provisions appear to be working to the benefit of some minorities, for the Roma they have had remarkably little effect.

The issue of repatriation agreements was raised in the Committee's concluding observations on the 1993 report of Germany. Considering the obligations under Article 2, clarification as to the agreements which sought to repatriate Roma and Sinti asylum seekers from Romania and Bulgaria was requested. In addition, the Committee sought information on the level of representation in national elected bodies and the cultural protection of those Roma and Sinti without legal German nationality.[35]

The Convention can be criticised on several counts. The lack of adequate enforcement is dealt with below and this is in part attributable to the wording of the text which, according to Meron, exacerbates the 'difficulties through its lack of precision'.[36] Furthermore, while it allows for special measures to be introduced to

---

29   *Ibid.* at para. 14.

30   Hungarian Helsinki Committee and the Roma Press Centre Regarding the Joint 14th, 15th, 16th and 17th periodic report of Hungary under Article 9 of the ICERD to the UN Committee on the Elimination of Racial Discrimination. For consideration at its 61th session, August 2002.

31   Concluding Observations of the Committee on the Elimination of All Forms of Racial Discrimination. 1 November 2002 A/57/18 para. 374,378.

32   CERD Ninth periodic reports of States Parties due in 1986, addendum, Spain 1 CERD/C/149/Add. 14.

33   CERD Tenth periodic report of States parties due in 1988 addendum, Czechoslovakia CERD/C/172/Add. 5.

34   CERD 69th session, 31 July–18 August. Questions put by the Rapporteur in connection of the 17th and 18th period CERD/C/UKR/18.

35   CERD Concluding Observations of the Committee on the Elimination of Racial Discrimination: Germany 15/09/93 A/48/18 paras 426–452.

36   Meron, T *Human Rights Law Making in the United Nations* (1986) Clarendon, Oxford at 44.

compensate disadvantaged groups, the introduction of such measures is ultimately at the discretion of the individual state. Given the economic difficulties of many of the Eastern European states and the comparative unpopularity of the Roma across Europe, there would seem little incentive in the Convention for any state to address the issue of special measures. The monitoring body has exhibited a tendency to make cautious suggestions for improvement, as discussed in the context of education in Chapter 5. Marcia Rooker found that the tone of the ICERD reports, particularly before the end of the Cold war, regarding discrimination against Roma, was cautious with a tendency to avoid directing blatant criticism at states.[37] Nevertheless, she notes a change in approach since 1992 with increasingly critical reports and condemnation of discriminatory practices and language.[38] Indeed, the reports demonstrate the wide range of discriminatory practices that Roma are exposed to including segregation in housing and education (contrary to Article 3), racial hatred (contrary to Article 4) and the denial of access to public services including courts (contrary to Article 5(c)).

In recognition of the unique situation faced by the Roma, the Committee on the Elimination of Racial Discrimination (hereafter CERD) adopted the first thematic recommendation of it kind in 2000. Recommendation XXVII on Discrimination Against Roma addressed racial violence including police acquiescence; discrimination in education including segregated schooling; living conditions; discrimination in public life and the media.[39] The recommendation arose out of the common criticisms and concern expressed in CERD reports and enables the Committee to apply a more structured, analysis of the treatment of Roma by State parties.

UNESCO Declaration on Race and Racial Prejudice

It is interesting to contrast the ICERD provisions with the non-binding UNESCO Declaration on Race and Racial Prejudice which includes a clear appreciation of the importance of minority identity. The Preamble to the Declaration notes the injustice of forced assimilation, included with apartheid and genocide as 'offences against human dignity'. Article 1 explicitly recognises the right of all individuals and groups to be different and Article 1(3) asserts the corollary right to maintain cultural identity.

The right to be different should be interpreted as enabling all individuals and groups to lead their lives 'without needing to abandon their essential identity'.[40] Article 5, concerning cultural identity, provides that every minority group has the right to decide the extent to which it desires to preserve and develop its own culture, or, if it prefers, to join the dominant culture.[41] The rights bearer in this context is clearly the group, rather than the member of the group, prompting Thornberry

---

37   Rooker, Marcia *The International Supervision of Protection of Romany People in Europe* (2004) Univ. of Nijmegen at 109.

38   *Ibid.* Chapter V.

39   CERD General recommendation XXVII *Discrimination Against Roma* adopted at 57th session on 16 August 2000.

40   UNESCO Explanatory report, Doc 20/C/18, annex.

41   *Ibid.* at 4–5.

to comment: 'The individualist bias in contemporary international law is here completely dissipated'.[42]

In the UNESCO Declaration group and individual rights are supplemental. The possible benefits of such an approach for the Roma were discussed in Chapter 2. Instead, of depending on political will to introduce special measures, the group has a right to maintain its cultural identity and a such is entitled to trump conflicting demands by the state. The sum total of the rights of the group members are clearly strengthened by the recognition of the group as rights-bearer and thus legal entity.

The application of de facto equality as a solution for minority problems

International law does recognise that equal treatment may result in unequal consequences and this has led to the recognition of affirmative action strategies. Special measures for minority groups can be defined as the requirement to ensure suitable means, including differential treatment, for the preservation of minority characteristics and traditions which distinguish them from the majority of the population.[43]

As Stavenhagen argues, minority groups need special measures to ensure real equality.[44] The promotion of such measures does not violate the principle of equality unless a person is subjected to invidious treatment as a consequence of such measures; such treatment results from a classification or distinction; and, that classification in the given context is unreasonable.[45]

Modern international law accepts in principle the notion of preferential treatment for disadvantaged groups and their members.[46] In the Advisory Opinion of the Permanent Court of International Justice in Minority Schools in Albania (1935) the court stated:

Equality in law precludes discrimination of any kind, whereas equality in fact may involve the necessity of different treatment in order to attain a result which establishes an equilibrium between different situations.[47]

The modern principle of positive action for such groups has gradually developed since the UN Charter and by 1970 it was possible to observe that:

---

42   Thornberry, P *International Law and the Rights of Minorities* (1991) OUP at 296.

43   According to Alfredsson and de Zayas 'Minority rights: protection by the United Nations' *HRLJ* 14 no 1–2 at 2.

44   Stavenhagen R *The Ethnic Question -Conflicts, Development and Human Rights* (1990) UN Univ. Press, Tokyo at 62.

45   Tomuschat, C 'Equality and non-discrimination in the common domain' in Eide *New Approaches to Minority Protection* (1993) MRG, London at 12.

46   See for example Article 2 CERD (below); UNESCO Convention against Discrimination in Education (1960) (Article 6) ILO Convention No 111 Concerning Discrimination in Respect of Employment (1958).

47   (1935) PCIJ Ser. A/B No 64 at 20.

Certain distinctions are legitimate if they are special measures designed to achieve rather than to prevent equality in the enjoyment of rights.[48]

Their purpose is to compensate for past injustices and such measures should cease once that compensation is realised.[49] In this way such measures are distinct from the measures included in the UN Declaration on the Rights of Persons Belonging to National or Ethnic, Religious and Linguistic Minorities and the Council of Europe Framework Convention for the Protection of Minorities[50] as the latter have the intention of enabling a lasting manifestation of difference.

Article 1 of ICERD states that in given conditions, special measures do not constitute discrimination. Article 2(3) advocates special concrete measures with the object of ensuring full enjoyment by such individuals of human rights and freedoms. It is further stated that such measures shall not lead to the maintenance of unequal rights and therefore should be of a temporary nature only.

The preference of the term 'racial group' in the ICERD is much narrower than the formulation in Article 27 of the ICCPR but it is generally regarded that a group will be considered a 'racial group' under the Convention if it can be regarded as ethnically discrete.[51] Meron argues that emphasis should be placed on the group's economic and political position rather than anthropological factors.[52]

The Convention goes further in actually requiring states to engage in affirmative action policies when the circumstances so warrant. Article 2(2) provides that in certain, unspecified circumstances:

> ... special and concrete measures to ensure the adequate development and protection of certain racial groups or individuals belonging to them, for the purposes of guaranteeing them the full and equal enjoyment of human rights and fundamental freedoms.[53]

The World Conference to Combat Racism and Racial Discrimination, echoed this position:

> Such specific measures should include appropriate assistance to persons belonging to minority groups, to enable them to develop their own culture and to facilitate their full development, in particular in the fields of education, culture and employment.[54]

While there is little guidance on the types of measures that States could use and the circumstances that could warrant the implementation of such measures, there is a

---

48   McKean *supra* n2 goes on to provide an example in the field of education where, international law would support the establishment of separate schooling, if required, in a separate language for a particular population group (*Study of Discrimination in Education*, UN Doc E/CN.4/Sub.2/181, para. 51 p24).

49   Lerner *supra* n6 at 168.

50   Discussed in Chapter 6 at 299.

51   Meron *supra* n36 at 39.

52   *Ibid.*

53   Article 2(2) *ibid.*

54   UN doc A/33/262 at 20–1 (1978).

clear recognition of the rights of groups as well as individual members of groups.[55] In this respect the Convention goes further than Article 27, discussed in Chapter 6, by providing specifically for affirmative action in the interests of protection of group identity.[56] Group identity is further recognised in Article 14 which allows groups as well as individuals to petition the Committee where the particular state has recognised the competence of the Committee to receive such complaints.[57] As Thornberry notes however, this clearly falls well short of a right to maintain a minority identity.[58]

The philosophy of the ICERD can be described as 'integrationist'.[59] It is unfortunate that the distinction between integration and assimilation is not always easy to draw. In the seventh report of Czechoslovakia the Czech representative had described the fact that re-education programmes had led to the removal of Roma from the locality as a 'favourable development'.[60] Doubts were raised by one committee member and it became clear that the distinction between integration and assimilation blurred when essential cultural practices were ignored.

ICERD's philosophy is reflected in Article 26 of the ICCPR. The Third Committee, preferring the phrase discrimination to 'distinction' recognised 'the word "discrimination" ... was used ... in a negative sense only, to mean a distinction of an unfavourable kind'.[61] Clearly, it has become apparent that even within the individual rights emphasis, there may be a need for special measures of a temporary nature to remedy unfavourable distinctions. This must be contrasted with the UNESCO approach in which group and individual rights are supplemental.

Affirmative action in practice

Affirmative action programmes have at their heart the disadvantaged situation of certain groups in society. The practice has been vigorously debated in the US where the limits of American individualism are tested. One critic argues:

> The practice of reverse discrimination undermines the foundation of the very ideal in whose name it is advocated, it destroys justice, law, equality, citizenship and replaces them with power struggles and popularity contests.[62]

The infamous *Bakke* case revealed a tautology: how can individual rights to equality be protected if one group of individuals is automatically given certain benefits not available to others? The case concerned a white applicant who had been denied a university place on two occasions due to the existence of policies favouring less fortunate groups. Justice Powell's literal view of equality did not encompass such programmes:

---

55   37 UN GAOR Supp (No 18) para. 468, UN Doc A/37/18 (1982).
56   Meron *supra* n36 at p37.
57   ICERD Article 14.
58   Thornberry *supra* n42 at 258.
59   *Ibid.* at 276.
60   CERD/C/91 Add 14, para. 393.
61   UN Docs A/C3/L. 1028/Rev.1 and Revelation 2; A/C3/SR 1181-5, 1202-7.
62   Newton, Lisa 'Reverse Discrimination as Unjustified' (1973) *Ethics* 83 at 312.

The guarantee of equal protection cannot mean one thing when applied to one individual and something else when applied to a person of another colour. If both are not accorded the same protection then it is not equal.[63]

Affirmative action is not a universally popular strategy for remedying past injustice. Much of the criticism is centred on the recognition of group rights and the artificial maintenance of group boundaries. It could also be argued that a marginalised group may be further stigmatised by its designation as needing such special treatment. It may encourage a feeling of resentment amongst other groups and the beneficiaries themselves may feel that they have been awarded a particular position as a token rather than through merit.

There is a recognition in international law that positive measure may be needed in order to achieve substantive equality but it is submitted that these obstacles and criticisms will not be overcome unless there is an acceptance of the failure of individual rights to support and promote minority identity. As Henrard argues:

> The fact that members of minorities do not have the power or ability to protect and promote their distinctive identity sufficiently, arguably enhances the need for their rights (as guaranteed) to be effective and also for genuine positive state obligations.[64]

Individual rights under the European Convention of Human Rights and Fundamental Freedoms (ECHR)

(i) Non-discrimination
It is apparent from the wording of Article 14 of the ECHR that the Convention is only concerned with discrimination relating to the other substantive rights contained therein: '… the enjoyment of the rights and freedoms set forth in this convention shall be secured without discrimination on any ground'. For example, in *Buckley* vs. *UK*, discussed below, the applicant alleged that her right to respect for family and home life (Article 8) had been interfered with and further that the cause of this violation resulted from legislation which discriminated against her on account of her Gypsy identity (Article 14).

Article 14 is the only provision in the Convention recognising, albeit implicitly, the adverse implications that may result from membership of a minority group. Discrimination is prohibited on specified grounds including association with a national minority, social and national origin as well as the more traditional aspects of race, religion and language. Article 14 will be violated when difference in treatment of analogous situations engaging a substantive Convention article does not have an objective and reasonable justification.[65] A justifiable distinction will require a legitimate aim and a reasonable and proportionate response.

---

63   *Regents of the University of California v Bakke* 438, US 265 (1978) at 280.
64   Henrard, Kristin *Devising an Adequate System of Minority Protection* (2000) Kluwer Int. at 151.
65   *Ibid.* p 74.

Case law suggests that in finding a violation of Article 14 it is not necessary for the court to find a breach of the substantive article.[66] Indeed, the decision of the ECHR in *Thilmmenos* v *Greece* suggests that the court are beginning to take a more flexible and creative approach when considering whether a substantive convention right has been engaged.[67] However, the interpretation of Article 14 has been criticised particularly when associated with deprivation of life or inhuman and degrading treatment. In this respect the Court's decision in *Anguelova* v *Bulgaria* is interesting.[68] The case itself concerned a 17 year old Rom who died in police custody following his arrest for attempted theft. The court found violations of Articles 2 and 3, 5 and 13 of the Convention. However, no violation of Article 14 was found as proof of racial discrimination 'beyond all reasonable doubt' could not be established. Judge Bonello, dissenting, reasoned that there was ample evidence of Bulgarian police hostility towards the Roma in this and previous cases.[69] However, the burden of proving discrimination in relation to the particular convention right was too onerous:

> It should, in my view, hold that when a member of a disadvantaged minority group suffers harm in an environment where racial tensions are high and impunity of state officials an epidemic, the burden to prove that the event was not ethnically induced, shifts to the government.[70]

Article 14 has also been criticised by several academic writers.[71] Sandra Fredman describes Article 14 as 'woefully inadequate as a constitutional equality guarantee'.[72] Timothy Jones similarly argues that the ECHR has had very little impact in the race discrimination field:

> A visitor from another planet reading the courts' judgements might be misled into concluding that Europe has been a haven of racial equality for the last 50 years.[73]

Jones goes on to argue that the Luxembourg authorities using the EU Race Directive may prove to be the principle protectors of rights in this respect.

Perhaps mindful of these criticisms, the ECHR subsequently found a breach of Article 14 coupled with Article 2 concerning the deaths of two Romani shot by Bulgarian police officers. In the landmark decision of *Nachova and Others* v *Bulgaria*, the court addressed the standard of proof issue in non-discrimination

---

66   *Belgian Linguistics Case* 1474/62 1 EHRR 252; *Airey* v *Ireland* ECHR 9 October 1979 Series A no 32, 16.

67   App 34369/97 (2001) 31 EHRR 15.

68   (2004) 38 EHRR 31.

69   See for example *Assenov* v *Bulgaria* (1999) 28 EHRR 652.

70   *Anguelova* v *Bulgaria* (2004) 38 EHRR 31 at O-I18.

71   See for example Livingstone, S 'Article 14 and the prevention of discrimination in the European Convention on Human Rights' [1997] *EHRLR* 25.

72   Fredman, S 'Why the UK Government should sign and ratify Protocol 12' (2002) 105 *Equal Opportunities Review* 21 at 23.

73   Jones, T 'The Race Directive: redefining protection from Discrimination in EU law' (2003) *EHRLR* Vol 5, 515–526 at 526.

allegations.[74] Given that the state rather than the individual is liable for discrimination under Article 14, the need to provide proof beyond reasonable doubt as in a criminal proceedings was questioned by the court. The impact of the decision in *Nachova* is significant as it extends the positive obligation on states to investigate every arguable claim of a violation of Article 14 without requiring the applicant to provide proof of discriminatory intent. Pleşe concludes:

> The Court has now lived up to its own mandate to provide a remedy to those in greatest need and assert its authority as a defender of the disadvantaged and the vulnerable.[75]

The change of interpretative approach to non-discrimination by the European Court of Human Rights is to be welcomed. It reflects broader developments in the EU including the change in onus of proof where an applicant can demonstrate evidence of discrimination. The judgement implicitly recognises the difficulty of proving racial discrimination and consequently the state's burden is to use best endeavours to investigate such complaints.[76]

A further prohibition on discrimination is contained in Article 20(2) ICCPR, which requires states to legislate against the advocacy of 'national, racial or religious hatred that constitutes incitement to discrimination, hostility or violence'. Alfredsson and de Zayas suggest that minorities would benefit from making more use of this provision in arguing that the source of their discriminatory treatment can be attributable to the advocacy of such hatred.[77]

The failings of Article 14 led to the introduction of Protocol 12 which came into force in April 2005 following the requisite 10 ratifications.[78] Article 1 contains a general non-discrimination clause which removes the requirement for the alleged discrimination to be 'within the ambit' of a substantive convention right. However, the approach of the protocol is brief and rather general and, as is typical with the Convention rights, it only applies to the activities of public authorities. Despite the obligation on public bodies to 'secure' these rights the extent of a positive duty on states to ensure full equality is clearly limited. According to the Explanatory notes, Article 1, Protocol 12 is 'not intended to impose a general positive obligation on the Parties to take measures to prevent or remedy all instances of discrimination in relations between private persons'.

Indirect discrimination, by which a particular policy or law has a disproportionately negative effect on members of a particular group, is not generally covered by Article 14.[79] Wintemute demonstrates that past judicial experiences suggest that the court is likely to restrict cases of indirect discrimination, considering factors such as

---

74   *Nachova* v *Bulgaria* App 43577/98 and 43579/98 (2004) 39 EHRR 37.

75   Pleşe, Branimir 'The Strasbourg Court finally redresses racial discrimination' *Roma Rights*, ERRC (2003).

76   *Supra* n74 para. 159.

77   Alfredsson et al. *supra* n43 at 7.

78   It has been ratified by Albania, Armenia, Bosnia and Herzegovia; Croatia; Cyprus; Finland; Georgia; the Netherlands; San Marino; Serbia and Montenegro; and Macedonia.

79   Gilbert, Geoff 'The burgeoning minority rights jurisprudence of the European Court of Human Rights' (2002) *HRQ* 24, 736–780 at 747.

resources and cost implications.[80] A wide margin of appreciation is likely to be given to states in these cases. This can be seen as a significant limitation the effectiveness of the anti-discrimination provisions. It fails to take into account the subtle ways that a state can discriminate against minorities and the disproportionate and often damaging effects of particular policies on minorities.[81]

Protocol 12 has not been embraced by the majority of Council of Europe states. There is a perception that the protocol is too vague and broad to be justiciable. According to the opinion of the UK Government, the Protocol contains 'unacceptable uncertainties' and it remains unlikely that ratification will follow without significant qualification.[82] While this view may be disputed by some writers, such as Wintemute, the number of ratifications suggests that Protocol 12 is a long way from making a significant difference in the field of anti-discrimination.

(ii) The right to respect for a particular lifestyle
The right to respect for private life guaranteed by Article 8 has been interpreted to cover the freedom to develop relationships in order to fulfil one's personality.[83] Marquand has distinguished between the right to adopt a particular lifestyle (which may fall outside the Convention) and the right to respect for a particular lifestyle.[84] But it seems clear that in some cases the European Court of Human Rights has been prepared to accept that 'respect' may entail a positive obligation on the part of the state.[85]

Article 8 is really the only provision in the Convention that may entail the protection of a particular lifestyle or culture. In *Beckers* v *Netherlands* (1991)[86] an application was bought by the occupant of a mobile home after he was evicted when he did not comply with the trades listed in a decree under the Mobile Homes Act (Woonwagenwet) 1986. Although declared inadmissible, the commission noted that as the applicant could not show association with a particular minority, the rules were not disproportionate to the aim of limiting mobile home occupation in the interests of preventing over-crowding in a small country. Such an approach suggested that members of minority groups, such as the Roma, could be given greater protection by Article 8.

---

80   Wintemute, R 'Filling the Article 14 "gap": Government ratification and judicial control of protocol No 12 ECHR: Part 2' (2004) *EHRLR* Vol 5. 484–499.

81   See for example the decisions of the ECHR in *Mutlu* v *Yildiz* 30,495/96 ECHR 17 October 2000 and *Kalin, Gezer and Tebay* v *Turkey* 24894/94, 24850/94, 24941/94 ECHR 18 January 2000. The disproportionate effect of Turkish security law on the Kurdish minority was not addressed by the Court.

82   See for example the report of the parliamentary Joint Committee on Human Rights 2004–05 session, 17th report para. 31.

83   *X v Iceland DR*5 at 86.

84   Marquand, C 'Human Rights protection and Minorities' (1993) *PL* at 365; *G and E v Norway*[35] at 30, 3 October 1983.

85   *Airey* v *Ireland* App 6289/73 2 EHRR 305 – the courts should be made available to any person who wishes to obtain a decree of judicial separation.

86   Application No 12344/86; Decision 25/2/91.

However, there have been a number of 'Gypsy' cases which suggest otherwise. The decision in *Buckley* vs. *UK* illustrates the limited protection of cultural identity offered under the provision and the need for a greater awareness of the importance of minority identity when balanced against the planning interest of the state.[87] In *Buckley*[88] the applicant, a Gypsy, had occupied her own land in caravans with her family without planning permission since 1988. She made two unsuccessful retrospective planning applications in 1989 and 1994. The local authority attempted to evict her and fined her for breach of the planning regulations when she refused to move. It was argued that she had alternative places to reside, particularly a public caravan site nearby. She alleged a breach of Article 8 coupled with Article 14 of the Convention.

The European Commission found in favour of the applicant under Article 8 of the Convention on the basis that her right to home life had been violated and that she had been deprived of realistic alternatives making the violation not 'necessary in a democratic society' (Article 8(2)). Both Commission and Court declined to look into the detail of Article 14 as the applicant had not been directly affected by the legislation introduced to restrict the lawful residence of Gypsies.

Both Commission and Court found that a 'home' under Article 8 did not need to have been lawfully established, providing the applicant could show continuity of residence. The Commission particularly understood the importance of the applicants Gypsy identity and recognised that Gypsies following a traditional lifestyle required special consideration in planning matters. The Court held that there had been a breach of Article 8(1) concerning respect for home life but added that in cases involving planning concerns and local needs, the Government would enjoy a wide margin of appreciation.[89] Furthermore, in finding that there was no violation of Article 8, the Court held that proper regard had been given to the applicant's needs and that on balance the means employed to achieve the legitimate aims pursued could not be regarded as disproportionate.[90]

The dissenting judgements of Judges Repik, Lohmus and Pettiti reveal a greater appreciation of the problems facing nomadic Gypsy people and greater weight is given to this aspect of identity when balanced against the State's margin of appreciation. In referring to a Council of Europe resolution on the cultural identity of nomads,[91] Judge Lohmus noted that 'living in a caravan and travelling are vital parts of gypsies' cultural heritage and traditional lifestyle.'[92] Though accepting that the planning objections were substantial, he nevertheless went on to stress the importance of different treatment in order to achieve equality in fact.[93] The opinion of Judge Pettiti is particularly interesting and well-informed. In taking a wider view

---

87   O'Nions, H 'The Right to Respect for Home and Family Life: the First in a Series of "Gypsy cases" to challenge UK Legislation' [1996] 5 *Web JCLI.*

88   App 20348/92; European Court of Human Rights, Strasbourg – judgement of 25 September 1996 in *HRLJ* vol. 17 no 11–12 at 420–427.

89   *Ibid.* at 423 para. 75.

90   *Ibid.* at 424 para. 84.

91   Committee of Ministers Resolution (75) 13.

92   *Supra* n88 at 426.

93   *Ibid.*

of the legislation affecting Gypsies in the UK he contended that there had been a violation of both Article 8 and Article 14:

> The discrimination results equally from the fact that if in similar circumstances a British citizen who was not a gypsy wished to live on his land, in a caravan, the authorities would not raise any difficulties, even if they considered his conduct to be unorthodox.[94]

The majority judgement of the court can be criticised on several grounds, particularly the failure to look at the cumulative effect of the legislation facing Gypsies in the UK which combines to make the establishment of family and home life near impossible.

There is also the spurious reasoning for the planning refusals. The planning inspector's initial concerns about highway safety and planning matters had all but disappeared from the final version placed before the court. The clear rationale was to restrict the number of Gypsy families living in the area.[95] Gypsies are often unpopular neighbours; however, unpopularity itself is not one of the permissible grounds for qualifying rights under Article 8(2).[96]

Overall the Buckley case verdict can be characterised as a missed opportunity. In the words of Judge Pettiti:

> The European Court had, in the Buckley case, an opportunity to produce, in the spirit of the European Convention, a critique of national law and practice with regard to gypsies and travellers in the United Kingdom that would have been transposable to the rest of Europe, and thereby partly compensate for the injustices they suffer.[97]

There have been several other Gypsy/Roma cases involving planning issues which reached the same conclusions as *Buckley*.[98] In a somewhat perverse application of Article 14, it was suggested in *Beard* v *UK* that while Gypsies deserved special consideration in planning considerations, exclusively affording Gypsies the right to live in caravans on their own land would undermine the principle of non-discrimination.[99] This approach is similar to the US Supreme Court in *Bakke* where non-discrimination was interpreted in a formal sense rather than a de facto sense to deny efforts to promote genuine equality of opportunity.[100]

The difficulty of reconciling planning policies with the interests of the travelling community has become an acute problem in the United Kingdom. In 1994, the duty on local authorities to provide adequate accommodation for those defined as

---

94   *Ibid.* at 427.

95   O'Nions *supra* n87.

96   This is of course crucial as many minority practices and beliefs face hostility from the rest of society – see for example *Dudgeon* v *UK* (1981) Series A No 45, 4 EHRR 149 concerning the ban on certain homosexual practices in Northern Ireland.

97   *Supra* n88 at 428.

98   See for example *Chapman* vs. *UK* (2001) app 27238/95, *Coster* v *UK* (2001) app 24876/94 and *Lee* vs. *UK* (2001) 25289/94.

99   (2001) App 24882/84 para. 106.

100   *Supra* n63.

'Gipsies' was removed and consequently a significant number of travelling people now occupy illegal encampments.

The Human Rights Act 1998 has added some weight to the claims that minority status should be afforded more weight in planning considerations. The case of *Clarke* [2001] suggested that the specific land use needs of Gypsies required special consideration in order to comply with Articles 8 and 14. Mr Justice Burton equated the denial of planning permission or eviction on the basis that alternative conventional housing existed with penalising a Christian, Jew or Muslim for refusing to work on certain days or eat certain foods.[101]

However, subsequent cases suggest that planning authorities pay lip service to human rights issues and this is facilitated by the balancing Act under Article 8. Decisions such as *Codona* v *Mid Bedfordshire DC* suggest that if the planning authority has considered all relevant options, including the applicant's aversion to conventional housing, this will satisfy the Article 8 proportionality test in most cases.[102] This is notwithstanding the statement by Newman J in Price:

> In order to meet the requirement to accord respect something more that 'taking account' of an applicant's gypsy culture is required. As the court in Chapman stated, respect includes the positive obligation to act so as to facilitate the gypsy way of life, without being under a duty to guarantee it to an applicant in any particular case.[103]

The decision of the court in *Chapman* recognised the Gypsy way of life as requiring particular respect under Article 8 and this has led to the emergence of a *European Standard* on the treatment of Gypsies and travellers under the Convention.[104] The subsequent decision in *Connors* vs. *UK* suggests that the court is now requiring a greater justification for interference with the Gypsy way of life.

Connors vs. UK: Narrowing the margin?

The case concerned the eviction of a family including four children from a local authority site. Under English law, Gypsies do not have security of tenure on caravan sites, making it comparatively easy for them to be evicted by site managers. The European Court ruled unanimously that a violation of Article 8 had occurred. They recognised that states had a margin of appreciation in housing policy but emphasised that the margin would be narrower where there was a great intrusion into the individual's personal sphere. Of particular significance is the concluding recognition:

> The vulnerable position of gypsies as a minority means that special consideration should be given to their needs and different lifestyle. There is a positive obligation upon Contracting States to facilitate the gypsy way of life.[105]

---

101   *Clarke* vs. *SS for Dept of Transport and the Regions, Tunbridge Wells BC* [2001] EWHC Admin 800. Para. 30

102   [2004] EWCA Civ 925

103   *R (Price) v Carmarthenshire CC 2003* EWHC 42 Admin para 19

104   App 66746/01 27 May 2004 (2005) 40 EHRR 9.

105   *Ibid.* para. 84.

The importance of the decision in *Connors* is clear. A narrow reading alone suggests that the Government will need to rethink policy on security of tenure on gypsy sites. However, a wider reading has implications for all Europe's Roma by suggesting that states will have to demonstrate that they have discharged a duty of respecting and enabling the Roma-Gypsy way of life. The decision-making process whereby planning inspectors and site managers pay lip service to human rights issues by making general enquiries of the particular applicants human rights needs and then going on to justify evictions as 'proportionate' should become a thing of the past. The margin of appreciation has been considerably narrowed when the Gypsy lifestyle is undermined. The House of Lords were asked to consider the impact of the decision in *Connors* in *Kay and Price*[106] concerning evictions from land occupied without permission. They held that only in very exceptional cases would there be a defence to an eviction from unlawfully occupied land under Article 8(2). The fact that the applicants were Gypsies an entitled to positive support from the state was expressly recognised as an exceptional circumstance.[107] However, the court confined the use of the Article 8(2) defence to cases where the applicants had occupied the land for a significant period of time such that it could be regarded as their 'home' under Article 8(1). As Gilbert argues, the European Convention is not designed to protect minority identity and it is potentially open for the court to strike out a minority rights claim as manifestly ill-founded.[108]

(iii) The rights of assembly and association
The twin rights of freedom of association and assembly have a dual quality in that while they inhere in all individuals, they can only be exercised collectively. The realisation of these rights can be seen as pivotal to the full realisation of individual rights such as freedom of expression and religion[109] as well as minority-based rights. The Universal Declaration,[110] ICCPR[111] and the ECHR contain proclamations of the right to 'peaceful' assembly and association.

Article 11 of the ECHR contains the basic right to freedom of association and assembly. Restrictions can only be imposed under Article 11(2) when they are prescribed by law; have a legitimate purpose and are necessary in a democratic society. The necessity test requires a balance of the individual's interests with those of the state in deciding whether such measures are proportionate to the legitimate aim pursued.[112] Henrard argues that Article 11 is indisputably important to members of minorities as it implicitly recognises, albeit in a limited way, a collective dimension.[113] However, as she recognises, the application of Article 11 in the

---

106   *Lambeth BC* v *Kay*; *Price* v *Leeds City Council* [2006] UKHL 10.

107   *Ibid.* para. 36 per L Bingham of Cornhill.

108   Gilbert *supra* n79 at 780.

109   C/E Freedom of Association Seminar organised by the Secretariat General of the C/E on collaboration with the Ministry of Justice for Iceland, Reykjavik 26–28 August 1993 at 14.

110   Article 20 UDHR.

111   Article 21 ICCPR.

112   *Handyside* v *UK* Judgement of 7 December 1976. Series A No 24 at p23, para. 49.

113   Henrard *supra* n65 at 83.

preservation and protection of minority identity has been limited. This can be seen clearly by the Roma experience. In the UK, the Criminal Justice and Public Order Act 1994 makes several inroads into this right by limiting the size of gatherings and by making trespassory assemblies illegal in the name of pubic order.[114] Residence restrictions apply to Roma across Eastern and Western Europe effectively preventing the full realisation of this right.[115]

The fact that a gathering may be peaceful will not hold much weight if there is a risk of public disorder. In *ARM Chappell* v *UK*[116] it was held that gatherings for spiritual events could be legitimately prevented if there was a real risk of disorder or violence, even when the disturbance was not created by the group in question. The interference with the right of Druids to conduct their solstice celebration was justified as necessary in a democratic society for the prevention of disorder and protection of rights and freedoms of others (Article 11(2)).

The extent of the Article has also been bought into question following the decision in *X v UK* where a prisoner was denied a right to receive visits from an acquaintance in order to discuss his medical condition.[117] In citing *Mc Feeley et al. v UK*, the court stated that 'The provisions did not concern the right ... to "associate" with other persons in the sense of enjoying the personal company of others'.[118] Although the decisions of the Court do not constitute binding precedent, it would appear that Article 11 is envisaged as being restricted to the right to form or be affiliated to a group pursuing particular aims, rather than merely a social collectivity.[119]

Nevertheless, the relevance of Article 11 to the preservation and dissemination of minority identity can be seen in the decision of *Sidiropoulos and Others v Greece* which concerned the rights of an ethnic organisation to establish an association 'the Home of Macdeonian Civilisation'. The Greek authorities had refused registration of the group on the basis that its central aim was to promote the idea that a Macedonian minority existed and to undermine territorial integrity. Both Commission and Court acknowledged there may be a wide margin of appreciation when restricting rights in the interests of public safety and national security. However, a violation of Article 11 was found on the basis that the state's response was disproportionate given the needs of the group members to promote their 'culture and spiritual heritage'.[120] While this decision demonstrates that the court will scrutinise state policies which restrict the rights of minorities to promote their culture, it is important to remember that there is no proactive obligation, inherent in Article 11, to facilitate that process. As Henrard recognises, states have a wide margin of appreciation concerning the application and implementation of Article 11 and 'De facto, it is in general relatively easy for a state to argue that it has complied with its obligations'.[121]

---

114 See assorted provision in Part V CJPOA 1994.
115 See below n127.
116 DR 53 at 241.
117 (1982) 5 EHRR 260.
118 DR 20 at 44.
119 *Ibid.*
120 ECHR Rep 10 July 1998 para. 41.44.
121 Henrard *supra* n65 at 89.

Freedom of expression

Article 10 of the ECHR guarantees the right to freedom of expression which, like Article 11, is very important right for members of minorities. It encompasses the right to communicate in ones own language and to disseminate opinions through the media.[122] It is linked to pluralism, democracy and tolerance and consequently incorporates the expression of difference and ideas that shock and disturb.[123]

The balancing act inherent in Article 10 appears to give little weight to the particular needs of minorities in terms of preserving and promoting their identity. In *Otto Preminger Institut v Austria* the Court acknowledged that religion may be crucial to the identity of a minority but was unwilling to give priority to that interest over the right of expression for a publisher of a blasphemous film.[124] In *Wingrove* vs. *UK*, the Court dealt with a similar issue but allowed expression to be restricted in pursuance of a legitimate aim, namely the protection of rights and freedoms of others.[125] Although the decision in Wingrove may provide some comfort to religious minorities, in reality it offers very little as the particular needs of minorities were not regarded as significant. Furthermore, the court acknowledged but did not dwell on the fact that UK's blasphemy laws only protected members of the Christian religion and thus could be infringing Article 14.

(iv) Freedom of movement

The Universal Declaration provides for the right to leave a country and to move freely within the borders of a given state.[126] The ICCPR goes further in including the right to choose residence. Article 2 of Protocol 4, ECHR states:

> 1   Everyone lawfully within the territory of a State shall, within that territory, have the right to liberty of movement and freedom to choose his residence ….

> 3   No restrictions shall be placed on the exercise of these rights other than such as are in accordance with the law and are necessary in a democratic society for the maintenance of 'ordre public', for the prevention of crime, for the protection of the rights and freedoms of others.

> 4   The rights set forth in paragraph 1 may also be subject, in particular areas, to restrictions imposed in accordance with the land and justified by the public interest in a democratic society.

Liberty of movement is still essential to the culture of many western travellers. Throughout Europe there have been many attempts to control the movement of

---

122   See, for example, *Informationsverein Lentia and others v Austria* ECHR 24 November 1993 Series A no 276.

123   *Handyside* v *UK* 1976 1EHRR 737 para. 49.

124   ECHR 20 September 1994 Series A no 295-A.

125   *Wingrove* v *UK* ECHR 25 November 1996.

126   Article 13 UDHR.

Roma and to set maximum limits on their number in particular areas.[127] The freedom to choose residence was successfully invoked in the German courts by a Turkish national residing in Berlin when his residence permit was stamped 'not authorised' in three specified districts.[128] However, the Commission indicated, in a case involving mobile-home dwellers, that Article 2 of Protocol 4 does not guarantee the right to choose a specific residence without title to the land.[129]

The relevance of this provision to travelling people depends on the region in question. While it may be asserted that the Roma have the state of mind of a nomad irrespective of their nomadic lifestyle,[130] it remains a fact that in much of Europe, Roma live sedentary lives in long-established housing. Nevertheless, the notion of freedom of movement is a contentious issue in two circumstances. Firstly, the situation of Roma in much of Western Europe does involve a nomadic element. In the UK, Department of Environment Statistics suggest that 32% of Gypsy families do not have an authorised stopping place.[131] It is inevitable that most of these families, as well as many families who do have an authorised abode, will be regularly moving. Such a move may occur for economic or social reasons or in response to police/local authority pressure.

The second situation where freedom of movement may be at issue concerns the right to reside and leave a country of residence. Such an issue is discussed in more detail in Chapter 4 (concerning citizenship rights in the Czech Republic). Case law from Strasbourg provides a clear indication that the Convention does not guarantee the right to enter a country and, as has previously been noted, distinctions between citizens and aliens do not fall under Article 14 of the Convention. Expulsion of aliens is not covered by the Convention unless it is 'collective'. The Human Rights Committee has taken a similarly restrictive approach by refusing to examine the interpretation of domestic law on expulsions unless there is evidence of bad faith.[132]

In either situation, the limitations of Protocol 4 are all too apparent. It only applies to persons lawfully on the territory of a state, enabling the German Government to agree to a bilateral treaty with Romania to repatriate those persons suspected of being of Romanian (particularly Romani) origin en masse.[133] Furthermore, the right can be restricted in the interests of public order and also in the 'public interest' – the definition of which appears uncertain. Protocol Four has not yet been ratified by the UK.

---

127 For example the French 'carnet de circulation' which restricts the movement of French travellers to specific regions; the Czech Jirkov rules (discussed in Chapter 4 below) and the designation provisions under the Caravan Sites Act 1968 in the UK.

128 *V wG Berlin*, 26 August 1977, discussed in Sieghart *supra* n5 at 182.

129 *Van de Vin and Others v Netherlands* (1992) Application No 13628/88, decision 8 April 1992.

130 Liégeois, J.P. *Gypsies. An Illustrated History* (1986) Al Saqi, London at 50–57.

131 D/E *Count of Gypsy Caravans*, (July 1994).

132 *Maroufidou v Sweden* (R 13/58) HRC 36, 160.

133 See Chapter 1 p 16.

(v) Peaceful enjoyment of property and possessions
Article 1 of Protocol 1 to the ECHR concerns the right to peaceful enjoyment
of possessions and prohibits the arbitrary deprivation and confiscation of such
possessions. Article 2 is concerned with the right to education and specifically
provides for parental freedom from unreasonable state interference with this right.
As far as Article 1 is concerned, it could be argued that 'possession' includes the
trailer/caravan home and related belongings.[134]

A right to enjoy the group culture?

Omitted from the wording of the ECHR, the right to enjoy and participate in cultural
life is included in the Universal Declaration and elaborated upon in the International
Covenant on Economic, Social and Cultural Rights.[135] Yet there is no mention of minority
cultures[136] in the formulation adopted by the UN. Article 15 merely provides:

> (1) the States parties to the present covenant recognise the right of everyone:
>
> (a) to take part in cultural life;
>
> (b) to enjoy the benefits of scientific progress and its applications;
>
> (c) to benefit from the protection of the moral and material interests resulting from any
> scientific, literary or artistic production of which he is the author.

This provision has not received much interpretative elaboration. For example, it
is unclear whether 'cultural life' would include the right to engage in traditional
practices which are at odds with the values maintained by the rest of society. The
right to cultural identity as such is omitted from the international human rights
documents, although it has been argued that such a right is unnecessary given the
extensive non-discrimination provisions.[137]

The protection of equality by the European Union

There has been a gradual emergence of a human rights culture in the EU to such an
extent that the protection of minority rights (albeit in an individualist paradigm) is
now implicit.[138] However, much of the focus has been directed a new and potential

---

134   Clements, Thomas and Thomas 'The rights of Minorities – A Romany perspective'
in *OSCE Bulletin* (1996) vol. 4, 4 pp 3–10 at 6.
135   Article 15, International Covenant on Economic, Social and Cultural Rights.
136   Although Article 27 does include the rights of members of minorities to enjoy their
own culture.
137   Donnelly, J 'Human Rights, Individual Rights and Collective Rights' in Berting
Human Rights in a Pluralist World (1990) Roosevelt Study Centre, Meckler, The Netherlands
at 58–9.
138   De Witte, Bruno 'The constitutional resources for an EU Minority Protection
Policy' 109–124 in Toggenburg (ed.) *Minority Protection and the Enlarged European Union:
The Way Forward* (2004) LGI Books at 123.

member states. As Bruno De Witte notes that respect for minorities is a fundamental value in the enlargement process but it is absent from the list of fundamental values for internal development. He concludes: 'For the EU, concern for minorities is primarily an export product and not one for domestic consumption'.[139]

In Eastern Europe the accession process has certainly led to some improvements. Gaetano Pentassuglia cites a number of examples where states have improved laws and policies towards minorities.[140] The clear picture that emerges is one of bilateral agreements and initiatives protecting minorities with strong political voices. The Roma, lacking this strong political voice, seldom benefit from such measures, notwithstanding the EU's criticism of the treatment of Roma in virtually all the accession states.[141] Furthermore, as Gabriel Toggenburg acknowledges, there is 'no safeguard against further decrease in the "minority-performance" of new member states now that the political carrot has been consumed'.[142] This point is echoed by De Witte arguing that once a country is accepted for membership its minority problems will be presumed resolved.[143]

The European Union has played an increasing role in the prevention of discrimination and protection of equality. Council Directive 2000/43/EC *implementing the principle of equal treatment between persons irrespective of racial or ethnic origin*[144] emphasises the importance of the international right to equality. This right goes beyond the initial freedoms of the European Community and extends to education, housing, healthcare and other social advantages.[145] McInerney contends that the directive provides a:

> Solid basis for the enlargement of the Union which must be founded on the full and effective respect of human rights since new accessions will bring into the Union new and different cultures and ethnic minorities.[146]

The directive includes both direct and indirect discrimination and encompasses harassment and instructions to discriminate. Harassment is given a broad definition and is not confined to intentional conduct. Under Article 2(3), harassment occurs:

> When an unwanted conduct relates to racial or ethnic origin takes place with the purpose or effect of violating the dignity of a person and of creating and intimidating, hostile, degrading, humiliating or offensive environment.

---

139   De Witte, Bruno 'Politics versus law in the EU's approach to ethnic minorities' in Zielonka (ed) *Europe Unbound. Enlarging and Reshaping the Boundaries of the European Union* (2002) Routledge at 139.

140   Pentassuglia, Gaetano 'The EU and the protection of minorities: the case of Eastern Europe' (2001) *EJIL* Vol. 12, 1 pp 3–38 at 26. See also Toggenburg *supra* n138.

141   The accession partnerships of Bulgaria, Czech Republic, Hungary, Romania and Slovakia included improvement in the situation of the Roma as a priority.

142   Toggenburg *supra* n138 at 8.

143   *Supra* n139 at 155.

144   Council Directive 2000/43/EC *Official journal L* 180 19 July 2000 P, 0022-0026.

145   Article 3.

146   McInerney, Siobhan 'Equal Treatment between persons irrespective of racial or ethnic origin: a comment' (2000) *EL. Rev.* Vol 25, 3 pp 317–323 at 320.

Provision is made in Article 5 for special measures to ensure full equality and to compensate for disadvantage attributed to previous inequality, otherwise known as positive action. However, the directive does not provide for a positive obligation on states in this respect. This omission is problematic and reflects the overall approach which seems aimed at procedural rather than substantive equality.[147] It is doubtful whether substantive equality can be realised in the case of the Roma in the absence of a positive duty on states to remedy past disadvantage and entrenched, discriminatory perceptions.

Positive action has been restrictively interpreted by the European Court of Justice. In the case of *Kalanke*,[148] the ECJ ruled against a policy aimed at providing priority for women where they were under-represented in a particular trade. This decision was mitigated by the more recent case of *Badeck* in which a flexible quota system was upheld providing it did not operate as a blanket policy privileging women applicants.[149] However, again in the case of *Abrahamsson*, the ECJ again afforded primacy to individual rights by rejecting a rule favouring female applicants.[150] This would suggest that the ECJ are operating from the premise of procedural rather than substantive equality and that much-needed measures to redress entrenched disadvantage are unlikely to receive much support. Indeed, Lilla Farkas suggests that special measures for the Roma minority in Hungary could be viewed with suspicion by the ECJ.[151]

Article 8 provides that the burden of proof should shift to the respondent where there is a prime facie case of discrimination supported by evidence. However, this does not apply to criminal cases. This may constitute a serious failing as the shifting of the burden in criminal cases would enable many more successful prosecutions which presently fail when the prosecuting authorities can not prove that the respondent acted with discriminatory intent.

Article 9 makes provision for victimisation which requires states to protect individuals from adverse treatment or consequences arising from a complaint or equal treatment proceedings. This may be particularly pertinent in cases where the authorities and police have been complicit in racially motivated discrimination; see for example the Bulgarian and Romanian examples discussed above.

The directive will be enforced nationally through the principles of direct effect, as Timothy Jones contends:

> There can be no doubt that the Race Directive is intended to confer rights on individuals and little doubt ... that its key provisions will be held unconditional and sufficiently precise.[152]

---

147   For further discussion see Barnard, C and Hepple, B 'Substantive equality' (2000) *Cambridge Law Journal* Vol 59, November pp 573–574.

148   Case C-450/93 *Kalanke v Bremen* [1995] ECR 1-3051.

149   Case C-158/97 *Badeck v Hessischer Ministerprasident* (2000) All ER (EC) 289.

150   Case C-407/98 *Abrahamsson v Fogequist* Judgement of 6 July 2000.

151   Farkas, Lilla 'Will the groom adopt the bride's unwanted child? The Race Equality Directive, Hungary and its Roma' *ERRC Notebook* (2003).

152   Jones, T *supra* n73 at 516.

In addition there is a five yearly reporting mechanism. Unfortunately, at the time of writing the reports of member states were not yet published but infringement action has been commenced against several European states.[153]

This failure of the proposed Roma Integration Directive, discussed in Chapter 6, has been attributed to the existence of this directive which, if implemented, should prohibit discrimination against the Roma in a variety of contexts including housing, employment and education. However, in many respects the Equality Directive is unlikely to secure this objective. The directive, as is common for EU directives and international human rights generally, establishes only minimum guarantees and while it allows for special measures there is no obligation on states to activate such measures where a group has been persistently marginalised.

In the specific context of employment, Council Directive 2000/78/EC *establishing a general framework for equal treatment in employment and occupation* is also significant. The latter extends the grounds of prohibited discrimination in the context of employment to people who are discriminated against by reason of age, disability, religion or belief or sexual orientation.

If fully implemented these directives could do help improve the education, housing and employment situation of the Roma, particularly in the new EU member states. The number of Romani men in full-time employment plummeted following the collapse of Communism. In Hungary for example the number of Romani men in employment fell from 85.2% in 1971 to 26.2% by 1994.[154] In some cases a decision to refuse a job to a Rom may not be evidence of discrimination but may reflect their lower educational attainment. The Equality Directive's holistic approach should address these issues in addition to discriminatory employment practices.

While the EU is becoming increasingly aware of the common problems facing minorities including the Roma, there have been many missed opportunities. This is particularly apparent from the accession process and the recent round of admissions to the Union. Peter Vermeesch observes that interest in the treatment of the Roma in the accession process stemmed from concern over the arrival in Western Europe of Roma asylum seekers from the East.[155] Toggenburg describes the Roma policy activities of the EU and the candidate countries as a 'charade'. He examines the reports of several accession states and concludes:

> It seems to me as if lip service can be paid to the Roma issue by the candidate countries' governments without it raising domestic political tensions or seriously straining the relations with the EU.[156]

---

153 der Boghossian, Anoush 'Implementing the EU Race Equality Directive' (2004) *Equal Opportunities Review* August, pp 15–17.

154 Kadar, A L, Farkas and Pardavi 'Legal Analysis of National and EU Anti-Discrimination Legislation: A comparison of the EU Racial Equality Directive and Protocol 12 with anti-discrimination legislation in Hungary' ERRC, Interights and the Migration Policy Group Budapest.

155 Vermeersch, Peter 'Minority policy in Central Europe: Exploring the Impact of the EU's Enlargement strategy' (2004) *The Global Review of Ethnopolitics* Vol 3, 2 pp 3–19 at 8.

156 Toggenburg *supra* n138 at 70.

International enforcement and monitoring

UN Special Rapporteurs

Perhaps the most effective means of monitoring the implementation of human rights standards is through the reports of special rapporteurs by the Commission on Human Rights and the Sub-Committee on the Prevention of Discrimination and Protection of Minorities. The results of the investigation carried out, for example, by Special Rapporteur Asbjorn Eide[157] were considered by the Sub-commission and became the basis for the UN Declaration on the Rights of Persons Belonging to National or Ethnic, Religious and Linguistic Minorities.[158]

International Covenant on Civil and Political Rights

The Human Rights Committee has the responsibility of overseeing the implementation of covenant provisions. A reporting system exists which has led to a series of General Comments on the interpretation of Covenant articles. The reporting procedure is rather weak with a lack of minority participation. To the extent that such participation exists it tends to be on an ad hoc basis and does not extend to involvement in the debates of the Committee.[159]

There is also a complaints procedure under which the parties may complain of non-compliance, provided both states have recognise the competence of the Human Rights Committee (under Article 41). Additionally, the Optional Protocol allows individuals to make complaints where the state has recognised Committee's competence and where all available domestic remedies have been exhausted.[160]

The Optional Protocol machinery is weak, particularly as it excludes a role for non-governmental organisations (NGOs). Its potential strength lies in the ability to invoke Covenant rights before a committee of experts. A summary of committee activities is included in the annual report under Article 45.[161] In drawing attention to the weakness of the individual complaints procedure, Pejic contends that it is:

> Unimaginable that the Committee could be used to solve minority problems similar to those in the former Soviet Union or the former Yugoslavia. The above reservations apply to the Committee on the Elimination of Racial Discrimination established under the CERD, as well.[162]

Without the involvement of NGOs the role of the individual complaints mechanism is very limited. Organisations such as the European Roma Rights Centre in Budapest, the Tolerance Foundation in Prague and Human Rights Watch in New York have

---

157   See for example Eide 'New Approaches to Minority Protection' MRG Profile 93/4 MRG, London.

158   UN GA Resolution 47/135.

159   Alfredsson and de Zayas *supra* n43 at 4.

160   Articles 1 and 2 Optional Protocol.

161   Article 6 Optional Protocol.

162   *Supra* n25 at 682.

been crucial in bringing the situation of Europe's Roma to the attention of the international community. Many Roma are illiterate or poorly educated and do not have access to free legal advice outside of such voluntary organisations. It would therefore be extremely unlikely for such a challenge to be mounted.

Committee on the Elimination of All Forms of Racial Discrimination

The Committee of 18 experts charged with overseeing the Convention on the Elimination of All Forms of Racial Discrimination has a tripartite function. It is empowered to consider state reports and make recommendations to the General Assembly; consider complaints bought by states against each other, and to consider the communications from individuals or groups.

The most effective measure to date has been the reporting system, with few states recognising the competence of the Committee to hear individual complaints under Article 14.[163] The Committee reports annually to the Secretary General of the General Assembly and can include recommendations and suggestions based on the consideration of the reports.[164]

In its consideration of state reports,[165] the Committee can request information from the state parties but, unfortunately, is unable to request information from other sources such as NGOs. It is poignant to note at this stage that most of the information pertaining to the effects of the Czech Citizenship Law contained in the following chapter has been documented by such organisations. In the absence of such documentation, international pressure may not have been so intense.

The Human Rights Committee and the CERD have been prepared to criticise states for failing to recognise the right to petition the Committee. In one example, a group of German Gypsies had complained to the European Court of Human Rights concerning discriminatory treatment in housing allocation. The CERD understood that Article 14 of the ECHR did not provide for a general right of non-discrimination and consequently the case would be inadmissible before the European adjudicators. If the state party had recognised the right of petition under Article 14 of the ICERD however, the Committee could have undertaken a full, judicial investigation.[166]

The European Court of Human Rights

The Court can receive complaints from individuals, NGO's or groups of people who claim to be the victim of a violation and have exhausted all domestic remedies under the new Article 35. In this sense the Convention is more liberal than both the preceding documents.[167] However it must be remembered that irrespective of the identity of the

---

163 Lerner, *supra* n25 at 69.

164 Lerner *supra* n6 at 59.

165 CERD Article 9.

166 *Summary Report of the 1196th Meeting: Germany 14/03/97* CERD/C/SR/1,196 para. 35.

167 Jacobs, F.G. *The European Convention on Human Rights* 1975 Oxford Univ. Press at 227 points out that applications have been brought by groups including companies, trade unions, churches and political parties.

complainant there must be *locus standi*, i.e., the individual, group or NGO must be a victim. The effectiveness of the European system can be seen in the decision in *Assenov* vs. *Bulgaria* (discussed below) in which the European Court found in favour of a Roma applicant whose rights had been violated.[168] The Court also held unanimously that the right of individual petition under Article 25 had been violated when members of the police attempted to dissuade the applicant from pursuing his case.

Obstacles to the realisation of individual human rights

Inadequate enforcement mechanisms

It can be seen from the above discussion that there are substantial weaknesses in the enforcement processes. These can be summarised as falling into two camps: inadequate consultation with minority groups and non-governmental organisations in the reporting process and secondly, the right of petition to being dependent on state recognition of the body's competence and the fact that such a right is often unavailable to group petitioners. Consequently, an individual who alleges a violation of a particular human right is often unable to rely on support from his or her group.

Lack of support from the group

An individual who alleges that their rights have been violated is presented with the unenviable task of challenging the political might of the state, first in the national courts and then before one of the international enforcement bodies. A member of an unpopular minority, such as the Roma, may find this task complicated by the dominant perception that he or she is an undeserving case. It may be difficult obtaining a good lawyer or obtaining the appropriate evidence, the victim may be hauled before the national media, or there may be deliberate attempts by law enforcement officials to dissuade the victim from pursuing their case. Some of these factors were raised before the European Court of Human Rights in *Assenov and Others v Bulgaria*.[169] The case concerned a family of Roma with Bulgarian nationality that alleged police mistreatment and a breach of Article 3 (concerning torture or inhuman or degrading treatment), Article 5 (unlawful detention), Article 6 (access to a court), Article 13 (denial of an effective remedy) and Article 25 (state hindrance of the right of individual petition). Following the Strasbourg application, law enforcement officials had attempted to intimidate the family into abandoning their case and two Bulgarian newspapers reported that a Roma gambler had 'put Bulgaria on trial in Strasbourg'.[170] It is difficult to see how in the present climate, a move to take legal action for a violation of a right will promote a wider climate of tolerance and equality. Indeed, as this case demonstrates, it may lead to further ostracism.

---

168 *Assesnov and Others v Bulgaria* 90/1997/874/1086, Judgement of 28 October 1998 C/E Strasbourg http://www.dhcour.coe.fr/eng/ASSENOV%20ENG.html.

169 *Ibid.*

170 *Ibid.* at para. 50.

Insufficient weighting given to the situation of the group as a whole in society

The inevitable consequence of an individualist approach to non-discrimination, is the absence of any enquiry into the particular situation of the group in society. As a result of the specific and abstract legalistic approach, a state can escape wider criticism for failing to address the root causes of discrimination in society. This can be seen clearly in the Buckley Case discussed above, in which the European Court of Human Rights was unwilling to examine the situation of the Gypsy minority in the United Kingdom outside the strict boundaries of the case. It is submitted that such narrow legal reasoning can lead to great injustice and it is for this reason that accountability through detailed state reports is so important. Unfortunately however, the monitoring procedure of the regional instruments does not provide for such effective scrutiny.[171]

As a result of the individualist approach, special measures depend on the political will of the state and hence the popularity of the group in question will be a relevant factor. It is easy to understand a state's unwillingness to consider an affirmative action policy when there are few votes to be won and many votes to be lost. The state is not under a duty to implement such measures to achieve de facto equality, as a result the unpopular minority is unlikely to benefit greatly from these provisions.

The significance of cultural identity is given little weight. Thus, in balancing the interests of the individual's culture with the state's need to protect public order or security, the individual stands alone against the state/society.

The failure of international human rights to protect minorities

The realisation of human rights for members of minority groups is fraught with difficulties. The present emphasis treats members of minorities as individuals, existing in a vacuum, removed from their culture, history and traditions. Special measures to counter discriminatory practices of the past are envisaged in the various international documents, particularly the ICERD. In practice however, they will depend on the willingness of the state to support the culture of the particular group. As Pentassuglia argues, the reach of special action measures is limited to levelling the playing field through temporary measures; they do not protect the identity of minority groups.[172]

All too often the law appears to be ethnically neutral but its effects are indirectly discriminatory, in that it has an adverse impact on members of a particular minority group. In the absence of international provisions protecting the identity of the group,

---

171 The OSCE is the only international organisation with a human rights agenda that examines a wide range of non-governmental evidence. The CSCE report *Romani Rights in Europe* (1998) New York contains the detailed information required to enable effective scrutiny. It is testament to the fact that a reporting process without recourse to non-governmental organisations, such as with the Convention on the Elimination of All Forms of Racial Discrimination, is unlikely to ensure accountability.

172 Pentassuglia, Gaetano 'Minority issues as a challenge in the ECHR' (2003) *German Yearbook of International Law* Vol 46 pp 401–51 at 435.

it would seem at best naive to expect states to show such concern, particularly in cases where the minority is relatively small, unpopular with the electorate and politically disorganised. The Roma minority in most states, with the exception of Romania and Bulgaria, tends to be smaller than other minority groups. Their geographical dispersion and lack of political organisation has made them particularly vulnerable to assimilationist pressures.

The human rights standards of non-discrimination and equality are important foundations on which a wider human rights culture has been developed. Nevertheless, individual human rights are often balanced against the collective rights of the state. The interests of different or 'outsider' cultures are presented at odds with the dominant culture and the emphasis on the individual cannot by itself redress this disparity.[173] The margin of appreciation under the European Convention allows the interests of minority groups to be weighed against factors of more prevalent public importance such as public order and the rights and freedoms of others, particularly in planning cases. The decision of the European Court of Human Rights in the Buckley case clearly illustrates the adverse consequences of the simple balancing act approach.

The lack of effective enforcement machinery under both the ICCPR and the CERD enables state parties to provide minimal constitutional protection to members of ethnically distinct groups while in practice efforts are made to promote assimilation in the name of integration.

There is no recognition in any of the instruments, including Article 27 of the ICCPR, of the possibility of ethnocide, i.e., the cultural destruction of the group.[174] Ethnocide consists of two elements, firstly the economic dimension and secondly, the cultural aspect. It occurs when government policies lead to the undermining of cultural identity of groups through measures such as language prohibition, erosion of land and resources and lack of support for cultural values and institutions. In reality, minority groups are often in such a marginalised position that they require active support from the state to maintain such attributes.[175] A failure to provide funding and other positive measures could thus constitute ethnocide.

At present, there is no obligation on states to recognise the existence of minority groups, surely a prerequisite to the realisation of non-discrimination. When looked at together with the limited recognition of group rights discussed in Chapter 6, the limitations of the present emphasis are obvious. There is no obligation on states to support the interests of minority groups and there is little to actively promote the maintenance of minority identity. Eide observes:

> Whether subjected to assimilationist ethno-nationlist domination or to a process of fusion, some groups seek to defend their own cultural identity, to maintain their own language and traditions. This can be done without any attempt to dominate others and without objecting to equal treatment in the common domain.[176]

173　See for example Sibley *Outsiders in Urban Society* (1982) Blackwell, London.
174　Stavenhagen *supra* n44 at 65.
175　*Ibid.* at 86.
176　Eide 1993 *supra* n45.

Eide goes on to argue that any approach to minority protection must comprise three elements: approaches which can safeguard equality between all human beings in society; promotion of group diversity when required to ensure the dignity and identity of all; and advancement of stability and peace, both domestically and internationally.[177] The emphasis on the rights of the individual contributes to the first of Eide's criteria but neglects the others. If one considers Claire Palley's observation that 'the aim of such approaches is to eliminate differences of treatment between group and group, and individual and individual' the conclusion is reached that, somewhat paradoxically, assimilationism may be encouraged by individualism.[178]

The examples of official prejudice at the beginning of this chapter remind us that even if the law does not wish to enter into questions of ethnicity, society regularly categorises people in this way. Many people are not treated and do not regard themselves merely as individuals. A Council of Europe report in 1995 asked Gypsy/ Roma women about ways of combating the discrimination they had experienced both as Roma and as women:

> The Roma/Gypsy women participating in the Hearing felt that their personal fulfilment could only be achieved by maintaining their most positive traditional and cultural values and their view of the world and life. They also felt that it would be wrong to impose other cultural models on Gypsy communities in an arbitrary fashion. They wished to be able to love and be respected in their own right and to receive social and economic support from the majority population while still preserving their culture and language.[179]

The European Committee on Migration accepted that the hostility shown towards the Roma in Europe is attributable to 'prejudices, deeply rooted in the collective memory, compounded by economic hardship and also the playing down of the cultural contribution Gypsies have made to Europe'.[180] It is difficult if not impossible, to conceive how the cumulative undervaluation of this culture can be redressed by an emphasis on individual rights.

The following two chapters look at particular contrasting examples of situations where the individualist emphasis of human rights instruments can be clearly seen to fail the Roma of Europe – the fields of citizenship and education.

---

177   *Ibid.* at 12.

178   Palley, Claire Constitutional Law and Minorities (1978) MRG, London at 7.

179   C/E *Hearing of Roma/Gypsy Women of West Central and East Europe* 30 September 1995 EG/TSI (95) 2 at para. 10.

180   European Committee on Migration the Situation of Gypsies (Roma and Sinti) in Europe (1995) C/E CDMG (95) 11 at para. 48.

Chapter 4

Citizenship in the Czech Republic

Introduction

As TH Marshall recognised, citizenship is fundamental to the application of political as well as social and economic rights.[1] Any examination of the situation of Roma in Eastern Europe today could not avoid the issue.[2] The Czech Government's response to the perceived 'Gypsy problem' is illuminating. Not only does it illustrate the extent of support for anti-Roma measures at all levels of a civilised society it also reveals a significant deficiency in international law. Despite international criticism, the Czech Government consistently argued that its citizenship law complied with international standards.

International law makes the application of some human rights contingent upon 'citizen' status, particularly in relation to political activity. Indeed, some states make minority recognition contingent upon citizenship.[3] Furthermore, the status of those declared 'non-citizens' is tenuous, with the ever-present possibility of expulsion. The dependant right of political representation is particularly important if the Roma are to achieve recognition. If the failed policies of the past are to be avoided, involvement at all levels of the political process must be regarded as essential.

The political title of 'citizen' while conferring many advantages is only one element of the wider debate of citizenship. Malloy has observed the tendency to conflate 'citizenship-as-desirable-activity' with 'citizenship-as-legal-status' – she notes that a concentration on the latter has resulted in neglect of the former.[4] Violence against Roma all over Europe suggests that even when afforded the legislative right to residence and political participation, they tend to be regarded as 'outsiders'. This appears to be more the case than with any other ethnic minority group, possibly because of their unwillingness to adapt and assimilate into the dominant lifestyle.[5]

---

1   Marshall, TH and Bottomore, T *Citizenship and Social Class* (1992) Pluto Press.

2   Citizenship criteria have also caused difficulties for the Roma elsewhere in Europe. A European Roma Rights Centre workshop noted particular problems in Croatia and Macedonia as well as in the Baltic states. In many cases this was due to lack of documents resulting from a mixture of inefficient administration and discrimination. ERRC Workshop 'Personal documents and threats to the exercise of fundamental rights among Roma in the FYR,' Igalo Montenegro 6–8 September 2000.

3   See Chapter 6 at 262.

4   Malloy, Tove *National Minorities in Europe* (2005) OUP at 45.

5   For discussion of reasons see 'Anti-Gypsyism' Chapter 15 in Hancock *The Pariah Syndrome* (1987) Karoma Ann Arbor.

With the transformation to democracy, the CEE states witnessed a significant rise in ethnic violence and discrimination directed at the Roma. In a written question to the Council of the European Communities in 1994, it was reported that:

> Violent attacks on gypsies in Eastern Europe have already caused the death of a considerable number of this minority group during the last three years. More than 400 houses have been set on fire in two years alone.[6]

The Czech Republic provides an illuminating case study. The new democratic state saw an immediate rise in racist attacks[7] which exceeded the combined total for Slovakia, Bulgaria and Romania.[8] Skinheads were blamed for many of these attacks but this is certainly not the entire picture.[9] Being 'at the bottom of the social ladder, Roma continue to face discrimination in housing, education and employment. They are often segregated in "special schools", denied residency permits and refused jobs solely because of their ethnicity'.[10] Those who do not participate or condone the ethnic violence often register their disapproval of the Romani residents in opinion polls.[11] Under the Nazi's, almost the entire Roma population of the Czech lands was systematically extinguished,[12] yet a poll in 1999 revealed that less than 25% of Czech respondents were aware of this.[13]

An analysis of the legislative attitude towards the Romani community in the former Czechoslovakia is used to set the context for the present developments but also to illustrate the comparable attitudes towards the Roma exhibited by Communists and Libertarians alike. It can be seen that the nature of the regime, while providing justification through ideology of particular treatment, is irrelevant to the general negativity of policies.

Individual rights guarantees alone, even if fully implemented, appear incapable of remedying many of the problems faced by the Roma in the Czech Republic. The Framework Convention for the Protection of National Minorities may go some distance

---

6   According to Mr Gerardo Fernandez-Albor in 94/C 102/47 *Official Journal of the European Communities: Information and Notices* (1994) Vol. 37 part 102, p21; see generally Human Rights Watch reports on Romania, Bulgaria, Czechoslovakia and Hungary; 'True, Tormented Pan-Europeans/Sad Gypsies' *Economist* vol. 321, 26 October 1991; Hockenos, Paul 'Racism unbound in the land of the Magyars' (1993) *New Politics* Vol. 4, 2.

7   Human Rights Watch Press release 8 June 1996 accompanying the report *Roma in the Czech Republic Foreigners in their Own Land* (1996) *HRW*, NY. In 1995, 181 attacks on Romanies were reported.

8   Crowe, Aileen 'The Czech Roma. Foreigners in their own land' (1996) *European Update Online* Vol. 4, No 2.

9   Bancroft, Angus *Roma and Gypsy-travellers in Europe* (2005) Ashgate at 141.

10   *Ibid.* referred to in Commission on Human Rights 53rd session Implementation of the programme of action of the second decade to combat racism and racial discrimination E/CN.4/1997/7 at 1F para. 30.

11   See Times-Mirror group survey of 13,000 respondents in Barany, Zoltan 'Democratic Changes Bring Mixed Blessings for Gypsies' in *Radio Free Europe* 15 May 1992, at 45.

12   It is estimated that 95% of Roma living in the Czech lands lost their lives during the war, Human Rights Watch *supra* n7.

13   US state department, 'Czech Republic' Country reports on Human Rights Practices 2000, 23 February 2001.

towards recognising the distinct cultural identity of ethnic groups but does not go far enough.[14] There is no right of effective political organisation (let alone citizenship) vested in members of ethnic minorities. Whilst, the Czech Citizenship Law attracted much international concern there was little in the normative human rights standards on which to base such criticism. Indeed, much of it occurred following the arrival of Czech Roma asylum-seekers in the West; suggesting that migration rather the denial of rights was the principal concern. Thus, international human rights were unable to offer much ammunition in the campaign to amend the law. It is argued that more ammunition would have been provided if the Roma were politically organised and if they were identified as a European minority with particular, albeit diverse, cultural values and traditions. The recognition of group rights may have facilitated such an approach and may well have prevented seven years of legal exclusion for the Czech Roma.

Historical Context of 'Gypsy Policy' in Czechoslovakia

Communism and the non-'Gypsy'

After the Second World War[15] only 600 out of an estimated 15,000 Roma remained in the Czech Republic.[16] Many had been exterminated; others had fled to Slovakia where the harsh conditions of compulsory labour at least provided some chance of survival.[17] There is no evidence of a specific Roma policy at this time but by implication the post-war industrial drives resulted in many Roma moving to urban areas.[18] Individual human rights had little place in the Marxist ideology espoused by Stalin. The focus was on the duties of the individual, rights, where they existed, were viewed as synonymous with the objectives of the state.[19]

A limited degree of autonomy was allocated to nationalities that could satisfy the basic Marxist criteria as explained by Milena Hubschmannova:

.Five markers of a nation were fixed: (common territory-history-language-culture-economic life). If an ethnic collectivity missed one of these markers, it was labelled as 'nationality or national group'. If it lacked more markers, it descended into the hierarchy of a mere 'ethnic group,' which was liable to get assimilated.[20]

---

14   For a full discussion see Chapter 6 at 299
15   For pre-war history of the Gypsies in the Czech lands see Guy, Will 'Ways of looking at Roms' Chapter 8 in Rehfisch *Gypsies, Tinkers and other Travellers* (1975) Academic Press, London.
16   Tolerance Foundation Report 25 May 1994 p 4 and Edginton 'The Czech Citizenship law: still causing problems for Roma' (1994) *Helsinki Federation for Human Rights Newsletter* Vol. 4 at 9.
17   See generally Kenrick and Puxon *The Destiny of Europe's Gypsies* (1972) Sussex Univ. Press and Hancock *supra* n5.
18   McCagg, William 'Gypsy Policy in Socialist Hungary and Czechoslovakia 1945-89' (1991) *Nationalities Papers* Vol 19, 3 pp 313−36 at 317.
19   Shestack, Jerome 'The jurisprudence of Human Rights' in Meron, T (ed.) (1984) *Human Rights in International Law: Legal and Policy Issues* Vol.1 Clarendon Chapter 3 pp 81–3.
20   Hubschmannova, M 'Three years of Democracy in Czecho-Slovakia and the Roma' in *Roma* No 38/9 (1993), p45.

When the Czech Socialist Republic (CSR) did turn its attention towards the Roma it was quickly determined that they were not a nationality as they lacked a common land, a common culture and distinct language.[21] The Romani language was demoted to being a 'hantyrka' – a concocted jargon.[22] An authoritative Czech language dictionary of the time defines a 'Gypsy' as 'a member of a nomadic nation, symbol for mendacity, trickery and vagabondage'.[23] The Roma (then popularly referred to as 'Gypsies') were thus regarded as a socially backward group who should be encouraged to assimilate.

Origins of the settlement policy
As a result of the policy decision that 'Gypsies' were not a nationality, the government introduced legislation on 'the permanent settlement of nomadic persons' in 1958; penal sanctions were introduced the following year.[24]

An estimated 6–7,000 'Gypsies' were nomadic in Czechoslovakia at this time and though the law was not confined to those labelled 'Gypsies,' it was generally regarded as indicative of an increasing animosity towards the Romani population.[25] The law, which was intended to offer improved accommodation and employment prospects for 'Gypsies,' failed for a number of reasons.[26] Firstly, there was a lack of suitable, available accommodation; when municipal authorities succeeded in finding such accommodation there were often many problems between the Romani and non-Romani residents, many of whom had waited years for such housing. Consequently, new ghettos developed where old ones had been demolished, often without running water or sanitation.[27] Czech employers added to the problem, ignoring the regulations which prohibited nomads from gaining employment until they had settled, often giving jobs to registered nomads without seeking approval beforehand.[28] These factors were compounded by the fact that local government officials failed to keep track of the movement of nomadic families and census statistics were allegedly altered in order to conceal the extent of the failure of the Act. By 1970, when full assimilation should have taken place according to the plans, over 70,000 Romanies were still living in extremely poor conditions in shanty-towns in Eastern Slovakia.

---

21   It is estimated that over 80% of Hungarian Gypsies speak no Romany dialect according to Barany (1992) *supra* n11 at 41.
22   Ulc, O 'Integration of the Gypsies in Czechoslovakia' (1991) *Ethnic Groups* Vol. 9 p110.
23   *Ibid.*
24   Bill No 74/1958 zb.
25   See for examples McCagg *supra* n18 at 119. Guy in Koudelka, J *Gypsies* (1975) Aperture, London (no pagination) and Kostelanick, D.J 'The Gypsies of Czechoslovakia. Political and Ideological Considerations in the Development of Policy' (1989) Studies in Comparative Communism Vol. xxii, 4 at 311.
26   In the UK, a similar problem had developed with the provision of adequate accommodation in the form of caravan sites for 'gipsies' (Caravan Sites Act 1968). Many local authorities simply had no available land and others were not prepared to accommodate these 'outsiders' – see O'Nions, H 'The Marginalisation of Gypsies' (1995) 3 *Web JCLI*.
27   Guy *supra* n25.
28   Kalvoda, J in Crowe, D and Kolsti, J *The Gypsies of Eastern Europe* (1991) M.E. Sharpe, Incorporated London at 97.

During his field-work, Will Guy found that 'Each adequate well and toilet had to serve over two-hundred Gypsies'.[29]

A new strategy under the same policy
In 1965, the CSR created the 'National Council for Questions of the Gypsy Population' and a resolution 'on organized dispersion of the Romanies' was introduced. It marked a renewed attempt at forcing assimilation by attempting to gain full employment of able-bodied men and liquidating the settlements while dispersing and relocating the inhabitants, often to the more prosperous Czech lands.[30] The previous restriction on free migration which previously applied to all registered nomads was now extended to all. The only Gypsies permitted to move were those in the planned resettlement and it was recommended that there should be a quota of 5% in any town, the largest quota being in the industrial heartland of Northern Bohemia.[31] Gypsies were classified arbitrarily according to the likelihood of their assimilation; there was no right of appeal.[32]

Once again the program was fraught with operational difficulties as many local authorities contended they had no available accommodation. As a result under 500 Gypsies were transferred in the first three years of the programme.[33] Hubschmannova comments that the Communist party were convinced that only by means of dispersion would they be assimilated.[34] This may imply recognition of a common culture which prevented assimilation in the absence of division and dispersal.

The policy of dispersal continued until 1989 when it was halted by the Velvet Revolution, with the task still far from over. Some 4,850 families were relocated from Slovakian shanties between 1972 and 1981,[35] but in 1983 there were still over 3,000 shanties remaining (10.5% of the Romani population in the Republic).[36]

If we describe improvement in terms of our Western values we find better housing, access to education and employment during the Communist era.[37] However as far as the intended beneficiaries were concerned these policies did little to improve their situation. While they had access to running water, they were often in substandard housing, their extended families had been divided and they were the subject of abuse and animosity from the non-Gypsy residents. Many Roma involved in relocation were evidently reluctant to abandon their old way of life. Zoltan Koren, a Public Prosecutor, wrote of this problem:

---

29   Guy *supra* n25. This is comparable to the holobyty accommodation discussed below p163.
30   Kalvoda *supra* n28 at 100.
31   Ulc, O 'Gypsies in Czechoslovakia. A case of Unfinished Integration' (1988) *East European Politics and Societies* Spring Vol. 2, 2 at 312.
32   Guy *supra* n25.
33   Kalvoda, *supra* n28 at 100.
34   Kostelanick *supra* n25 at 313.
35   Imrich Farkas 'Transformation of our fellow Gypsy citizens' *Pravda*, Bratislava 23 September 1982 p5.
36   Kostelanick *supra* n25 at 314.
37   Guy, Will 'The Czech lands and Slovakia: another false dawn?' in Guy (ed) *between past and future. The Roma of Central and Eastern Europe* (2001) Univ. of Hertfordshire Press pp 285–323.

It is a generally known fact that the main obstacle in accomplishing the charted goal of elevating the Gypsy population are the Gypsies themselves.[38]

The Prague spring 1968

The liberalisation of attitudes following the Prague spring led to the establishment of the Union of Gypsy Romanies, the first organization of its kind in Czechoslovakia, which promoted a variety of cultural activities and tried to address the hostility towards the Gypsies from the non-Gypsy population.[39] Even the media became involved in the project with Gypsies increasingly being referred to as 'Rom' and an issue of Demografie being devoted to Gypsies in 1969.[40]

It is clear that obtaining nationality status was regarded as essential to the realisation of basic human rights at that time. The President of the Union of Gypsy Romanies, Miroslav Holomek, became involved in the political struggle to advance the concept of a separate Gypsy nationality. There were more than 5,000 members of the Union before the first conference in 1969, suggesting elements of a common culture that had a wide base of support. Hubschmannova has argued that a clear nationality consciousness was evidenced by the success of the Union.[41]

Following the Soviet invasion in 1973 and the subsequent period of 'normalization,' the Union was disbanded as they had 'failed to fulfil their integrative function'.[42] The resettlement policy was renewed and demands for recognition as a nationality fell silent again.

Charter 77: Demands for human rights

Charter 77, a temporary human rights organization, was established to bring human rights concerns in Czechoslovakia to the attention of the international community following the ratification of the Helsinki accord in January 1977. Many of the people involved in the project went on to gain political power in the new democracy in 1989.

Document 23 of the report was titled 'the situation of the Gypsies in Czechoslovakia'. The Gypsies were described as one of the largest minorities in Czechoslovakia but legally the Gypsy identity was denied and they did not exist. The high illiteracy rate and poor housing conditions which Gypsies experienced were highlighted, as was the practice of sterilization carried out on Gypsy mothers with consent often being obtained in 'suspicious circumstances'.[43] With the support of some illuminating evidence they described the Gypsies as 'the least protected of all citizens – a Third World culture in the midst of a European culture'.[44]

Unsurprisingly the Government took little notice of the Charter 77 report and resisted any suggestion that Gypsies/Roma should be given nationality status. Similarly, when the World Congress of Gypsy-Romani in Geneva made appeals to

---

38   Quote in Ulc *supra* n31 at 318.
39   See generally Kalvoda *supra* n28 at 277.
40   Reported in Demografie, vol. 11 no 4.
41   Kalvoda *supra* n28 at 278.
42   Guy *supra* n25.
43   Ulc *supra* n31 at 315.
44   Powell, C 'Time for another Immoral panic? The case of the Czechoslovak Gypsies' (1994) *Int. J Soc L* Vol. 22, at 106.

recognise the nationality of the Gypsies, as had occurred in Poland and Hungary, the media was used to show success stories of assimilated Gypsies.[45]

Policies of benevolence or racism?

McCagg concludes in his article that despite allegations of genocide by Charter 77 the evidence reveals that the Communist Government in Czechoslovakia was driven by welfare objectives rather than a more sinister racist ideology.[46] However, the evidence suggests rather the opposite. The Communist strategy regarded the Roma as a collection of social undesirables and only once assimilated could they be considered full Czechoslovak citizens. Yet assimilation failed to succeed and this was in part due to the state's failure to recognise their particular cultural identity and particular values and needs.

The 1958 Settlement Bill was clearly understood by the Municipal Authorities to refer to Gypsies. The Gypsies were targeted as a group based on the classification of local officers who used methods such as skin colour, large families and language difficulties (all indicators that they were regarded as a separate nationality that could be easily identified). They were identified as a separate nationality (albeit arbitrarily) and discriminated against as a separate nationality, yet in the eyes of the law they did not exist as a nationality. This enabled the policies of dispersal and assimilation to be pursued with a belligerent rigour ignoring the interests of those affected.

Statistics suggest that health-care and education were adversely affected by the Communist policies. The average life-span of a Rom born in 1980 was expected to be 13 years less than that of a gadjo,[47] 20% of Roma children were born retarded as a result of poor pre-natal care[48] and a massive proportion will attend special schools designed for children with mental health difficulties.[49] These facts do not suggest that the authorities have been motivated by concern for the welfare of Romany families over the past 30 years. The disapproval of the Romani culture is captured in this statement printed in Demografie in 1962:

> Under socialism it is totally unthinkable to build some 'socialist and nationalist' Gypsy culture from the fundamentals of something which is very primitive, backward, essentially often even negative and lacking in advanced tradition .... The Question is not whether the Gypsies are a nation but how to assimilate them.[50]

Perhaps the best example of an attitude primarily routed in racism is the process of sterilization, carried out without informed consent. Helsinki Watch reported:

> ... the government reportedly took specific steps to encourage the sterilization of Romany women in order to reduce the 'high unhealthy' Romany population and, as a result, a

---

45   Reported in Rudé *Právo* 21 June 1986.

46   McCagg *supra* n18 at 329.

47   Kalibova cited in Powell *supra* n44.

48   Kalvoda *supra* n28 at 288.

49   Up to 50% in some areas, see Kalvoda *supra* n28 at 288 and Kostelanick *supra* n25 at 316.

50   *Demografie* (1962) pp 80–1.

disproportionately high number of Romany women were sterilized, often in violation of the existing safeguards and of their rights to non-discrimination on the basis of ethnicity or sex.[51]

Romany women were given a financial incentive to undergo sterilisation of between 5 and 10 times that offered to other women.[52] Helsinki Watch concluded that Government policy, though it did not specifically refer to the Roma, sought to lower their birth rate.[53] Most surprisingly there is evidence to suggest that the practice of sterilisation continued.[54] In November 2005, the Ostrava District Court found that a Romani woman coercively sterilised in 2001 had been unlawfully deprived of her dignity.[55] A subsequent report by the Czech Ombudsman found:

> The problem of sexual sterilization − carried out either with unacceptable motivation or illegally − exists, and that Czech society stands before the task of coming to grips with this reality.[56]

Sterilization and cultural genocide

Charter 77 referred to the process of institutional discrimination as 'cultural genocide', i.e., the intent to destroy the culture, language or religion of an ethnic, racial or religious group.[57] It was further asserted that sterilization practices were in danger of breaking Article 259 of the Penal code on genocide.[58] While cultural genocide is not included in the Convention on the Prevention and Punishment of the Crime of Genocide (1948), Article II of the convention states that (d) imposing measures designed to restrict births within the [national, ethnical, racial or religious] group' with intent to destroy that group, amounts to Genocide which is an international crime.[59] Similarly Article 259 (1) (b) of the Czech Penal Code states:

> Whoever seeks to destroy fully or partially any national, ethnic, racial or religious group; … takes measures in order to prevent reproduction among the group … will be subject to punishment of between 12 and 15 years in prison or the death sentence.

While there is some supportive evidence to amount to a policy of genocide it is unlikely that the requisite intention to destroy could be proved. Improved housing

---

51   Human Rights Watch *Struggling for Ethnic Identity − Czechoslovakia's Endangered Gypsies* (1992) HRW, NY at 19.
52   *Ibid.* at 29; Ulc *supra* n22 at 116; Ofner, P 'Sterilisation Practice in Czechoslovakia' in *O'Drom* April (1990) at 268/9.
53   *Supra* n51 at 20.
54   Centre for Reproductive Rights *Body and Soul, Forced Sterilisation and Other assaults on Roma Reproductive Freedom in Slovakia* (2003) p 119.
55   ERRC 'First Court victory in Central Europe on Coercive Sterilisation of Romani Women' 11 November 2005 ERRC.
56   As reported by European Roma Rights Centre 'Coercive Sterilisation of Romani Women: organisations welcome Ombudsmans report' 10 January 2006.
57   Cassese, Antonio *Human Rights in A Changing World* (1994) Polity Press at 76.
58   *Supra* n51 at 31.
59   For discussion see Chapter 6 p 272.

and employment conditions could be cited to show that the Government was trying to improve rather than destroy the Romani identity.

If nothing else this debate serves to indicate the thin line dividing the welfarist concern for the situation of the Roma and the desire to 'ethnically cleanse' the society of 'unsavoury elements'.

The new democracy: Human rights for all

It has already been noted that human rights protection has been directly associated with the recognition of the Roma as a nationality within Czechoslovakia. Following the Velvet Revolution of 1989 Roma were given the status of minority which had been sought for so long yet the instant improvement in their circumstances did not follow as predicted. The Government issued 'Principles of the governmental policy of the Czech and Slovak Federal Government toward the Romany Minority'. The first principle states:

> Alongside the basic hypothesis of eliminating societal inequality of Romanies in the CSFR is the all-sided respect of the rights and free declaration of the Romany nationality. The Romany national minority is equivalent to other national minorities in the CSFR ....

On the other hand, however, unrestrained freedom of expression resulted in increased abuse and violence towards unpopular groups, most prominently Roma. This coupled with the decrease in socio-economic benefits following the revolution has led many to conclude that they were better off under the Communist regime.[60] Tomias Haisman, head of the Federal Department of Human Rights and Humanitarian Issues 1990–92, explains the incompatibility of the post-Communist state and Romany rights. He argues that the key concepts which symbolised the new Czechoslovakia were freedom, democracy and the market economy: 'You extend these concepts to the Roma people and you have a real horror story'.[61] Haisman contends that freedom enables the Roma to express themselves which is not necessarily conducive to good relations with non-gypsy neighbours; in turn their freedom means freedom to take action against the Roma. In this analysis democracy is perceived as the codification of the present status quo and the assertion of the will of the majority over the minority; the free market is seen as entrenching the position of the Roma at the bottom of the economic ladder.[62] On 24 November 1991 a large group of fascists marched on the centre of Prague shouting slogans such as 'Gypsies to the gas chambers!' and 'Czechs for Czechs,' local Gadje residents reportedly clapped in approval.[63] In 1992, there were 26 deaths of Roma in racially motivated attacks before the break up of the federal state.[64]

---

60   Ulc *supra* n22 at 115.

61   Hockenos *Free to Hate* (1993) Routledge, NY at 221.

62   *Ibid.*

63   *Supra* n51 at 3.

64   Crowe, David *A History of the Gypsies of Eastern Europe and Russia* (1995) St Martins Press: NY at 64. Ian Traynor gives a figure of 32 Czech Roma deaths since 1989 'Czech Gypsies fear Ghetto Wall' *The Guardian*, 20 June 1998 p 16.

The new constitution came into force on 1 January 1993, the date of the controversial split of the federal Republic. The Preamble states that the Government are:

> ... determined to build, protect and develop the Czech Republic in the spirit of the inviolable values of human dignity and freedom, as a homeland to equal, free citizens who are conscious of their obligations towards others and of their responsibility toward the whole, as a free and democratic state based on a respect for human rights and on the principles of a civil society ....[65]

Article 10 of the Constitution gives direct binding effect to the European Convention on Human Rights and the Constitution is accompanied by the Charter of Fundamental Rights and Freedoms which is based on the Convention. Article 3 of the Charter states that the rights shall be guaranteed to all without distinction as to race, colour, national or ethnic origin, membership of a minority, etc. and goes on to state that everyone shall have the freedom to choose their nationality, any form of influencing that choice being prohibited. The Charter also goes further than the Convention by guaranteeing freedom of movement and settlement.[66]

In relation to citizenship, the Constitution and adjoining Charter also make positive claims: Article 12 of the Constitution establishes that no citizen may be deprived of citizenship against their will and Article 14(4) of the Charter states that no citizen can be forced to leave the country. It is clear that unless otherwise stated the Charter of rights extends to all people on Czech soil whether or not they are citizens of the Czech Republic (Article 42(2)). The theoretical commitment to human rights of the Czech Government cannot be doubted; the acid-test is how far these words show a real, practical commitment. The treatment of the Roma as the country's most unpopular minority provides an indication of the strength of this commitment.[67]

The Jirkov rules
Soon after the division of Czechoslovakia, municipal authorities in the Czech Republic began to introduce rules designed to limit the stay of Romani visitors in their area. The moves were a result of fear that Romanies would begin to come over the border to gain work.[68] It is difficult to comprehend why this movement should suddenly occur after a policy aimed at forcing dispersal to Czech lands had taken three times as long as intended because the Roma in the settlements were unwilling to be relocated. It can only be assumed that the authorities seized the opportunity of reducing the indigenous Romani population by intimidation and discrimination.

The Jirkov rules, so called after the town where they were first introduced, restricted the residence of people staying with non-family members (using the Czech sense of the word rather than the extended family of the Romani communities) to five

---

65   Blaustein and Flanz 'Constitution of the Czech Republic' Chapter 3, Article 25 *Constitutions of the World* (1971) Dobbs Ferry NY.
66   Article 14(1) of the Charter of Fundamental Rights and Freedoms.
67   Times-Mirror group survey of 13,000 respondents Barany *supra* n11 at 45 (1992).
68   Powell *supra* n44 at 115.

days in any six-month period following registration with the municipal authority.[69] Permission was required for any period longer than three days.[70] Under the ordinance local police were empowered to check the identity of any person in an apartment between 6 am and 12 pm. Although the rules did not make specific mention of a target group, the explanatory text says that the objective was to 'regulate' the migration of Roma.[71] It has been suggested that in practice the regulations were used to send all Roma residents who were not registered as Czech citizens back to Slovakia, regardless of whether they had ever lived there.[72]

Many other localities were quick to follow in the footsteps of Jirkov and although the ordinance and following decrees were interdicted by the Government in February 1993, the pace with which they developed is indicative of a deep hostility towards the Roma which had survived the transition to democracy. Indeed, public opinion polls listed this hostility along with international criminality and the fear of Communism as matters of particular concern in the new democracy.[73] The influence of the Jirkov regulations on the new Czech Citizenship Law suggests that such attitudes are not unique to the general public.

The rights of the citizen

There is little theoretical discussion of the legal aspects of citizenship. The work of the sociologist T.H. Marshall provides a good starting point for any conceptual analysis.[74] Marshall provides three basic dimensions to the concept of citizenship. Firstly, the political dimension which includes that right to participate in political affairs, as a voter and representative. Secondly, the social dimension which consists of the right to enjoy basic minimum protection from the social welfare system provided by the state, and finally; the civil dimension which provides the rights necessary for individual freedom.[75] It has since been argued that notions of citizenship are broader today than Marshall's analysis conveyed and this may include recognition of the cultural dimension of citizenship.[76]

These may be the three basic components of 'citizenship' but there is an obvious danger in making comparisons between states about the specific rights which citizens are afforded. Many states value the concept differently, stressing, for example, the political dimension while denying the social dimension. Marshall's analysis is clearly rooted in Western conceptions of 'citizenship' and while it is necessarily limited by this fact it is apparent that the new democracies are adopting Western approaches to

---

69   *Ibid.*

70   Hubshcmannova *supra* n20 at 32.

71   *Ibid.*

72   Powell *supra* n44 at 116.

73   Ulc, O 'The Plight of the Gypsies' (1995) *Freedom* Review vol. 26, 3 at 27.

74   'Citizenship and Social Class' in TH Marshall *Class, Citizenship and Social Development* (1976) Doubleday, NY

75   Marshall, TH and Bottomore, Tom *Citizenship and Social Class* (1992) Pluto Press

76   Malloy, Tove *National Minorities in Europe* (2005) OUP at 45.

citizenship by linking it with a variety of rights, particularly the political and social rights mentioned.

There are two distinct ways in which an individual can be regarded as a non-citizen. Both lead to institutionalised discrimination and the second has the force of law behind it. The legislative denial of citizenship is addressed in several international human rights documents. However, a person may also be deprived of effective citizenship if they are designated as 'outsiders' and 'aliens' by other members of the society, irrespective of their legal status. In his book on European citizenship, Paul Close examines the meaning of 'real citizenship':

> Citizens are those people who have acquired full citizenship rights -the full range of legal rights necessary for full membership of (or full inclusion within) society. But such rights in themselves are insufficient for real citizenship. Citizens are divided between those who are able to realise citizenship rights and those who are unable; between those who really enjoy and experience full inclusion, participation and membership and those who do not. Between those who have sufficient enabling resources to allow them to be included as full members of society and those who have insufficient, between those who enjoy the power to be real citizens and those who do not.[77]

i) De facto denial of citizenship

This occurs when other members of the state regard a class of people as not being true-citizens. In some ways this is an inevitable consequence of the development of nation-state ideology, with the only true members of the State being perceived as ethnically homogenous.[78] While intolerance towards ethnic minorities may appear to be growing in Eastern and Central European states, the Roma tend to be the victims of ethnic intolerance from all sections of society − not simply the dominant ethnic group. The fact that they appear unwilling to assimilate, unlike many immigrant minorities, makes them ripe for such criticism.

Roma are often lumped with foreigners in racist dicta. In this respect it is interesting to note that the UNHCR identified their role in the Czech Republic in 2001 as focusing on three areas: asylum-seekers, refugees and the Roma.[79] Of course, one would expect the UNHCR to concentrate their efforts on asylum seekers and refugees but the inclusion of one particular ethnic group, the Roma, as a separate priority for the refugee agency illustrates the perception of Roma as outsiders and aliens.[80] In Romania it has even been suggested that the former Communist president Ceausescu was in fact Romani because his behaviour was so alien and abhorrent.[81] This attitude can also be seen in the UK with reference to nomadic or semi-nomadic

---

77   Close, Paul *Citizenship, Europe and Change* (1994) Macmillan, London at 52.

78   Habermas, Jurgen 'Citizenship and National Identity: Some Reflections on the Future of Europe' (1992) *Praxis International* Vol.12, 1 pp 1−19 at 2−3.

79   UNHCR Country Operations Plan. Czech Republic 5 April 2002.

80   Interesting that in 2001 the UNHCR work in CR concentrated on three areas: asylum, seekers, refugees and the Roma.

81   Human Rights Watch *Destroying Ethnic Identity. The persecution of Gypsies in Romania* (1991) HRW NY.

travelling people. Settled residents may be threatened by what is regarded as an alien lifestyle which opposes the values that they hold dear: owner occupation, deference to authority and the work-ethic.[82] As a result discrimination is able to flourish unhampered by any debate as to the human rights implications. It is apparent that Czech Roma are regarded as aliens on both counts: because of the large-scale migration from Slovakia and because their lifestyle is so incomprehensibly different from that of Gadje and, as a result, is perceived as being inferior.

One notable effect of the entrenched discrimination and racism that Roma encounter is the denial of identity. This can be clearly seen with regard to the census results. Indeed, the number of Roma willing to identify themselves as such decreased between 1991 and 2002 – only 11,716 Roma admitted to their identity in the most recent census (the true figure is officially estimated at 250,000–300,000).[83] This figure suggests that many Roma suffer from low self-esteem and are not able to enjoy their identity. The pressure to assimilate is intense, yet the dominant society is hostile to this objective and prevents integration by maintaining discriminatory housing and educational practices and by denying employment to those with darker skins.[84]

Segregation is also evidence of the de facto denial of citizenship. The number of Roma living in segregated, sub-standard housing in the Czech Republic is, according to Ina Zoon, 'growing exponentially'.[85] Many do not have adequate documentation having been transported from Slovakia in the Communist industrial drives and this lack of paperwork makes them vulnerable to eviction.[86] In addition, the 1993 Citizenship law mean that many Roma without de jure citizenship lost access to social benefits including rent allowance and child benefit. There has been insufficient acknowledgement by central government of these problems. In its response to the critical Committee on the Elimination of All Forms of Racial Discrimination report, the government claimed that, apart from the Usti Nad Ladem wall, they were unaware of other examples of isolation.[87] Such central indifference has allowed municipal authorities to introduce criteria which limit the ability of Roma applicants to qualify for social housing, including a good character or moral behaviour requirement and full employment conditions.

As a consequence, many evictees and those unable to access social housing now occupy accommodation known as 'holobyty', characterised by the absence of public services, extreme over-crowding and insanitary conditions. 'Holobyty' flats are

---

82   For examples reported in the media see O'Nions *supra* n26.

83   Radio Prague 'Ever less citizens consider themselves members of a Roma community' 5 July 2001.

84   See for example Open Society Institute EU Accession Monitoring Program: *Minority Protection in the Czech Republic* (2001) Open Society Institute.

85   Zoon, Ina *On the Margins. Roma and Public Services in Romania, Bulgaria and Macedonia* (2001) Open Society Institute at 163.

86   *Ibid.* at 164.

87   CERD Additional Information Pursuant to Committee *Decision*: *Czech Republic* CERD/C/348 21 January 1999 para. 1.

overwhelmingly inhabited by Roma.[88] Zoon argues that discrimination is inherent in the municipal housing process:

> If it is true that government officials do not target Roma for evictions and do not single them out to be moved to segregated area, it is incredibly difficult to explain how Roma account for 60%, 80% or even 100% of the 'holobyty' tenants when they constitute less that 3% of the Czech population.[89]

In 2001, the Human Rights Committee expressed concern over discrimination against the Roma including the high rate of unemployment, special schools and the lack of initiative to improve their socio-economic situation. A range of recommendations exclusively focused on the situation of Czech Roma including the need to adopt special measures, particularly in the field of education.[90]

ii) Legislative discrimination

Van Gunsteren, in his analysis of conceptions of citizenship, has noted that there has been a new tendency in modern times for states to assist individuals in attaining the criteria to apply for citizenship 'by helping them to obtain the qualities required for admission, but also by removing the obstacles and lowering the demands'.[91] His label of the present model as 'Neo-Republican citizenship' requires that states recognise the community of the 'citizen' as but one of many communities that the individual may belong to and, further, that these communities should be enabled to develop their identity without sacrificing their citizen status.[92] One may therefore expect that a modern democracy should assist disadvantaged individuals and groups to reach the criteria set for citizenship so that they can access the rights and duties which the status provides. Furthermore, community interests and objectives should not be eroded when an individual strives to join the community of citizens. The OSCE's Commissioner on National Minorities has issued a number of principles which should apply in states considering new citizenship laws:

> Citizenship forms the basic bond between a person and state. For the individual, citizenship means he or she is wholly welcome in the state, a full member of the political community. For the state, citizenship underscores the loyalty of the person and confers certain duties and responsibilities on him or her. In granting citizenship, the state should take into account a person's long term (and often life-long) residence on its territory and should furthermore use citizenship to promote bonds of loyalty to the new political community.[93]

---

88   Barbora Bukovská 'Difference and Indifference: Bringing Czech Roma Ghettoes to Europe's Court' (2002) Eumap.org http://www.eumap.org/journal/features/2002/may02/czechromaghettoes.

89   *Supra* n85 at 181.

90   CCPRE/C/CZE/2000/1 May 2000.

91   Van Gunsteren, H 'Four Conceptions of Citizenship' in van Steenbergen, *The Condition of Citizenship* (1994) Sage, London at 37.

92   *Ibid.* at 45.

93   CSCE *Human Dimension Seminar on Roma in the CSCE Region* (1994) CSCE at 10.

People become citizens of the state in which they live either as a result of birth or by naturalisation. Domestic legal systems tend to be based on the principle of *jus soli* or *jus sanguinis*. The former grants citizenship on the basis of birth, whereas the *jus sanguinis* principle affords citizen status on the basis of descent, i.e., through a long-established link with the state in question.[94] Whichever method is applied may be crucial and a person is unlikely to form any bond or loyalty towards the state unless they are afforded the title of citizen. The sense of bonding conferred by citizenship status is emphasised by many writers.[95] Marcia Rooker explains the significance of acquiring legal citizenship as follows:

> Citizenship is the consolidation of the tie between an individual and a state. A citizen can always return to his country, can influence the governing of the country and participate in economic and social life. Citizenship makes the tie between state and individual even stronger. To deny an inhabitant citizenship or deprive him of it will alienate that person from the State.[96]

International human rights provisions are generally not contingent on the issue of citizenship but there are certain rights which may be denied to non-citizens; particularly significant is the right to vote and thus participate in the political life of the state. Robert Blackburn notes:

> The right of every citizen to vote and take part in the political process of a state is the foundation of its democracy. It is a citizen's right which is of immense symbolic as well as practical importance, for it enshrines the principle of political and civil equality ....[97]

The right to vote is crucial if the geographically dispersed Czech Roma are to have their voice heard in any effective way. This can be seen clearly following the results of the parliamentary elections of 1996 where the Republican Party captured 18 seats with an extreme-right agenda. Among his manifesto promises and populist rhetoric, the party's leader, Miroslav Sladek, had called for the deportation of Czech Roma.[98]

The issue of nationality has generally been left to the domestic jurisdiction of the state, outside the sphere of international law.[99] Brownlie observes that international law does not support a contention that the deprivation of nationality is illegal.[100]

---

94   The *jus soli* method is applied in French naturalisation criteria. This can be contrasted by the German approach where less people are eligible to become full citizens.

95   Barbalet, J.M. suggests citizenship defines or distinguishes between those who are and those who are not members of a common community or society in *Citizenship Rights, Struggle and Class Equality* (1988) Open University Press at 18.

96   Rooker, M *Stateless and Marginal* (1995) Unpublished conference paper, The Netherlands.

97   Blackburn, R 'The Right to Vote' in Robert Blackburn (ed.) *Rights of Citizenship* (1993) Mansell, London.

98   CTK 1996 quoted in O'Nions, H 'Czech Citizenship Restrictions and the Roma' conference paper presented at Roma Studies Day SSEES June 1997.

99   Donner, Ruth The Regulation of Nationality in International Law (1994) Helsinki Finnish Society of Sciences and Letters.

100   Brownlie, I *Principles of Public International Law* (1990) Clarendon, Oxford at 405.

Yet the usual test will be a genuine and effective link with the state concerned. In the leading case of *Nottebohn* a German national working in Guatemala had attempted to acquire the nationality of Liechtenstein in order to avoid the possible confiscation of his property should a war break out between Germany and Guatemala. Following Guatemala's declaration of war, Nottebohn's property was confiscated and Liechtenstein brought a claim on his behalf before the International Court of Justice.[101] According to the International Court of Justice, a state must act 'in conformity with this general aim of making the legal bond of nationality accord with the individual's genuine connection with the State'.[102] In this case, no genuine connection had been shown and the claim was unsuccessful.

Article 15 of the Universal Declaration of Human rights gives everyone the right to a nationality but does not impose a corresponding obligation on a particular State to uphold that right.[103] This provision was considerably watered down by the drafting of the ICCPR which merely provides that every child has the right to acquire a nationality.[104] Most writers on the subject of nationality echo the view that there is no rule of international law imposing a positive duty on States to grant nationality,[105] although some argue that there may be a negative duty not to create statelessness under international law.[106] As far as territorial transfers are concerned, there is however, evidence of a strongly supported principle that nationality is linked with territorial occupation. Brownlie contends that 'the evidence is overwhelmingly in support of the view that the population follows the change in sovereignty in matters of nationality'.[107] More specifically, Chan asserts that the issue of nationality in such cases will depend on a 'genuine and effective link', in most cases established by residency.[108] Thus, there is evidence of a principle but not a rule that on the dissolution of Czechoslovakia, those residing in the Czech Republic would acquire Czech nationality.

There is clearly a gap in international protection where an individual has lost their nationality and as a result is denied effective representation and nationality based privileges such as welfare provision.[109] The difference between de facto and de jure statelessness has given rise to such a gap. In his 'Report on Nationality including Statelessness' in 1952, Manley Hudson noted:

---

101 ICJ Nottebohm Case (1956), 6 April General List no 18.

102 *Ibid.*

103 Chan, Johannes MM 'The Right to a Nationality as a Human Right' (1991) *HRLJ* Vol.12, 1 pp 1–2 at 2.

104 Article 24(3) ICCPR.

105 Lillich, Richard B 'Civil rights' in Meron *supra* n19 at 154, Weis *Nationality and Statelessness in International Law* (1979) Sijthoff and Noordhoff at 198.

106 Chan, *supra* n103 at 11.

107 Brownlie, I 'The Relations of Nationality in Public International Law' (1963) *BYIL* 284 at 320.

108 Chann *supra* n103 at 12.

109 Batchelor, Carol. A 'Stateless Persons: some Gaps in International Protection' (1995) *Refugee Law Vol.* 7, 2 pp 232–259 at 238.

Purely formal solutions ... might reduce the number of statelessness persons but not the number of protected persons. They might lead to a shifting of statelessness 'de jure' to statelessness 'de facto'.[110]

The 1954 Convention Relating to the Status of Stateless Persons,[111] the first international document dealing specifically with the increasing rise in the number of refugees and stateless persons, did not concern itself with the problem of de facto statelessness. The 1961 Convention on the Reduction of Statelessness paid little attention to the issue, despite the advice of the High Commissioner for Refugees who considered the inclusion of de facto statelessness to be essential if the convention was to have any meaningful effect.[112] Nevertheless, the legislative competence of a state is limited by some of the provisions contained therein. Article 1 of the Convention provides that a state shall grant its nationality to a person born on its territory if that person would otherwise be stateless. This provision is extended by Article 4 by which a state should grant its nationality if one of the parents of a stateless person was born on its territory. Particularly relevant to the Czech situation is the principle providing that a state shall not deprive a person of their nationality if they would otherwise be stateless.[113] However, this right is subject to the qualification that the person has not acted in a manner which is prejudicial to the interests of the state.[114]

Despite the weakness in the wording of such principles and the lack of state support for the convention generally,[115] the Special Rapporteur on Nationality and State Succession of the International Law Commission contends that limits are placed on the discretion of states in the context of state succession and, specifically, naturalisation.[116] In particular he refers to the general principles against discrimination on the grounds such as sex, race and religion; he also refers to Article 9 of the Convention:

In the event of State succession, this provision must be understood as a prohibition of any arbitrary policy on the side of the predecessor state when withdrawing its nationality from the inhabitants of the territory affected by state succession.[117]

110   Hudson, M *Report on Nationality including Statelessness* International law Commission 4th session UN Doc A/CN.4/50 21.2.52 at 49.

111   28.9.54 UN Treaty series Vol. 360 at 131. This convention has not been signed by the eastern European countries with the exception of Yugoslavia and Slovenia – Marie, Jean Barnard 'International instruments relating to human rights. Classification and status as of 1.1.95' (1995) *HRLJ* at 75.

112   Dr P Weis in Conference on Elimination or Reduction of Future Statelessness 1959 Un Doc A/CONF 9/3 (13.2.59) 3. The final vote on the text was reached at Un Doc. A/CONF. 9/Sr.23 (11.10.61).

113   Article 8.

114   Article 8(3)(a)(ii).

115   As of 1 January 1995 the Convention has 18 State parties and only four signatories, see above.

116   Special Rapporteur of the International Law Commission, Mr Mikulka, in Doc A/CN/.4/467 on 17 April 1995 at para. 85.

117   *Ibid.* at 154 para. 85.

His report also finds that the criteria of habitual residence and domicile are the most frequently used in practice.[118] In response to the Council of Europe's criticism however, the Czech Government were clear that territorial integrity and sovereignty should trump any assumed obligation to comply with these principles:

> Public rights cannot be guaranteed on succession, because they represent the innermost 'hard core' of sovereignty of a new State and may be regulated only by the successor State.[119]

At a regional level, the European Convention on Nationality entered into force in 2000.[120] Article 3 preserves the principle of territorial sovereignty and allows each state to determine nationality according to its own laws. However, it also requires states to develop these laws in line with international principles including the avoidance of statelessness and the arbitrary deprivation of nationality. Discrimination on grounds of nationality is prohibited by Article 5.

The situation of state succession is specifically addressed by Article 18 which requires states to take account of the genuine and effective link with the state concerned, habitual residence of the individual at the time of succession, the will of the person concerned and the territorial origin of the person. As of August 2006, only 15 Council of Europe states have actually ratified the Convention. Despite criticism by the UNHCR, the Czech Republic chose to wait until 2004, by which time their own citizenship law had been largely amended to conform to the requirements.[121]

The lack of clear international guidance on the subject of state succession and nationality transfer is clearly problematic. However, from the confused picture there are several clear strands that emerge as established principles, the breach of which will attract international condemnation and will demand satisfactory justification. An obligation to reduce or eliminate statelessness is one such principle. It is argued that the elimination of statelessness will only be successful if the 'nationality of the individual is the nationality of that State with which he is, in fact, most closely connected'.[122] Furthermore, shortly after the Czech citizenship amendment, discussed below, the Committee on the Elimination of All Forms of Racial Discrimination specifically addressed the issue in their *Recommendation on Discrimination against Roma* which instructed State parties to 'ensure that legislation regarding citizenship and naturalisation does not discriminate against members of Roma communities'.[123]

---

118   *Ibid.* at 154.

119   'Comments of the Czech Republic to the Report by the Council of Europe experts on the citizenship laws of the Czech Republic and Slovakia' in *supra* n146 at 103 para. 32.

120   *European Convention on Nationality* 6 November 1997 European Treaty Series/166.

121   UNHCR *Country Operations Plan. Czech Republic* 5 April 2002 UNHCR.

122   Hudson *supra* n110.

123   CERD General recommendation XXVII *Discrimination Against Roma* adopted at 57th session on 16 August 2000.

Political developments in the Czech Republic

The new republic and constitution

On 1 January 1993 the Republic of Czechoslovakia ceased to exist and was formally split into the Czech Republic and the Republic of Slovakia. The Czech Republic has its own constitution of December 1992 and has ratified the European Convention on Human Rights and Fundamental Freedoms. In June 1994, the Republic became a member of the Council of Europe and 10 years later became a member of the European Union.

The Charter on Fundamental Rights and Freedoms contains some provisions going beyond the international legal standards including Article 3 which is comparable to Protocol 12 of the European Convention in that it prohibits any 'distinction as to race, national or social origin ... membership of a minority'. Chapter 3 of the constitution contains 'the rights of minorities' containing a list of rights vesting in citizens who constitute minorities.[124]

The Czech Citizenship Law

The new Citizenship Law came into effect with the new constitution on 1 January 1993.[125] Law 40/1992 is not particularly unusual in the requirements it lays down for acquiring citizenship. It has however; become controversial for the effects it has had on many Slovak state citizens who, despite residing in the Czech region for many years, were immediately defined as immigrants. Indeed, as Tibor Papp observes, the law illustrates the ethnocentric conception of nationhood which continues to characterise the Czech state identity.[126] The Tolerance Foundation's *Report on the Czech Citizenship Law* details the immediate effect of the Act:

> The new law means that there are people who were born in the Czech territory and/or have lived there for decades – including those who were forcibly moved there from Slovakia by the communist regime – who before January 1993 had all the rights of citizenship, today are deemed foreigners in their own land.[127]

Reflecting Marshall's analysis of 'citizenship,' social benefits from education to health care ceased to be available from June 1994 to those who could not prove citizen status. One month later the preferential procedure for Slovaks applying for citizenship in the Czech Republic ended so that they were treated the same as any other foreign national in the application process.[128]

The law built on the old Citizenship Law 165/1968 which established dual citizenship: everyone became a member of the federation of Czechoslovakia and

---

124 Blaustein and Flanz *supra* n65.
125 Law 40/1992 on 'the acquisition and loss of citizenship'.
126 Papp, Tibor *Who is in, Who is out? Citizenship, Nationhood, Democracy and European Integration in the Czech Republic and Slovakia* EUI Working Paper RSC No 99/13 European University Institute, Florence at 14.
127 *Report on the Czech Citizenship law* (May 1994) Tolerance Foundation, Prague at 2.
128 Article 18 of Law 40/1993.

could additionally opt for citizenship of one of the two federal states. Only the federal citizenship was considered legally significant at the time and the state citizenship was not even used on identity documentation.[129] Under law 40/1992 the category of federal citizenship was abolished with state citizenship becoming the relevant factor. It is hardly surprising then that many Czech Roma were defined as Slovak. It is estimated that as many as 150,000 Roma had to re-apply for citizenship in their country of permanent residence.[130] This amounted to what, the European Roma Rights centre contend, was the first act of forced mass statelessness in Europe since the Second World War.[131] Indeed, there have been suggestions that the citizenship law was a deliberate effort to rid the Czech Republic of the Roma population.[132] The criteria that applicants needed to establish created a wealth of problems for the applicants and deserve closer examination.

i) Permanent residence in the Czech Republic for at least five years
This provision was reduced to two years as a concession for Slovak citizens until July 1994.[133] This may seem a relatively straightforward requirement,[134] but there were some obvious difficulties with respect to Romani residents. Primarily, it is often difficult for a family to prove they have been in permanent residence, especially as many of the dwellings allocated to them as part of the resettlement program were overcrowded[135] and sub-standard and thus were not registered as permanent dwellings with the Local Authority.[136] Another problematic factor was the increase in violence towards Romani residents which meant that many were forced to flee or were harassed into leaving their residence.

ii) The clean criminal record requirement (Article 7 (1c))
The so-called 'Gypsy-clause' also had to be satisfied in any application for permanent residence. It stated that persons should not have been sentenced for an intentional criminal offence in the previous five years. The law notably failed to draw any distinction between minor crimes and more serious offences; most crimes are intentional under the Czech penal code. Ina Zoon, a Czech human rights lawyer, observes:

> It is somewhat of a paradox that in ignoring the severity of the offense and focusing exclusively on when the sentence is pronounced, the citizenship law would allow a person

---

129   *Ibid.* at 6.
130   Powell *supra* n44, at 117.
131   ERRC 'Statement of the ERRC on acceptance into NATO of Czech republic, Hungary and Poland' 1997, ERRC.
132   *Ibid.*; Open Media Research Institute Daily Digest 17 September 1992.
133   Article 18.
134   Chan *supra* n103 at 9. Denmark, Italy, Netherlands, Norway and Sweden all require 5 years residency for naturalisation. The figure is 10 years in Spain and Germany. The new citizenship legislation in Latvia, following the vote for independence, set the residency requirement at sixteen years, with dire consequences for many of the estimated 50% of foreigners living in Latvia – Close *supra* n77 at 77.
135   The Czech housing regulations specified at least 8 m² for each occupant.
136   Tolerance Foundation *supra* n127 at 18.

convicted of crimes against humanity after the Second World War to obtain citizenship while at the time barring a person convicted of a minor offense from obtaining citizenship.[137]

This provision only applied to people living in Czechoslovakia with Slovak state citizenship, it did not apply to Czechs who were abroad in 1968 and thus did not have to apply for state citizenship under the law 165/1968. It disproportionately affected the Romani population, many of whom have been involved in minor offences. It has been argued that Roma criminality has direct links with high levels of unemployment following the collapse of communism. Will Guy notes that semi-legal or illegal activities where and consequence of pandemic unemployment among Roma.[138] Zoon and Siroka argue that the link between crime and poverty is:

> not merely a matter of legal theory. There is a clear connection between the tragic social condition of the Roma community and the predominant type of criminal offences.[139]

One writer estimated that approximately half the Roma denied Czech citizenship may fail to satisfy the so-called 'Gypsy clause'.[140] The evidence collated by Zoon and Siroka suggests that there is inherent bias in the criminal justice system with Roma more likely to have their papers checked, to be arrested and prosecuted.[141] Such concerns have also been raised by the US State Department and various UN bodies including the Human Rights Committee, the CERD and the Committee against Torture.[142] The Tolerance Foundation found that 45% of their sample of 208 Roma who failed to obtain citizenship had no criminal record and 35% of the survey were indicted for theft under Article 247 of the penal Code and other petty crimes.[143]

The Council of Europe criticised the law on the basis of the prohibition of retroactive penalties in Article 7 of the European Convention. The United Nations[144] and the Chairman of the Office of Security and Cooperation in Europe also expressed disapproval.[145] The Council of Europe experts further criticised the law for depriving people of their right to vote on the basis of legislation that was not in force on the date that the crime was committed.[146] They considered the clean criminal record requirement to be arbitrary in that it unjustly discriminated between former Czechoslovak citizens

---

137 Tolerance Foundation *supra* n127 at 16.

138 Guy *supra* n37 at 296.

139 Tolerance Foundation *The Non-Czech Czechs* (1995) at 15.

140 Ulc *supra* n73 at 29.

141 Tolerance Foundation (1995) *supra* n139 at 11.

142 US State department report Bureau of Democracy, Human Rights, and Labor, Country Reports on Human Rights Practices – Czech Republic 2000 23 February 2001; *Concluding Observations: Czech rep* 14 May 2001 CAT/C/XXVI/Concl.5/Revelation 1 para. 8(b); CCPRE/C/CZE/2000/1 May 2000.

143 *Ibid.* at 18.

144 United Nations High Commission for Refugees The Czech *and Slovak Citizenship laws and the Problem of Statelessness* (1996) UNHCR, NY.

145 Chairman Smith, OSCE Letter to the Interior Minister 13.5.96.

146 Council of Europe Report of the Experts of the Council of Europe on the Citizenship laws of the Czech Republic and Slovakia and their Implementation 2 April 1996 DIR/JUR (96) 4 at 26 para. 80.

and disproportionate in its impact on the Roma. While the clean criminal record requirement was usual in naturalisation criteria for foreigners generally, in the case of state succession it was considered to be discriminatory if a person could show established ties with that country.[147] Statistics issued by the Tolerance Foundation indicate that over half of those Roma denied citizenship were born and have remained on Czech soil; over 80% had lived in the Czech Republic for more than 20 years.[148] The UNHCR also issued a report condemning the law in which reserved particular criticism for the apparent intransigence of the Czech Government.[149]

iii) The requirement to master the Czech language (s7(1)(d))
The imprecise wording of this requirement gave rise to several difficulties. For example, it was not clear how mastery should be interpreted or whether illiterate applicants were automatically excluded. Much depended on the discretion of the particular administrative officer.

The harshness of the provision was mitigated by s10(2) which stated that s7(1)(d) did not apply to former Slovak citizens. However the Tolerance Foundation have evidence suggesting that language ability was often relevant to the success of the application. One representative from the Ministry of Interior stated in obvious contradiction 'It is true that the Slovaks don't have to be "examined" but they still have to "prove" that they have mastered the Czech language by speaking Czech when they apply for citizenship'.[150]

Such difficulties should be viewed in the light of numerous practical problems that Roma applicants experienced, including high levels of illiteracy and lack of awareness as to their rights. In response to the legislation the Roma Democratic Congress asserted:

> The Czech law on acquiring and losing citizenship will take away from tens of thousands of people their right to a homeland, will deny them their basic rights and threaten their existence.[151]

Despite many apparent problems with the legislation, the Czech Constitutional Court rejected attempts to abolish the law on the grounds that it violated the constitution.[152] International institutions[153] have however been vociferous in their

---

147   C/E *supra* n146 at p10 para. 21(e) and pp 24–25 paras 73–87.

148   Tolerance Foundation (1994a) *supra* n127 at 4.

149   UNHCR *supra* n144.

150   Tolerance Foundation (1994a) *supra* n127. Interview with Mrs Goluskinova February 1994 at 22.

151   Press Conference on 30 June 1994 see Czech Republic Embassy report on minority rights (1994) Czech Embassy, London.

152   13 September 1994 Dec P1.US 9/1994 of Czech Constitutional Court. Article 87 of the Czech constitution allows the court to annul a law or part of a law if it contravenes the constitution or an international agreement – Matscher, F and Liddy, J 'Report on the Legislation in the Czech Republic' (1993) *HRLJ* Vol.14 No 11–12 at 442–6 at 443.

153   An overview of these criticisms can be found in Schlager, Erika 'UNHCR Report says Czech Citizenship Law violates international law; Council of Europe experts say Czechs Violate Rule of Law' (1996) *CSCE Digest* June pp 5–6.

criticisms of the legislation and in 1996 an amendment was introduced by MP Jiri Payne to mitigate the harshness of the clean criminal record requirement. Yet the amendment which gave the Ministry of Interior discretion to wave the clean criminal record requirement in less serious cases did not end the international disapproval.[154] The permanent residence requirement remained unaltered and the discriminatory nature of the clean criminal record requirement simply became discretionary rather than mandatory. Chairman Smith of the CSCE compared the amendment to telling Charter 77 dissidents that of course they had a right to free speech -providing they got a waiver of the Minister before exercising it.[155]

The Czech Government initially claimed that only 200 Roma had been denied citizenship. While the exact figures remain elusive, this figure is clearly a blatant underestimate. The Equal Rights Programme established by the Tolerance Foundation found over 400 people whose applications had been refused and that from a sample of 99 cases, 92% of those denied citizenship did not possess a Slovak passport either. The Roma Democratic Congress initially estimated that at least 77,000 Czech Roma would lose citizenship as a direct result of the legislation,[156] (the figure is now thought to be somewhere between 10,000 and 25,000).[157]

Article 16 of the Czech Criminal Code allows a foreigner to be expelled by the police for a misdemeanour or crime. Expulsions by judicial decision can also occur for serious crimes if the person is a non-citizen irrespective of citizenship elsewhere.[158] The US State Department reported that 851 'Slovak' people had been expelled administratively or judicially by the first half of 1997.[159]

It would appear that scant regard was paid to Article 12 of the Czech Constitution which states that 'no-one can be deprived of their citizenship against their will'. The Czech authorities argue that such an Act was essential to maintain sovereignty and contend that reasonable and preferential measures were adopted in order to enable all former Slovak citizens to claim Czech citizenship. In making this assessment though the authorities, perhaps conveniently, failed to consider the particular difficulties common to the Roma and the entrenched prejudice of many people charged with processing applications. The 'Equal Rights Program' discovered many examples of Roma applicants being refused citizenship on dubious grounds before there was any right of appeal.[160] In some cases applicants were refused because they had not obtained the correct identification documents or for criminal offences committed over 5 years previously and, in at least one case, as a result of a 'regrettable misunderstanding' when officials failed to consider all the relevant circumstances.[161] A 1995 survey by

---

154   Chairman Smith of the OSCE has written to the Interior Minister criticising the amendment for failing to redress the ex post facto increase of criminal penalties (dated 13 May 1996).

155   *Ibid.*

156   Press Conference 30 June 1994 *supra* n151.

157   *Supra* n10 at 26.

158   Article 57 Czech Criminal Code.

159   *Supra* n166.

160   Tolerance Foundation *A Need. For Change. Analysis of 99 Individual Cases* (1994) November, Tolerance Foundation, Prague.

161   *Ibid.* at 24–6.

the Roma National Congress revealed that 90% of Czech Roma saw no reason to remain in the Republic.[162]

In 1997, the Czech Supreme Court ruled on the legality of citizenship denial for minor criminal offences.[163] The applicant had been sentenced to expulsion following the theft of $4 worth of sugar beet. He had lived in the Czech Republic since he was three months old and had been raised in Czech orphanages. His lawyers successfully argued that his private and family life had been violated contrary to Article 8 of the European Convention on Human Rights and that such measures were 'not necessary in a democratic society'. It was held that the offence did not meet the threshold for what constitutes a criminal offence for the purpose of the Citizenship law and the applicant should have his residence rights reinstated. The same year saw renewed international criticism following the arrival of Roma asylum seekers in Europe and the exodus of an estimated 1200 Czech Roma to Canada.[164]

The 1999 Amendment[165]
Some four years after the original amendment, the European Roma Rights Centre estimated that 10,000 Roma remained stateless and the US State department estimate the number could be as high as 20,000.[166] In 1999, a more significant amendment was enacted so that persons in the territory at the time of dissolution can apply for citizenship by declaration. The amendment still causes concern as it requires persons to have remained in the Czech Republic since dissolution. Documentation will be crucial if residency is to be demonstrated and those people who went abroad, including those who sought asylum and those that returned to Slovakia, as well as people expelled by the Czech police or judiciary will be precluded from applying. As a result of this law expulsions of 'Slovak' citizens who have committed offences are no longer been imposed.

Further, while the citizenship amendment has ended much of the criticism over de jure citizenship denial, the UN Committee Against Torture recognised that discrimination and segregation remain commonplace.[167] A new Law on Ethnic and National Minorities which includes rights to bilingual signs, minority language education and municipal minority councils, entered into force in July 2001. The Commissioner for Human Rights described the law as change of direction whereby

---

162 Roma National Congress Report on the Situation *of the Roma in Europe* (1995) RNC, Hamburg at 21.

163 May 1997. Again I am indebted to Mark Thieroff of the Equal rights Programme, Prague for this information.

164 Siklova, Jirina and Miklusakova, Marta 'Law as an instrument of discrimination Denying Citizenship to the Czech Roma' 1998 *East European Constitutional Review* Vol 7 No 2; Bancroft *supra* n9 pp 110–118.

165 Amendment no 194/1999 to the Act on Acquisition and Loss of Citizenship.

166 Fekete, Liz 'Newsletter of ERRC' No 3 1999, 1 March 2000; US State department 'Czech Country Report 2000' February 2001.

167 Conclusions and Recommendations of the Committee against Torture: Czech Republic. 14/05/2001. CAT/C/XXVI/Concl.5/Revelation 1 (Concluding Observations/ Comments).

members of minorities are afforded a right to have the state obligations fulfilled.[168] The law is to be welcomed but it is unlikely to benefit the Roma given that most of the rights are contingent upon a 10% minority population threshold.

Options for those denied citizenship

Czech residents from Slovakia who did not obtain citizenship status had two possible alternatives to remaining in the Czech Republic as a foreigner. Many non-Czech citizens may still possess Slovakian identity documents and could elect to return to Slovakia. However, one of the conditions of applications was that any Slovak citizenship should have been surrendered before the application for Czech citizenship. As a result there are many non-Czech citizens who became stateless and were unable to return. The second route that opened for many non-citizens was to emigrate. Indeed, the second half of the 1990s witnessed many Roma leaving the Czech Republic in search of a more secure future and applying for asylum in Western Europe and Canada.[169]

Remaining in the Czech Republic as a 'foreigner'

In the Czech Republic a person who is not a Czech citizen is necessarily a 'foreigner' and must comply with the Act on Foreigners Stay and Residence[170] or risk expulsion. Under the Act there are three forms of legal stay for a non-citizen:

1) short-term stay (intended for tourists) up to 180 days,
2) long-term residence (work, studies, medical treatment) for up to 1 year, and
3) permanent residence which is generally only available to family members who reside permanently in the Czech Republic.

Permanent residence was also subject to the clean criminal record requirement and is necessary in order to obtain health and unemployment benefits; if a father does not have permanent residence then the whole family may be deprived of these benefits.[171] Statistics gathered by Human Rights Watch suggested that 80% of Roma were unemployed in 1998.[172]

Return to Slovakia

Roma who decided to return to Slovakia are likely to face conditions of extreme poverty and hardship. One observer from the International Helsinki Federation for

---

168   Commissioner for Human Rights in Open Society Institute EU Accession Monitoring Program: Minority Protection in the Czech Republic (2001) OSI at 156.
169   O'Nions 'Bonafide or Bogus' (1999) 3 *Web JCLI.*
170   Law 123/1992.
171   *Supra* n10 at 26.
172   Human Rights Watch 'Czech Republic. Human Rights Developments' (1998) *HRW.*

Human Rights was alarmed by the high level of deprivation in one camp of over 600 people living in wooden units of 12 to 14 people. The report revealed that there was no public transport to the camp and that the rubbish had not been emptied for over a year. The one positive aspect was that the site had a school, financed by local money from Roma entrepreneurs.[173] This camp was regarded by the Roma guide as being one of the better ones with 'The Roma of a neighbouring village living in dug out holes in the ground, covered by plastic sheets'.[174] Rising poverty in the ghettos has led to an increase in crime, alcoholism and deteriorating relationships with the non-Gypsy community.[175] Although the situation in Slovakia has improved somewhat there remain significant problems in terms of unemployment, educational disadvantage and poverty.[176]

Furthermore, for many non-Czech citizens the option of returning is unrealistic as well as undesirable. Many left Slovakia during the industrial drives and no longer have family or territorial links with Slovakia.[177] For those who surrendered their Slovakian citizenship or who cannot obtain necessary identity documentation the situation is even more disconcerting. In their analysis of 99 cases, the Equal Rights Program, found that 92% of those interviewed had failed to acquire citizenship and did not possess a Slovakian passport while 8% had been released of their Slovakian citizenship to make them de jure stateless.[178] None of those surveyed had a permanent residency permit under the Foreigners Act which would have allowed them to claim state benefits or employment without a work permit. Until recently there was no guarantee that those who remain in the Czech Republic without a residence permit would not be expelled; their existence was precarious in a hostile country.

Those that did emigrate abroad or return to Slovakia either voluntarily or through expulsion will now find that they are unable to take advantage of the amendment as they cannot satisfy the residency test.

Emigration to the 'safety' of the West

The alternative for many of the Czech non-citizens was to emigrate and seek prosperity abroad in Western Europe, often Germany[179] and more recently, the United Kingdom and Canada. In 1993, the Czech Government detained 24,000 people attempting to depart illegally for Germany, a significant number of who were Roma.[180] Evidence tends to suggest that those who succeed in illegally entering Germany may soon discover that their problems are only just beginning.

---

173   Young, J 'Is Slovakia Ready for the Potential Influx of Roma Denied Czech Citizenship?' in *Promoting Human Rights and Civil Society in Central and Eastern Europe* (1994) No. 4 at 2/3.

174   *Ibid.* at 3.

175   Mann, A *The Romanies in Slovakia: Local History and Minorities* training course, Slovakia C/E (1994) at 5.

176   Human Rights Watch World *Report* (2002) *HRW*, New York.

177   Tolerance Foundation (1995) *supra* n139 at 21.

178   Tolerance Foundation *supra* n157 at 17.

179   Roma National Congress *supra* n162 at 21.

180   Edginton, Bella 'To kill a Romany' (1994) *Race and Class* Vol. 35, 3 pp 80–83.

Following the reunification of Germany racist attacks increased ten-fold in 1991 and the terror increased through 1992 to over 2,000 incidents of right-wing violence.[181] The prejudice is particularly intense towards Roma, Turks, Vietnamese, Poles and black Africans.[182] On the political platform, Roma have not yet been acknowledged as a 'national minority' and there are numerous examples of official prejudice. A member of the Bremen state Parliament referred to the Nazi Holocaust and stated 'it's a pity that not more of them were murdered' and one Green Party Council supervisor likened the Romani Holocaust to the disappearance of the dinosaurs, saying 'We cannot help everybody we've hurt through history .... The Romani culture is not worth protecting'.[183] Furthermore, Germany was the only nation to vote against a United Nations Resolution on the 'Protection of Roma' in 1992 on the basis that the Roma are not considered a minority and they should not be afforded special positive treatment.[184] Germany is thus unlikely to provide the security that the Romani refugees from Eastern Europe are seeking.[185]

Canada became a popular destination for Roma following the airing of a Czech television documentary on 5 August 1997 which depicted a country of tolerance with a special program to assist Romanies.[186] Precise figures as to the number of Rom moving to Canada in the late-summer and autumn of 1997 remain elusive: the European Roma Rights Centre in Budapest stated that thousands were preparing to move[187] and the Helsinki Commission noted 1,100 arrivals in September 1997.[188] By the end of August 1997 the homeless shelters of Toronto were full to capacity of Czech asylum seekers.[189] A significant number of these arrivals returned to the Czech Republic in the following months after finding that their relatives were not given permission to join them.[190]

In one three-day period in October, some 200 Roma arrived in Dover from the Czech Republic and Slovakia.[191] Soon after, the tabloid Sun newspaper reported that

---

181   Hockenos *supra* n61 at 28/9; Bancroft *supra* n9 pp 100–102.

182   *Ibid.* at 39.

183   Quoted in RNC *supra* n162 at 16.

184   United Nations Commission on Human Rights Res. 62/1992 *Protection of Roma*; Written question E-207/1994 to the European Commission, *Official Journal of the European Communities: Information and Notices* (1994) 37 349 24.

185   See for example Resolution ResCMN (2003)3 on the implementation of the Framework Convention for the Protection of National Minorities by Germany adopted bye the Committee of Ministers on 15 January 2003

186   'Gypsies go to heaven' 5 August 1997 TV NOVA; 'Gypsy Accuses "Arrogant" Canada' *Toronto Star*, 24 August 1997 pA2.

187   Goldston, James 'Claiming civil rights for Roma' (1997) *Christian Science Monitor* 3 September editorial.

188   Helsinki Commission, CSCE, 'Letter to the Czech Deputy Foreign Minister,' 7 October 1997.

189   CFRB Radio, 22 August 1997 18.30; RFE/RL *Newsline* vol. 1 no 101, Part II August 22nd 1997 estimates that 20% of the hostel residents are Roma.

190   Radio Prague E-news 'Romanies come home' 15 June 1998, reported that 600 of the 1,500 Romani asylum seekers have now returned to the Czech Republic.

191   Transcript of CBC news Report Broadcast 20 October 1997 by Don Murray, London.

'3,000 gipsies' were heading for Britain from Slovakia to use the 'cushy benefit system'. Many failed to arrive after news spread that the welcome would not be as warm as they had been led to believe following another favourable Czech television documentary.[192] The extreme-right organisation, the British National Party, was quick to try to mobilise local anger by demonstrating at the port of arrival, although they received little support from the Dover residents. The visa requirement for Czech citizens coming to Canada was quickly reinstated[193] and the period of application for asylum seekers in the UK was similarly reduced by immigration minister Mike O'Brien, from 28 days to five in response to the wave of these allegedly 'economic migrants'.[194]

It now appears that most of the migrating Rom were from the Czech Republic rather than Slovakia and the majority were quickly sent back to France. After the initial scare-mongering had subsided,[195] several newspapers were forced to recognise, albeit reluctantly, something of the discrimination faced in the Czech Republic. Three Romany families were eventually granted asylum. In one case, following the recent murder of a Romany woman in a racially motivated attack,[196] the High Court ruled that the family were victims of discrimination and would probably face persecution on their return.[197]

Once a date had been set for EU accession, visa restrictions against the Czech Republic became untenable. Consequently the UK Home Office stationed immigration officials at Prague airport in an effort to weed out potential asylum-seekers. In 2004, the House of Lords overruled the decision of the Court of Appeal and held that such a practice was contrary to international law and the principle of non-discrimination.[198]

Conclusion: What next for the Czech Roma?

Before 1990 the Roma lacked minority status in the Czech Republic. Today, the Czech Charter on Fundamental Rights and Freedoms follows the language of the regional human rights instruments, paying little more than lip-service to the effective recognition and protection of minority identity. A new notion of Czech citizenship

192   Lee 'Man whose tale prompted scores of Gypsies to follow him to Dover has no regrets' *Times* 23 October 1997, Fisher 'Now Czech TV sending Gypsies to UK' *Toronto Sun* 26 October/7th 1997.

193   Appleby 'Visiting Czechs need Visas' *Globe and Mail*, Canada, 8 October 1997; Schneider 'In bid to restrict Gypsies, Canada Limits Czech visitors; visa controls reinstated to curb refugees' *Washington Post*, 10 October 1997 A31.

194   CTK (Czech news agency), Prague, 27 October 1997.

195   Note the headline in *The Independent* 'Gypsies invade Dover, hoping for a handout' 20 October 1997 p1; *The Telegraph* talks of the 'Dover Nightmare' on 20 October 1997 p 2.

196   CAROLINA No 277 'Young woman dies after racially motivated attack' 20 February 1998.

197   CAROLINA No 279 'Romany family granted asylum in Great Britain' 6 March 1998.

198   *R (on the application of European Roma Rights Centre) v Immigration Officer, Prague Airport* [2004] UKHL 55 [2005] 2 A.C. 1 [2005] 2 W.L. R. 1.

is based on ethnic homogenisation in which the Roma are defined as Outsiders.[199] In the absence of effective recognition individual Roma lack political space and are insecure and powerless, as evidenced by the reluctance to identify oneself as Roma in the recent census. Disengagement with majority society has become entrenched. The strength of Kymlicka's argument that the protection of some group-based rights may be a necessary prerequisite to the adequate protection of individual rights can be seen clearly here.[200] While the Czech authorities can point to an impressive charter of individual freedoms, such freedoms cannot be realised in the climate of discrimination and intolerance in which all Czech Roma find themselves. The Roma minority has been officially recognised and has become increasingly visible as a result. In this situation, an emphasis on the rights of the individual is ineffective and may be counter-productive if one considers the effects of seemingly neutral citizenship criteria. The Tolerance Foundation explains the way in which the citizenship law indirectly discriminates against the Roma:

> The law was aimed at limiting the Roma population's possibility of acquiring citizenship because it imposed a set of requirements that are particularly difficult for this ethnic groups to comply with.[201]

Human rights are not dependent solely on questions of citizenship, but it may be argued that their realisation becomes a fiction without basic guarantees protecting identity and personal security. Rainer Bauböck questions whether Marshall neglected cultural dimensions of citizenship, the recognising of which would entail a degree of special minority rights and possibly cultural autonomy.[202] Using the example of minority languages he concludes that cultural citizenship is indeed missing from Marshall's analysis and identifies this to be a significant omission as it may prevent the other dimensions of citizenship from being fully realised.[203] Special treatment is urgently required to provide de fact equality and to redress the entrenched prejudice of the legislature and the general public.

The recent wave of migration bought the Czech human rights record to the forefront of international media. The European Community continually expressed concern about the treatment of Czech Roma. The Agenda 2000 report noted that the Roma:

> Are the target of numerous forms of discrimination in their daily lives and suffer particular violence from skinheads, without adequate protection from the authorities or police. Their social situation is often difficult (though sociological factors to some extent account for

---

199   Bancroft argues that while Czech citizenship does reflect the notion of an ethnically homogeneous society it has also been constructed so as to exclude the economically redundant *supra* n9 at 156.

200   Kymlicka, W *Multicultural Citizenship* (1995b).

201   Tolerance Foundation *supra* n127 at 40.

202   Bauböck, Rainer 'Cultural Citizenship, Minority Rights and Self-government' pp 319–348 in Aleinikoff, T Alexander and Klusmeyer, Douglas (eds) *Citizenship Today. Global Perspectives and Practices* (2001) Carngeie Endowment for International Peace, Washington DC.

203   *Ibid.* at 325.

this), alongside with any discrimination they may suffer from the rest of the population, notably over access to jobs or housing.[204]

Their treatment was critically monitored before accession. Indeed, evidence documented by Will Guy suggests that the change in the law was directly attributable to concerns over accession.[205] In March 1998 the European Parliament threatened to block the approval of EU associate members' entry criteria, stating that Romany integration must be moved from a medium to a short-term objective.[206] The UN Committee on the Elimination of All Forms of Racial Discrimination was equally critical, expressing concern over the level of segregation, discrimination in housing, employment and civic life and the six-fold rise in racially motivated attacks between 1994 and 1996.[207]

Aware of these criticisms,[208] the Czech Government have begun to address the problem by establishing an inter-ministerial 'Commission On Romany Community Affairs' which includes Romani representation.[209] One of the Commission's first missions was a visit to Ostrava to discuss the problems of unemployment and poor housing and in 1998, the 1958 Act outlawing nomadism was finally repealed.[210] There are signs that the causes of discrimination are beginning to be addressed and the profile of the Roma is being gradually raised. Initiatives to recruit Romany police officers have been explored[211] and a deputy Mayor was been found guilty of encouraging racial hatred and issued with a fine when he banned Roma from using a public swimming pool.[212] The 2000 Concept strengthened the work of the Commission.[213] Yet there remain questions over the willingness to implement the necessary measures. The 1999 EU Phare programme financed Roma advisers, assistants and social workers but no government funding was allocated afterwards.[214] Budget issues plague the commission, regional meetings were abandoned in 1998 due to lack if funds and therefore assistants were appointed from the top down without regional support. Later in 1998, allegations of apartheid were directed at the Usti Nad Labem municipal authority, who began constructing a wall to segregate Roma and non-Roma inhabitants.[215] The Czech Government failed to take action to

204   CTK 17 July 1997 'EC Points to Romany human rights in Czech Republic'.

205   Guy *supra* n37 at 303.

206   CTK (Czech news agency) Brussels 3 March 1998.

207   UN 52nd session CERD, reported in ERRC Press *Statement on the Concluding Observations Concerning the Czech Republic of the UN CERD* March 1998.

208   Pehe, Jiri 'Attitude to foreigners, emigres must change' *Prague Post* 24 June 1998. The writer, parliamentary adviser to the president, writes that in order for the Czech Republic to be fully accepted as a European state there must be vast improvements in the attitude to foreigners. He highlights as as 'outrageous example' the Czech Citizenship Law.

209   CTK (Czech news agency) 'Czech cabinet drafting legislation to solve Romanies problems' 16 January 1998.

210   RFE/RL 'Czech senate Revokes Anti-Romany Law' 5 March 1998.

211   Radio Prague e-mail service 'Romanies invited to join police force' 7 March 1998.

212   CTK 20 February 1998.

213   Approved by Government resolution No 599, June 2000.

214   OSI Roundtable, Prague 22 March 2001.

215   Traynor, Ian *supra* n64.

prevent the construction of the wall although they were legally empowered to do so. Finally, in November 1999, the wall was removed and the government converted the area into an all-Roma neighbourhood and financially assisted non-Roma who moved into a new neighbourhood. Although the citizenship law has now been amended, de facto denial still exists and is maintained through segregation and a discriminatory criminal justice system.[216]

Any measure to improve the situation of the Czech Roma must consider the daily denial of human rights to which they are subjected. Individual rights amount to little more than rhetoric in a climate of entrenched prejudice and discrimination. Positive protection for minority identity and special measures are urgently needed alongside individual rights to give real meaning to constitutional guarantees. Tibor Papp argues that if Ralf Darendorf's assertion that the 'true test of the strength of citizenship rights is heterogeneity,' is accurate, the Roma minority becomes the real test of Czech citizenship. He concludes that thus far the Czechs barely manage to get a passing grade.[217]

---

216   See for example US State Dept *supra* n142.

217   Papp Tibor *supra* n126 at 18 quoting Dahrendorf, Ralf 'The changing quality of citizenship' in Bart van Steenberger *The Conditions of Citizenship* (1994) London, Sage at 17.

Chapter 5

The Education of Roma and Traveller Children: The Development of an Intercultural Pedagogy

Education is empowerment. It is the key to establishing and reinforcing democracy, to development which is both sustainable and humane and to peace founded upon mutual respect and social justice. Indeed, in a world in which creativity and knowledge play an every greater role, the right to education is nothing less than the right to participate in the life of the modern world.[1]

Introduction

A strictly individualist emphasis also gives rise to problems with respect to the right to education. Regarded as a social right, rather than a civil/political right, education is housed between the related rights of health and culture in Articles 13 and 14 of the United Nations International Covenant on Economic, Social and Cultural Rights (hereafter ICESCR). It will be recalled that the second of the two international covenants is not regarded as imposing immediate obligations on the signatory states. This is an uncomfortable position for many writers who argue that education is a prerequisite to the realisation of other human rights, such as freedom of expression and religion.[2]

Improvements have been made in the provision of education for Roma and other travellers, particularly since the European Community Resolution On *school Provision for Gypsy and Traveller Children* in 1989.[3] It can be seen that much of this improvement derives from a greater recognition of the different needs of minority groups in the education process. There are still many obstacles to be overcome and the Roma are still categorised as one of the most poorly educated groups in Europe. It is believed that only 30–40% of these children attend school with any regularity[4]

---

1   United Nations Economic and Social Council 'Progress report on the implementation process of the education for all objectives' A/52/183, E/1997/74 18 June 1997 Introduction.

2   Many writers from the Developing World and developing countries in particular have argued that economic and social rights should have priority. Only when the basic living conditions are achieved through the provision of economic and social rights, it is argued, can there be the necessary equality for civil and political rights to flourish – see Cassese, Antonio *Human Rights In a Changing World* (1990) Polity at 59–60.

3   22 May 1989. EC Res. 189/C 153/02 (No C153/3-4) 1989.

4   *Ibid.*

and up to 90% of adults in some regions are illiterate.[5] Many children who do begin school will discontinue their studies; this is most notable in the transition to secondary school.

The Roma are disadvantaged in the education system for a variety of reasons.[6] A crucial factor is the attitude of educators as exemplified in national education policies; in too many cases the education system has been used to promote assimilation. Discrimination is commonly evidenced at all levels of the education process. However, this is not the only problem as many Roma live in conditions of extreme poverty which can make schooling a practical impossibility.[7] In addition, some Roma parents have tended to disapprove of formal education and considered it to be unnecessary for the traditional lifestyle. The reasons for this negative attitude will be explored in this chapter.

Is formal education important for the Roma?

This question may appear to yield an obvious answer, yet for a Romani child the benefits of education may not be self-evident. Roma pupils rarely learn anything of their culture, language or values in a classroom. They are presented with a stark choice of denying their cultural identity and perhaps consequently suffering rejection at home, or rejecting the educational system.[8] One observer in the former Federal Republic of Germany noted 'only those Sinti who disguise their origin and who avoid contact with the group, have succeeded in learning a trade requiring prolonged apprenticeship or studies'.[9]

When one considers these factors the reluctance to attend regular school exhibited by many Roma is understandable. Paradoxically, however, these difficulties can only be addressed and surmounted when Roma children attend mainstream schools. Once those involved in the provision of schooling begin to understand more of the traditions and history which frame the Roma culture, in all its forms, they can begin to overcome the prejudices and discrimination which has subverted attempts at understanding in the past.

The value of education as a key to realising other rights such as accommodation and employment cannot be overstated. Unemployment is a major problem for Roma

---

5   Liégeois and Gheorghe *Roma/Gypsies: A European Minority* (1996) Minority Rights Group, London at 12.

6   Research by the OECD in 1983 lists several categories of disadvantaged students. The Roma fall into several categories – including membership of ethnic minorities; economically disadvantaged and geographically disadvantaged. OECD *The Education of Minority Groups* (1983) Gower, Hampshire at 11.

7   Kyuchukov, Hristo 'Transformative education for Roma (gypsy) children: an insider's view' (2000) *Intercultural Education* Vol 11, 3 pp 273–280. See also United Nations Development Program report *Avoiding the Dependancy Trap* (2003) UNDP, Bratislava at 53.

8   Liégeois, J P *Roma, Gypsies, travellers* 1994 C/E: Strasbourg passim and Advisory Council for the Education of Romany and Other Travellers, *The Education of Gypsy and Traveller Children* (1993) University of Hertfordshire Press passim.

9   Papenbrok, Marion quoted in Liégeois School Provision for Ethnic Minorities: *The Gypsy Paradigm* (1988) Interface, Univ. of Hertfordshire Press at 111.

throughout Europe.[10] The installation of market economies in the former Communist countries of Eastern Europe has worsened this situation; the new emphasis on a competitive workforce has enabled employers to reduce costs by dismissing workers for flimsy reasons. Poor qualifications and an irregular work history provide excuses for employers who do not wish to hire or retain dark-skinned employees.[11]

Equality of opportunity in education

Education should enable opportunity and the realisation of potential, but as Rainer Bauböck and Kristin Henrard note, it is also important to the development of self-esteem and identity.[12] Furthermore, if delivered sensitively and appropriately, it can break down barriers and prejudice between communities. Liégeois states: 'The ultimate goal of any school is to give each child the means and tools he requires in order to achieve autonomy'.[13] Respect for diverse cultural values and opinions are integral to this approach. Many older Roma see little need for education and may perceive it as a threat to their culture. This is especially true if they speak a minority language and the child will be instructed in the majority language.[14] In these circumstances, education can operate to destabilise communities. It is for this reason that the majority education system must be sensitive to the needs of minority cultures, instructing pupils about the foundations of their identity rather than alienating them.

Assimilationist and pluralist education strategies contrasted

The education of minorities, as Thornberry recognises, is often marked by a tension between integration and separation:

---

10   International Helsinki Federation for Human rights *Annual Report* 1997 IHF Vienna, indicates the frequency of Roma unemployment across Europe. The report highlights particular unemployment problems in Greece, the Czech Republic and Hungary. See more recently the UNDP report *supra* n7.

11   The International Committee on the Elimination of Racial Discrimination noted that unemployment of Czech Roma was between 70 and 80% and this was largely attributable to their poor education and labour skills. UN CERD Summary *record of the 1254th meeting*: *Czech Republic* 11 March 1998 para.55CERD/C/SR.1254.

12   Bauböck, Rainer 'Cultural Citizenship, Minority Rights and Self-government' pp 319–348 in Aleinikoff, T Alexander and Klusmeyer, Douglas (eds) *Citizenship Today. Global Perspectives and Practices* (2001) Carngeie Endowment for International Peace, Washington DC at 329; Henrard, Kristin 'Education and multiculturalism: the contribution of minority rights?' (2000) *Int. Journal on Minority and Group Rights* Vol 7 pp 393–410 at 394.

13   Liégeois *supra* n8 at 208.

14   Office for Standards in Education (OFSTED), *The Education of Travelling Children*, (1996) at 20 and Advisory Council for the Education of Romany and Other Travellers *supra* n8 above passim.

If integration is pushed too far, the result is assimilation and the disappearance of the minority as a distinct culture. A policy of separation, on the other hand, can lead to a ghetto culture of withdrawal from society.[15]

It is clear that policies which on the surface appear non-discriminatory may result in de facto inequality. Hawes and Perez note that the British 'open door' policy of the 1970s did nothing to encourage the enrolment of travelling people.[16] Specific funding was required in order to focus on the particular needs of travellers, many of who did not have a legal place of abode and whose interests were consequently outside the net.[17]

The assimilationist ideology, which regards ethnic affiliation as potentially dysfunctional, was dominant in many education systems until recently.[18] Such a perspective emphasises a belief in the common culture to the detriment of minority characteristics and values. In his study of US educational policy, James A. Banks is critical of the assimilationist approach to education:

> When assimilationists talk about the 'common culture,' most often they mean the Anglo-American culture and are ignoring the reality that the US is made up of many different ethnic groups, each of which has some unique cultural characteristics that are a part of America.[19]

Nathan Glazer sees a policy of 'benign neutrality' in respect of ethnic issues as the best way of promoting equality and universalism in education.[20] Will Kymlicka's critique of the 'benign neglect' strategy has already been discussed in Chapter 2.[21] The question remains as to how far a state or education authority can remain neutral to the needs and interests of all minority groups, particularly when such a policy involves endorsing the majority language.

Liégeois argues that educators have paid little attention to the education provided in the family unit, concentrating solely on the formal state education system. The education provided at home, he contends, has the same objectives as formal education, namely autonomy, responsibility and a sense of community.[22] However, he observed that school can destabilise minority identity:

> It can easily and effectively participate in assimilating the minority groups subjected to it, all the more so as attendance is often compulsory. Yes, school can 'form' a child – but its role may be conforming, reforming or deforming.[23]

---

15   Thornberry, Patrick 'Article 12' in Weller (ed.) *The Rights of Minorities* (2005) OUP at 392.

16   Hawes and Perez *The Gypsy and the State. The Ethnic Cleansing of British Society* (1996) School of Advanced Urban Studies, Univ. of Bristol at 67.

17   *Ibid.* at 71.

18   Liégeois *supra* n9.

19   Banks, James A. *Multi-ethnic Education. Theory and practice* (1981) Allyn and Bacon, Mass. at 68.

20   Glazer, Nathan 'Cultural pluralism: the social aspect' in Tumin and Plotch *Pluralism in a Democratic Society* (1977) Praeger, NY pp 3–24.

21   See Chapter 2 at 52.

22   Liégeois 1998 *supra* n18 at 64.

23   *Ibid.* at 175.

Many writers have thus begun to explore pluralist education policies. The pluralist ideology recognises cultural differences as significant in the development of education policy.[24] A dramatic re-organisation of the curriculum is advocated so that minority values form an intrinsic part of the mainstream educational policy. Furthermore, it is recognised that different ethnic groups have different cognitive styles and that these styles must be part of any educational assessment process.[25]

As far as minority cultures are concerned, equality of opportunity can only be achieved if there are measures to enable plurality and diversity rather than assimilation. Holly Cullen has pointed out that pluralism and equality of opportunity are both important objectives of a good education system.[26] To a large extent it is a question of resources, particularly in states where there are many ethnic minority groups making competing claims for resources. Equally important though is the political will of the dominant state system. The provision of special education measures to Roma and travelling people is unlikely to be popular with non-Roma[27] and if there is no effective lobbying to produce culturally appropriate, better quality education this need can easily be forgotten.[28] There are of course many other areas, not just education, which require special measures and education may often be ignored. A common complaint is that education is discussed without reference to accommodation, the absence of which is often a major factor in poor school attendance by Roma children.[29] Acton and Kenrick also observe that sedentarism is regarded as being an essential prerequisite to the provisions of education. Their research notes the unsettling effects of policies aimed at preventing nomadism:

> ... historical experience ... would seem to indicate that it is not nomadism in itself, but only frequent forced evictions, or discrimination against nomads, that is an obstacle to education.[30]

---

24   See for example Novak, Michael 'Cultural Pluralism for Individuals: a Social Vision' in Tumin and Plotch (eds) *supra* n20 at 25–57.

25   Banks *supra* n19 at 63 highlights research by Ramirez and Castaneda concerning the learning styles of Mexican-American youths, and a study by Stodolsky and Lesser which supports the notion that the cognitive approaches of ethnic groups differ.

26   Cullen, 'Education Rights or Minority Rights?' (1993) *IJLF* Vol 2 pp 143–177 passim.

27   Turgeon, L claims that the 1956 Kadar Government in Hungary had to play down affirmative action measures to assist the social situation of Gypsies in order to retain majority support. See 'Discrimination Against Gypsies' in Wyzan, M (ed.) *The Political Economy of Ethnic Discrimination and Affirmative Action* (1990) Praeger, NY at 158.

28   This may explain why many of the advancements in traveller education are attributable to the action of voluntary organisations rather than part of a focused national strategy.

29   Liégeois *supra* n8 at 7. Tom Lee, Secretary to the Romany Guild in the UK, asserts: 'To discuss education before stopping-places is like putting the cart before the horse.'

30   Acton and Kenrick in Liégeois *supra* n18 at 100. This conclusion receives support from Italian and French sources in the same report.

Indeed, nomadic Roma and travellers may see themselves as victims of double discrimination as they are often unable to access education, particularly at secondary level.[31]

Nonetheless, the significance of education for any minority group cannot be overstated. If sensitively delivered, it provides the tools which these children need to maintain their culture, reducing discrimination and the potential of assimilation. The pluralist approach however, can be criticised for promoting and exaggerating difference at the expense of unity.[32] If there is no universal conception of rationality, replaced by a belief in relativism, then the logical outcome of pluralist education policy, it is argued, would be ethnic segregation.[33] There is also concern that pluralism in education would prevent critical commentary on illiberal practices.[34] This has led to the middle-ground 'multi-ethnic' approach:

> ... multi-ethnic education is intended to reduce discrimination against ethnic groups and to provide all students with equal educational opportunities .... Ethnic groups anywhere are the intended beneficiaries by modifying the school environment to reflect the diversity of multi-ethnic populations.[35]

Multi-ethnic or 'intercultural' education recognises that pluralism may exaggerate cultural differences but also that the role of these groups is greatly underestimated in the assimilationist approach. Freedom of choice is essential. Banks envisages an open society in which individuals are free to maintain their ethnic identity:

> Multi-ethnic theorists feel strongly that during the process of education the school should not alienate students from their ethnic attachments but help them to clarify their ethnic identities and make them aware of other ethnic and cultural alternatives.[36]

Most educationalists recognise that this does not imply a separate education for each culture but rather it requires cross-cultural awareness. The classroom can be the perfect environment for the acknowledgement and exchange of different cultural values. Research in Romania found that over 70% of children were unwilling to have Roma children as friends whereas 93% of the Roma children wanted to have ethnic Romanians as their classmates.[37] Indeed, the negative attitudes of Gadje are one of the major obstacles (if

---

31   Derrington, Chris and Kendall, Sally *Gypsy Traveller Students in Secondary Schools* (2004) Trentham Books, Stoke-on-Trent.

32   Assimilationists argue that it could lead to the 'Balkanization of society' by increasing separatism and segregation.

33   Zec, Paul 'Multicultural Relativism: what Kind of Education is Possible?' (1980) *Journal of Philosophy of Education* Vol. 14, 1 pp 77–86.

34   Jeffcoate, Robert *Ethnic Minorities and Education* (1984) Harper and Row, London at 120–121.

35   OECD *supra* n6 at 297.

36   Banks *supra* n19 at 71.

37   Research cited in Cozma et al. 'The education of Roma Children in Romania: description, difficulties, solutions' (2000) *Intercultural Education* Vol 11, 3 pp 281–288 at 287.

not the major obstacle) to educational success.[38] A multi-ethnic, intercultural strategy would facilitate the dialogue needed to address these problems and research suggests that it may promote tolerance of different cultures.[39] This approach is supported by Council of Europe Recommendation R (2000) 4 on the education of Roma/Gypsy children in Europe which supports the need for modified teaching materials for all pupils which would incorporate the Roma/Gyspy culture and history.[40]

Modification of the curriculum remains a crucial issue. The multi-ethnic ideology requires that the curriculum respects the diversity of each child and that teachers are skilled and sensitive to the needs of ethnic cultures.[41] Such an approach is grounded in a collective rights perspective but also entails recognition of the complementarity with and, in cases of conflict, supremacy, of individual rights.

A review of some of the policies operating in Europe reveals a conflicting message. On the one hand there are serious problems in accessing quality education, on the other hand there have been some positive steps taken, usually by individual schools and teachers. Recent initiatives in the European Community and the Council of Europe suggest that Roma education is now being taken seriously and a brighter picture is emerging.

An overview of education strategies in Europe

Spain

Article 3.3 of the Spanish Constitution states that the diverse range of cultures, languages and traditional institutions which make up Spanish heritage will be the objects of special respect and protection.[42] Article 27 provides the equal right to education.

It has been estimated that the number of Spanish Roma or 'Gitanos' is somewhere in the region of 650,000–800,000.[43] They are the largest minority group in Spain. Half live in Andalucia, usually in out of town districts without basic amenities such as electricity, water and sewerage. Accommodation is often in caves dug out of hillsides or in shanty towns.[44] Throughout Spain Roma occupy the poorest strata of society with high unemployment and extremely deprived housing conditions.[45]

---

38   Zamfir, C and Zamfir, E *The Gypsies: Between ignoring and Worrying* (1993) Bucaresti: Alternative Publishing House.

39   See for example Noorderhaven and Halman 'Does Intercultural Education lead to more cultural homogeneity and tolerance?' (2003) *Intercultural Education* Vol 14, No 1, pp 670–76.

40   Council of Europe Recommendation R4 of the Committee of Ministers On the Education of Roma/Gypsy Children in Europe (2000).

41   *Supra* n19 at 70.

42   'Spanish Constitution' in Flanz and Blaustein Constitutions of the Countries of the World (1971–) Dobbs Ferry: New York.

43   Liégeois and Gheorghe *supra* n5 at 7.

44   Muñoz Enrique, 'Some Facts Concerning the Situation of Andalucia' in Advisory Council for the Education of Romany and Other Travellers *supra* n8 (eds) at 115.

45   The Gypsy Council for Education, Culture, Welfare and Civil Rights, The first Romani Congress of the European Union Seville 18–21 May 1994.

Schooling for the Spanish Roma has improved greatly over the past two decades but, as is the case throughout Europe, there remain numerous obstacles to be overcome.[46] In a country in which half of the Gitano population are under eighteen,[47] it is estimated that some 75% are illiterate. Secondary attendance levels are very poor although primary school attendance has increased from around 40% in 1992[48] to 74% in 2001–02.[49] The drop-out and failure rates remain comparatively high, particularly from the age of eleven.[50]

While free, compulsory education is open to all in Spain, Spanish educators have persistently failed to provide de facto equality of opportunity based on the special needs of the most disadvantaged groups in Spanish society.[51] Compensatory education schemes which attempt to redress entrenched inequalities appear to make little real difference; concentrating on socialisation skills and looking at future employment prospects.[52] There have been some low key initiatives aimed at redressing these problems but they are seldom sufficient, for example in Madrid a scheme was established so that all schools with public financing had to enrol at least two immigrants, Roma or children from marginalised neighbourhoods in each class.[53] Bridging schools offered to Roma children in order to help them adapt to mainstream schooling, have been a failure.[54] Again the emphasis on this type of education is corrective and remedial rather than supportive of minority culture.

Gozalo Yagües refers to the lack of pre-school provision which could attempt to redress immediate disadvantage that children from economically unstable backgrounds will face when they begin primary school.[55] Furthermore, he argues:

There is also inequality of opportunity in the educational process, because from the pedagogical point of view teaching and instruction methods are scandalously inadequate and there is a lack of differentiation and adaptation of programmes of study and methods suited to the interests, lives, values and particular features of the Gypsy community.[56]

---

46   Concepción Gozalo Yagües, 'Spain: Analysis of the Schooling Situation of the Gypsy Community' in Advisory Council for the Education of Romany and Other Travellers *supra* n8 at 110.

47   The Gypsy Council for Education, Culture, Welfare and Civil Rights *supra* n45.

48   European Community Conference Working Party for Gypsy Education 'Europe 92' (1992) GCEWCR, UK at 17.

49   European Monitoring Centre on Racism and Xenophobia *Roma and Travellers in Public Education. An overview of the situation on the EU member states.* May 2006 at 27.

50   *Ibid.* at 27.

51   Advisory Council for the Education of Romany and Other Travellers (eds) *supra* n8 at 111.

52   *Ibid.* at 116.

53   Zoon, Ina 'The situation of Roma in Spain' in *Monitoring the EU Accession process: Minority Protection* (2001) Open Society Institute.

54   Etxeberria, Felix 'Education and Roma children in the Basque region of Spain' (2002) *Intercultural Education* Vol 13, 2 pp 291–304 at 294.

55   *Supra* n51 at 111.

56   *Ibid.*

The Spanish Roma evidently face a number of obstacles in accessing education and this is now being addressed by the Ministry of Education and Culture's 'Gitano Development Plan'. The plan includes recommendations that elements of Gitano culture be incorporated into primary curricula in an intercultural approach and further that intercultural mediators are trained to improve relations.[57]

Slovakia

Slovakia now has the highest concentration of Roma in the world (estimated at half a million,[58] amounting to approximately 12% of the total population). A report in the Helsinki Monitor describes 'Gypsies' and 'Hungarians' as the 'natural enemies' of the Slovak state:

> The result is growing social isolation of the Gypsies in their ghettos ... such isolation excludes these minorities from social and political life and from defining national priorities and long-term national goals.[59]

Bakker notes that the extent of anti-Roma prejudice constitutes a big obstacle to the resolution of the 'Roma question'.[60] It will thus come as no surprise that education of Roma has not been a priority with estimates indicating that up to 80% of Roma children attend special schools.[61]

The dissolution of Czechoslovakia led to a new constitution and equal rights legislation, but there was simultaneously a large increase in unemployment and poverty.[62] Additionally, a major problem in the development of schooling is the self-denial of the Roma minority status in the census, a consequence of centuries of prejudice including the Romani Porajmos[63] and recent increases in right-wing violence and anti-Roma hostility.[64]

---

57   As reported in *supra* n49 at 74.

58   Liégeois and Gheorghe *supra* n5 at 7. Official statsitics suggest a lower figure of 3.6% of the 5 million population.

59   Kusý, Miroslav 'Minorities and regionalization in Slovakia: Regionalization as a solution for the Hungarian minority issue in Slovakia' (1996) *Helsinki Monitor* Vol. 7. 1.

60   Bakker, E. 'The economic situation of Slovakia's minorities' in Trifunovska, S (ed.) *Minorities in Europe: Croatia, Estonia and Slovakia* (1999) TMC Asser, The Hague pp 189–207.

61   Report on the Commissioner's visit to the Slovak Republic 14–16 May 2001, Comm DH(2001)5 Council of Europe.

62   Mann, A.B. *Training Course for Teachers As Part of Pilot Project No 2*: 'The Analysis of the Questions of Minorities Issue and of the Possible Response of History Teaching and History Textbooks Design,' Council of Europe. 14–17 September 1994 at 14. (DECS/SE/BS/Sem (94) misc 6).

63   Advisory Council for the Education of Romany and Other Travellers Education for All: *Working for Equal Rights*, Advisory Council for the Education of Romany and Other Travellers. (1995) at 23, a mere 80,000 Gypsies in Slovakia classified themselves as such in a recent census.

64   *The Economist*, 'His struggle/Slovak Prime Minister under Fire over Gypsy Comments,' 18 September 1983. Slovak Prime Minister Vladimir Meciar was allegedly

Around 20% of Roma children in Slovakia do not complete their primary education, although recent initiatives aimed to improve this situation. Despite these positive steps there remain some deeply entrenched problems. The Government has recognised the need to provide an integrated education and have been working on developing the curricula to reflect Romani language and culture, this remains an enormous task.[65] Although legislation does provide for mother-tongue teaching for minorities, this does not extend to Romanes despite the fact that an estimated that 70% of Slovak Roma speak it.[66] Roma history and culture are typically not part of teaching in elementary or secondary schools. The pioneering work of the Roma Education Initiative is documented below[67] but Martina Kubánová agues that there is a lack of monitoring of successful projects and an absence of political will to change these practices. Indeed, she provides examples of extremely slow progress – Roma teaching assistants were experimentally tested for over 10 years before they received government backing and the widespread adoption of pre-school classes has been mooted since the early 1990s.[68]

In April 2003, the Slovak cabinet approved priorities aimed at proving integration of Roma[69] and money has been allocated for this purpose but a significant emphasis is placed on the Roma's behaviour. Indeed, one of the Government's educational goals is stated as:

> the gradual modification of values within Romany families so that education becomes an accepted value and precondition for resolving social, cultural and economic problems, with support from the Roma themselves.[70]

The plans notably lack concrete initiatives to tackle and prevent discrimination.[71] Given the international criticism of the Slovak Government's failure to respond to the challenge of Roma education it is surprising that the EU accepted Slovakia for membership in 2004. Anna Meijknecht concludes that the EU has lowered its

---

referring to Gypsies when he expressed concern at the number of 'socially unadaptable and mentally backward populations'.

65   *Ibid.* In one special school in Rudnany some 98% of the pupils are of Romani origin. See also Brearley, Margaret The Roma/Gypsies of Europe: A Persecuted People (1996) Jewish Policy Research Paper No 3 December 1996 at 31–32.

66   Article 3 of Act 29/1984 as discussed by Meijknecht, Anna *Minority Protection. Standards and Reality.* Implementation of Council of Europe standards in Slovakia, Romania and Bulgaria (2004) RMC Asser Press, The Hague at 154; ERRC *Time of the Skinhead. Denial and Exclusion of Roma in Slovakia* January 1997 ERRC, Budapest at 54.

67   See p 249 below.

68   Martina Kubánová 'The missing link: monitoring and evaluation of Roma-related policies in Slovakia' August 2005 *eumap.org Journal of the Open Society Institute.* See also Tanaka, Jennifer 'Economic Development Perspectives of Roma – looking critically at reality and the Social Impact of Development Measures' August 2005 *eumap.org.*.

69   Open Society Institute Report Monitoring the EU Accession process. Minority protection in Slovakia (2001), OSI.

70   Report submitted by the Slovak Republic pursuant to Art. 25 para. 1 of the FCNM ACFC/SR (1999) 008, 4 May 1999 at 27.

71   *Supra* n66 at 75.

requirements with regard to human rights, as it will take decades for Roma integration to be realised.[72]

Bulgaria

The Bulgarian situation is similar to that found in Slovakia. According to a recent United Nations Development Report, 32% of Roma children in Bulgaria do not attend school (compared to the national average of 8%). Only 5% will have the opportunity to attend secondary education.[73] There are also estimated to be 105 schools where the student body is entirely Roma, a consequence of segregated, ghetto-like neighbourhoods.[74] Although a desegregation program was initiated by Roma NGO's and adopted by the Government in 1998 the use of special schools is still prevalent.[75] Indeed, this has been explicitly recognised in the Bulgarian report to the Advisory Committee for the Framework Convention on National Minorities.[76] Gerganov et al. observe that education is not viewed as a two-sided process where minorities and the majority can learn about each other.[77] The minority is expected to adapt to the school whereas the school does not need to consider the specific needs of minority pupils.

Article 36(1)B of the constitution allows minorities the right to use their own language alongside compulsory study of Bulgarian. Romanes can be studied as an optional course in schools but Meijknecht reports that few children seem to study Romanes or Romani and attributes this to lack of textbooks and teachers and the Government's objective of integration.[78] There remains a significant disengagement with the educational process and illiteracy levels have actually risen from 11.2% in 1992 to 14.9% in 2001.[79] In the past it is certainly true that attitudes of the national government have done little to support successful projects. The PHARE programme funded a highly successful Intercultural Education project from 1995 to 1998 involving 200 teachers in 35 schools. High quality teaching materials and textbooks covering Roma history and culture were produced yet the project fell into decline and the materials were not reproduced because of lack of funding and additional support from the government.[80] In the past the Bulgarian Government have repeatedly

---

72   *Supra* n66 184.

73   *Supra* n7 at 54.

74   Danova, Savelina 'Patterns of segregation of Roma in education in Central and Eastern Europe' in *Separate and Unequal* (2005) Public Interest Law Initiative at 3.

75   *Supra* n66 at 57.

76   Report submitted by Bulgaria pursuant to Article 25 para. 1 of the Framework Convention for the Protection of National Minorities ACFC/SR (2003)001, 2003 at 26.

77   Gerganov, Varbanova and Kyuchukov 'School adaptation of Roma children' (2005) *Intercultural Education* Vol 16 No 5 pp 495–511 at 495.

78   *Supra* n66 at 169.

79   UNDP *supra* n7 at 31.

80   This is documented by the Open Society Institute Research on Selected Roma Education Programs in Central and Eastern Europe (2001) OSI, New York.

attributed lack of educational success and involvement to the attitudes of the Roma themselves yet the success of focused projects presents a different picture.[81]

There have been some efforts by the Bulgarian Government to address this issue and lessons were learnt from a successful NGO project in Plovdiv which established a summer pre-school course for bilingual children with a professional teacher and a Roma assistant. A project funded by The World Bank and Open Society Institute but largely organised by Romani activists from Drom Organisation commenced in 2000 in a Romani settlement in Vidin. Within three years 700 children were being transported from the settlement to an integrated school.[82] The project also introduced school counsellors who focused on the needs of the new children, supplemental classes, extracurricular events and assistance to Romani parents.[83] Research has demonstrated positive educational and social results in culturally mixed rather than separate classes with Roma students coming to see higher education as both possible and desirable.[84] Subsequently the Public Education Act 2002 made pre-school education obligatory with financing from the state budget.[85] On October 10th 2003 the *Action Plan for Implementation of the Framework Program for Equal integration of Roma in the Bulgarian Society* was introduced with state funding of approximately 135 million euros.[86] The Plan was originally established in 1999 but little was done to implement it for four years when the EU accession process was looming.[87] It refers to the need to implement recently adopted anti-discrimination legislation, specifically in the context of discriminatory treatment by the police and teachers. Money is primarily earmarked to combat unemployment but also to fund teaching assistants and textbooks and improve access to healthcare.[88] Nevertheless, significant problems remain in implementing these objectives and in October 2004, the Bulgarian parliament rejected that Draft Law for Educational Integration of

---

81   See the response of the Bulgarian Government to questions by the Committee on economic, Social and Cultural Rights *Summary record of the 30th Meeting: Bulgaria 23 November 1999* UN Doc E/C.12/1999/SR.30 1999 at para. 49.

82   Russinov, Rumyan 'Desegregation of Romani Education: Challenges and Successes' in *Public Interest Law Initiative supra* n74 at 15.

83   Kanev and Vassileva 'Local initiatives: desegregation in Bulgaria' in PILI *supra* n74 at 230–2.

84   Open Society Institute *supra* n80 at 509; *ibid.* at 234 shows that success depends on supplementary support and involvement of all interested parties.

85   UNDP *supra* n7 at 61.

86   The Framework Program had been introduced in 1999 but there was little political will or financial support at the time. Many of the criticisms and problems remain, see Human Rights Project, Bulgaria Press Release 'Roma public officials in Bulgaria criticise the policy of the Government in Open letter to the prime minister' May (2004).

87   Kanev and Vassileva 'Local initiatives: desegregation in Bulgaria' in PILI *supra* n74 at 221.

88   A critical perspective on the plan is offered by the Human Rights Project, Bulgaria's press release 'The Government Worked Out its action plan for the Roma Minority but it rises [sic] number of questions' 16 October 2003.

Minority Children which explicitly included a special fund for the desegregation of Roma children.[89]

The UK

The education of travelling people in the UK has been a story of slow, progressive success, which received a significant set-back in 1994 with the introduction of the Criminal Justice and Public Order Act which criminalises Gypsies and travellers who do not have a legal place of abode.[90] The Department of Education and Skills have recognised that one in five travellers has no legal or secure place to stay.[91] The success of traveller schooling can be clearly attributed to the dedicated work of a small number of volunteers and teaching professionals, it has never been seriously addressed by legislation.

The Plowden Report of 1967 described Britain's travelling community as 'probably the most deprived children' requiring 'special attention and planned action' to remedy their educational disadvantage.[92] The first Gypsy caravan school was founded by Thomas Acton in 1967, but, despite particular initiatives and extensive lobbying by the National Gypsy Education Council and the Advisory Council for the Education of Romany and other Travellers (ACERT), most of the changes over the next 20 years were of an ad hoc nature.

Following extensive research by the West Midlands Traveller Education team between 1970 and 1972, Christopher Reiss concluded that: 'The educational plight of the Gypsies has changed little since the 1870's'.[93] Acton recalls that the Department of Education and Science began to introduce short courses for teachers who might meet travellers in school but, paradoxically, there was little effort from the department to ensure that such children attended school.[94]

Government reports and academic commentary on the education of minorities continued to highlight the travelling community as experiencing severe educational disadvantage.[95] The Department of Education and Science's *Education of Travellers' Children* report of 1983 suggested that as many as 10,000 Gypsy children were still

89   Human Rights Project, Bulgaria Press Release 'Bulgaria: Roma children not children of Bulgaria, Decides Parliament' 11 October 2004 www.bghelsinki.org.

90   O'Nions, H 'The Marginalisation of Gypsies' (1995) 3 *Web JCLI*. For details of the evolving UK education policy see Acton and Kenrick *The Education of Gypsy/Traveller children in Great Britain and Northern Ireland. A report prepared for the Commission of the EC* Unpublished.

91   Dept for Education and Skills (2003) *Aiming High: Raising the Achievement of Minority Ethnic Pupils* London: DfES.

92   Central Advisory Council for Education *Children and their Primary Schools* (1967) HMSO.

93   Reiss, C *Education of Travelling Children* (1975) Macmillan p 14.

94   Acton, Thomas Romani Studies *at the University of Greenwich* Course Information, Univ. of Greenwich.

95   See for example HMI *The Education of Travellers Children* 1983 DES and the Swann report -*Education for All: the report of the Committee of Inquiry into the Education of Children from Ethnic Minority Groups* 1985 DES; Jeffcoate *supra* n34 at 72.

not getting any educational provision, especially at secondary level. Two years later, the Swann report was particularly critical of traveller education provision:

> In many ways the situation of Travellers' children in Britain today throws into stark relief many of the factors which influence the education of children from other ethnic minority groups – racism and discrimination, myths, stereotyping and misinformation, the inappropriateness and inflexibility of the education system and the need for better links between homes and schools and teachers and parents.[96]

In response to the criticisms of the report, many local authorities began appointing advisers to develop a multi-cultural education policy.[97] Nevertheless, the concerns exhibited in the Swann report can be seen clearly in the preference among travellers for on-site education. Bridging schools such as that offered in Avon were rarely successful;[98] segregation was an easier option for all concerned. Robert Jeffcoate observed that due to their nomadic existence and traditional hostility towards formal education, Gypsies were the only ethnic minority presenting a 'prime facie case for segregation in education'.[99]

By the late 1980s the emphasis had shifted firmly from voluntary provision to provision within the state education system and the number of teachers grew greatly. In 1990, s210 of the Education Reform Act came into force allocating specific funding for traveller education projects.[100] Such funding replaced the ad hoc grants made under the 'no area pool' provisions and suggested that the Government was aware that the different needs of travelling children needed to be addressed through specifically targeted resources. However, the sheer number of projects competing for resources has meant that many projects are under funded. Research by Hawes and Perez reveals that seven local education authorities lost more that 20% of their grants in April 1993 which inevitably led to job losses and reorganisation.[101] By the mid-1990s Acton contends there were around 500 specialist teachers besides many more who had Gypsy children in their ordinary classes. Nevertheless, further cuts in the specific funding of education projects have followed, compounding the effects of the Criminal Justice and Public Order Act 1994.[102] In 2003, OFSTED estimated that around 12,000 secondary -age traveller children were not registered at any school in

---

96   Swann report *supra* n95.

97   Hawes and Perez *supra* n16 at 69. One encouraging example which demonstrates that a simple idea can be very effective occurred in Cornwall when a Craft, Design and Technology class was asked to design a bender tent and thus consider the sociological and technological issues of nomadism. See Taylor, William. H 'Ethnic Relations in all-white Schools' in Tomlinson and Craft *Ethnic Relations and Schooling: Policy and Practice in the 1990's* (1995) Athlone Press, London p 106.

98   Hawes and Perez *supra* n16 at 70 and Chapter 4.

99   Jeffcoate *supra* n34 at 115. Such reasoning can be criticised for its failure to understand the causes of this 'traditional hostility' as they manifested themselves in discrimination and racism in the classroom.

100   s210 Education Reform Act 1988.

101   Hawes and Perez *supra* n16 at 80–1.

102   *Ibid.* at 83–5.

England.[103] Hatley-Broad demonstrates the common theme of invisibility with the traveller population omitted from some key national surveys and strategies.[104] This invisibility appears to extend to the national curriculum which generally overlooks the needs of ethnic minority learners.[105]

From defect to deficit theory

The failure of school systems to accommodate Roma and traveller children can be attributed to two different, but equally divisive, education strategies. Communist defectology determined the segregation of many children to special educational establishments on the basis that they had particular leaning difficulties making them unsuitable for mainstream education. Roma pupils found themselves in such schools because of poor command of the state language and culturally insensitive testing criteria.[106]

The special school situation is slowly changing – in some areas Roma teaching assistants have been introduced and there have been modifications to the traditional primary system to cater for the particular educational needs of the Roma. However, we then see evidence of another compensatory model of education based on deficit theory.[107] This approach emphasises educational equality but regards cultural difference as something to be rectified rather than supported. When integrative methods are applied, the focus is on the majority language and there is no legitimacy afforded to minority cultural values, tradition and language. As the recent report by the EU Monitoring Centre on racism and Xenophobia recognises:

> Such 'benevolent' segregation is not preferable to the provision of additional support to the school in the form of specially trained teachers, appropriate teaching material and intercultural mediators. Support measures should be functionally linked to normal school activities facilitating the full integration of pupils into the normal educational process.[108]

A European problem?

The experiences of Roma school children across Europe reveal the same problems. Along with general difficulties caused by poverty and unemployment, there often exists a lack of awareness on the part of education authorities; inappropriate, culturally-insensitive, education policies; and an inability to cope with the particular demands of this student body. Successful initiatives tend to be attributable to the work

---

103   OFSTED *Provision and Support for Traveller Pupils* (2003) London: HMSO.

104   Hatley-Broad, Barbara 'Problems and good practice in post-compulsory educational provision for Travellers: the Wakefield Kushti Project' (2004) *Intercultural Education* Vol 15, pp 267–281.

105   Verma, G.K. and Pumfrey, P.D. *Cultural Diversity and the Curriculum* (1993) Falmer Press, London.

106   Kanev et al. *supra* n83 at 234.

107   Igarashi, Kazuyo 'Support programmes for Roma children: do they help or promote exclusion?' (2005) *Intercultural Education* Vol 16, 5 pp 443–452 at 446.

108   *Supra* n49 at 47.

of a few committed individuals rather than a targeted, coordinated policy. Indeed, often those responsible for policy are reluctant to claim expertise in the area.[109]

In 2005, the European Parliament called on member states to implement desegregation programmes within a predetermined period of time to enable access to quality education and to prevent the rise of anti-Romani sentiment amongst school children.[110]

Obstacles to educational access

The Roma experience numerous obstacles in terms of access and success in education. Some inevitably arise from cultural differences, others from the inefficiencies of the school system and others still, from the discrimination shown in the classroom by teachers and fellow pupils. Overarching all of these obstacles, as recognised by the United Nations Development Programme report, is the common theme of poverty.[111]

Cultural difficulties

1. Parents' illiteracy means lack of family support for formal schooling plus the need for the child to be economically productive at a comparatively young age
The importance of formal education is not so obvious when considered in the context of the Roma community in which most children will live and work and where education is only essential so far as it improves the ability to earn or parent. Education is provided through close family networks where children work alongside their parents, learning their skills, from an early age.[112] The educationalist John Ogbu's 'cultural-ecological' theory of minority education emphasises the community forces, including family dynamics, which can play a significant part in undermining educational success. While not denying the existence of racism and discrimination in the education process, Ogbu was controversially concerned about neglecting the destabilising role of the minority itself.[113] Certainly, the Roma family structures and the community itself are often blamed for failing to support mainstream education. This argument may be overstated but it is prevalent and deserves some analysis. Felix Etxeberria identifies the main features of a traditional Roma education

---

109   Ms Lenner, the German Government's representative on Roma and Sinti education, is reported as saying to a European conference on education 'I am not an expert in the education of Sinti and Rom children nor am I in anyway responsible for this education' ACERT *The Education of Gypsy and Traveller Children* (1993) Univ. of Hertfordshire Press at 57.

110   European Parliament Resolution *on the situation of the Roma in the European Union* 28 April 2005 RC-B6-0272/2005.

111   UNDP *supra* n7 at 53.

112   Okely, J *The Traveller-Gypsies* (1983) Cambridge Univ. Press at 160–164.

113   Ogbu, John 'Adaptation to minority status and school experience' (1992) *Theory into Practice* Vol 31, 4 pp 287–295. For comment on this view see Foster, Kevin 'Coming to terms: a discussion of John Ogbu's cultural-ecological theory of minority academic achievement' (2004) *Intercultural Education* Vol 15, 4 pp 369–384.

including the importance of family life, oral communication, experiential learning and the importance of particular values, notably experience, initiative, solidarity, one's word, respect for one's elders and defence of the family.[114] The differences between these two styles of education are considerable, as Romani academic Tracy Smith argues:

> The conflict which exists between mainstream education and traditional Romani gypsy education is located in the opposing structures, values and interests which are used to support and maintain social cohesion in two very different societies.[115]

Mainstream education as presently constructed provides few additional skills which are regarded as valuable and which mitigate the absence of a young wage-earner from the family unit. As a consequence, Roma school pupils may also experience discrimination from their families.[116] A Spanish Gitano representative writes of this internal prejudice:

> In his peer group they will consider him as 'apayado' (Gorgified). They will be contemptuous of him in the belief that he no longer has 'picardia' (a commonly used term in certain Spanish Gypsy contexts to express irony and sharpness of word and deed) and he will perhaps be the target of the typical bitter, and even pitiless humour that we usually reserve for the Gorgios. That is to say that, little by little, they will begin treating him as if he had stopped being a Gypsy.[117]

The lack of parental literacy is also a major problem in increasing education. The Amman Affirmation on Education for All notes that improvement in adult education is crucial:

> In all societies, the best predictor of the learning achievement of children is the education and literacy level of their parents.[118]

Ogbu's solution to these 'negative' community forces is for the child to learn the dominant educational values. However, this may underestimate the way that the school system privileges particular perspectives and is unlikely to be successful in a climate of discrimination. Indeed, recent research has shown that many Roma parents accept the need for formal education but they are concerned about bullying from pupils and teachers. In some cases these concerns have led parents to support segregated, ghetto schools where the majority of students are Romani.[119] Successful

---

114 Etxeberria *supra* n54 at 295.

115 Smith, Tracy 'Recognising Difference: The Romani "Gypsy" Child socialisation and education process' (1997) *British Journal of Sociology of Education* Vol 18, 2 pp 243–257 at 244.

116 Liégeois *supra* n22 at 177 looks at the loss of Gypsy identity through regular school attendance.

117 European Community Conference *supra* n48 at 20/1.

118 The Amman Affirmation, adopted at the mid-decade meeting of the International Consultative Forum on Education for All, Amman from 16 to 19 June 1996, reprinted in *supra* n1 Annex.

119 Danova *supra* n74 at 8.

integration projects have demonstrated that when parents feel that their child is safe at school they are willing to move their child from ghetto schools.[120]

2. Nomadic travellers

It is a practical impossibility for many nomadic travellers to obtain consistent education for their children. While nomadism is primarily confined to West European Gypsies in countries where the provision of education to travellers generally is hailed as something of a success, e.g., in the UK, the provision of education to nomadic families is still regarded as problematic.[121] It has previously been noted that it is not the nomadic lifestyle itself that present problems, but rather the threat of constant eviction.[122] Research by Derrington and Kendall on the experiences of Traveller secondary school pupils demonstrates the acute difficulties that constant eviction and instability poses.[123] Indeed, the child's education is often cited as a crucial reason why nomadic families adopt a sedentary or semi-sedentary lifestyle.[124]

3. Economic instability leads to poor social skills

The inferior standard of living of many Roma families, particularly in Spain and Eastern Europe, creates its own difficulties for the child faced with entirely new surroundings. Nicolas Jimenez Gonzalez, a Spanish Gitano speaking of the situation facing Roma boys starting school:

> The lexicon of Spanish words used by his family is undoubtedly smaller and, what is more, if he lives in a shanty he will not know how to use certain instruments that he will find in a school, such as a light switch, washbasin, toilet, etc.[125]

In many countries funded pre-school education has been abolished. Poverty inevitably means that parents may not be able to provide the school uniform and books which will further alienate the child at school.[126] In other cases parents cannot afford to transport their child to school and persistent lateness is frowned upon by teachers and attributed to tardiness.

Etxeberria observes a different but related problem which has equally damaging effects on the education of Roma children, namely the dependancy trap. He argues that the Roma exhibit a 'passive sense of victimisation' which is characterised by an over-reliance on charity and state support.[127] Caution is needed therefore in providing sufficient resources to encourage opportunity and self-development without promoting reliance and reducing autonomy.

---

120   Russinov *supra* n82 at 16.
121   OFSTED (1996) *supra* n14 at 20.
122   *Supra* n29.
123   Derrington and Kendall *supra* n31 passim.
124   Davies, Elizabeth *Housing Gypsies* (1987) Dept. of Environment.
125   OFSTED *supra* n14 at 19.
126   Save the Children Denied a Future. *The Right to Education of Roma, Gypsy and Traveller Children* (2001) Save the Children, UK Summary at 40.
127   Etxebberia *supra* n54 at 298.

4. Difficulties of adapting to schooling in the dominant language

Rajko Djuric of the International Romani Union cites difficulties with the dominant language as an 'immediate disadvantage' for many Romani children particularly in Eastern Europe.[128] A French school teacher interviewed by Cotonnec recognised three separate linguistic spheres: the traveller version, standard oral French and written French: 'In theory the teacher has a command of the last two, but not of the first: the children are in the opposite situation'.[129]

The Czech Government have acknowledged that the language difficulty represents a serious factor in access to education. However, there is still evidence of misunderstanding and insensitivity in this respect. The attitude of Ladislav Goral, a Czech official, is far from atypical; he observed that language was a major problem, but then defended the lack of pre-school provision by suggesting that the fault lay with the Roma culture: 'because for the Romani person time doesn't exist and they don't know the value of education'.[130]

An increased focus on pluralism and group based difficulties in accessing schooling has led to a general recognition, emphasised by various international conventions and statements, that preliminary education requires some instruction to be taken in the mother tongue. Dr Tove Skutnabb-Kangas concludes:

> High levels of bilingualism and biculturalism benefit every child, but for minority children, bilingualism is a necessity. High level bilingualism can be achieved but it requires the adoption of the principle of institutional support for minority languages, which, without such support, are less likely to develop to a high level than are majority languages.[131]

Henrard also notes that when one language is used as the main medium of instruction, a seemingly equal starting point can have significant disadvantages for those not taught in their mother tongue.[132] Yet the UNDP report cautions against the use of minority language teaching in the absence of proficiency in the official state language:

> If Roma language is perceived as a substitute rather than as a supplement to majority language proficiency, it will reduce educational end employment opportunities and will promote further isolation, and subsequent ghettoisation, of the community.[133]

---

128 *Supra* n125 Opening address. Hartmann, 'Information File' 16 (1994) Interface 16 – A Romani teacher of Roma children in Cologne mentioned the following specific problems exhibited by the students: irregular attendance, insufficient grasp of the German language and significant gaps in general knowledge.

129 Cotonnec, Alain 'Group scolaire de Clayes-sous-bois' (1983) *Journeés d'études sur la scolarisation des Enfants Tsiganes*, Ministère de l'Education natioanle. Caen, Ecole normale du Calvados.

130 Central Europe on-line 'Czech official says government is doing its part to help the Roma' 10 October 1997.

131 Skutnabb-Kangas Tove Language, *Literacy and Minorities* (1990) Minority Rights Group, London at 31.

132 *Supra* n12 at 395.

133 UNDP *supra* n7 at 59.

The significance of minority language teaching in schools is gradually being realised in national education policies and this reflects the requirements in Articles 12 and 14 of the FCNM. It was also specifically endorsed by Council of Europe Recommendation R (2000) 4 of the Committee of Ministers on the Education of Roma/Gypsy children in Europe.[134] The Czech constitution recognises the right of citizens constituting minorities to education in their own language[135] and there have been suggestions that some teachers should learn the Romani language. However, at present the pre-school education initiative still devotes resources to enabling Romani children to catch up with the linguistic abilities of the majority Czechs. In some areas with a high proportion of Roma, an adviser who is Rom may assist with translation and understanding.[136]

The Slovak Minister for Education, attending a conference on the Roma in Eastern and Central Europe in 1992, advocated mother tongue teaching for the Roma as it was found to facilitate the learning experience.[137] Nevertheless, in a 1996 resolution the Roma were the targets of a programme for citizens in need of special care, and measures under the policy included alternative teaching programmes with 'an emphasis on better Slovak language instruction'.[138] A policy of integration as adopted in Bulgaria and Slovakia can often hamper efforts to deliver mother-tongue language provision.[139] The absence of Romani teachers also presents an added complication.

Inability of the school system to cater for minority groups

In the 1995 Hearing of Roma/Gypsy Women of West, Central and East Europe the delegates asked the European countries to consider the cultural specificity of the children when making educational provision. It was felt that this must include recognition of the Romani language and culture in the school curriculum.[140] A more recent Save the Children report examining state education practices across Europe concludes:

> There are still almost no references in mainstream curricula to the history of the Roma peoples in Europe and their participation in key historical processes, despite a presence that dates back some 600 years.[141]

---

134   Council of Europe Recommendation R (2000) 4 of the Committee of Ministers On the Education of Roma/Gypsy *children in Europe* Para 12.

135   Czech Constitution, Charter Article 25 (2) in Blaustein and Flanz *supra* n42.

136   Central Europe on-line 'Czech official says government is doing its part to help Roma' 10 October 1997.

137   Project on Ethnic Relations Conference Report the Romanies in Central and Eastern Europe: *Illusions and Reality* (1992) Stupava, Czechoslovakia at 19.

138   *The Resolution of the Government of the the Slovak Republic to the proposal of the activities and measures in order to solve the problems of citizens in need of special care* 30 April 1996, Ministry of Labour, Social affairs and Family.

139   Meijknecht *supra* n66.

140   Gimenez Adelantado, *A Hearing of Roma/Gypsy women of West, Central and East Europe*, Council of Europe. 29–30 September 1995 at 3, para. 13. (EG/TSI (95) 2).

141   *Supra* n126 Summary at 33.

In the UK, an LEA survey of travelling children on school rolls in 1967–70 revealed some worrying attitudes amongst teachers, many of which continue to be expressed today:

> Most teachers saw traveller children as socially and culturally deprived and disadvantaged. There seemed a widespread belief that the travellers had no culture or even sub-culture as such but merely a way of life-and one which met with general teacher disapproval … several thought that education could play a role in preventing the children from having to follow in their parents footsteps.[142]

This inflexible and ignorant approach from some school authorities is deeply entrenched and many families are still reluctant to send their children to school as a result. One mother in Leicester stated in 1993:

> I never had no education, and I do not want my children being educated. They do not teach them Gypsy ways, they teach them travelling's bad. And they teach them bad ways. All my children's trusty but them gaujo children's not. They got no respect.[143]

Research on other minority experiences in education supports the view that children withdraw from school in late primary and secondary level if they feel that what they are learning is irrelevant to the life they are leading.[144]

It is apparent that most of the problems that teachers raise about the behaviour of the Roma student occur because of the collision between two very different cultures. Romani culture and language are transmitted orally,[145] reading and writing are unfamiliar concepts and yet they will be expected to progress at the same level as children who are familiar with books and show confidence in basic writing skills.[146] Similarly, Romani children have been bought up with distrust for Gadje society and separation is maintained between the two cultures. Entering an alien environment inhabited by a majority of total strangers is difficult for every child, but the difficulty is compounded when there is imbued, mutual distrust.[147]

Generally, it would appear that teachers are insufficiently trained in educating minorities and that school curricula fail to incorporate anything of the Romani

---

142   Reiss *supra* n93.

143   Rhys Morris D *The Education of Gypsy and Traveller Children in the European Community* (1995) Unpublished MA thesis, Leicester University School of Education, Leicester UK at 25.

144   Cunnington (1991) cited in Smith, Tracy *supra* n115 at 249.

145   Although in some countries, such as Finland, the Romany has been written – dictionaries and grammar books have been developed to assist in teaching: as observed by Myntti, Kristian 'National Minorities and Minority legislation in Finland' in Packer, J and Myntti, K (eds.) *The Protection of Ethnic and Linguistic Minorities in Europe* (1993) Abo Akademie Univ.: Finland at 93.

146   Lee, 'Alternative Education: Lessons from Gypsy Thought and Practice' (1991) *British Journal of Educational Studies* Vol 39 at 315.

147   *Ibid.* at 316 and Zatta 'Oral Tradition and Social Context: Language and Cognitive Structure Among the Rom' in Salo, MT 100 years of Gypsy Studies (1990) Gypsy Lore Society. Cheverly, Maryland at 74.

culture.[148] The pupils are alienated and are thus bound to be disruptive and unenthusiastic; the teachers are confused and unsympathetic.[149] There is often a stalemate and it is the traveller's schooling that will suffer. Jimenez Gonzalez, a Spanish Gitano representative, reports that there is no account taken of the different values of the Gypsy students and few teachers have any familiarity with their culture, interests and language:

> All this prepares for and conditions methodological, pedagogical and didactic assumptions which place Gypsy students in an inferior position, denigrate them and show contempt for them.[150]

Specialist staff from the British Traveller Education service expressed dismay at the lack of cultural awareness and interest exhibited by many teachers the absence of intercultural teacher-training can be seen in the responses of several British teachers in research by Derrington and Kendall:

> One senior teacher expressed the view that traveller children may be better off having their own segregated provision, with specialist teachers, until they were ready to be assimilated into mainstream education. Another was adamant that 'They will behave and act like any other pupil in the school!'[151]

The same research also found that many traveller students did not want aspects of their culture to be discussed in class, rather they were concerned to be treated equally (without regard to their difference).[152] This cultural denial is understandable when we consider Charles Taylor's arguments concerning the misrecognition that results when cultural identity is not respected.[153] It is easy to see how this could manifest itself as denial in a classroom context. Ian Hanock has observed that denying traveller identity may be a coping strategy in order to avoid abuse and social exclusion.[154]

Skutnabb-Kangas highlights the importance of minority language teaching in schools alongside the dominant language.[155] She notes that immersion into a foreign language regularly results in poor academic achievement.[156] It is inevitable that it will also encourage disinterest and result in irregular attendance. Her report is critical of assimilationist educational strategies, noting their effects on the minority culture:

---

148   Liégeois *supra* n8 Chapter 15.

149   The question of whether students need to see themselves reflected in the curriculum in order to learn effectively is critically addressed by Glazer, Nathan *We are All Multi-culturalists Now* (1997) Harvard University Press at 49.

150   The Gypsy Council for Education, Culture, Welfare and Civil Rights *supra* n45.

151   Derrington and Kendall *supra* n31 at 64.

152   *Ibid.* at 99.

153   See Chapter 2 at 40.

154   Hancock, Ian 'The struggle for control of identity' (1997) *Transitions* Vol 4, 4 September.

155   Skutnabb-Kangas *supra* n131.

156   *Ibid.* at 19.

Ethnicism and linguisicism are more sophisticated but equally sufficient weapons as biological racism in committing ethnocide, the destruction of the socio-cultural (often including linguistic) identity of a group.[157]

Resource allocation is a significant problem. The ad hoc, localised nature of many of the measures to improve traveller schooling often means that funding can be subject to the vagaries of the market and that there is little opportunity for long-term secure planning for projects. Some successful pilot projects fail to receive financial support from national governments and are forced to rely on support from the SOROS Foundation and Open Society Institute. The Save the Children report expresses dismay at the lack of progress despite numerous successful local initiatives and projects.[158]

Daily discrimination at school by pupils, parents and teachers

A report on the status of Romani education in the Czech Republic[159] revealed an extremely worrying factor in discrimination against Romany children at school; that of teacher acquiescence.[160] Over a five-month period, the researcher witnessed school practices in seven key areas and interviewed teachers, teaching assistants, school directors and others involved in providing education for Roma children. Conway found that with regard to classroom racism: 'It is fair to say that the basic school teacher does not want to, or does not know how to deal with the Romani child'. One special-school teacher stated: 'I get embarrassed when the other teachers won't take things from Romani children's hands, because they're afraid of getting lice or fleas'.[161] The results of Conway's research echo the findings of a European Commission investigation which culminated in the 1989 *Resolution on School provision for Gypsy and Traveller Children*.[162]

The effects of the teachers' acquiescence in racist stereotyping and bullying are considered in the Czech report with reference to the work of Trevor Holme, an educational psychologist. Holme looks at the effects of labelling a child rather than their behaviour, for example 'You're stupid' or 'You're a thief'. He contends that the effects of such behaviour by teachers is: 'damaging and hurtful ... reduces self-esteem ... makes the young person think he/she has to change their whole personality

---

157   Skutnabb-Kangas *supra* n131 at 13.

158   *Supra* n126 Summary at 42.

159   Conway, L, *On the Status of Romani Education in the Czech Republic* (1996) Citizens' Solidarity and Tolerance Movement (HOST) Prague.

160   Literature on the education policy in the United Kingdom in the 1970s reveals similar racist stereotyping and acquiescence from teachers – see Jeffcoate *supra* n34 at 102. The Czech Republic is a fledgling democracy and it is probably fair to say that teachers have no adequate training on how to counter prejudice which has existed for generations.

161   *Supra* n159 at 33.

162   *Supra* n3; Liégeois *supra* n18 passim.

not just their behaviour'.[163] Derrington and Kendall's research found that 80% of surveyed Traveller pupils had encountered racist abuse and bullying.[164]

Rhys Morris looks to a study by the Spanish anthropologist Tomas Buezas on the 'Attitudes and Prejudices of Teachers and Pupils Regarding Other peoples and Cultures'. He found that teachers often reinforce the prejudice of their pupils and that Gitanos inspire the most prejudice from teachers and pupils alike. He found that 5% of teachers and 11.4% of pupils claim that given the choice they would banish the Gypsies from Spain.[165] It is likely that many more would prefer not to share their classroom.

There is a disproportionate number of exclusions and suspensions of traveller pupils in the UK.[166] One Scottish study found that much perceived indiscipline by Scottish Traveller pupils could be attributed to bullying and racism from other students.[167] There is also a tendency to equate poverty with stupidity, with teachers exhibiting low expectations of Roma children, hence the widespread diagnoses of special educational needs in the UK[168] and the use of special schools and classes elsewhere.[169] Low expectations become a self-fulfilling prophecy as students come to view themselves as failures and extricate themselves from the educational process.[170]

The attitudes of non-Roma parents also cause problems for two principle reasons. Firstly, because of prejudiced passed on to their children but also where they voice objection to integrated education. In some cases parents have withdrawn their children from mixed-schools and in a few of these examples schools have chosen to retain segregated teaching in order to placate this racism.[171]

A common consequence: Special schools and segregation

As a result of the perceived difficulties of educating Roma in the mainstream school system, many children across Europe have been referred to special schools.[172] Some of these schools are established primarily to cater for children who have learning

---

163   *Ibid.* at 34 and Holme, 'The Importance of Self-esteem' and 'Enhancing Self-concept' (1994) 363 TMH (Teacher training manuals).

164   Derrington and Kendall *supra* n31 at 178.

165   Rhys Morris *supra* n143 at App. 3. The extent of Spanish Anti-Roma sentiment is also noted by Etxeberria *supra* n54 at 297.

166   DfEE *Tackling Truancy Together: A strategy document* (1999) London: DfEE.

167   Lloyd et al. 'Teachers and Gypsy Travellers' (1999) *Scottish Educational Review* Vol. 31 pp 48–65.

168   Derrington and Kendall *supra* n31 at 168 note that 50% of their sample of secondary school children were on the SEN register.

169   Save the Children *supra* n126 and Smith *supra* n115 at 250

170   Open Society Institute *supra* n80

171   *Ibid.* See also Danova *supra* n74 at 7.

172   This is not simply a problem in the CEE countries. The report by Liégeois *supra* n18 at 83–86 has examples of segregated schooling in the the Federal the Republic of Germany, France and the UK. The Council of Europe's Commissioner on Human Rights also found examples in Finland, Denmark and Greece. Comm DH(2006)1 Council of Europe. ERRC

difficulties and often they have a disproportionately high number of Romani pupils on their records.[173] Often, discriminatory IQ tests are used to designate Roma pupils as having particular educational needs and in some cases financial incentives are offered to attract Roma pupils away from mainstream schools.[174] In the Czech Republic one study revealed 12 different tests in operation at 63 testing centres.[175] Acton argues that the nature of assessment tests, used throughout Europe, reveals less about the ability of the candidates than the ethnocentric perspectives of the testers.[176] In most cases the quality of education offered at such schools is inferior and the curriculum is reduced.[177]

The common practice of Roma attending special schools was noted in the report on education in the Czech Republic by Conway.[178] In an interview with Central *Europe On-line*, Milan Pospisil, Secretary of the Czech Council of Nationalities, recognised the problem of poor educational achievement in the special schools.[179] Pupils will rarely complete their elementary (primary) level of schooling and the gap between elementary and secondary is so great that very few students are able to bridge it.[180] The Advisory Committee on the FCNM has recently expressed concern that children are still being placed in such schools on the strength of psychological tests. The tests have been revised but the Committee expressed concern that the revisions may not have been adequate.[181]

In Slovakia, the 'Osobitna Skola' or special schools are used in a similar way to segregate Roma children from other pupils. The Roma Participation Program found that many of these children come from out − of-town ghettos and that such segregation serves to reinforce prejudice and disadvantage experienced by the Roma pupil.[182]

Campland: Racial segregation of Roma in Italy (2000) demonstrates that many Roma have no education or are segregated due to camp life.

173   Conway *supra* n159 at Chapter 1.

174   Cahn et al. 'Roma in the educational systems of Central and Eastern Europe' (1998) ERRC Report; Danova *supra* n74 at 5 and Rostas and Nicoara 'Advocacy Strategies to combat segregation' in *supra* n74 at 115–6.

175   Jiri, D and Palatova, H 'Results from research on the use of pyschological tests in pedagogical pyschological advice centres' (1998) *Vychovne poradenstvi* No. 16 at 31.

176   Acton, T (1984) quoted in Liégeois *supra* n18 at 85.

177   Open Society Institute Research on Selected Roma Education Programs in Central and Eastern Europe (2001) found that the curriculum in remedial schools in the Czech Republic was 95 pages, compared to 336 pages for the regular curriculum.

178   *Ibid.*

179   Central Europe on-line 6 Novmeber 1997. Interview by editor Bruce Konviser.

180   Information received by the International Committee on the Elimination of Racial Discrimination suggests that 20% of Roma children attend special schools compared to 3% of children from the majority. *Supra* n11 at para. 57.

181   Advisory Committee on the Framework Convention for the Protection of National Minorities (2005) *Second Opinion on the Czech republic* 24 February 2005 ACFC/INF/OP/II (2005)002 para. 146.

182   Zubak, Lubomir and Lagryn, Antonin 'Roma are tired of being studied' Roma Participation Program Reporter See App 2. Glazer *supra* n149 at 136 argues that educational segregation reinforces separate ethnic perspectives on life in general.

Special schools have also been used in Hungary to segregate difficult Roma children who are linguistically or otherwise disadvantaged in mainstream education. In 1985, 36% of children in schools for the mentally impaired were Rom and 15.2% of all Rom school children were in such schools.[183] In certain crisis areas the percentage has been much higher – in the area of Ercsi 90% of pupils were Wlach Roma who speak Romani as their mother tongue.[184] It has been noted that where integrative efforts were attempted Roma children were ridiculed and despised by the other students and that such initiatives were seldom successful.[185] An investigation by Human Rights Watch in 1995, found that some children were not examined before being placed in the remedial class and the reintegration of these children was rare.[186]

A 2003 amendment to the Law on Education introduced a ban on segregation and efforts have been made to integrate at least 10% of the disadvantaged pupils each year.[187] These initiatives have been supported by generous grants for schools and community groups from the Phare programme.[188] Following the decision in the Ferenc Pethe case, discussed below, the National Integration Plan was established with the aim of achieving complete desegregation by 2008. The plan includes special assistance for Romani education and designated financial support. It also includes guidance to schools and specifically endorses an intercultural approach where majority children must be taught about the culture of local minorities.[189] Yet progress remains slow and in some cases there is de facto segregation within mainstream school system.[190] Lilla Farkas notes that primary schools often persuaded Roma parents to educate their children at home and that a substantial number of Roma children may be virtually excluded from school as a consequence.[191]

In the first legal challenge of its kind, a group of 14 Roma challenged discriminatory practices in Ferenc Pethe primary school. Around half the 531 pupils at the school were Roma, 207 were assigned to completely separate classes, 38 to classes for pupils with mental handicap and only 5 to integrated classes. For 10 years the Roma pupils were not permitted to enter the cafeteria or gymanzium in the main building and attended separate graduation ceremonies. A reporter for the Hungarian newspaper

183   Crowe, D *A History of the Gypsies of Eastern Europe and Russia* (1995) St Martins Press, NY at 95.

184   Reported in *Népszabadság* 2 February 1996.

185   According to the head of the Experts' and Rehabilitation Committee for Learning Skills Examination of Fejér County quoted in *Népszabadság*, 2 February 1996.

186   Human Rights Watch *Rights denied: The Roma of Hungary* (1995) HRW NY passim.

187   Report of the Commissioner for Human rights *On the Human Rights Situation of The Roma, Sinti and Travellers in Europe* CommDH (2006)1 Council of Europe at para. 53.

188   Mohácsi, Viktória 'Government Initiatives: Hungary's school integration program' in PILI *supra* n74 at 239

189   Article 48 Public Education Act 2002.

190   Nemeth, Szilvia Roma Education Initiative *Annual Research and Evaluation Report Hungary* (2005)

191   Farkas, Lilla 'Education, Education and More education' (2004) eumap.org, *Journal of the EU Monitoring and Advocacy Programme*, Open Society Institute.

Magyar Narancs found that the exclusion was requested by non-Romani parents.[192] The plaintiffs were successful at each stage of the legal process, culminating in a decision by the Supreme Court in 2002 which found violations of the Constitution, Civil Code, the Public Education Law 79/1993 and the Law on the Rights of National and Ethnic Minorities 77/1993.[193] In a more recent judicial decision, the Debrecen Appeal Court found that efforts to integrate seven primary schools by the Miskolc local council without redrawing the catchment areas amounted to a violation of equal treatment as it constituted de facto segregation and was contrary to Equal Treatment Directive 2000/43/EC.[194] In 2006, the Committee on the Rights of the Child welcomed measures aimed at desegregated education but continued to express concern about the disadvantage and stigma faced by Romani children, particularly in access to services, in Hungarian society.[195] The Committee recommended, inter alia, additional measures in education to eradicate social exclusion of Roma children.[196]

In Bulgaria, the legal segregation of schooling for Romani children was abolished in 1992. Nevertheless, as Marushiakova and Popov observed, 'Gypsy-schools' continued to exist against the wishes of the vast majority of Bulgarian Roma.[197] Linguistic and socio-economic disadvantage combines to prevent the Rom from attending 'normal' schools, with the result that many are thereafter unemployable.

While educational segregation in itself does not necessarily contravene the non-discrimination criteria of international human rights instruments, providing it is both in accord with the accepted standards of mainstream education and if it is voluntarily undertaken,[198] it presents several obvious disadvantages. Such schools are often unpopular with Roma parents: there is very little choice involved for the child who may have been ostracised and alienated in the mainstream school; issues of intolerance between Roma and Gadjes cannot be addressed at an early age and thereby the potential for animosity and xenophobia is increased; and finally, they prevent schools from addressing the important demands and needs of cultural minorities.

Indeed, international criticism of this practice has led to some significant changes in this area in the last five years. In the Czech Republic, Slovakia and Bulgaria efforts have been made to promote integration. However they have often faced obstacles from non-Roma and they are seldom adequately funded. In October 2004, The Bulgarian parliament rejected that Draft Law for Educational of Minority Children

---

192   'Graduation in separate ways' *Magyar Narancs* 19 June 1997.

193   ERRC 'Roma Sue School in North-eastern Hungary: the submission against the principle of the Ferenc Pethe Primary school, Tiszavasvari, Hungary' (1998) *Roma Rights*.

194   Decision of 9 June 2006 reported by Public law Interest Initiative 'Press release: Appeal victory for Roma in Miskolc, Hungary'.

195   Committee on the Rights of the Child 41st session *Concluding Observations: Hungary* CRC/C/Hun/CRC/C0/2, 27 January 2006.

196   *Ibid.* Paras 62 and 63.

197   Maurushiakova, Elena and Popov, Vesselin '"Gypsy schools" in Bulgaria' (1994) *Promoting Human Rights and Civil Society* Newsletter No 4 p5.

198   Cullen *supra* n26 at 155.

which explicitly included a special fund for the desegregation of Roma children.[199] In the Basque region of Spain, policies have recently been announced recognising the need for an intercultural approach which rejects remedial provision, but again, implementation of these policies is fraught with difficulties.[200]

It is possible for segregated schools to present excellent standards of education for their Rom pupils. One such example is the Gandhi Gimnazium, a residential school in Pécs, Hungary, which was established at the initiative of local Roma organisations. The school's director, János Derdák, himself of Romany origin, defined the aim of the school as to create an elite among Romanies who will work in the interest of their country.[201] The syllabus incorporates Romani culture alongside Hungarian culture through the traditional curriculum and the expectations of the students are high.[202] This school is certainly nothing like the special schools for students with learning difficulties and significant educational needs. The Ghandi school is not without its critics, even among the Roma community. Indeed, some former pupils felt that they had been 'cocooned' from the real world and that a separate education had not prepared them for life in the discriminatory, competitive environment that awaited them.[203] As Luciak recognises, separate schooling may have beneficial short-term effects for the student but there may be longer-term problems in the absence of intercultural dialogue and understanding.[204]

The Alternative Foundation Trade school in Szolnok[205] is another initiative supported by the National Minority Self-Government of the Gypsy population, aimed at enabling disadvantaged school pupils to gain the necessary skills for specific trades.[206] The trade school was established in 1996 and is open to both Roma and Gadjes; the success of the project has led to its adoption in other Hungarian regions.[207] The head teacher of a Gypsy secondary school in Budapest argues that separate schools are needed not just because of the level of discrimination in mainstream education:

---

199   Human Rights Project, Bulgaria Press Release 'Bulgaria: Roma children not children of Bulgaria, Decides Parliament' 11 October 2004 www.bghelsinki.org.

200   Etxeberria *supra* n54 at 296.

201   TAZ 'Pécs is home to first all Romany High school' 14 November 1994, p 11. Tragically, János Derdák died in a car accident in January 1999. Katz, Susan 'Emerging from the cocoon of Romani pride: The first graduates of the Gandhi Secondary School in Hungary' (2005) *Intercultural Education* Vol 16, 3 pp 247–261.

202   CSCE *Human Dimension Seminar on Roma in the CSCE Region* 1994 CSCE, Warsaw at 26.

203   Katz *supra* n201 passim.

204   Luciak, Mikael 'Minority schooling and intercultural education: a comparison of recent developments in the old and new EU member states' (2006) *Intercultural Education* Vol 17, 1 pp 73–80 at 78.

205   Csillei, Béla 'Roma opportunity' The Alternative Vocational Foundation school of Szolnok 1998 Hungary. Unpublished paper.

206   Three trades were selected for the 1996 programme: computer operator, park caretaker and road maintenance skilled worker.

207   Csillei *supra* n205 at p 11.

We learn in a different way and require teachers to teach in a different style, but we also need to develop a real knowledge of our own culture, our own language and our own history. These things are not taught in normal Hungarian schools.[208]

At present, there remains an insufficient number of well-educated Roma in most countries. This means that the special school system is open to abuse by educators who know little of the Romany culture. Segregated schooling must be approached with caution. Where it is run by and for the Roma, it can be viewed as an example of collective rights in practice. However, it evidently contradicts principles of equality and can serve to undermine tolerance. The Roma Education Program, financed by the Soros Foundation places the emphasis on integration rather than separation:

They are not separated in society and need to know how to communicate with non-Gypsies, to learn about their own cultures as well as their own.[209]

There is a catch-22 situation. Discrimination prevents many Roma from completing school. Yet at the same time, how is this discrimination to be addressed if not from an early age through the education system?

Czech special schools in the European Court of Human Rights

In 2006, the European Court of Human Rights issued a judgement in the case of a group of 18 Czech Roma from Ostrava who had been educated in special schools.[210] The applicants contended that the practice amounted to racial segregation contrary to Article 14 which had deprived them of the right to an education as guaranteed by Article 2 of Protocol 1.

The Court recognised that indirect discrimination which did not specifically target a particular minority could fall within Article 14 if it had disproportionately prejudicial effects on that minority. However, they deferred to the views of educational psychologists on the matter of suitability of these pupils to mainstream schooling and seemingly accepted the legitimacy of the practice of sending the majority of Roma pupils to such schools. While acknowledging the concerns regarding the prevalence of special schools for the Roma the Court was not empowered to look beyond the facts of the present case. A proactive approach to non-discrimination would have enabled the Court to reflect the concerns of other international bodies including the Advisory Committee of the FCNM. The decision is to be lamented and again highlights some of the flaws of an individualist approach to human rights in which there is little room to recognise the inherent disadvantage experienced by members of particular minority groups. The use of culturally insensitive testing methods was not addressed by the majority and the disadvantage experienced by Roma entering the education system as a result of factors beyond their control – such as poor housing, high unemployment and inadequate health care, was again beyond

208   Jozsef Choledroczi interviewed by Simon Evans 'Separate but Superior?' *Hungary Report* Archive 2.05, 22 July 1996.
209   Ferenc Arato interview by Evans *ibid.*
210   *DH and Others* v *Czech Republic* App 57325/00 Judgement of 7 February 2006.

the Courts remit. Significant weight was attached to the presence of consent by the parents without any consideration of the possibility of misinformation, financial incentives to attend special schools and the extent of parental illiteracy. Separate and ethnically homogenous schools are compatible with human rights standards if they are based on free, informed parental choice and if the education is of a good standard. However, as Petrova observes 'With respect to the Roma ... it is very unlikely that somewhere in Central and Eastern Europe such a primary school exists'.[211] The Court was also unable to agree that affirmative action was required through an enlightened approach to Article 14 in order to achieve genuine equality of opportunity for children attending special schools.[212] As shown in Chapter 3, this lack of compulsion to provide affirmative action measures is attributable to the individual emphasis of international human rights norms.

Judge Cabral Barreto, who has adopted a purposive approach to the concept of non-discrimination in similar cases, offered the only dissenting opinion. He reasoned that the Czech Governments own recognition of discrimination is obvious from the statistics – namely that 80–90% of special school pupils are of Romany origin.[213] Furthermore, he opines that the states differential treatment made matters worse for the pupils and therefore could not be interpreted as a form of beneficial affirmative action designed to redress educational disadvantage. An appeal has now been lodged before the Grand Chamber.

A similar case concerning segregation in Croatia was filed with the European Court of Human Rights in 2004. The application was made by 15 Roma children forced to attend racially segregated classes within mainstream schools. These classes offered a substantially reduced curriculum. Allegations of racial discrimination were rejected by the Croatian courts and the applicants now claim violations of Article 3 (inhuman and degrading treatment), protocol 1 Article 2 (the right to education), Article 6 (the right to a fair trial), Article 13 (the right to an effective remedy) and Article 14 (non-discrimination).[214]

The International Human Right to education

The basic right of every child to an education is laid down in a variety of international instruments. The United Nations Convention against Discrimination in Education (1960) prohibits segregated education and the provision of inferior standard education to certain persons or groups.[215] Article 5(1) recognises the right of national minorities to carry on their own educational activities, including school maintenance,

211   Petrova, Dimitrina 'From segregated to Integrated Education of the Roma in Europe' in Public Interest Law Initiative *supra* n74 at 27.

212   See the comments of Judge Costa in para. 6 of his concurring opinion.

213   See the dissenting comments of Judge Cabral Barreto para. 2.

214   ERRC Press Release 'Croatian Romani Children Sue at European Court of Human Rights over Racial Segregation in Schools' ERRC.

215   Article 1(b) Convention against Discrimination in Education (1960) Adopted by the General Conference of the United Nations Educational, Scientific and Cultural Organization on 14 December 1960.

providing that the state is not obliged to provide financial assistance, that attendance is optional and that it is not exercised in a way that would make the minority unable to understand the dominant language. Admissions processes that deny equal access to education for the Roma and the inferior curriculum offered in segregated schools would thus appear to breach the Convention. However, in response, states could argue that segregation is voluntary and is therefore expressly permitted by the CDE. Furthermore, the CDE does not prohibit separate schooling based on disability, the rationale offered for separate schools by several CEE states.

Henrard argues that the obligations in Article 5(1) should be interpreted purposively such that states may be obliged to finance schools for minorities if state schools are not sufficiently pluralistic as this is compatible with the obligation to respect parents' ideological and philosophical convictions in educational choice.[216]

Following on from the CDE, Article 13 of the Covenant on Economic, Social and Cultural Rights defines the purpose of education to include the promotion of 'understanding and tolerance among all nations and all racial, ethnic or religious groups'.[217] Yet there is no recognition of, and thus no recommendations for alleviating, the specific educational problems faced by certain minority groups. Both the ICESC and the Convention on the Rights of the Child (CRC) provide that free primary education must be compulsory, but there is no requirement as to the quality of such provision.[218]

Elaboration of the Covenant provisions can be found in Article 29 CRC which expressly recognises the significance of culture and family life. Article 29(1)c provides that *the education of the child* shall be directed towards:

> the development of respect for the child's parents, his or her own culture, identity, language and values, for the national values of the country in which the child is living, the country from which he or she may originate, and for civilisations different from his or her own.

However, the provision omits a guarantee of multi-cultural or mother-tongue education. Article 30, which provides for the interests of members of minorities, does so only in a negative formulation comparable to Article 27 of the ICCPR. Article 2 reiterates the basic principle of non-discrimination in relation to any of the substantive rights, but it is somewhat surprising to note that there is no express provision dealing with the quality of education. The implementation of the Convention is examined

---

216 Henrard *supra* n12 at 407.

217 Article 13(1) International Covenant on Economic, Social and Cultural Rights (1966).

218 *Ibid.* Article 13(2)(a) and Article 13. CRC Article 28 provides a) make primary education compulsory and available free to all; b) encourage the development of different forms of secondary education, including general and vocational education, make them available and accessible to every child, and take appropriate measures such as the introduction of free education and offering financial assistance in the case of need; c) make higher education accessible to all on the basis of capacity by every appropriate means; d) make educational and vocational information and guidance available and accessible to all children; e) take measures to encourage regular attendance at schools and the reduction of drop-out rates.

by a series of reports on its implementation by state parties every three years.[219] There is no opportunity for an individual to take a case against a signatory state for breach of obligations under the Convention. However, the Committee overseeing the implementation of the Convention has issued critical reports that recognise the educational disadvantage suffered by members of some minority groups.[220] Following the report of the Czech Republic, the Committee found:

> ... no adequate measures have been taken to prevent and combat all forms of discriminatory practices against children belonging to minorities, including Roma children, and to ensure their full access to health, education and other social services. The committee is concerned that the principles and provisions of the Convention are not fully respected as regards to Roma children, in particular those who are in detention or otherwise institutionalised.[221]

The issue of segregation is also dealt with by the Convention on the Elimination of All Forms of Racial Discrimination.[222] Indeed, segregation and discrimination in education is prohibited by Article 5 ICERD. The ICERD also accepts special measures of temporary duration in the interests of remedying the disadvantageous positions of some minorities:

> Special measures taken for the sole purpose of securing adequate advancement of certain racial or ethnic groups or individuals requiring such protection as may be necessary in order to ensure such groups or individuals equal enjoyment or exercise of human rights and fundamental freedoms shall not be deemed racial discrimination, provided, however, that such measures do not as a consequence, lead to the maintenance of separate rights for different racial groups and that they shall not be continued after the objectives for which they were taken have been achieved.[223]

Thus, temporary initiatives, which seek to establish special educational programmes or develop the curriculum in order to recognise the contribution of the Roma in society, would not constitute a form of discriminatory treatment contrary to international law. The Committee on the Elimination of Racial Discrimination has expressed greater condemnation of educational policy than the other UN treaty bodies.[224] It has been critical of the Czech Government's measures in education and employment with respect to the Roma minority.[225] Their 1998 report noted that the level of education and

---

219   United Nations Convention on the Rights of the Child (1989) Article 44.

220   On the composition of the Committee see Article 43 of the Convention on the Rights of the Child (1989)

221   United Nations Concluding Observations of the Committee on the Rights of the Child: Czech Republic 27/10/97 CRC/C/15/Add. 81 para. 15.

222   ICERD Article 3 provides, inter alia, that state parties undertake to prevent, prohibit and eradicate all practices of racial segregation and apartheid.

223   Article 1(4).

224   Rooker, Marcia *The International Supervision of Protection of Romany People in Europe* (2004) Univ. of Nijmegen at 202.

225   The Czech Governments initiatives in the field of education and other areas in respect of the Roma can be found in the Resolution of Government of the the the Czech Republic of 29.10.97 No 686 on the report on the situation of the Romani community in the Czech Republic and on the present situation in the Romani community (1997).

vocational skills was comparatively low, while unemployment was correspondingly much higher than the average. However, in keeping with their obligations under the Convention, the Czech Ministry of the Interior had instructed every local authority to create a post of 'Roma assistant and advisor'. Roma assistants are being trained to 'bridge the gap between teachers and pupils and also to encourage Roma parents to overcome their mistrust of the school system'.[226] Nevertheless, the Committee expressed concern that only the basics of Roma culture and language were taught at a small number of teacher-training colleges. It was added that 'To promote the social integration of members of the Roma population, greater importance should be given to education in their mother tongue'.[227]

Thus, the Committee implicitly recognised that the goal of integration is dependent, to some extent, on the maintenance of minority identity through instruction in the minority language. In 2001, the Committee revisited these issues and again expressed concern that segregation of the Roma continued and that it may amount to a violation of Article 3 of the CERD.[228]

The extent of concern has been such that the Committee adopted its Recommendation XXVII on Discrimination Against Roma in 2000. In the field of education, the Recommendation requires states to avoid segregation, to raise the quality of education and attainment in schools and to improve retention. States are requested to take urgent measures to train educators, assistants and teachers from among the Roma community and to include Roma culture and history in teaching materials.[229]

Research by Marcia Rooker examining the reports of the international treaty bodies in the field of education demonstrates a patchy picture of suggestions and recommendations falling short of concrete proposals for action.[230] In 2000, the UN Committee on the Rights of the Child reviewed the situation in Slovakia and expressed concern at the use of segregated education for the Roma. Yet its recommendations, as noted by Rostas and Nicoara, are weakly worded, suggesting that the state party design measures to ensure that Romani children have 'equal access to opportunities to attend regular education and supportive education if necessary'.[231] It was only when the Human Rights Committee reported in July 2003[232] that the tone changed to one of condemnation by which time other European states were introducing desegregation strategies to some extent as a response to perceived EU accession demands.

In the past, international human rights provisions have focused on the availability of education, particularly at primary level, but they have avoided the issue of content

---

226 United Nations CERD Summary *Record of the 1254th Meeting: Czech Republic* 11 March 1998 CERD/C/SR.1254. Paras 12 and 13.

227 *Ibid.* Mr Diaconu (Country Rapporteur) para. 27.

228 *Concluding observations of the Committee on the Elimination of Racial Discrimination: Czech Republic* CERD/C/304/Add. 109 1 May 2001.

229 Paras 23 and 26 respectively.

230 Rooker *supra* n224, Chapter VII.

231 Rostas and Nicoara *supra* n174 at 118 and *Concluding Observations of the Committee on the Rights of the Child: Slovakia* 23 October 2000 CRC/C/15/add. 140.

232 *Concluding Observations of the Human Rights Committee: Slovakia* 22 August 2003 CPR/CO/78/SVK.

and quality of such education. This has allowed states a wide margin of appreciation. However, the recent CERD recommendation on Discrimination Against Roma recognises these failings and specifically advocates the need for an intercultural pedagogy.[233]

Regional human rights provisions on education

The ECHR as originally drafted did not deal with any right to education per se. This deficiency was remedied by Protocol 1, Article 2 in 1952:

> No person shall be denied the right to education. In the exercise of any functions which it assumes in relation to education and to teaching, the State shall respect the right of parents to ensure such education and teaching in conformity with their own religious and philosophical convictions.

A member state that has ratified the First Protocol can be challenged in the European Court of Human Rights if they fail to respect the right to education.[234] Article 2 is not as extensive as the provision in the Convention on the Rights of the Child and as such appears to serve a very limited purpose in isolation. Giving the limited wording of Article 2 it may perhaps be more prudent to mount a challenge in conjunction with Article 14 of the *ECHR* which prohibits discrimination in the implementation of the convention on grounds which include national or ethnic origin. The *Belgian Linguistics Case*[235] centred on the interplay of these two provisions in addition to a separate application under Article 8 for interference with family life. The case concerned an application from French speaking parents challenging the Belgian school system which had divided the country into various regions and denied access in some regions to French language instruction. The court found that denial of the right of access to instruction in the minority language was a breach of the two provisions. As far as Article 8 was concerned there was held to be no right to be educated in the language of one's parents by the public authorities or with their aid.

Cullen criticises the restrictive interpretation of the Court and highlights the earlier decision of the Commission, which found a violation where the subsidies to minority language schools in unilingual areas had been withdrawn and studies completed in minority language were not recognised by the education system.[236] The cultural protection of minorities in the education system does not appear to have been particularly advanced by the Court's interpretation.

Multi-ethnic education is implicitly endorsed in the Council of Europe's Framework Convention on the Protection of National Minorities, discussed in Chapter 6 below.[237] Article 12 requires states to 'where appropriate, take measures

---

233   Para. 18.

234   Article 34 of the ECHR allows the Court to hear individual or group applications alleging a violation of a protocol right.

235   *The Belgian Linguistics Case* (1962) 1 EHRR at 252.

236   Cullen *supra* n26 above, at 171.

237   C/E Framework Convention on the Protection of National Minorities H (95), October 1995.

in the field of education and research to foster knowledge of the culture, history, language and religion of their national minorities and of the majority'. Intercultural dialogue is also referred to in Article 6 of the FCNM.[238] To this end, opportunities for teacher training and access to text books shall be developed to enable a policy of equal opportunities for all.[239] Thornberry notes that the 'climate of tolerance and dialogue' envisaged in the explanatory report will have a potential impact in many aspects of the curricula, notably with the avoidance of negative stereotypes and enhanced intercommunal contacts.[240] Having analysed the travaux preparatoire and reports by the Advisory Committee, Thornberry finds that the intercultural approach is inherent in Article 12:

> The mere removal of offensive stereotypes from textbooks is not enough. What is required is a more active policy of presenting minority culture in a fair and balanced fashion, highlighting the contribution of the group to the cultural richness of the nation as a whole.[241]

The right to learn and communicate in the mother tongue is also expressly recognised by Article 14 when numbers and resources demand it.[242] While encouraging for the future of multi-ethnic education there is no imposition of positive obligations on states and mother-tongue teaching will depend on resources, numbers and demand. It is thus submitted that in practice, the absence of positive rights for minority groups to be educated bilingually, can significantly undermine an intercultural objective. The Czech Government have already noted that bilingual education provision for the Roma has not been regarded as particularly important as there has been no 'demand' for it from Roma parents.[243]

Segregation in education has been a constant cause for concern for the Advisory Committee. The Advisory Committee has repeatedly expressed criticism of the Czech Republic's treatment of Roma, although the recent report praises recent legislative changes aimed at desegregating Roma education.[244] In the case of Austria, the Committee welcomed the abolition of the special, remedial school regime and it recommended that other states could learn from these measures.[245] However, in its 2000 opinion on Hungary, the Advisory Committee continued to express deep concern about Roma education, including the use of special schools for mentally

---

238   Ad hoc Committee for the Protection of National Minorities (CAHMIN) Explanatory rep on the FCNM H (1995) 010, 1995 para. 48.

239   *Ibid.* Articles 12(2) and (3).

240   Thornberry *supra* n15 at 374.

241   *Ibid.* at 381.

242   *Supra* n144 Article 14(1) states: 'The parties undertake to recognise that every person belonging to a national minority has the right to learn his or her minority language'.

243   This comment from the Czech Governments report to the ICERD was criticised by the Committee: ICERD *Summary Record of the 1255th Meeting: Czech Republic 30 March 1998* CERD/C/SR.1255.

244   Advisory Committee on the Framework Convention for the Protection of National Minorities, *Comments of the Government of the Czech republic on the 2nd opinion of the Advisory Committee* GVT/COM/INF/OPII (2005) 002.

245   Advisory Committee Opinion on Austria ACFC/INF/OP/I (2002) 009 para. 93.

disabled children which were considered to be incompatible with Art. 12(3).[246] They also noted de facto increasing separation of schools, mainly due to the attitudes of non-Roma parents and the reluctance of Roma parents to send their children to kindergarten which appears to express a lack of confidence in the educational system. The Committee referred the Hungarian authorities to Recommendation No. R (2000) 4 of the Committee of Ministers on the education of Roma/Gypsy children in Europe.[247] Very similar comments are made in relation to the report from Slovakia,[248] yet the Committee seemed satisfied that the Government was improving equal access to regular schools. The Committee, like the CERD, specifically endorses an intercultural approach.[249]

The non-binding European Charter for Regional and Minority Languages contains a provision for the appropriate forms and means for teaching regional and minority languages at all appropriate stages.[250] This provision applies to non-territorial languages such as Romani. However, Article 7(5) enables them to be interpreted in 'a flexible manner, bearing in mind the needs and wishes, and respecting the traditions and characteristics of the groups which use the languages concerned'.[251] The Charter also includes extensive provision for education in the mother tongue.[252] The Standing Conference of Local and Regional Authorities of Europe, Resolution on Gypsies in Europe: *the role and responsibility of local and regional authorities* requests that the Committee of Ministers encourage ratification of the charter and application of its principles in respect of non-territorial languages.[253] Given the resources and the determination that the charter demands for the provision of minority languages in education it is perhaps unsurprising that there have been comparatively few ratifications.

The Organisation on Security and Co-operation in Europe and its offices in the Czech Republic, Poland and the US has been concerned with the situation affecting Roma and other travellers throughout Europe for some time. For the Eastern European countries which have only recently joined the Council of Europe it was a welcome opportunity to be included in discussion on the future of Europe, political co-operation and the protection of human rights. The Document of the Copenhagen Meeting (1990) provided a comprehensive provision on the rights of national minorities, something which had, until recently, largely been over-looked by the Council of Europe.[254] The importance of 'special measures' are stressed in

246   Advisory Committee on the Framework Convention for the Protection of National Minorities Opinion on Hungary, adopted on 22 September 2000 ACFC/INF/OP/I (2001)4 23 November 2000 para. 41.

247   *Ibid.* at para. 42.

248   Advisory Committee on the Framework Convention for the Protection of National Minorities *Opinion on Slovakia*, adopted on 22 September 2000 ACFC/INF/OP/I (2001)1.

249   *Ibid.* para. 41.42.

250   Article 7(1)(f).

251   Article 7(5) European Charter for Regional and Minority Languages.

252   *Ibid.* Article 8.

253   SCLRAE Res 249 (1993) on Gypsies in Europe: the Role and Responsibility of Local and Regional Authorities para. 10.

254   CSCE *supra* n202.

Article 31 of the Copenhagen document 'for the purposes of ensuring to persons belonging to national minorities full equality with the other citizens in the exercise and enjoyment of human rights and fundamental freedoms'. Groups of experts have examined and reported on the human rights of Roma in Bulgaria, Czechoslovakia, Hungary and Romania and Article 40 of the Copenhagen Document refers to the particular problems of the Roma (Gypsies) in the context of racism and xenophobia. In the following conferences in Geneva, Moscow and Helsinki the treatment of Roma and travellers was raised regularly.[255]

The Human Dimension Seminar on Roma in the CSCE region took place in September 1994. It represented a natural progression but also serves as a very welcome review of the situation of Roma throughout Europe, its topics for discussion included ethnic violence, administration of justice, mobility and citizenship. The 47-page consolidated summary illustrates the strength of concern for this minority group internationally.[256] In an introductory address the Deputy Secretary General of the Council of Europe observed the importance of a policy based multiculturalism:

> We all proclaim our commitment to human rights. The acid test of their effectiveness lies where the most exposed and vulnerable members of society are concerned. After all their past suffering, the Roma are entitled to be recognised at last as full members of a democratic, pluralistic and multicultural European society which we want to build together.[257]

On the subject of education the summary identifies the need for better teacher training and pre-school schooling where available and a number of projects have been funded to find the best ways forward.[258]

The Hague recommendations on the education rights of national minorities

Drafted by the Inter-Ethnic Relations Foundation which assists the High Commissioner on National Minorities, the recommendations elaborate on the existing international commitments in the field of minority education. The importance of mother-tongue teaching is emphasised as necessary for minorities to maintain their identity.[259] Indeed, Article 12 emphasises that the primary curriculum should, wherever possible, be delivered in the child's mother tongue and states are required to improve training and facilities so that qualified teachers are available.[260] The participation and consultation of minorities at all levels of education policy and delivery is viewed as important to the success of such programmes.

Article 19 elaborates upon commitments in the Copenhagen Document by endorsing the need for an intercultural approach to education by which states are

---

255   Liégeois *supra* n8 at 285–6.

256   CSCE *supra* n202 at 10,

257   *Ibid.* at 9 para. 9.

258   *Ibid.* at 25.

259   Article 1 The Hague Recommendations regarding the Education Rights of National Minorities 1996 OSCE.

260   *Ibid.* Article 14.

required to ensure that the compulsory general curriculum includes information about minority history, culture and traditions.[261] While the recommendations are not legally binding they provide a framework for states to consider when developing minority education. They also provide an indication of current thinking in this field and endorse the need to involve and integrate minority values and beliefs within the mainstream educational process.

Article 116 of the Treaty of the European Union Article identified the EU's jurisdiction in the education field. There have also been many projects throughout the community which have been aided by both European Community and/or Council of Europe funding.[262]

The resolution of the Council of Ministers of Education of 22 May 1989 *On School Provision for Gypsy and Traveller Children*[263] instructed states to make every effort to give support for educational establishments in providing schooling for these children. Teaching methods suggested included support for distance learning programmes, use of new technological aids, improved teaching materials and 'consideration for the history, culture and language of the Roma and travellers'. Improvements for teacher training were advocated, including using teachers of a traveller origin when possible. In many areas highlighted as needing dramatic improvement, the Community resolution will be welcome.

On school provision for gypsy and traveller children[264]
The member states reported on implementation of the resolution at the end of 1993 and eventually, in 1996, the Commission's findings were published. It will come as little surprise, given the history of exclusion and assimilation, that the respondent states had very little information on the number of travellers/Gypsies who fell outside the education system. Nevertheless, illiteracy levels were considered as high as 90% in Greece and 80% in French speaking Belgium.[265] Poor school attendance was a common problem, particularly in relation to secondary school. The UK report bore out the earlier conclusions of Liégeois,[266] revealing that 47% of Gypsy children were not enrolled at secondary school.[267] The report recognised that the low literacy level was a major problem and yet most States had failed to construct a national policy on Roma/Gypsy education.[268]

---

261   Para. 34 Document of the Copenhagen Meeting of the Conference on the Human Dimension of the CSCE 1990.
262   The Council of Europe has raised the profile of the Gypsy minority by holding seminars and documenting reports on subjects including: Education, teacher training and Roma women. They have also funded the Interface collection of journals on Gypsy and Traveller Education.
263   *Supra* n3; the report by Liégeois *supra* n18 provided the impetus for the Council of Ministers Resolution.
264   European Commission On School Provision for Gypsy and Traveller Children (1996) COM (96) 495 Brussels.
265   *Ibid.* at 24 Paras 61 and 23 para. 56.
266   Liégeois *supra* n18 at 255.
267   *Supra* n264 at 25 para. 66.
268   *Ibid.* at 27.

More recently, the Equal Treatment Directive 2000/43/EC, as discussed in Chapter 3, has widened the scope of anti-discrimination law and clearly applies the concept of indirect discrimination and harassment to education policy. A legal complaint against segregated classrooms in Romania based on the directive failed to lead to widespread reform of the educational system.[269] However, the more recent decision of the Debrecen Appeal Court in Hungary, discussed above,[270] demonstrates that the Directive may be having some effect where de facto segregation is maintained. Nevertheless, the EU Network of Independent Experts on Fundamental Rights remains sceptical regarding the use of the Directive as a mechanism for achieving de facto equality for the Roma. They call for a proactive integrative approach in addition to special measures aimed at ensuring the protection of Roma ethnicity and identity.[271]

The EU accession process also resulted in greater monitoring of minority policies in the CEE states. Yet these commitments were eventually watered down and states were given membership while still retaining discriminatory education policies.[272]

EU funding has proved essential to the success of several educational projects across Europe. The Community Action Programme to Combat Discrimination includes in its eight priority areas, Roma and traveller integration in education and employment and the European Social Fund helps fund a variety of initiatives. The PHARE programme has also been instrumental in funding a range of educational projects in the CEE countries yet it is interesting to note the findings of the UN Development report found that the impact of such projects was typically far smaller than expected.[273] The Lisbon Summit of 2000 targeted social inclusion for marginalised communities, specifically including the Roma. Various benchmarks and targets have been established pursuant to the objectives of the summit including a benchmark of 85% of 22-year-olds having completed secondary education.[274]

It is apparent that EU resources have contributed to many positive educational initiatives but it is essential that these programmes are monitored and, where successful, implemented by member States. The EU Equal Treatment directive may target discriminatory education practices but it lacks vision in that it fails to address some of the subtle difficulties faced by members of minorities and it does not compel states to take action in order to redress entrenched prejudice.

---

269 Discussed in Rostas and Nicoara *supra* n174 at 128.

270 *Supra* n194.

271 De Schutter, O and Verstichel, A *The Role of the Union in Integrating the Roma: Present and Possible Future* EURAC Research (2005) at 25.

272 Rostas and Nicoara *supra* n174 discuss the attitude of the European Commission to the Slovak education policy. They note that in 2001 the Commission exhibited strong concern over the under-representation of the Roma whereas in 2003 the language had been substantially diluted with reference to 'persistent problems relating to the Romani minority'.

273 UNDP *supra* n7 at 9.

274 'Council Conclusions of 5 May 2003 on reference levels of European average performance in education and training (Benchmarks)' *Official Journal* C 134 of 7 June 2003 identified in *supra* n49 at 104.

Examples of positive educational initiatives

There are some encouraging examples of education policies targeting the Roma. These policies tend to adopt a flexible, culturally sensitive approach to education which respect the specific needs of the community and seeks to provide education within a cultural framework. A blanket policy of educational neutrality in respect to minorities is felt to be inadequate and potentially disruptive.

Positive initiatives

Distance learning initiatives, such as that offered by the National Centre for Distance Learning (CNED) in France have been very effective in providing education for Nomadic travelling peoples. The provision of education for minorities is complicated in France due to the Republics denial of ethnic minority identity and the resultant lack of census and statistical data. The provision of education to nomadic travellers in France has always been a particular problem.[275] Preparatory and elementary courses are offered by the CNED and the Antennes Solaires Mobiles Units.[276] The CNED scheme provides a personal tutor who follows the development of the pupil with a flexible learning approach based on the individual's own progress. The curriculum is specifically targeted towards the cultural needs of the travelling community and the skills of pupils are developed rather than rejected from the school environment. The Director of the Centre is clear about the importance of the travellers' culture in the programme:

> To accept the traveller's way of life is to concede that the school should go with him, and allow him to reconcile the various constraints of a shifting base, travel and unconventional living conditions.[277]

A wide range of teaching materials and resources are used in order to maintain the pupils' interest, including audio-tapes and videos. Rhys Morris summarises the advantages of this approach thus:

> They make education available right across the geographical, linguistic and age spectrums of the client group, with passage into adulthood not being a barrier to acquiring a vocational training for those requiring a second chance.[278]

Although the 'Besson law' of 2000 provided local authorities with a duty to provide encampments for travellers there is evidence to suggest that many authorities have not complied with this duty and recent legislative changes in the law on Internal

---

275   Ministry of Education, Dept of Schools 'Synthesis of the Investigations into the schooling of Traveller children 2002–2003' 2004 found that enrolment rates approached 85% of sedentary but only 60% of non-sedentary children. Although the figures are reportedly much lower according to the ERRC *Always Somehwere Else. Anti-Gypsyism in France* November 2005 ERRC, Budapest.

276   *Supra* n246 at 31 para. 94.

277   Plessis, J.C. *School Provision of Gypsy and Traveller Children – Distance Learning and Pedagogical Follow-up*, Council of Europe (1992) at 30 (C/E DESC/EGT (90) 47).

278   Rhys-Morris *supra* n143 at 52.

Security 2003 criminalise unauthorised camping.[279] This measure will undoubtedly complicate the work of mobile and distance educational initiatives and are likely to lead to greater educational disadvantage as experienced by travellers in the UK following the Criminal Justice and Public Order Act 1994.

While the provision may be criticised for isolating the pupil, it should be recognised that the alternatives for the pupil are likely to be far from satisfactory and may well result in the child receiving no formal education.[280] Distance learning initiatives have also been reported in the United Kingdom and Italy.[281]

In the UK, the West Midlands Consortium Education Service for Travelling Children provides a pupil record transfer system which allows a record of the traveller's previous education to be monitored when s/he enters a new school. It also includes a resource centre for both teachers and pupils; field welfare officers; advisory and support teachers and help with transport if needed. The Information Pack illustrates a refreshing awareness of the central problems of traveller education:

> Travellers are not a homogeneous group and we need to be aware of different experiences, traditions, language, histories and work patterns. Children in school bring a cultural experience/background and a personal history we need to be responsive to, assessing and meeting their needs appropriately ... in this way schools can, given awareness and understanding of the travelling communities, ensure formal education skills add to and enhance family education skills and do not seek to replace them.[282]

The service attempts to establish pre-school places as well as higher education for the post-16 pupils. Class teachers and support teachers work as a partnership. The information stresses that often the class teacher will work with a small group or one of the traveller pupils if necessary while the support teachers instructs the rest of the class. This practice is intended to help create a bond between the teacher and the Gypsy pupils giving them confidence in the school system.

The situation of the Romanian Roma has traditionally been very poor with the post-Ceausescu years characterised by economic impoverishment and anti-Romani pogroms.[283] Yet there has been some limited educational success in recent years which should serve to encourage educationalists in other CEE states. In 1998, the Romanian Ministry of Education revealed that as many as 59% of women and 44% of male Roma are illiterate.[284] The following year, the Government's Strategy

---

279   Bresson law no 90-449 of 31 March 1990, *Journal Officiel* 2 June 1990 as amended by Law no 2000-614 of 5 July 2000. Law no 2003-239 on internal security of 18 March 2003, *Journal Officiel* no 66 19 March 2003.

280   Alcaloïde, M and Gramond, B 'France The General Situation' Advisory Council for the Education of Romany and Other Travellers (eds.) *supra* n8 at 42. It was estimated that in 1979 some 65% of children of school age were not in attendance.

281   *Supra* n264 at 31 paras 95–6.

282   West Midlands Consortium. *Education Service for Traveller Children*, Information Pack.

283   Cahn *supra* n174.

284   *Xinhua* 'Gypsies' Situation in Romania' 5 October 1998, Bucharest. Roma are estimated to comprise around 10% of Romanian society (see Appendix 1), yet in Romanian orphanages they amount to between 40 and 80% of children – Brearley *supra* n65 at 29.

for improving the condition of the Roma, included a number of initiatives, most notably the employment of a highly qualified Roma expert in every county and specific education programs. Unlike Slovakia and Bulgaria, the issue of minority language teaching for Roma has been treated more seriously and there have been opportunities to study Romanes and Roma history in both primary and secondary schools since 1999. Consequently the number of pupils attending school has increased significantly. There are also some schools where Romanes is offered as the medium of instruction for three to four hours per week. The Romanian Government has also used affirmative action strategies to reserve a number of University places for talented Roma students.[285] Unfortunately, progress in Romania is still hampered by a lack of political will. Georgi Ivanov, Romanian Secretary of State for Minority Issues admitted that Romania had not implemented anything further and attributed this to a lack of political interest. As is true in much of the region, the extent of racist violence and police brutality are officially denied.[286]

The Roma education initiative[287]

The Open Society Institute's *Step by Step* program, which commenced in 1999, and the more recent Roma Education Initiative has been instrumental in changing attitudes and policies towards the education of Roma. The operation of the projects was monitored between 2002 and 2005 in eight CEE countries including Hungary, Slovakia and Bulgaria.

The focus of the different projects varied from promotion of the use of Roma Teaching Assistants in the Czech Republic to a much more far-reaching equal opportunities project aimed at changing the emphasis of the entire education system in Romania.[288] In the Slovak Republic projects were implemented in four different Slovak regions aimed at integrating Roma pupils using methods such as Roma teaching assistants, teacher-training and the addition of Roma culture into the curriculum. The findings of the programmes are largely positive with improved participation in Kindergarten, improved progress and results at all levels and greater participation from Roma parents. The attitudes of teachers towards segregated education changed and more began to regard it as a disadvantage.[289]

All projects reported improvements in the self-esteem of Roma pupils and a beneficial impact on the relationship between Roma and non-Roma communities.

---

285   Open Society Institute AP *Report on Romania* (2002) Open Society pp 517–518.

286   Meijknecht *supra* n66 at 82.

287   The website giving details and reports on all the programmes is available at: http://www.osi.hu/esp/rei.

288   The Open Society Institute's initial documentation provide an overview of the projects and a summary of initial findings, *supra* n80. Each of the country reports can be found on the website: http://www.osi.hu/esp/rei/.

289   Barurikova, *Zita REI Annual research and Evaluation Report Slovakia* (2005) OSI at 16.

Recent international progress

In recent years, there have been a number of privately funded educational projects aimed at improving the educational experience of the Roma. The Roma Education Initiative is the most comprehensive effort to date to gather research in this field and it is expected that the Roma Decade will see more movement in this area. The Hungarian Government has demonstrated the political will to improve access to education and the Phare programme has supported their efforts with specific funding for schools and community groups that are committed to the integration agenda.[290]

In 1994, the European Union established the Socrates education programme to run from January 1995 to December 1999. The Comenius chapter encompassed three action fields, one of which is on the education of migrant workers, occupational travellers, Travellers and 'Gypsies'.[291] The programme allows for financial assistance to be given to projects which aim to increase participation of Gypsies and travellers; to improve their schooling; to meet their specific needs and capacities and to promote inter-cultural education for all children. Inter-cultural teaching is an essential part of the Socrates programme, with support given to projects incorporating multi-culturalism into the curricula and teaching practice. The guidelines also note that in connection with Gypsy and traveller children, priority should be afforded to primary and secondary education, the transition from school to work, the training of Gypsy intermediaries and the use of open and distance learning.[292]

In 2002, the Council of Europe began 'the education for Roma Children in Europe' project pursuant to Recommendation (2000) 4 which focused on improving access to education through the standardisation of teaching materials and the use of Roma mediators or assistants. The data collected by the Project found that Roma mediators or assistants were used in Austria, Bulgaria, Croatia, Czech Republic, Finland, France, Hungary, Italy, Latvia, Lithuania, Poland, Romania, Slovakia, Spain, Sweden and the UK.[293] The roles of the mediators/assistants and the extent of the scheme varied across the region. There had also been some criticism from the mediators themselves as to the low status and uncertainty of the role. However, the Council of Europe is keen to expand the use of mediators as essential to supporting the educational experience of Roma children. The need for an intercultural approach to minority teaching is now firmly situated on the European agenda as noted in the recent European Monitoring Centre on Racism and Xenophobia report on *Roma and Travellers in Public Education.*[294]

---

290   *Supra* n188.

291   SOCRATES, Action 2 14 March 1995 *Official Journal of the European Communities* 20 April 1995.

292   The SOCRATES project and its implications for the education of travellers and Gypsies is discussed in 'Programme' 1995 *Interface* Vol. 19 p 3–5.

293   C/E the Situation of Roma School Mediators and Assistants *in Europe* DGIV/EDU/ROM (2006)3.

294   *Supra* n49 Key Findings at 93.

Concluding observations: The intercultural solution

Romani children are at a clear disadvantage in the educational process. Pre-school places which enable Romani pupils to catch up with their future classmates have had significant success but they are not routinely available.[295] Many governments are beginning to recognise their need but a shortage of teachers and a perceived lack of demand from Romani parents provide excuses for inadequate provision.[296]

The traditional focus on non-discrimination has not ended inequality in education. Indeed, it has failed to get to grips with the problems facing minorities. Nowhere is this more apparent than in the recent decision of the ECHR in the Czech Schools case.

The previous emphasis on individualism and neutrality is now being questioned and it is no longer presumed that absenteeism is attributable to social backwardness. An educationalist from French-speaking Belgium noted:

> Once we perceive the correlation between persistent illiteracy, daily school attendance, and failure to progress beyond primary level, we cannot but admit how inappropriate basic teaching has been to the needs of Gypsy and traveller children, sedentary or not.[297]

The Roma have been the victims of assimilationist educational strategies which promote one national vision for education while applying deficit theory. Conversely, but again relating to deficit theory, they have also been the victims of segregation on a grand scale. While segregation has now been prohibited in legislation across the CEE, the process of integration remains slow and the barriers are now so entrenched that educators are resorting to internalised segregation whereby Roma pupils are educated in the same building but not in the same class.

The obstacles to achieving educational success for the Roma are widely understood.[298]

Education in the mother tongue is now regarded by leading educationalists, such as Skutnabb-Kangas, as essential. However, as Hristo Kyuchukov recognises, the bilingualism of Roma children is rarely viewed as an advantage because of the low status of the Romani language throughout the world.[299] The focus on individual human rights and the assimilation of minority cultures has been prevalent in the education policies of many states. In the past, there was little in the international human rights standards to provide strong argument in favour of intercultural

---

295   See the findings of the Open Society Institute *supra* n80 and the various Roma Education Initiative project reports available at http://www.osi.hu/esp/rei/.

296   The Czech Government have increased pre-school provision to 66 classes in 1997–98. However 45 of these classes were still in special schools for special need children. The Committee on the Elimination of Racial Discrimination noted that only 10% of Roma children attended such pre-school classes. *Supra* n11 at para. 57.

297   European Commission On School Provision *for Gypsy and Traveller Children* (1996) COM (96) 495 Brussels at 44 para. 179

298   See for example: Hegedus, András 'The tasks concerning Gypsy Children's Socialisation at school' *Social Cohesion, Szolnok* (1998); Derrington and Kendall *supra* n31 passim and Open Society Institute *supra* n177.

299   *Supra* n7 at 273.

teaching. This position is now changing; international organisations such as CERD and the European Union now understand that education cannot be offered in a neutral, value-free manner without undermining the human rights of members of non-dominant groups. Mother tongue teaching for minorities is regarded by many educationalists as fundamental but an intercultural approach requires both majority and minority to be exposed to such teaching. The invisibility of the Roma in the majority curriculum is well documented. 'Colour-blind' strategies for educating all students equally have been rejected as unsuitable in a world where people are far from being colour-blind.[300] Furthermore, an intercultural education needs to embrace anti-racism so that intolerance can be confronted in the classroom.[301] Luciak defines this enlightened approach:

> Intercultural education aims to deepen students' knowledge and appreciation of different cultures, to reduce prejudices, to pinpoint the interdependence of the world community, and-if it encompasses an anti-racist approach-to facilitate a critical awareness of institutional discrimination and the origins of societal inequalities.[302]

Segregation and separation cannot be sustained. Racism needs to be challenged in the classroom in a climate of inter-cultural respect, in keeping with the United Nations' recently elaborated policies on human rights education.[303] In developing the multi-ethnic strategy, consultation and co-operation are essential pre-requisites. As far as possible Roma should be involved in the development of policy and the delivery of education programmes. This not only serves to demonstrate legitimacy but also provides role models and understanding of particular problems which cannot be learnt from a teacher-training programme. At present, the high level of illiteracy means that there is a shortage of Roma in a position to offer teaching. Therefore, it is desirable to develop the role of teaching assistants and mediators.[304] Banks argues that excluded groups must be included in shaping educational policy so that the necessary reforms become institutionalised in the education system.[305] Furthermore, the dangers of assessment without regard to the cultural backgrounds of pupils have been well documented by Conway.[306] Testing must be done in a way that is sensitive to cultural, social and economic disadvantage.[307] A blanket

---

300   Gillborn, David 'Race' *Ethnicity and Education* (1990) Unwin-Hyman, London at 199. This study concerning Afro-Carribean students in the education system bears out the findings of researchers on Romani education in that teachers who believed they were 'treating everyone the same' were actually applying stereotypes which discriminated heavily against minority students.

301   Lawson et al. 'Teacher training and multiculturalism in a transitional society: the case of the Slovak Republic' (2003) *Intercultural Education* Vol 14, 4 pp 409–420 at 416.

302   Luciak *supra* n204 at 75.

303   The United Nations Decade for Human Rights Education, proclaimed by the General Assembly in Res. 49/184 of 23 December 1994, is to end in 2004.

304   *Supra* n264 at 37.

305   Banks *supra* n19 at 83.

306   Conway *supra* n159 at Chapter 2

307   Lowden, Gordon 'Assessing children with learning difficulties' in Williams, Phillip (ed.) *Special Education in Minority Communities* (1994) Open Univ. Press at 99.

approach to school testing which fails to recognise the educational inequality of some groups may be reconcilable with liberal principles of equal treatment but it does not meet the demands of equal opportunity in a multi-ethnic framework. This is gradually been recognised with the revision of discriminatory testing methods in several CEE countries.[308] Labelling Roma children as handicapped on account of their lifestyle has been a popular approach in education policy. It is keeping with the goal of assimilation in that the group are regarded as socially disadvantaged and hence targeted for improvement. The cultural aspects of the pupils' identity are underplayed in a way that stifles identity and denies access to individual rights such as expression and association.[309] Again, it is apparent that individual rights cannot be viewed in isolation from the cultural identity of groups.

The different learning needs and particular problems arising from a position of economic and social disadvantage characterise the schooling problems of Roma and travellers across Europe. Increasingly it is recognised that this problem can only be remedied through particular group-targeted action programmes.[310] The regions that have noted the greatest problems with educational achievement in these communities are those that have continued to push for a blanket, culturally insensitive education policy. More Roma teachers, classroom assistants and mentors are urgently needed.[311] Successful initiatives have shown the difference this can make to Roma schooling both in terms of educational progress, parental attitudes and support. Yet the recent history of poor quality, segregated schooling means that such developments cannot be realised on a satisfactory scale. In the short term improved teacher training and support materials are required so the characteristically low expectations of teachers can be challenged. Flexible learning approaches, which recognise the competing demands on young Roma students, are needed. One obvious development that could improve access to education is free pre-school education.[312] Indeed, there is a growing literature on positive teaching initiatives and the results of these programmes needs to be disseminated and funded.

It is important to be cautious in adopting a standard approach to Romani education. Heterogeneous communities require diverse and flexible approaches to schooling. What is important is that there is both national and international coordination of such projects. This will improve the quality of education as well as identify common mistakes. Unfortunately, at present there is far too much duplication of unsuccessful policies and, while there have been successive seminars to discuss teacher training in the Council of Europe;[313] there is insufficient national coordination and responsibility. Successful approaches are often voluntary or isolated experiments,

---

308   See *supra* n49.

309   On the disruption of minority identity see Liégeois *supra* n18 at 70–71.

310   See for example the SOCRATES programme above at 214.

311   This was recognised by the Council of Europe Recommendation R (2000) 4 of the Committee of Ministers on the Education of Roma/Gypsy *children in Europe* paras 14.15 and 20.

312   Save the Children *supra* n126 Summary pp 52–3.

313   See for example, European Teachers' Seminar, (1992) *Towards Intercultural Education – Training for Teachers of Gypsy Pupils*, Council of Europe, Benidorm, Spain 9–13 June 1989.

with little national focus. Inevitably many of these projects are under-funded and poorly resourced.[314] In this respect the programmes of the Decade of Roma Inclusion will be viewed with interest. The Decade established a Roma Education fund and specifically acknowledges the need for monitoring and scaling up of successful pilot projects among the eight CEE countries.[315] It is to be hoped that the Decade will take existing successful projects and broaden their application rather than duplicating the work of the Open Society and Roma Education Initiative. Of course, it must be remembered that access to education alone will not be a panacea for all the problems of the Roma – significant difficulties will remain in access to employment, housing, health and political representation. Intercultural education will go someway to ameliorating these problems but it certainly cannot solve them.[316]

---

314   A letter to Romnet from an American Journalist, John Smock, who worked in a Romani school in Spain echoes these concerns. Although Smock describes the school as culturally sensitive and educationally progressive, he is compelled to conclude that the 'school seems designed to keep the Romani children out of the mainstream schools as much as to address their special needs by giving them a special school' Letter to Romnet dated 13 October 1998.

315   'Roma Education Fund: a concept note' in *Roma and Expanding Europe: Challenges for the* Future Conference by World Bank and Soros Foundation, Budapest 30 June–31 July 2003.

316   Luciak *supra* n204 at 79.

Chapter 6

The Protection of Minorities in
International Human Rights Law

Introduction

The importance of international human rights law in the protection of the rights of minorities has not been universally accepted.[1] As a result, such protection has, in the past, been patchy and inadequate. Recent history has shown the world that minority rights cannot be ignored and that rather than increasing irredentist tendencies they may be a prerequisite for the peaceful stable societies which benefit us all.

In a detailed study on the rights of minorities, Special Rapporteur Eide identified three crucial components in the protection of minorities: respect for the equality of all human beings; group diversity when required to ensure the dignity and identity of all; and an approach which aimed to advance stability and peace, both domestically and internationally.[2] The first of these complimentary[3] issues has been dealt with in Chapter 3 which raised serious questions over the ability of international law to protect minorities when grounded in a purely individualist foundation.

This chapter will focus on the promotion of group diversity under international law. It will aim to clarify the types of groups protected and the extent of that protection while critically evaluating its effectiveness with reference to Eide's third point.

Minority rights and non-discrimination can be viewed as two sides of the same coin. The United Nations Sub-Commission on the Prevention of Discrimination and the Protection of Minorities distinguished them as follows:

1. Prevention of discrimination is the prevention of any action which denies to individuals or groups of people equality of treatment which they may wish.

2. Protection of minorities is the protection of non-dominant groups which, while wishing in general for equality of treatment with the majority, wish for a measure of differential

---

1   Sohn, Louis B 'The rights of minorities' in Henkin, L *The International Bill of Rights* (1981) Columbia Univ. Press, NY at 271. Vierdag for example doubts the need for a minority rights regime, arguing that the full realisation of non-discrimination provisions would negate the need for such special measures. Vierdag, E. W *The Concept of Discrimination in International Law* (1973) Nijhoff, The Hague at 158.

2   Eide, A *New Approaches to Minority Protection* (1993) MRG, London at 12.

3   McKean, W describes non-discrimination and the provision of special measures for minority groups as 'complementary methods of attaining equality of treatment for all persons' in *Equality and Non-discrimination under International Law* (1983) Clarendon, Oxford at 86.

treatment in order to preserve basic characteristics which they possess and which distinguish them from the majority of the population.[4]

The legal status of the group

International legal provisions concerned with the interests of groups are varied and numerous. However, the right of the group as distinct from its members is rarely recognised let alone protected.[5] It would appear that great efforts have been expended, particularly since the establishment of the United Nations, to avoid the creation of a group entity. The Western tradition with its central focus on the rights of individuals is clearly reflected in the international norms of equality and non-discrimination. But even the provisions concerning the protection and preservation of minority cultures and characteristics contained in Article 27 of the ICCPR refer to 'persons belonging' to minorities rather than the rights of the group per se.

The protection of the existence of certain types of minority groups is covered by the Convention of the Prevention and Punishment of the Crime of Genocide of 1948. Until recent events in the former Yugoslavia and Rwanda, the convention had been regarded as largely symbolic; governing extreme forms of minority-focused violence. The use of the treaty to protect the identity of ethnic groups and to promote their characteristics in the face of assimilation will be proved limited. Additionally, Article 1 of the ICCPR refers to the inherent and inalienable right of all peoples to self-determination. *Peoples* it can be seen are not purely a collection of unassociated individuals, and the right to self-determination can only be claimed by a people and not by an individual or dissociated group. Its use as a vehicle for the promotion of minority rights in a non-colonial setting, discussed in Chapter 7, has been limited and is likely to remain so.

The definition of minority

A major difficulty with affording special rights for particular minority groups – the problem of defining a minority, has hounded international lawyers and academics since the League of Nations first became concerned with minority protection.[6] Sixty years later there is still no accepted definition as to what constitutes a minority in international law. The Declaration on the Rights of Minorities in 1992 contains no definition.[7] Furthermore, the international human rights documents use various terms, from 'ethnic, linguistic and religious' minorities (in the ICCPR) to 'national' minorities (in the *C/E* Framework

---

4   UN Doc E/CN.4/52 Section V (Sub-commission, 1st session 1947).

5   Baron describes this difference in terms of 'rights of minorities' which are concerned with equality and opportunity for individual members of the group, and 'minority rights' referred to as the rights of groups to a degree of autonomy, for example in the provision of education and cultural establishments; Baron, S *Ethnic Minority Rights Some Older and Newer Trends* (1985) Oxford Centre for Postgraduate Hebrew Studies at 3.

6   Packer, J 'On the Definition of Minorities' in Packer and Myntti (eds) *The Protection of Ethnic and Linguistic Minorities in Europe* (1993) ABO Akademie Univ. at 24–7.

7   UN Res. 47/135 of 18 December 1992.

Convention and the OSCE documents). This lack of definition is generally blamed on the complexity of the subject. However, other commentators point to the traditional antipathy and 'fear' that talk of minority rights invokes in national governments.[8]

In trying to reach a consensus in this complex area, it is possible to delineate some common criteria:

i) A distinct non-dominant group

The Sub-Commission on the Prevention of Discrimination and Protection of Minorities suggested the following definition in 1954:

> The term minority shall include only those non-dominant groups in a population which possess and wish to preserve ethnic, religious or linguistic traditions or characteristics markedly different from those of the rest of the population.[9]

Thus, there must be an element of unity within the community to the extent that a non-minority member could not easily acquire the minority identity. The nature of distinction is not specified and the group does not need to be distinguished in the physical sense, i.e., the members do not need to live together in a geographically separate location.[10]

On the same point, a minority must be distinguished from a loosely defined collection of disadvantaged individuals. In a memorandum on the definition of minorities, the UN Secretary-General noted: 'Communities are based on unifying and spontaneous (as opposed to artificial or planned) factors essentially beyond the control of the members.'[11]

The most commonly cited definition was developed by Francesco Capotorti, Special Rapporteur for the Sub-Commission on the Prevention of Discrimination and Protection of Minorities, in a special study on minorities in 1977:

> A group numerically inferior to the rest of the population of a State, in a non-dominant position, whose members – being nationals of the State – possess ethnic, religious or linguistic characteristics differing from those of the rest of the population and show, if only implicitly, a sense of solidarity, directed towards preserving their culture, traditions, religion or language.[12]

The Capotorti definition was revised in 1985 by Judge Jules Deschenes of the Human Rights Committee, although it remains substantially the same.[13] Both definitions

---

8   Packer *supra* n6 at 25–6.

9   UN, Report of the 10th Session of the Commission on Human Rights, 18 ESCOR Supp. 7, UN Doc E/2573 at 48–9 (1954).

10   Ramaga, Phillip. V 'The Group Concept in Minority Protection' (1993) *HRQ* Vol. 15 pp 575–588 at 575.

11   *Definition and* Classification of Minorities (Memorandum) UN.Doc. E/CN.4/2/85 at para. 18.

12   Capotorti, Francesco Study on the Rights of Persons Belonging to Ethnic, (1991) *Religious and Linguistic Minorities* UN Doc. E/CN.4/Sub.2/384 (Rev1. 1979) at 96 in UN Human Rights Study Series 5.

13   Deschenes, J UN Doc E/CN.4/subs2/1985/31 of 14.5.85 at para. 181.

incorporate the same elements of objective and subjective classification. The former refers to 'nationals' of the state, the latter to 'citizens' – illustrating a clear intent to exclude non-nationals from minority status. The Deschenes definition has further been criticised[14] for including a limitation to the aim of achieving equality in fact and law.[15]

ii) A specific homeland

Commentators often regard minorities as associated with a specific homeland and this can be damaging for groups such as the Roma who do not have this association. Indeed, the Roma community were excluded from negotiations on the future of Yugoslavia as they had no territorial boundaries over which to negotiate.[16] Alcock notes that 'Almost all minorities have a homeland in which they are concentrated,'[17] he then focuses exclusively on the 'almost all' without regard to non-territorial groups. The diversity of the Roma people across a large variety of borders is discussed in Chapter 1 and the absence of a 'protector-state' to defend their interests may indeed be the principal reason for their comparatively poor economic and social status. The Roma are unlikely to benefit from bilateral treaties and their unique political vulnerability may necessitate some sort of transnational approach to Roma culture and identity.[18] Territorial connection is not featured as an essential component of a minority in these definitions and the issue of territory, although a relevant factor, should not act as a prerequisite for minority status.[19]

iii) Numerical inferiority

This requirement appears to be uncontroversial when defining minorities.[20] The maximum number that can constitute a minority is clearly established at less than 50% of the total population of the state.[21] The only area of disagreement appears to relate to the minimum number of people who could constitute a minority group.[22] Capotorti manages to evade this question by indicating a test of reasonable

---

14   See for example Packer *supra* n6 at 56.

15   Deschenes *supra* n13.

16   Project on Ethnic Relations Countering Anti-Roma Violence in Eastern Europe, (1994) *The Snagov Conference and Related Efforts*, PER, Princeton NJ at 6.

17   Alcock, A 'A New Look at the Protection of Minorities and the Principle of Human Rights' (1977) *Community Development Journal* vol. 12, 2.

18   See for example the bilateral treaty of September 1992 between Germany and Romania on the repatriation of Romanian Rom for a negotiated price. Reported in Open Media Research Institute Daily Digest, 3 November 1992. European Parliament Motion for a Resolution Doc B3-1503/92 on the Agreement between Germany and Romania on the forced repatriation of Romanian Gypsies.

19   Ramaga *supra* n10 notes that the absence of a physical collectivity (i.e., in geographically dispersed communities) should not negate the existence of a minority.

20   Although the issue of apartheid in South Africa clearly illustrates that this approach is not absolutely satisfactory.

21   Sohn *supra* n1.

22   Shaw, M 'The Definition of Minorities in International Law' (1991) *Israel YBHR* Vol. 20 pp 13–42 at 37.

proportionality where the effort involved in implementing special measures should not be disproportionate to the benefit to be derived from it.[23]

iv) Excluded categories

There has been a general expectation among commentators and states that the rights conferred by Article 27 are only available to 'citizens' or 'nationals' of the particular state.[24] The Central European Initiative's Instrument for the Protection of Minority Rights adopted in 1996 adopts this approach 'reaffirming that the protection of national minorities concerns only citizens of the respective state'.[25] As a result certain groups will be unable to claim protection. The excluded groups include refugees, aliens and migrant workers, all of which are provided for in customary law and other international law treaties.[26] The exclusion of non-nationals can be criticised for leaving a loop-hole where protection is needed most[27] and in its General Comment the Human Rights Committee expressed disapproval at this interpretation:

> In this regard, the obligations deriving from Article 2.1 are also relevant, since a State party is required under that article to ensure that the rights protected under the Covenant are available to all individuals within its territory and subject to its jurisdiction, except rights which are expressly made to apply to citizens, for example, political rights under Article 25. A State party may not, therefore, restrict the rights under Article 27 to its citizens alone.[28]

In respect of the United Nations Declaration on the Rights of Persons Belonging to National or Ethnic, Religious and Linguistic Minorities, the definition advocated by Mr Chernichenko emphasised that minorities should include non-citizens who permanently resided in a given state.[29]

v) The problem of loyalty

The issue of the loyalty of minorities to the state has been raised by several commentators and can be seen in the UN Sub-commission's fifth session definition.[30] However, the criterion of loyalty can no longer be regarded as part of the definition of a minority. As Thornberry argues it would mean that there was no such thing as

---

23   Capotorti 1991 *supra* n12 at 12, 96.

24   Report of the Third Committee, GAOR 16th session, agenda Item 35, at 14. UN Doc A/5000/Annexes (1961-2).

25   CEI Instrument *for the Protection of Minority Rights* (1996) at 4, Centre for Information and Documentation, Trieste, Italy. Though, ironically, Article 7 of the instrument recognises the specific problems faced by the Roma and emphasises a commitment to their rights.

26   Thornberry *Minorities and Human Rights Law* (1987) MRG, London at 7.

27   Ramaga *supra* n10 at 580.

28   HR1/GEN/1/Rev.1/at 38 (1994) at para. 5.1.

29   Commission on Human Rights, Sub-commission on the prevention of discrimination and protection of minorities 48th session *Report of the Working Group on Minorities on its second session* para. 131E/CN.4/Sub.2/1996/28.

30   Capotorti (1991) *supra* n12 at p 6 para. 23.

a disloyal minority and it would enable an intolerant state to argue that Article 27 does not apply as the particular group had not exhibited sufficient loyalty.[31] Bruegel supports this argument by contending that such a clause would make the provision of minority rights into a charitable event.[32]

vi) Community unity

There is an obvious requirement that the members of the group itself do not wish to be assimilated. While the Roma may not be a universally homogeneous group with uniform value systems, their refusal to accept the majority goal of assimilation can be seen in virtually every state in which they live. Capotorti notes:

> With respect to the indigenous populations and to the Gypsies, for example, the available information suggests that their imperviousness to the encroachment of the dominant culture is due to the strong attachment to their own traditions. Any attempt to impose assimilation would lead to conscious and deliberate resistance.[33]

This refusal to assimilate in such adverse circumstances may present ample evidence of a desire to exist as a group. Shaw comments that: 'It is also axiomatic that a group that has survived historically as a community with a distinct identity could hardly have done so unless it had positively so wished'.[34]

The two poles of minority identity

The coupling of the objective and subjective elements of the definition give effect to what Alfredsson describes as the 'two poles' of minority identity.[35] In the Lovelace case, the Human Rights Committee considered whether minority status could be lost on marriage to a non-member and affirmed the subjective element:

> Persons who are born and brought up on an [Indian] reserve, who have kept ties with their community and wish to maintain these ties must normally be considered as belonging to that minority within the meaning of the Covenant.[36]

It has been argued that the definitional difficulties should not be considered a bar to special minority protection. It would appear that in most cases recognising a group as a minority does not present a particular difficulty and it is clear that international

---

31   Thornberry   International   Law   and   the   Rights   of   Minorities   (1991) Clarendon, Oxford at 166.

32   Bruegel, A 'A Neglected Field: The Protection of Minorities' (1971) *Revue des Droits de L'Homme* Vol 4, 413, at 440.

33   Capotorti 1991 *supra* n12 at para. 255.

34   Shaw *supra* n22 at 40.

35   Alfredsson, Gudmundur 'Emerging or Newly Restored Democracies – Strengthening of Democratic Institutions and Development' paper presented at *Workshop 1: Human Rights, Fundamental Freedoms and the Rights of Minorities, Essential Components of Democracy*, Conference on Parliamentary Democracy, Council of Europe (1991) at 10.

36   *Report of the HRC Lovelace v Canada* (1981) No 24/1997 2 *HRLJ* 158 (1981).

law will not treat as conclusive the status ascribed to groups by the particular state in which they live.[37]

It is submitted that there is nevertheless a need for some international codification in this area. States at present can easily evade the protection of unpopular or small minorities and if necessary can invoke the lack of international clarification to support their domestic policies.

Capotorti found that the Roma are rarely recognised by states as being a legal minority targeted with special measures aimed at equality and non-discrimination:

> It is important to remember that in most cases the groups recognised as 'minorities' or as communities which are to benefit from special treatment are well-defined groups. Certain groups, including those which are scattered throughout the territory of a country, seldom appear among those forming the subject of recognition by the State with legal effect. Such is the situation, for instance, of the groups described as 'Gypsies' in a large number of European countries.[38]

It is evident that there is a vast amount of material and debate within the United Nations on exactly what constitutes a 'minority' group and it would seem unlikely for any precise definition to be enumerated in the near future. The minority status of Roma is problematic when looked at in relation to some of these definitional proposals, particularly in relation to the absence of a specific territory. It is submitted however, that the development of a precise definition, while encouraging debate, is unnecessary to show that Roma/Gypsies are and should continue to be regarded in the international legal system as a 'minority'. International documents regularly refer to the Roma or Gypsy minority.[39] When considering the Romanian state report, the Committee on Economic, Social and Cultural Rights stated:

> The Committee is concerned about the realization of the right to education and of the right to take part in cultural life by one of the largest minorities in Romania, namely the Gypsy minority ....[40]

Introducing a Conference on the Roma in Europe, Peter Leuprecht, Deputy Secretary General of the Council of Europe, noted:

> Let us not hide behind legal hair-splitting as to whether this or that definition of minorities applies to the Roma. Let us be honest. We all know that the Roma are a minority and a particularly vulnerable one.[41]

---

37   Capotorti (1991) *supra* n12 para. 570.

38   *Ibid.* at para. 77.

39   For example see CSCE *Roma* (Gypsies) *in the* CSCE Region Report of the High Commissioner on National Minorities (1993) CSCE.

40   Committee on Economic, Social and Cultural rights *Concluding Observations on Romania* UN Doc. E/C.12/1994/4 (1994) at para. 12 see further para. 15.

41   CSCE *Human Dimension Seminar on Roma in the CSCE Region*, Consolidated Summary. 20–23 September 1994 at p 7 para. 7. CSCE, Warsaw.

While the criteria adopted by Capotorti and Deschenes suggest similar strategies for ascertaining the existence of a minority group, it can be seen that the definition of the Roma minority fits uncomfortably within these definitional parameters and it should perhaps be emphasised that the most important aspect is 'the exposition of a distinct culture and way of life as compared with the majority culture and living conditions should be seen as a decisive criterion for determining the nature of a minority'.[42]

This is the main reason why those people who have experienced the diverse lifestyle of the Roma of Europe recognise this minority status.[43]

The background to minority recognition

Most early minority treaties were concerned with the treatment of religious minorities.[44] However, Capotorti notes a change of attitude in the nineteenth century which saw an increased range of minority provisions contained in various multilateral instruments.[45] Despite this increased concern, attributed primarily to the number of wars in this period, there was little attention paid to the situation of ethnic and linguistic minority groups until the League of Nations was created following the First World War.[46]

League of Nations

Before the adoption of the United Nations Charter which contained no provision for the rights of minorities or their members, minority rights had been frequently on the agenda of bilateral treaties between the Allied nations and the Eastern and Central European states. The treaties were not of a universal application, applying only between the Allied nations and the particular signatory state.[47] Indeed, it has been noted that none of the Allied powers were willing to accept the treaty obligations themselves.[48]

The treaty obligations shied away from providing an enforceable collective right but the emphasis was certainly on minority rather than individual rights. Thornberry

---

42   Heinz, W *Indigenous Populations, Ethnic Minorities and Human Rights* (1988) Quorum Verlag, Berlin at 1. This is also the main approach of the definition advocated by Fawcett in 1979. He defined a minority group as having 'a common will – however conditioned-to preserve certain habits and patterns of life and behaviour which may be ethnic, cultural, linguistic or religious, or a combination of them, and which characterise it as a group. Further, such a minority may be politically dominant or non-dominant' in Fawcett, J.E.S *The International Protection of Minorities* (1979) MRG, London at 4.

43   It can also be argued that well-established travelling groups such as Irish travellers satisfy this definition and more recent groups such as 'new age travellers' may, over time, be able to claim a similar status.

44   Heinz *supra* n42 at 22–3.

45   Capotorti 1991 *supra* n12.

46   Heinz *supra* n42 at 24–5.

47   Bagley, TH (1950) *General Principles and Problems in the Protection of Minorities.* Imprimeries Populaires, Geneva at 68.

48   Macartney, C.A. 'League of Nations' Protection of Minority rights' in Luard (1967) *The International Protection of Human Rights* Thames and Hudson, London at 23.

describes the League's minority regime as 'the most extensive developed by the international community.'[49]

The need to protect the interests of minorities appears to have stemmed from fears about European security rather than from a benevolent concern for the plight of disadvantaged groups.[50] Nevertheless, numerous bilateral treaties were in evidence, aiming to provide much more than equality of treatment, extending to special teaching in the mother tongue where there was a sufficient number of a linguistic minority.

Although the minorities referred to in the treaties were not generally regarded as collective entities,[51] there was a clear understanding that a simple non-discrimination approach was insufficient[52] and groups as well as individuals were given the right to petition the League (a right unfortunately absent in the United Nations Covenants that followed).

The minority provisions established by the League have been criticised for their cumbersome procedures and lack of real enforcement powers[53] and it is clear that the treaties were only concerned with the protection of certain minority groups.[54] Most of the newly created and enlarged states were reluctant to implement the treaty provisions regarding them as a serious incursion into their sovereignty.[55] Furthermore, policing of the treaty provisions apparently created problems for some allied powers most of who were also involved with their own minority problems.[56]

Nevertheless, there is considerable symbolic if not practical significance in the recognition of the importance of minorities as a fundamental aspect of international law. Each particular state undertook that the treaty provisions 'shall be regarded as fundamental laws, and that no law, regulation or official action shall conflict or interfere with these stipulations, nor shall any law, regulation or official action prevail over them'.[57]

---

49   Thornberry (1991) *supra* n3 at 40.

50   Macartney *supra* n48 at 24.

51   Capotorti *supra* n12 at para. 101.

52   Article 9 of the Polish Treaty states that minorities are to be afforded an equitable share of the funds for education, religious or charitable purposes, See Green, L. C 'Protection of Minorities' in Gotleib (ed) Institute of Canadian Affairs at 190.

53   During the first 10 years, 773 petitions were received of which 292 were found inadmissible, action was taken by the League in two cases. Three case decisions were given by the Permanent court of Justice and two further advisory opinions were issued (Fawcett *supra* n39 at 29) See also generally Claude, I *National Minorities. An International Problem* (1955) Harvard Univ. Press, Mass. at 33–6.

54   Wolfrum argues that many of the existing minority groups such as Gypsies and Jews were actually excluded from the protective measures as they were not 'racial groups;' see also Ramaga, Phillip. V 'The Bases of Minority Identity' (1992) *HRQ* Vol 14 pp 409–428 at 416 he argues that Jews were regarded as racial groups, he goes on to look at the deliberate omission of 'race' from the minority criteria in Article 27.

55   Baron *supra* n5 18–9; Thornberry (1991) *supra* n at 47; Sacerdoti, G 'New Developments in Group Consciousness and International Protection of the Rights of Minorities' (1993) *Israel YBHR* Vol 13, 1 pp16–146 at 120; Claude *supra* n53 at 35–6; Poulter, S 'The Rights of Ethnic, Religious and Linguistic Minorities' (1997) *EHRLRev* Vol 3 pp 254–266 at 255.

56   Green *supra* n52 at 195.

57   *Protection of Linguistic, Racial or Religious Minorities by the League of Nations: Provisions contained in the various International Instruments at present In Force,* Series

The controversial application of special measures for minority members highlighted the importance of the distinction between equality in law and equality in fact, the recognition of which remains fundamental to the realisation of non-discrimination and equality. The treaties stated that:

> Equality in law precludes discrimination of any kind; whereas equality in fact may involve the necessity of differential treatment in order to obtain a result which establishes an equilibrium between different situations .... The prohibition against discrimination, in order to be effective, must ensure the absence of discrimination in fact as well as in law.[58]

Successful initiatives of the period included the establishment of minority schools in several countries; the rehabilitation of some neglected groups and minority involvement in the political affairs of countries such as Czechoslovakia and Latvia.[59] It is also interesting to note that although the main beneficiaries were citizens of the particular state, limited protection was also available to those people who were not citizens.[60]

It will become apparent that much of the post-war reluctance to improve minority rights has been based on the fear of secessionist demands and irredentism. These fears were not realised before the demise of the League system, rather its' demise appears to have been the result of its' selective application[61] coupled with the appropriation of minority rights ideology in the Second World War.[62] Goronwy Jones contends that Hitler's use of minority rights as a vehicle for the expression of Nazi ideology marked the nail in the coffin for the group rights vocabulary of pre-war Europe.[63]

The new age of human rights for all

The advent of the United Nations saw the emphasis change from minority rights to individualism in human rights discourse.[64] There was no mention of minorities

---

of L.O.N Publications, I.B Minorities, 1927, I.B. 2 (C.l.110.1927 I, annex) at 42 – cited in Capotorti *Supra* n12 para. 101.

58 *Treatment of Polish Nationals in Danzig* 1932 Series AB/44, 39–40 (2 W.C.R 814–5) at 19 and 20.

59 Lerner, N (1991) *Group Rights and Discrimination in International Law* Martinus-Nijhoff, Dordrecht at 11.

60 Distinction is discussed in *Treatment of Polish Nationals in Danzig supra* n58.

61 Green *supra* n52 at 197.

62 Lerner notes that all the treaties lost their force following the War with the exception of the Aaland Islands agreement *supra* n59 at 14.

63 Jones, G 'The UN and the Domestic Jurisdiction of States: Interpretations and Applications of the Non-intervention Principle' (1980) International Affairs Vol. 56, 4 pp. 685–686; Geroe and Gump also note the post-war rejection of minority rights concepts which refused to soften until the mid-1960s and Bilder, R 'Can Minorities Treaties Work?' in Dinstein and Tabory (1992) *The Protection of Minorities and Human Rights* Martinus-Nijhoff, Dordrecht at 67.

64 *Supra* n59 at 14.

in the Charter to the UN or the Universal Declaration[65] and despite the General Assembly's recognition that 'the United Nations cannot remain indifferent to the fate of minorities,'[66] there is evidence of a clear intention to subsume issues of collective identity into the individual rights of non-discrimination and equality.[67]

A draft minority provision prepared by the Sub-Commission did not receive endorsement by the Human Rights Commission,[68] but the issue was not laid to rest. In the Third Committee of the General Assembly, representatives of the USSR, Denmark and Yugoslavia submitted draft recommendations for the inclusion of a minority rights article.[69] The Yugoslav delegate stressed the importance of the collective dimension:

> In order to secure the protection of individuals who formed a community, that community must first of all be recognised and protected. Thus, the principle of the recognition and protection of nation minorities as communities must appear in the Declaration of Human Rights. The cultural and ethical rights of all persons belonging to a national minority ... depended upon the recognition of the minority itself as an ethnical group.[70]

Such approaches were ultimately unsuccessful. Thornberry notes that minority rights tended to be viewed as alternatives to individual rights. Mrs. Roosevelt, the US delegate, gave her opinion that 'the best solution of the problem of minorities was to encourage respect for human rights'.[71] Consequently, as Inis Claude observes:

> ... the United Nations Charter was formulated without consideration of the questions of principle which are presented by the existence of national minorities in a world dominated by the concept of the nation state.[72]

Optimists, such as Mrs. Roosevelt, apparently believed that problems concerning the treatment of minority groups could be successfully addressed through the individualistic perspective.[73] The principle of self-determination featured in the

---

65 Nowak notes that there were a number of draft proposals to include such a provision in the Declaration and that the USSR's abstention in voting on the UDHR was attributable to the absence of such a provision. (1993) *UN Covenant on Civil and Political Rights CCPR Commentary* Engel, Kehl at 481.

66 UN GA Res. 217 C [III] 10 December 1948.

67 The explanation given for the lack of minority provision is that they are inherently incompatible with the universalist nature of the Declaration. According to Szabo this masks the real motive for its omission, namely the uncertainty of the relationship between individual and collective rights; Szabo, I *Cultural Rights* (1974) A.W Sitjhoff, Leiden at 109 – he goes on to argue that in ignoring the difference between groups in an attempt to forge unity in a divided world, the United Nations policy risks increasing division and tension between groups, at 113.

68 UN Doc E/CN.4/SR.74, 5 (by 10 votes to 6).

69 GAOR 3rd session, part 1, 3rd Committee Annexes, UN Doc A/C.3/307/ Rev. 2, 45–6.

70 UN Doc A/C.3/SR.161, 720.

71 UN Doc A/C.3/SR.161, 726; noted in Thornberry (1991) *supra* n31 at 136–7.

72 Claude *supra* n53 at 113.

73 Baron *supra* n5 at 22.

Charter but its aim, as discussed below, was strictly limited and may be of little use to minorities who do not comprise *peoples*.

It is evident that concern about minorities had not disappeared altogether. The Sub-Commission on the Prevention of Discrimination and Protection of Minorities was established in 1947 to look into ways of addressing specific minority problems. In 1953, the Economic and Social Council recommended that in the preparation of international treaties and decisions, 'special protection should be paid to the attention of any minority which may be created thereby'.[74] The issue of the rights of minorities had subsequently resurfaced in the 1948 Genocide Convention.

The Genocide Convention

The measures contained in the Convention on the Prevention and Punishment of the Crime of Genocide have been described as '*supra*-positive'[75] in that their force does not depend on their recognition in domestic legal systems. The International Court of Justice has stated that the principles contained therein are part of customary law: 'recognized by civilized nations as binding on states, even without any conventional obligation'.[76]

Until recently considered as largely a symbolic document, the Convention is a major step in the 'enforceable' international human rights code. Disapprobation for the crime of genocide is universally acknowledged and despite occasional examples of genocide in the latter half of this century, no nation would ever admit to endorsing such a policy.[77]

Recent activities by the International Court of Justice and International Tribunals on War Crimes in the former Yugoslavia and Rwanda have shown that the Convention has much more than a symbolic role to play. In the case bought by Bosnia and Herzegovina against Yugoslavia relying on Article IX of the Convention, the ICJ ruled that the Convention was binding on both state parties despite the latter's submissions that the matter was a civil war and thus of domestic jurisdiction only.[78] The International Criminal Tribunal for the Former Yugoslavia was established in 1993 to investigate complaints of offences against humanity including allegations of genocide.[79] Proceedings against more than 90 individuals have been successfully concluded.[80] The International Criminal Tribunal on Rwanda has also had some

---

74   ESC res. 502 F [XVI].

75   Van Boven, Theodoor. C 'Distinguishing Criteria of Human Rights' in Vasak (ed.) *The International Dimensions of Human Rights* (1982) Vol. 1 UNESCO, Paris at 47.

76   ICJ Advisory Opinion on Reservations *ICJ Reports*, (1951) at 15.

77   Higgins, R *Problems and Process: International Law and How We Use It* (1994) Clarendon, Oxford at 19.

78   ICJ Case No. 105 Concerning Application of the Convention on the Prevention and Punishment of the Crime of Genocide (*Bosnia and Herzegovina v Yugoslavia*) (Preliminary Objections) Judgement of 11 July 1996. See ICJ Website: www.icj-cij.org/.

79   UN Security Council Res. 827, 25 May 1993.

80   Statute of the International Tribunal (adopted 25 May 1993) as amended 13 May 1998 Article 4; Resolution 1166 (1998) adopted 13 May 1993 by Security Council

success especially in its interpretation that sexual offences were capable of amounting to genocide under the International Convention.[81] The need for an effective tribunal to investigate crimes against humanity has led to the replacement of the ad hoc tribunal's with an International Criminal Court (hereafter ICC). The definition of genocide contained in Article 5 of the draft statute has been taken directly from the Convention.

The crime of genocide consists of a strictly prescribed mens rea requiring the intention 'to destroy, in whole or in part, a national, ethnical, racial or religious group, as such'. There are five acts which constitute genocide when coupled with the necessary mens rea: Killing members of the group; causing serious bodily harm to group members; deliberately inflicting of the group conditions of life calculated to bring about its physical destruction in whole or in part; imposing measures intended to prevent births within the group; forcibly transferring children from the group to another group.[82]

The convention is clearly concerned with the collective right of the specified groups to exist. Genocide cannot be committed against one or even a small number of individuals. The proposed inclusion of cultural genocide[83] would have increased the scope of collective rights to a limited protection against the erosion of group identity. Cultural genocide was considered in the drafting of the Convention.[84] It was defined to encompass prohibition of the use of a group's language in schools or in publications; and destroying or preventing the use of libraries, museums, schools, historical monuments and places of worship or other cultural institutions and objects of the group.[85] When applied to travelling people, 'cultural institutions and objects' could have been interpreted to include the elimination of the travelling way of life through the closure of authorised stopping places; or the compulsory dispersal of densely populated minority regions. Several delegates in the drafting process accepted that the destruction of culture could have the same effect as physical destruction of the group and that, in any event, destruction of minority culture was often the precursor to physical genocide.[86] It is thus unfortunate that the provision did not survive the drafting stage.

---

at its 3,878th meeting. Human Rights Watch Looking for Justice. *The war crimes chamber in Bosnia and Herzegovina* (2006) Vol. 18, 1 February 2006. See also Factsheet on the International Criminal Tribunal for the Former Yugoslavia, PIS-FS 49. Public Information Services, The Hague, The Netherlands.

81   *The Prosecutor v Akayesu* Case No. ICTR-96-4-T. 2 September 1998. Statute of the Tribunal, Article 2 specifically addresses genocide.

82   Convention on the Prevention and Punishment of the Crime of Genocide (1948) Article 2.

83   Mentioned in General Assembly resolution 96, (1) of 11 December 1946.

84   Support for the proposal was given by the USSR, Czechoslovakia and Poland; Heinz *supra* n39 at 36.

85   Article III of the Draft Convention on the Prevention and Punishment of the Crime of genocide (E/794) in Capotorti *supra* n12 at p37, para. 220.

86   The views of the delegates are analysed in detail by Morsink, Johannes 'Cultural Genocide, the Universal Declaration and Minority rights' (1999) *HRQ* 21 pp 1009–1060.

Thornberry notes the views of the USA and France that the subject of cultural genocide should be dealt with under minority protection. In the latter case this was apparently related to concern over excessive interference in the political affairs of states.[87] Other arguments against the inclusion of cultural genocide related to the imprecision of the definition which it was feared could diminish the value of the convention as a whole.[88]

Article 1 of the International Covenant on Civil and Political Rights:
Self-determination

The opening provision of the ICCPR states:

> All peoples have the right to self-determination. By virtue of that right they freely determine their political status and freely pursue their economic, social and cultural development.

Thus, Article 1 is conferring a collective right on 'peoples'.[89] An individual cannot claim a violation of their right to self-determination and from this we can deduce that the allegation that international law should and does only protect the interests of individuals is misleading. A focus on individual rights here would clearly be at odds with the emphasis in Article 1, as Drost observes:

> These equal rights of peoples do not coincide with the human rights of persons. A people can be associated with a great number of persons together but it cannot be identified with any particular person. In international relations a people constitutes a collective entity of human beings, which differs entirely from the single entity of the human person.[90]

'Peoples' as well as 'citizens' are groups of people, united by a degree of common identity and heritage, and both categories are routinely used in international law to confer particular rights.[91]

Cristescu has identified several key components which would indicate that a particular group amounts to a 'people' as distinct from a 'minority'.[92] The relationship with a specific territory appears to be the most definite requirement. However, Baehr also lists the criteria which he considers as necessary to indicate a people and his list does

---

87   Thornberry 1991 *supra* n31 at 72.

88   *Ibid.* at 73.

89   White, Robin C.A. 'Self Determination: Time for A Re-Assessment?' (1981) *Neth Int 'l L Rev* Vol.28, 2 at168.

90   Drost, Pieter N (1965) *Human Rights as Legal Rights* A.W. Sijthoff, Leyden at 193.

91   Kymlicka, W *Multicultural Citizenship* Oxford Univ. Press at 124–6 in exposing the liberal contradiction between individualism and citizenship, he notes that citizenship is an 'inherently group-differentiated notion' which is necessary to protect peoples cultural membership. If the dominant group in society are benefiting from the collective right of citizenship, it is illogical to deny collective rights to smaller units.

92   Cristescu, A *The Rights to Self-Determination: Historical and Current Developments on the Basis of United Nations Instruments* (1981) UN Doc E/CN.4/Sub.2/404/ Rev.1 at para. 279.

not include a territorial component, although he does note that often the group will seek to preserve or achieve recognition in the form of political autonomy or statehood.[93]

Cassese added two additional criteria to Cristescu's list, namely that the group must be of dimensions comparable to other national groups within the state (not simply a minority) and that the people are constitutionally recognised as having a distinct legal status within the Constitution.[94] The latter point can be criticised particularly for giving room to states who want to avoid the consequences of a people asserting their right of self-determination.[95]

The Human Rights Committee have distinguished the collective right of self-determination from the minority provision under Article 27[96] and in so doing have underlined the fact that a minority may not necessarily be a people and vice versa.

There has been much international caution in developing this sphere which is clearly attributable to its association with political secession.[97] However, the issue of territorial integrity versus secession arises less in the case of internal self-determination, discussed further in Chapter 7, and defined by RapporteurEide as:

> ... the right of a people to control significant aspects of its internal matters (culture, education, property relations, social matters and welfare) while external maters (defence against armed attack from third states, international trade relations, diplomatic intercourse) are left in the hands of a larger political entity, e.g., a federal State.[98]

Article 27 of the International Covenant on Civil and Political Rights

> In those states in which ethnic, religious or linguistic minorities exist, persons belonging to such minorities shall not be denied the right, in community with the other members of their group, to enjoy their own culture, to profess and practice their own religion, or to use their own language.

At the fifth session of the Commission on Human Rights in 1949, the limitations of a focus on non-discrimination were recognised and the importance of 'differential treatment ... in order to ensure [minorities] real equality of status with the other elements of the population' was acknowledged.[99]

---

93   Baehr, Peter. R 'Human Rights and People's Rights' in Berting (ed.) (1990) *Human rights in a Pluralist World: Individuals and Collectivities* Roosevelt Study Centre, Meckler The Netherlands at 100–101.

94   Cassese, A 'The Self-determination of Peoples' in Henkin (1981) *supra* n1 at p 92–427 at 95.

95   Kiss, A 'The Right to Self-determination' (1986) *HRLJ* Vol.7 No 2–4, p165–17 at 173.

96   Human Rights Committee General Comment No 18 (Article 27) (1994), para. 3.1. HR1/GEN/1/Rev.1 at 38 (1994).

97   *Ibid.* at 106; Kiss *supra* n95 at 168.

98   Eide, A 'National Sovereignty and International Efforts to Realise Human Rights' in Eide (ed.) *Human Rights in Perspective* (1992) Blackwell pp 3–30 at 16.

99   Commission on Human Rights Fifth Session 1949, A/2929, Chapter 6, s183 quoted in Bossuyt *Guide to the* 'Travaux Preparatoire' *of the International Covenant on Civil and Political Rights* (1987) Martinus-Nijhoff at 493.

Article 27 is symbolically the most important minority provision in international legal instruments and the drafting process helps to reveal illuminating insights into the scope of the provision and expression of many of the fears surrounding recognition of collective rights. During the debate of the draft provision in 1961, views were expressed by some members supporting assimilation policies. One representative contended that there were no minorities in the entire American continent,[100] and the Australian delegate suggested that aborigines were too primitive to constitute a minority.[101] Given the frequency of the expression of such views it in not surprising that the final version is deficient in many respects. It is in fact somewhat surprising that such a provision survived the drafting process at all.

The first draft of Article 27 stated that:

> Ethnic, religious and linguistic minorities shall not be denied the right to enjoy their own culture, to profess and practice their own religion or use their own language.

Despite the negative formulation of the draft, there was a clear recognition of group rights vesting in the minority rather than in the members as individuals.[102]

Following debates questioning the juridical personality of minorities, the Sub-Commission adopted a different construction, protecting the rights of 'persons belonging to minorities'.[103] Some disappointment has been expressed regarding this change of emphasis. Bruegel comments:

> Here all the objections against any positive steps in this field have been collected in a resolution supposed to define the positive steps which are desirable. Small wonder that the representative of a Jewish organization taking part in the proceedings felt obliged to say that under the conditions of this resolution no minority of any kind could ever achieve any rights.[104]

The Covenant refers to 'ethnic, religious or linguistic' minorities rather than 'national' or racial minorities. The terms 'religious' and 'linguistic' are self-explanatory; 'ethnic' is used instead of 'racial' to refer to all biological, cultural and historical characteristics, rather than inherited physical characteristics.[105] Capotorti notes that the choice of wording reflects a desire to incorporate both national and racial groups within the obligation under Article 27.[106]

100 3rd Committee of the GA A/C.3/SR.1103, SR.1104; A/5000, paras 116–126.

101 *Ibid.* para. 26.

102 Sohn *supra* n1 at 273.

103 UN Docs E/CN.4/Sub.2/112 (1950); E/CN.4/Sub.2/SR.55 at 5–7 (1950); E/CN.4/Sub.2/SR.57 at 2–3 (1950); E/CN.4/358 at 19–23 (1950).

104 Bruegel *supra* n32 at 425.

105 E/CN.4/Sub.2/SR.48; E/CN.4/Sub.2/119 para. 31.

106 Capotorti *supra* n12 para. 201.

The individual emphasis

The final version of Article 27, following an amendment by a British delegate, refers to 'members of minorities' rather than the minority itself as the rights bearer. Capotorti provides three reasons for this individual emphasis: the historical background of the Second World War and the abuse of the pre-existing minorities regime; the need for a coherent formulation which has been couched in terms of the individual as rights bearer against the state as rights upholder with no room for other collective entities; and for political reasons to prevent friction between the minority and the state.[107] He subsequently warns against dismissing or under-estimating these sound reasons.[108] Manfred Nowak goes further by attributing the final wording to 'the fear marking the entire historical background of Article 27 that effective, collective protection of minorities might threaten national unity in some states'.[109]

A collective dimension is added however, by the phrase 'in community with the other members of their group'. Although the intention of this addition appears to have been to avoid a concern that any individual could claim the benefits of the rights for minorities,[110] the effect is to recognise that the rights of members of minorities are not independent and can only be fully realised within the security of the group.[111] Thus, Article 27 can be described as having a 'double effect,'[112] which establishes collective goods realisation through individual rights.[113] The HRC General Comment recognises that the protection of minority identity is dependent on recognition of the group.[114]

The double-effect approach however is limited by the failure to recognise a collective right of petition under the Optional Protocol of 1976. The problems with the petition rule can be seen in *Mikmaq Tribal Society v Canada*,[115] where the Human Rights Commission declared the petition inadmissible as the petitioner could not show that he was authorised to bring the case on behalf of the group.

This raises a further problem in that there is no obligation on member states to recognise minorities legally,[116] despite the argument that the allocation of resources may depend on such recognition by the state. In delineating his desirable criteria for a minority Convention, Roth regards the recognition of minorities as the fundamental

---

107   *Ibid.* paras 207–9.

108   *Ibid.* at para. 210.

109   Nowak *supra* n65 at 495.

110   Bossuyt *supra* n99 at 495 s186.

111   Hailbronner, K 'The legal status of population groups in a multinational state under public international law' in Dinstein and Tabory *supra* n63 at 133.

112   Capotorti 'Are Minorities Entitled to Collective International Rights?' in Dinstein and Tabory *supra* n63 at 508.

113   Alfredsson and de Zayas 'Minority rights: Protection by the United Nations' (1993) *HRLJ* Vol 14 1–2 at 2.

114   HRC *supra* n96 para. 6(2).

115   *Mikmaq Tribal Society v Canada* Complaint No 78/1980 HRC Report, GAOR 39th Session Supplement No 40, UN Doc A/49/40, Annex 16 (1984).

116   Stavenhagen, R (1990) *The Ethnic Question – Conflicts, Development and Human Rights* UN Univ. Press, Tokyo at 62.

'linchpin' to rights recognition.[117] Jackson-Preece observes that giving states the right to determine whether minorities 'existed' allowed them to redefine national minorities to avoid the international obligations.[118]

France has issued a reservation under Article 27 stating that 'France is a country in which there are no minorities'.[119] This is on the basis that the application of the principles of equality and non-discrimination under Article 2 of the 1958 French Constitution provide that all people must be treated equally, without distinction as to race, colour, national origin, etc. With a very restrictive conception of equality confined to the procedural domain, it is thus contended that there are no minorities in France.[120] Similarly, France has also refused to ratify the Framework Convention discussed below.

Special measures

A refusal to see minority problems in any way other than from an individual perspective has meant that it is possible to regard Article 27 purely in a narrow, negative formulation which affords no entitlement to special measures such as government funding or specific education initiatives. Henrard argues that a 'positive' reading of Article 27 can be gleaned from state practices and reports to the HRC.[121] However, the wording of Article 27 alone does not spell out this positive duty. Stavenhagen is particularly scathing in his verdict:

> When Article 27 of the ICCPR states that persons belonging to minorities shall not be denied certain rights, it does not go far enough .... In a world of polyethnic nation-States, these rights can only be guaranteed by the active involvement of Governments in their implementation.[122]

Indeed, a majority of the Human Rights Commission rejected a proposal which purported to ensure to national minorities the right to use their native language, to possess their own schools, libraries, museums and other cultural and educational institutions.[123]

---

117   Roth, S (1991) 'Toward a Minority Convention: Its Need and Content' *Israel YBHR* Vol 20 pp 93–126 at 102.

118   Jackson-Preece, Jennifer (1998) *National Minorities and the European Nation States System* OUP at 129.

119   Alfredsson and de Zayas *supra* n113 at 7.

120   Heintze, Hans-Joachim 'Minority issues in Western Europe and the OSCE High Commissioner on National Minorities' (2000) *Int. Journal of Minority and Group Rights* Vol 7 pp 381–392 at 384. The Greek Government have also denied the existence of minorities in Greece with the exception of the Muslims of Western Thrace – Weber, Renate 'Minority Rights: Too Often Wronged' (1995) *Human Rights and Civil Society* 2 No 1 at 1.

121   Henrard, Kristin (2000) *Devising an Adequate System of Minority Protection* Kluwer at 170.

122   Stavenhagen *supra* n116 at 65.

123   Proposal E/CN.4/L.222 (SU) was rejected by 8 votes to 4, with 4 abstentions in the 9th Session of the Commission (E/CN.4/SR.371, p. 6).

However, in a detailed investigation into the scope of Article 27, Capotorti rejected such a narrow focus arguing that a refusal to recognise some special rights would render the application of Article 27 'meaningless'.[124] It is widely accepted that rights under the ICCPR should be immediately implemented,[125] and an interpretation which does not favour special rights would be at odds with the goal of immediate, rather than progressive, implementation.

The need for positive measures was also supported by the Committee on Human Rights in 1994 with the adoption of a General Comment on Article 27 which aims to clarify the interpretation of its scope.

Paragraph 6.1 states that each State party is:

> Under an obligation to ensure that the exercise and existence of [the rights declared by Article 27] are protected against their denial or violation. Positive measures of protection are, therefore, required ... also against the acts of other parties within the state party.

Paragraph 6.2 goes further in establishing that positive measures to correct past discriminatory treatment and inequality may 'constitute a legitimate differentiation ... if based on reasonable and objective criteria'.[126] This policy is clearly compatible with Article 1(4) of the Convention on the Elimination of All Forms of Racial Discrimination (discussed below).

There is no attempt by the committee to elaborate on the type of positive measures that a state should undertake.[127] The committee presumably felt that it was impossible to make up a prescription containing the most effective ways of eliminating past discrimination and achieving de facto equality in a vast variety of different types of minority needs. This failing might also be regarded because of the individualistic approach which in attempting to avoid any claims of rights inherent in a particular collectivity, has the effect of viewing minority issues as subjective and therefore requiring individual remedial measures rather than national programs for alleviating poverty and discrimination. It would be difficult to manipulate the individualistic language of Article 27 to stretch to any program of special group-orientated measures without undermining the rights of each individual member to choose their own ends.

Universality of the minority question

The final version of Article 27 clearly does not regard minority questions as a universal problem. The opening 'In those states in which minorities exist' seems at odds with the general purposes of the International Covenants which aim to secure universal respect for human rights. There is clearly opportunity here for any member state to refuse to acknowledge the existence of minority groups within the state

---

124 Capotorti *supra* n12 at 16.

125 Thornberry *supra* n31 at Chapter 18.

126 CCPR/C/21/Rev.1/Add. 5 26 April 1994.

127 Although commentators such as Hailbronner *supra* n111 at 134 suggest measures such as the right to use their own language and establish schools and newspapers she does not suggest where the responsibility for funding such initiatives would rest.

and while it has been reiterated that the protection of Article 27 does not depend on national classifications[128] there must be some conflict with notions of territorial integrity.[129]

Although Article 27 refers to 'persons' rather than nations or citizens, immigrant groups would appear to be excluded from the Article 27 provisions.[130] The rationale for this omission may be the expectation that immigrant groups should adopt the values of their new society and become fully integrated. This approach seems at odds with the needs of minority groups who may be fleeing cultural persecution in their home country and who do not satisfy the stringent requirements for political refugees.[131] The approach is also clearly at odds with a general comment under Article 40 of the Covenant on the position of aliens.[132]

In conjunction with other covenant provisions

After examining the rights contained in Article 27 and the Declaration, Nigel Rodley argues persuasively that Article 27 adds nothing new to the range of other rights contained in the Covenants which could be used to protect the cultural identity of individuals. He cites Article 2(1) and Article 26 on non-discrimination, which when read in conjunction with Article 18, would guarantee the rights to practice a particular religion to a member of a minority group.[133] Similarly, in relation to language, Article 26 can be read to provide the same protection as Article 4(3) of the declaration. The response of the European Court of Human Rights in the Belgian Linguistics Case adds weight to this approach; the absence of education provided in the French minority language in a Dutch unilingual region, constituted discrimination on the grounds of language.[134]

The cultural rights of members of minorities present more of a problem for Rodley's theory. Article 15 of the Economic Social and Cultural Covenant contains a progressive guarantee of the right to one's culture but this would seem to fall short of the standard in Article 27 which is of immediate effect. Article 19 of the ICCPR

---

128   General Comment No 18 (1994) *supra* n111 para. 4.

129   *Ibid.* para. 3.2 states that the enjoyment of rights under Article 27 'does not prejudice the sovereignty or territorial integrity of a State party'.

130   Report of the 3rd Committee, GAOR 16th Session, Agenda item 35, at 14. UN doc A/5000/Annexes (1961–62). Such an approach is strongly criticised by Nowak *supra* n65 at 488–9.

131   Ramaga, P 'The Group Concept in Minority Protection' (1993) *HRQ* 15 at 575–588.

132   General Comment 15/27 of 22 July 1986 (Position of Aliens). Para. 7 states that 'in those cases where aliens constitute a minority within the meaning of Article 27, they shall not be denied the right, in community with the other members of their group, to enjoy their own culture, practice their own religion and to use their own language'.

133   Rodley, Nigel 'Conceptual Problems In the Protection of Minorities: International Legal Developments' (1995) *HRQ* 17 at 57.

134   *Belgian Linguistics Case* 1474/62 1EHRR p252.

guarantees freedom of expression which could cover most of the artistic element of culture and language,[135] but this is only one element of any culture.[136]

John Packer looks at minority rights protection as essentially an issue of freedom of association.[137] Clearly, the approach taken by the Human Rights Commission in *Lovelace* vs. *Canada*[138] would support his contention. The committee had to consider whether Ms Lovelace, a Maliseet Indian, was a member of that tribe after marrying and subsequently divorcing a non-Indian. Applying Article 27 the Committee found that her rights were interfered with as she had been denied access to the other members of her community with which to enjoy her culture (essentially a matter of freedom of association).[139]

Nevertheless, the inclusion of an article dealing specifically with minorities has important implications. On one hand it could be seen as oppositional to the general emphasis dealing purely with individuals[140] and may therefore appear to be suggesting that minority rights are in conflict with individual human rights and that there is no compatibility. On the other hand, Article 27 essentially delineates the importance of the rights of members of minorities and indicates that an individualistic approach alone will be deficient in providing de facto equality. This fundamental importance is seen in the absence of a limitation provision where 'necessary to protect public safety, health, or morals or the fundamental rights and freedoms of others'.[141]

Consideration of State reports by the Human Rights Committee

It is interesting to note the Human Rights Committee makes frequent criticisms of state inaction under Article 27 in respect of the Roma minority. A selection of examples is presented here.

---

135 Prof. de Varennes gave evidence to the Sub-commission Working Group on Minorities that contravention's of freedom of expression, including language, constituted some of the most direct threats to minorities. Examples were given of the prohibition of the Chinese language in Indonesia; the restrictions on the language of the Kurds in Turkey and in Algeria where the Berber language was restricted in certain sections of the private sphere: Sub-Commission on the Prevention of Discrimination and Protection of Minorities 48th session *Protection of Minorities* (1996) para. 29 (E/CN.4/Sub.2/1996/28).

136 Rodley *supra* n133 at 59.

137 Packer *supra* n6 p23-65.

138 *Lovelace* vs. *Canada* No 24/1997 2 *HRLJ* 158 (1981).

139 Lovelace actually lost the case as there was a reasonable and objective justification for the legislation which was consistent with the rest of the Covenant, i.e., to protect the identity of the Maliseet tribe.

140 Article 1 is the exception and is something of an anomaly.

141 The original draft intended for the Declaration and proposed by the Sub-commission in 1947 included such a limitation in the interests of public order and security (E/CN.4/52 at 9 (1947)). However, Ramaga notes that an interference with Article 27 may be justified if there is a reasonable and objective justification and consistency with other convention provisions: Ramaga, Phillip. V 'Relativity of the Minority concept' (1992) *HRQ* Vol 14 pp 104–119 at 112.

Following the report of Romania in 1993, the Committee were concerned about the problem of discrimination and ethnic violence towards people from minority groups. It noted:

> This situation is especially threatening to vulnerable groups, such as the Roma (gypsies). The Committee is concerned that the Government has not been sufficiently active in combating such discrimination or effectively countering incidents of violence committed against members of minority groups.[142]

Here the two-pronged effect of Article 27 is clearly visible. The Committee are concerned with the condition of the Roma as a collectivity but they then adopt individualistic wording when criticising the absence of measures to prevent discrimination. The Committee went on to advocate the need for positive measures to counter discrimination in the media, particularly regarding the Roma.[143]

Following the Bulgarian report, the Human Rights Committee expressed concern over the disadvantages faced by the Roma community in Bulgaria;[144] and in their comments to the Hungarian Government the Roma minority were again singled out as the particularly vulnerable victims of prejudice and discrimination.[145] Such concern was not purely related to the central and Eastern European states however, with Ireland being similarly criticised in respect of the lack of electoral and public affairs participation amongst travelling people.[146]

Elaboration of Article 27: The Declaration on the Rights of Persons Belonging to National or Ethnic, Religious and Linguistic Minorities

Following a recommendation by Professor Capotorti,[147] the Sub-Commission has been involved in developing a draft Declaration on the Rights of Persons Belonging to Minorities. Following a three-year study by Special Rapporteur Asbjorn Eide,[148] a Declaration was finally adopted in 1993.[149]

---

142 *Comments of the HRC on the Report of Romania*, Part D para. 9 5.11.93 (CCPR/C/79/Add. 30).

143 *Ibid.* para. 14.

144 *Comments of the HRC on the Report of Bulgaria*, Part D, para. 8 3.8.93 (CCPR/C/79/Add. 24).

145 *Comments of the HRC on the Report of Hungary*, Part D, para. 10 3.8.93 (CCPR/C/79/Add. 24).

146 *Comments of the HRC on the Report of Ireland*, para. 23 3.8.93 (CCPR/C/79/Add. 21).

147 Capotorti *supra* n12 at Add 5, para. 59.

148 Eide 'Protection of Minorities: Recommendations to the UN Sub-Commission' in *supra* n2.

149 *UN Declaration on the Rights of Persons Belonging to National or Ethnic, Religious and Linguistic* Minorities UN General Assembly Res. 47/135.

In carrying out his study into constructive and peaceful ways of resolving minority problems, Eide was asked to '... accord special attention to and to provide information on the specific conditions in which the Roma (gypsies) live'.[150]

The Declaration should be viewed as a reinforcement of the weak provisions in Article 27. It contains no definition of minorities but it does list a number of basic principles which, if implemented, would serve to greatly improve the situation of most minority groups. The Working Group on the Protection of Minorities collects information on state constitutions and domestic legislation in order to assess the extent of minority protection.[151] In addition, short studies concerning the interpretation of the Declaration's core principles are being undertaken.

The preamble considers that:

> The promotion and protection of the rights of persons belonging to national or ethnic, religious and linguistic minorities contribute to the political and social stability of States in which they live.[152]

The individual emphasis is still dominant, but Article 1 goes into new territory by requiring states to protect the identity of minorities as well as their existence (which is effectively guaranteed by the Genocide Convention).[153] A vast range of subjects dear to the hearts of minorities are covered in the nine articles. These include:

- education, which should promote awareness of the minorities traditions and culture,[154]
- participation in cultural, religious, social, economic and public life as well as the right to participate in decisions concerning the minority at a national and, where appropriate, regional level;[155] and
- the right to associate and maintain contact with other members of the minority group.[156]

In contrast to Article 27, there is a clear positive obligation on states to take:

> Necessary measures to create favourable conditions to enable persons belonging to minorities to express their characteristics and to develop their culture, language, religion, traditions and customs, except where specific practices are in violation of national law and contrary to international standards.[157]

---

150   ECS, Commission on Human Rights Protection of Roma (gypsies) 1992/65 E/CN.4/1992/L. 72.

151   Eide *supra* n2 at 6.

152   For full text see *HRLJ* vol. 14 No 1–2 at 55–6.

153   Article 1(1): 'States shall protect the existence and the national or ethnic, cultural, religious and linguistic identity of minorities within their respective territories, and shall encourage conditions for the promotion of that identity'.

154   Article 4(4).

155   Article 2(2) and 2(3) respectively.

156   Article 2(5).

157   Article 4(2).

It is interesting to note that the state can only evade this obligation if the practices of the group are contrary to international standards as well as domestic legislation. Thus, it would appear to be outside the spirit of the declaration for a state to fail to support the travelling lifestyle of nomadic Roma/Gypsies on the basis that national legislation prohibits unauthorised stopping and camping.

In this respect the Declaration is symbolically very important. Eide notes that it marks a departure from the common domain where equality is the predominant value. The separate domain envisaged by the Declaration is about the lasting manifestation of difference and it is not confined to remedial measures aimed at ensuring equality for all.[158]

The Declaration does contain a number of significant weaknesses and can be criticised for doing too little too late – a seemingly inevitable consequence of international compromise. Minorities were not consulted during the drafting process[159] and by looking at the measures omitted from the Declaration the deficiencies are all too apparent. There is no definition of minorities, enabling a subjective interpretation by states anxious to avoid a guarantee of basic minority rights for non-nations and new ethnic collectivities.[160] The emphasis of the wording is on 'should' rather than 'shall' or 'will' and the provisions are qualified with the words 'where possible,' enabling a more gradual and possibly partial implementation of these essential measures. There is also, perhaps unsurprisingly, no right of minority autonomy included in the Declaration, thus the protection of minority identity is again at the hands of the particular state rather than an inalienable right of the group. Furthermore, Rodley argues that the goal of the Declaration as a whole is unclear and the same results could be obtained through the application of Article 26 of the ICCPR to a particular minority issue.[161] Sigler's observations concerning Article 27 are equally applicable to the new Declaration. He noted:

> The Covenant represents a minimalist version of minority rights. Minority rights are not promoted by such a provision. Minorities are not given special economic, social or political advantages, nor is their position made secure against majority culture, language or religion. Certainly, no kind of autonomy is envisaged by the 1966 covenant, not are minorities entitled to any institutional safeguards.[162]

---

158   Eide, A 'Peaceful group accommodation as an alternative to secession in sovereign states' in Clark and Wiliamson (1996) *Self-Determination. International Perspectives* Macmillan pp 87–110 at 100.

159   Alfredsson and de Zayas *supra* n113 at 3.

160   Thornberry, P 'International and European Standards on Minority Rights' in Miall (1994) *Minority Rights In Europe: The Scope for a Transnational Regime* Pinter pubs, London at 17 notes that Germany has insisted that the Declaration is limited to nationals and citizens of Germany, thus denying such rights to the large number of immigrant and refugee minority groups.

161   Rodley *supra* n133 at 57.

162   Sigler, J (1983) *Minority Rights: A Comparative Analysis* Greenwood Westport at 79.

There are significant 'shortcomings' in both UN minority provisions, but as Jackson-Preece argues, together they provide a floor for international thinking on minority questions.[163]

Thus, there are clearly a number of serious deficiencies in the Declaration. Yet there is some cause for optimism as there have already been some positive consequences. For example, in Hungary, it formed the basis for a new law on National and Ethnic Minorities[164] and was extended to provide for minority self-government in minority dominant regions. The Romanian Law on Education adopted in 1995 provides for the right of national minorities to receive education in their mother tongue at primary level and it further provides for the teaching of history and traditions of the national minority.[165] Furthermore, Professor Yacoub has contended that the Declaration could be a useful negotiating tool for minorities, reducing the desire to undermine political integrity.[166] Neither Article 27 nor the Declaration distinguish between citizens and non-citizens and, according to Professor Thornberry, it could therefore be used to prevent denial of citizenship.[167]

Other international provisions concerned with minority rights

Activities of UNESCO

The Declaration of International Cultural Co-operation affirmed that every people have the right and duty to develop their own culture.[168] Most importantly, UNESCO has recognised the importance of education in the development of minority culture and identity.[169] The UNESCO Convention on Discrimination in Education states that:

> It is essential to recognise the rights of members of national minorities to carry on their own educational activities, including the maintenance of schools and, depending on the educational policy of each State, the use or teaching of their own language.[170]

Drafted in 1960 when the importance of specific minority rights was hotly contested, this is clearly a weak provision. The rights of members of minorities are described as 'essential' at the outset, but it also appears that they may be watered down 'depending

---

163   *Supra* n118 at 131.

164   Sub-Commission on Prevention of Discrimination and Protection of Minorities 48th session Protection of Minorities Report of the Working Group on Minorities in its Second Session (1996) para. 22. (E/CN.4/Sub.2/1996/28).

165   *Ibid.* at para. 35.

166   *Ibid.* at para. 16.

167   *Ibid.* at para. 143 see also Prof. Eide at para. 145.

168   UNESCO Records of the General Conference, 14th Session 1966. Resolutions pp 86–89.

169   Hannum, H *Autonomy, Sovereignty and Self-determination: The Adjudication of Conflicting Rights* (1990) Pennsylvania Press at 460–1.

170   Article 5(c).

on the educational policy of each state'. The provision of education for minorities will be discussed in Chapter 5 in detail.

The non-binding UNESCO Declaration on Race and Racial Prejudice goes beyond the protection afforded by many of the binding documents by explicitly recognising the right to be different and the right to identity for both individuals and groups (including ethnic minorities). Article 5 is particularly relevant here as it recognises a right to cultural identity and the development of cultural life for groups.

However, the declaration has been criticised for its blanket approach which affords the right of identity to majority, dominant groups and minority groups alike.[171]

The 1989 Convention on the Rights of the Child

This document is unusual in that it has received widespread international support, being ratified by 192 states as of May 2006.[172] Article 30 provides for the protection of a child belonging to an ethnic, religious or linguistic minority. The Committee has so far failed to make use of Article 30 and has dealt with minority issues under the other Convention articles dealing with specific matters such as education, non-discrimination and development.[173]

Minority rights and discrimination

The issue of minority protection frequently emerges in the field of racial discrimination and intolerance. On the whole the policy has been individualist and is discussed in Chapter 3. However, there are certain provisions which specifically note the needs of members of minority groups for special measures and action to achieve de facto equality for the group. The approach taken by the Convention on the Elimination of All Forms of Racial Discrimination recognises the need for 'affirmative action,' which is deemed not to constitute discrimination under Article 1(4), providing that it does not:

> As a consequence, lead to the maintenance of separate rights for different racial groups and that they shall not be continued after the objectives for which they were taken have been achieved.[174]

Distinctions between citizens and non-citizens are permitted under the Convention.[175] Such a deliberate omission opens up a loop-hole in that states can argue that

---

171   See for example Henrard, Kristin *Devising an adequate system for minority Protection* (2000) Kluwer at 203.

172   UNHCR *Convention on the Rights of the Child* http://www.ohchr.org/english/countries/ratification/11.htm.

173   *Ibid.* at paras 80–1.

174   Article 1(4) International Convention on the Elimination of All Forms of Racial Discrimination.

175   Article 1(2) CERD. In *Demba Talibe Diop v France No 2/1989* (1991) *HRLJ* Vol 12 at 300 – the Committee could find no violation where a Senegalese lawyer living in France was denied a license to practice at the Bar.

discriminatory treatment is not based on ethnic characteristics but rather on lack of citizenship. Meron recommends that the state should have the burden of proving that such discriminatory treatment was based exclusively on alienage: 'The use of the citizenship exception as a pretext for discrimination could thus have been avoided'.[176] The situation of the Roma in the Czech Republic (discussed in Chapter 4) illustrates the way in which citizenship criteria can be manipulated to exclude unpopular minority groups.

The International Labour Organization 'Discrimination (Employment and Occupation) Convention' 1958 (no 111)

Covering discrimination in employment, an ILO Commission of Inquiry has been concerned with the situation of specific minority groups on several occasions, including one enquiry which recommended greater respect for the minority languages of the Magyar and Roma minorities in Romania.[177]

Regional Minority Protection

The Organisation on Security and Cooperation in Europe
The Conference, now 'Organisation', on Security and Cooperation in Europe (hereafter, OSCE) has made considerable developments in international cooperation in the fields of human rights as well as in security and military issues. In 1994, 53 states had made political commitments to implement the CSCE initiatives contained in the Helsinki Final Act of 1975[178] and the numerous follow-up meetings.[179]

The Conference Process
The CSCE focus on cultural rights is essentially individualistic. The Helsinki Final Act contains detailed provisions on individual rights to culture but the provision dealing with collective rights to culture and identity is by comparison, short and 'unsophisticated'.[180] Over the past 20 years a clear development has taken place regarding the attitude of CSCE states to the problem of minorities. Helgesen notes that the Vienna Concluding Document[181] was something of a landmark in the changing attitudes of member states: 'For the first time in the CSCE Process, all

176 Meron, T *Human Rights Law Making in the United Nations* (1986) Clarendon Oxford at 44.
177 Sub-Commission *supra* n164 at para. 94.
178 Final Act of the Conference on Security and Co-operation in Europe, 1 August 1975 reprinted in 14 *ILM* 527.
179 Eide (1993) *supra* n2 at 7.
180 Helgesen, January 'Protecting Minorities in the CSCE Process' in Rosas and Helgesen (eds) *The Strength of Diversity Human Rights and Pluralist Democracy* (1992) Martinus-Nijhoff at 162.
181 Concluding Document of the Vienna meting of the Conference on Security and Cooperation in Europe, 4 November 1986 − 7 January 1989, reprinted in 28 *ILM* 527.

(but one) of the participating states really wanted to comply with these fundamental values'.[182]

The Vienna document[183] goes further than previous documents in explicitly requiring that 'legislative, administrative, judicial and other' measures be adopted. This development continued pace during the run up to the Copenhagen meeting, which took place in a post-Communist Europe, and bought a new range of ideas and approaches to the subject of minority rights.

The Copenhagen document on the Human Dimension[184] has been 'hailed as a veritable European charter on democracy,'[185] Part IV focuses entirely on the protection of minorities. It recognises that the protection of the rights of persons belonging to minorities 'is an essential factor for peace, justice, stability and democracy in the participating state'. The main areas of concern are minority languages, education and political participation in a climate of pluralism. The right to education is linked to the rights of minorities to 'develop their culture in all its aspects free of any attempts at assimilation against their will'[186] and in furtherance of these objective, members of national minorities are given the right to establish their own educational institutions and to seek voluntary financial contributions and public assistance.[187]

As far as political participation is concerned there is an implicit recognition that majoritarian democracy may not be sufficient to protect the interests of minorities;[188] 'appropriate local or autonomous administrations' are envisaged.[189]

The situation of the Roma in Europe was specifically highlighted as a cause for concern. The document declares:

> The participating states clearly and unequivocally condemn totalitarianism, racial and ethnic hatred, anti-Semitism, xenophobia, and discrimination against everyone as well as persecution on religious and ideological grounds. In this context, they also recognise the particular problems of Roma (gypsies).[190]

The states pledged to take the measures to provide necessary laws to protect against discrimination and ethnic violence, and to promote tolerance and understanding particularly through education.

In 1991, the Geneva Meeting of Experts on National Minorities was similarly concerned about the rise in discrimination and xenophobia and reiterated paragraph 40:

---

182   Helgesen *supra* n180 at 168.

183   *Supra* n179.

184   Document of the Copenhagen Meeting of the Conference on the Human Dimension of the CSCE, June 29th 1990 reprinted in (1990) *HRLJ* at 232.

185   Glover, A 'The Human Dimension of the OSCE: From Standard setting to Implementation' 1995 *Helsinki Monitor* No 3 at 2.

186   *Supra* n184 at para. 32.

187   *Ibid.* at para. 32.2.

188   Hannum, H 'Contemporary Developments in the International Protection of the Rights of Minorities' (1991) *notre* Dame Law Review Vol 66 pp 1431–1448 at 1442.

189   Para. 35.

190   *Supra* n184 Chapter IV, para. 40.

In this context they reaffirm their recognition of the particular problems of Roma (gypsies). They are ready to undertake effective measures in order to achieve full equality of opportunity between persons belonging to Roma ordinarily resident in their State and the rest of the resident population. They will also encourage research and studies regarding Roma and the particular problems they face.[191]

In the Document of the Helsinki Follow-up Meeting (1992), the participating states agree to consider taking appropriate steps to address the escalating issues of intolerance and discrimination.[192] The need to promote human rights education and cross-cultural training and research were stressed. Furthermore, the participating states:

> Reaffirm, in this context, the need to develop appropriate programmes addressing problems of their respective nations belonging to Roma and other groups traditionally identified as Gypsies and to create conditions for them to have equal opportunities to participate fully in the life of society, and will consider how to co-operate to this end.[193]

By 1991 the Yugoslav crisis revealed the extent of the CSCE's inability to respond to international security threats. Rady argues that previous unwillingness to elaborate on collective rights contributed to this failure.[194] The negotiators involved in reaching a settlement in Yugoslavia were forced to adapt the framework of collective rights in both political and territorial spheres as well as the more traditional cultural sphere.[195]

In 1994, The Budapest Declaration established the Contact Point for Roma and Sinti issues within the Office for Democratic Institutions and Human Rights (hereafter ODIHR). The contact point facilitates contacts between states on issues facing Roma and Sinti and provides information on the initiatives and programmes concerning them,[196] a newsletter has been established to communicate these developments.

It is evident that the OSCE process has raised the profile of minority rights issues generally,[197] in particular the plight of the Roma.[198] Many minority rights activists and commentators point to the OSCE's fieldwork missions as evidence of its continued importance in the field of minority protection.[199] Nevertheless, recent Conferences

---

191   CSCE Report of the Geneva Meeting of Experts on National Minorities 1990, Chapter VI.

192   CSCE Document of the Helsinki *follow-up Meeting* 1992 Chapter IV, para. 35.

193   *Ibid.*

194   Rady, M 'Minority rights and Self-determination in Contemporary Eastern Europe' (1993) *Slavonic and East European Review* Vol 71, 4 pp 717–727 at 722.

195   *Ibid.* 722–724.

196   CSCE Budapest Document 1994, towards A Genuine Partnership in a New Era, Budapest decisions viii, 4. para. 23. For details on the work of the Contact Point see ODIHR *From Budapest to Lisbon* 1996 at 34–5 CSCE

197   Thornberry in Miall (ed.) *supra* n160.

198   See for example CSCE *supra* n41.

199   Neukirch, Simhandl and Zellner 'Implementing Minority Rights in the framework of the CSCE/OSCE' in Council of Europe Mechanisms for the Implementation of Minority Rights (2005) C/E at Chapter 7.

have recognised the urgent need to focus on methods of implementation. The Budapest document of 1994 decided to concentrate efforts on improving the co-operation framework in order to improve the effectiveness of the effectiveness of the Conference documents.[200]

The following year, a Conference dealing specifically with Implementation was held in Warsaw.[201] No negotiated document resulted from the meeting, the purpose being to record the problems faced by participating states in meeting their political obligations, and make suggestions for their solution.[202] Representatives from non-governmental organisations are invited to take part in working groups and plenary sessions and may raise problems of concern in specific states'.[203]

The work of the High Commissioner on National Minorities
The office of the High Commissioner was established in 1992 following the Helsinki Summit.[204] The High Commissioner acts as an early warning mechanism for situations of minority conflict and also examines the situation of minorities issuing specific reports and recommendations.[205] The role of the High Commissioner is confined to situations involving minorities and there is no jurisdiction over individual rights.[206] The reports and recommendations are non-binding but they do have strong political influence and may prove more use than the Framework Convention. In relation to political participation, the Commissioner has gone further than Article 15 of the Convention in advocating the development of specialised organs to deal with legislation concerning minorities.[207]

In 1993, the High Commissioner undertook an investigation of the situation of the Roma throughout Europe.[208] He was asked by the Committee of senior officials 'to study the social, economic and humanitarian problems relating to the Roma population in some participating states and the relevance of these problems to the mandate of the High Commissioner'.[209] The report advocated greater respect for individual rights

---

200   CSCE *supra* n196 decisions viii, 4.

201   OSCE Implementation Meeting on Human Dimension Issues, Warsaw 2–19 October 1995.

202   For the relationship between the Implementation Meeting and the Budapest document as well as recent concerns with problems affecting the Roma see Estebanez, Maria 'The OSCE Implementation Meeting on Human Dimension Issues 1995' 1996 *Helsinki Monitor* 7 No 1.

203   Glover *supra* n185 at 3.

204   Helsinki Decisions of 10 July 1992 *HRLJ* 13 at 289.

205   (1992 *ILM* Vol 6 1385; Packer, J paper given to *Minority Rights in the* 'New' *Europe*' Conference, Univ. of Central Lancashire. November 1996.

206   CSCE Helsinki Document 1992 *The Challenges of Change: Helsinki Summit Declaration, II, 5 (c)*

207   Letter of the OSCE High Commissioner on National Minorities to Slovak Republic, CSCE Communication No 36, Vienna, 14 November 1994.

208   The only example to date of a non-territorial minority to be investigated by the Commissioner.

209   CSCE *Roma* (Gypsies) *in the* CSCE Region Report of the High Commissioner on National Minorities (1993) CSCE.

coupled with measures recognising the identity and specific needs of the Roma. Such measures '… may also include special government policies for addressing Roma-related issues in such areas as employment, education, health care, and general welfare'.[210]

The Council of Europe

Notwithstanding the absence of a specific minority provision in the European Convention on Human Rights, the Council of Europe has played a vital role in many recent initiatives concerning the treatment of the Roma.[211] Studies and conferences have been established with funding from the Council along with the OSCE which have dramatically increased awareness of the issues facing the Roma community. Many of these reports and seminars, as well as the Interface Collection which receives Council of Europe funding, are referred to throughout this book, but the aim of this chapter is to focus specifically on international human rights provisions and their weaknesses, and thus it is not the place of this chapter to make a detailed assessment of the Council of Europe's activity in their non-judicial/legislative capacity.

The European Convention on Human Rights and Fundamental Freedoms (1950) contains no substantive provision dealing with the rights of minorities comparable to Article 27.[212] The only mention of minorities is found in Article 14 which prohibits discrimination on the grounds of association, inter alia, with a national minority. Members of minorities may seek to protect their identity under one of the substantive Articles, such as Article 11 concerning freedom of association and assembly or Article 9 on freedom of religion, coupled with Article 14[213] but this is clearly an individual procedure and cannot be pursued by collectivities. The solution of minority problems through individual rights enforcement has already been addressed from a critical perspective in Chapter 3.

The Framework Convention on the Rights of Persons Belonging to National Minorities

The movement towards a specific minority rights convention in Europe began 30 years ago when the Committee of Ministers considered a draft protocol to the European Convention on 'persons belonging to national minorities'.[214]

---

210   *Ibid.* at 5.1 para. 2.

211   For further details see Council of Europe Council of Europe Activities on Travellers and Gypsies CDMG (92) 10 Revelation 2 (1993).

212   In *G and E v Norway* (1983) 9278/81 *and* 9415/81, DR 35/30, the commission stated: 'the convention does not guarantee specific rights to minorities … [though] under Article 8(1), a minority group is, in principle, entitled to claim the right to respect for the particular lifestyle it leads as constituting "private life", "family life" or "home"'. Marquand notes that the 'convention organs have been careful not to find that there are minority rights when to do so may upset the political balances of the states in which the minority is present' in 'Human Rights Protection and Minorities' (1994) *Public Law* pp 359–366 at 365.

213   See for example *Buckley* vs. *UK* (1992) 20348/92.

214   Report of the Committee of Experts on Human Rights to the Committee of Ministers, adopted on 9 November 1973 (C/E, DH/Exo (73) 47), discussed in Capotorti *supra* n12 at 11.

In more recent times the debate gathered momentum with the increase of minority-based conflicts, particularly in the former Yugoslavia. A steering committee was established in 1991 to consider the best way for the Council of Europe to address this deficiency.[215] The following year, the Parliamentary Assembly noted:

> 7. There have been more and more colloquies and conferences of every kind. The extreme diversity of situations has now been properly recorded, described and analysed, as have the very great variety of problems raised and the difficulties, both legal and political, involved in solving them.
>
> 8. All of this is no longer enough. These analyses and these conclusions that nothing can be done are no longer acceptable. There is an urgent need for international decisions and commitments which can rapidly be implemented in the area concerned. Peace, democracy, freedoms and respect for human rights in Europe are at stake.[216]

In 1993, the Parliamentary Assembly recommended an additional protocol on the rights of minorities to the European Convention.[217] This document included a definition of the term 'national minority'[218] and went as far as providing for local or autonomous authorities for national minorities.[219] The Vienna summit of October 1993 saw the Heads of State advocating legal commitments for minority protection, and a draft protocol to complement the ECHR in the cultural field was commenced by the ad hoc Committee for the Protection of National Minorities.[220] In February 1995 the Framework Convention for the Protection of National Minorities was opened for signature requiring 12 ratification's to bring it into force.[221] The Convention entered

---

215   Following Parliamentary Assembly Recommendation 1134 (1990); see also Committee of Ministers Recommendation No *R (92)* 10 on the implementation of rights of persons belonging to national minorities.

216   Parliamentary Assembly Recommendation 1177 (1992) on the rights of minorities (23rd sitting) paras 7–8.

217   Parliamentary Assembly of the Council of Europe Recommendation 1201 (1993) on an additional protocol on the rights of minorities to the ECHR, reproduced in Klebes, H 'Draft Protocol on Minority rights to the ECHR' (1993) *HRLJ* 14 pp 140–144 at 144.

218   The definition reiterated in Recommendation 1255 (1995) (Parliamentary Assembly 3rd sitting) refers to 'a group of persons in a state who: a) reside on the territory of that state and are citizens (my emphasis), b) maintain long-standing, form and lasting ties with that State, c) display distinctive ethnic, cultural, religious or linguistic characteristics, d) are sufficiently representative, although smaller in number that the rest of the population of the State in which they live, e) are motivated by a concern to preserve together that which constitutes their common identity, including their culture, their traditions, their religion or their language'.

219   Article 11. Special Rapporteur Mr. Bindig noted that this provision in particular was controversial and resulted in a cautious approach by the Vienna Commission at the summit (Report on the protection of the rights of Minorities Doc.7572 1996).

220   Adopted by Committee of Ministers at the 95th Ministerial session on 10 November 1994. For details of the background see the Explanatory report to the Framework Convention (1995) H (95) 10.

221   Council of Europe Framework Convention for the Protection of National Minorities and Explanatory Report (1995) H (95) 10.

into force on 1 February 1998 and has now been ratified by 35 states. Three Council of Europe states have omitted to sign or ratify the convention – France, Andorra and Turkey.

The Convention situates minority rights protection squarely within the human rights paradigm. Marc Weller observes a fundamental shift from the security dimension of minority rights towards the promotion of a harmonious and inclusive society.[222] Democracy is embedded with divergent values and identities which are able to co-exist peacefully in a spirit if pluralism.[223] As evidence of this shift he points to co-governance whereby minority constituencies are entitled to participated fully in public decision making and to have equal opportunities in all aspects of public life.

> Although described as rights according to members of minorities, there is clearly a collective dimension envisaged and the state obligations go beyond the negative formulation of Article 27 ICCPR.

The Convention, like the OSCE, prefers the term 'national minority' to the ICCPR formulation of 'religious, linguistic and ethnic minority'. It is clear that the Convention rights have been greatly influenced by the OSCE, particularly part IV of the Copenhagen document, although the final, legal commitments have clearly watered down the political obligations.[224]

There is no definition of 'national minority' in the Framework Convention. The Explanatory Report notes that 'it is impossible to arrive at a definition capable of mustering general support of all Council of Europe member states' and advocates a 'pragmatic approach'.[225] By contrast, a proposal to the Human Rights Commission by the Soviet delegate to replace 'ethnic, linguistic or religious minority' with 'national minority' in Article 27 of the ICCPR had not been accepted. He defined national minority as 'an historically formed community of people characterized by a common language, a common territory, a common economic life and a common psychological structure manifesting itself in a common culture'.[226] The rigid application of these criteria is certainly not a prerequisite for the minority status in the Council of Europe documents if we compare the approach taken in the influential OSCE process. The OSCE has also shied away from elaboration in this respect, although Helgesen notes that there is agreement on the only distinct implication being that the individual must be a national of the given state in order to enjoy the particular protection.[227]

---

222 Weller, M (ed.) *The Rights of Minorities in Europe* (2005) OUP at 624.

223 For introductory commentary see Heintze, Hans-Joachim 'Article 1' and Malloy, Tove 'Title and preamble' in Weller *ibid.*

224 Gilbert, Geoff 'Council of Europe and Minority Rights' (1996) *HRQ* Vol 18 pp 160–189 at 186.

225 *Supra* n221 at 12, para. 12. See also Heintze *supra* n223 at 82–5.

226 UN Doc E/CN.4/SR.369 (1953) at 16. This is akin to Stalin's criteria for a nationality discussed in the Chapter 4 on Czech Citizenship.

227 Helgesen *supra* n180 at 163; see also Mullerson, R 'Minorities in Eastern Europe and the Former USSR: Problems, Tendencies and Protection' (1993) *MLR* 56, 793–811 at 807.

The link between citizenship and minority status is of fundamental importance and Helgesen's conclusions are evidenced in Part IV of the CSCE Geneva report which states that 'the participating states affirm that every person belonging to a national minority will enjoy the same rights and have the same duties of citizenship as the rest of the population'.[228] If the same approach were to be adopted by the Council of Europe,[229] non-citizens would be outside the ambit of the Convention;[230] a consequence that would considerably undermine its significance. Gilbert observes that this could be particularly problematic for the Roma who are generally regarded as a minority but who may be excluded from nationality legislation.[231] He argues that whether Roma constitute a 'national minority' in this sense could prove to be debatable.[232]

Indeed, Tove Malloy's recent work *National Minority Rights in Europe* excludes Roma altogether on the basis that national minorities are autochthonous communities, i.e., native to a particular region which was once either independent or belonged to a neighbouring state.[233] Contrary to the evidence, Malloy considers the Roma and Sinti to be nomads who, until 1989, were largely confined to Eastern Europe and whose present adverse circumstances are economic and can thus be solved by economic strategies rather than minority protection.

This approach was taken in the drafting of the Hungarian minorities' law, discussed in Chapter 7, where citizenship is listed as one of the criteria for membership of a national or ethnic minority.[234] It should be reiterated that the use of bilateral treaties which may serve to promote the status of minority groups in their host countries will be unlikely to improve this situation – the Roma's absence of a homeland state removes a powerful bargaining tool in minority negotiations between states. The Treaty of Good Neighbourliness and Friendly, Co-operation between the Slovak Republic and the Republic of Hungary incorporated the obligations under

---

228   1991 *ILM* 30 1692.

229   Wheatley argues that: 'At the most basic level, a "national minority" group must encompass less than half the population of the State (i.e. be a "minority"), and members of the group must be nationals of the State … sharing some ethnic, linguistic or cultural factor which distinguishes them from the majority' in 'The Council of Europe's Framework Convention on National Minorities' (1996) 5 *WebJCLI*.

230   Klebes, Heinrich implies that 'national' means minorities resident within the particular territory who are citizens of that State, Klebes, H 'The Council of Europe's Framework Convention for the Protection of National Minorities' (1995) *HRLJ* Vol 16 92, 114.

231   One cannot have a Hungarian and a Roma nationality. Berman, Stephen 'Gypsies: A national group or a social group' (1994) *Refugee Survey Question* Vol 13, 4 p51 at 60–61.

232   Gilbert *supra* n224 at 176–7; see also Klebes *supra* n230 at 143 who notes that an alternative approach of linking the minority with a territory rather than a State may similarly exclude 'gypsies'.

233   Malloy, T *National Minority Rights in Europe* (2005) OUP at 22–4.

234   Chapter 1, S1 Act LXXVII of 1993 *on the Rights of National and Ethnic Minorities*.

the Framework Convention into the mutual responsibilities of the treaty.[235] The Hungarian Status Law went further and controversially sought to extend Framework Convention rights to the estimated five million Hungarians living outside Hungary.[236] Such initiatives demonstrate the strength which can come from association with a specific territory or nation, something the Roma are unable to use.

The explanatory report to the FC has been used by some states to suggest that recognition of the protected minorities is a matter to be determined by the state. Article 3 of the Explanatory report makes minority identity both a subjective matter, for the individual, and an objective matter.[237] However, since the Convention has entered into force it has become apparent that the interpretation of 'national minorities' is not the sole preserve of the signatory states. Those states, such as Denmark, that have attempted to confine the convention to specified minorities and states that have made citizenship a prerequisite to Convention protection,[238] have been rebuked by the Advisory Committee.[239] However, there remains a great deal of divergence among states as to which minorities they accept as requiring Framework Convention protection.[240]

It is similarly evident from the reports of the Advisory Committee that the situation of non-territorial minorities, particularly the Roma, will be scrutinised in the monitoring process. Indeed, the majority of reports issued to date make specific reference to the continued discrimination and disadvantaged experienced by the Roma. Nevertheless, there has been criticism that the Advisory Committee has not been sufficiently proactive in calling states to account for non-recognition of minorities, including the Cypriot and Danish Roma.[241]

Content of the Framework Convention
Article 1 clearly establishes that the protection of minorities and their members constitutes a fundamental element in international human rights law. It is apparent from the Explanatory Report that this does not constitute recognition of collective rights,[242] with the general emphasis on 'persons belonging to minorities' as in the ICCPR. Any notion of minority rights is situated squarely within the human rights paradigm.[243] Nevertheless, the Convention does contain rights which, although

---

235   Article 15(4)(a) *Treaty on Good Neighbourliness and Friendly Cooperation between the Slovak Republic and the Republic of Hungary* (1995).

236   Hungarian Status Law Act LXII on Hungarians Living in Neighbouring Countries (2001).

237   Dimitras, Panayote Elias 'Recognition of minorities in Europe: Protecting Rights and Dignity' (2004) *Minority Rights Group International Briefing* at 3.

238   Austria, Estonia, Switzerland and Poland have issued declarations linking national minority status to citizenship.

239   Phillips, A (2002) *The Framework Convention for the Protection of National Minorities: A policy analysis* Minority Rights Group International.

240   Heintze 'Article 3' in Weller *supra* n222 at 113.

241   *Supra* n237.

242   *Supra* n221 at 12, para. 13.

243   Thornberry, P (2004) *Minority Rights in Europe* Council of Europe Publishing at 100.

couched in individual terms, clearly apply to collectivities per se and could only be enforced by such collectivities.

Special measures are envisaged by the Convention if necessary to combat discrimination and to ensure de factor equality. As Gilbert states 'equal treatment should take precedence over simple non-discrimination'.[244]

Article 5 asserts:

1. The parties undertake to promote the conditions necessary for persons belonging to national minorities to maintain and develop their culture, and to preserve the essential elements of their identity, namely their religion, language traditions and cultural heritage.

2. Without prejudice to measures taken in pursuance of their general integration policy, the parties shall refrain from policies or practices aimed at assimilation of persons belonging to national minorities against their will and shall protect these persons from any action aimed at such assimilation

Gilbert argues that, if justiciable, Article 5 could only be enforced by the group, to talk of purely individual rights to maintain and develop culture is meaningless.[245] Furthermore, he identifies a positive obligation arising from Articles 5 and 15 to ensure that minorities are directly involved in identifying their needs and a correlative obligation on the state to provide the resources to realise them.[246] He goes on to argue that such special measures are particularly appropriate to the Roma who have suffered 'entrenched discrimination' and 'institutionalized racism'.[247]

The Convention expands some of the individual rights contained within the ECHR, such as freedom of expression and association. It also develops specific minority – centred rights such as rights to practice religion and language and advocates improvement in representation in a variety of contexts – including media, politics and education. Article 16 prohibits expulsion and forced eviction, something to which the Roma are particularly vulnerable as recognised by the UN Committee on Economic, Social and Cultural Rights.[248] Although the Advisory Committee has offered little analysis of Article 16, the evictions of many Greek Roma from land designated for Olympic Games developments will obviously invite some comments. The actions of the Greek authorities led to a violation of the rights to family life and housing under Article 16 of the European Social Charter.[249]

On the whole, the Convention can be criticised as suffering from the same flaws as the UN Declaration on the Rights of Persons Belonging to Minorities, discussed above. The language focus is typically progressive rather than immediate and there is little positive action required from states. Steketee argues that the lack of concrete obligations is a recognition that a 'one size fits all approach' would fail to address

---

244 Gilbert *supra* n224 at 156.

245 *Ibid.* at 183.

246 *Supra* n223 at 158.

247 *Ibid.* at 171.

248 General Comment No 4 'The right to adequate housing, Article 11(1)' 6th session, 1991 Report of the CESCR on the Right to Adequate Housing para. 3.

249 See Committee of Ministers ResChS (2005) 11–8 June 2005.

the diverse needs of minorities across Europe.[250] However, in a powerful critique of the Convention, Alfredsson identifies a variety of shortcomings which undermine the validity and legitimacy of the Convention:

> These shortcomings include the programmatic formulation of the FC, the limited scope of the special measures called for in order to eliminate discrimination and to achieve dignity and equal rights, weak wording and frequent qualifications in the text, the absence of group rights, a monitoring instance relying only on the examination of State reports, political control over the monitoring body, and the apparent opening for States to arbitrarily identify minorities which are entitled to protection under the FC, thus implying the rejection of other groups.[251]

The opening lines of Articles 8–11 state that 'The parties undertake to recognize ....' rights ranging from freedom of religion to expression, language and name respectively. Thus there is no duty placed on states to ensure the conditions necessary for the promotion of these rights. Education is seen as a matter for the minority and incurs no state financing obligation,[252] although the state shall take measures, *where appropriate*, to increase general awareness about minority cultures.[253] The application of these rights remains essentially a private matter between the individuals and their community and will thus depend on the resources and status of the community.[254]

Several of the articles include the clause 'within the framework of their legal systems' which undermines the importance of the right to which it is attached. Klebes notes that such a restriction implies, contrary to the European Convention on Human Rights, that national law prevails in cases of conflict and that there is no obligation on parties to adapt the national law to comply with the Convention rights.[255]

The anti-discrimination provisions go further in requiring the state to take:

> Appropriate measures to protect persons who may be subject to threats or acts of discrimination, hostility or violence as a result of their ethnic, cultural, linguistic or religious identity.[256]

---

250   Steketee, F 'The Framework Convention: a piece of art or a tool for action?' (2001) *Int. Journal of Minority and Group Rights* Vol 8 pp 1–15 at 4.

251   Alfredsson, Gudmundur 'A frame an incomplete painting: a comparison of the Framework Convention for the Protection of National Minorities with international standards and monitoring procedures' (2000) *Int. Journal of Minority and Group Rights* Vol 7 pp 291–304 at 292.

252   *Supra* n221 Articles 13(1) and (2) respectively.

253   *Ibid.* Article 12.

254   Similarly Article 14 concerns the right of members of minorities to use their own language. The explanatory report states categorically 'there can be no exceptions to this' but then goes on to say '... this paragraph does not imply positive action, notably of a financial nature, on the part of the State' *supra* n221 at 21 para. 74.

255   Klebes *supra* n230 at 94.

256   *Supra* n221 Article 6(2).

The Framework Convention and the Draft Protocol: A comparative critique[257]

It is illuminating to compare the text of the Convention with the Parliamentary Assembly's draft protocol.[258] Although the protocol can be criticised for associating minority status with citizenship it is a much more proactive document. Article 10 concerning the right to use the minority language is clearly weaker than the Draft protocol which provides for the right to use minority languages 'in publications and the audiovisual sector'. Furthermore, the latter provides that:

> In the regions in which substantial numbers of the national minority are settled, the persons belonging to that minority shall have the right to display in their language local names, signs, inscriptions and other similar information visible to the public.[259]

The minority language provisions in the Protocol are developed from the Charter on Regional and Minority Languages and as a result they aim to impose clear, immediate obligations on the state. Article 8 of the draft protocol provides a right to receive education in the mother tongue at an appropriate number of schools and state educational and training establishments. The language of the corresponding provision in the Framework Convention is more tentative and hinged with provisos giving the state a very wide margin of appreciation.[260]

Article 6 of the draft gives persons belonging to a national minority the right to set up their own organisations, including political parties, whereas the rights under the Framework Convention to assembly and association are vague and consequently weak.[261]

Perhaps the most far-reaching term of the Parliamentary Assembly's draft related to the right to local autonomy or special status. Article 11 states:

> In the regions where they are in a majority the persons belonging to a national minority shall have the right to have at their disposal appropriate local or autonomous authorities or to have a special status, matching the specific historical and territorial situation and in accordance with the domestic legislation of the State.

---

257 Comparative Table of the provisions of the Framework Convention for the Protection of National Minorities and the Parliamentary Assembly's proposal for an additional protocol to the European Convention on Human Rights (Doc AS/Jur (1994). 63 of 22 November 1994) reproduced in *HRLJ* 16 No 1–3 at 108–113.

258 Recommendation 1201 (1993) on an Additional Protocol on the Rights of National Minorities to the European Convention on Human Rights, full text reproduced in (1993) *HRLJ* 14 at 144.

259 *Ibid.* Article 7.

260 Article 14 of the Framework Convention states "(2) In areas inhabited by persons belonging to national minorities traditionally or in substantial numbers, *if there is sufficient demand*, the parties shall endeavour to ensure, *as far as possible, within the framework of their education systems*, that persons belonging to those minorities have adequate opportunities for being taught the minority language or for receiving instruction in this language (my emphasis).

261 *Supra* n221 Article 7.

This may explain the reluctance of the Vienna Commission to endorse the draft protocol. It has been frequently observed that:

> The sensitivity with regard to autonomy in whatever form is still very strong in quite a number of Member States of the Council of Europe. There is widespread fear of the spiral 'cultural autonomy, administrative autonomy, secession'.[262]

A right to an effective remedy 'before the State authority' is provided by Article 9 of the Draft Protocol, but there is no such right contained in the Framework Convention. The method of monitoring implementation through 'national legislation and appropriate government policies' is through the supervision of state reports by the Committee of ministers; there is no supranational enforcement mechanism.[263] An Advisory Committee has been established to assist the Committee of Ministers under Article 26.

The monitoring mechanism cannot be regarded as an enforcement mechanism and has been subject to much criticism. It is clear that a minority cannot directly petition the European Court of Human Rights and that implementation will depend on the particular state's commitment to minority rights, hardly a suitable guarantor in such matters.[264] Furthermore, as with the UN 'Declaration on the Rights of Persons Belonging to Ethnic, Religious and Linguistic Minorities,' there is no duty on states to officially recognise their minority groups.[265] Capotorti notes that 'international protection of minorities does depend on official recognition of their existence'.[266] Despite the fact that the presence of sufficient elements indicating a minority will attract the international rules,[267] several commentators have indicated that such recognition is essential for the full realisation of rights under the Convention.[268]

The Parliamentary Assembly have expressed the opinion that the Convention is weakly worded and are continuing to press for the inclusion of a draft Protocol on cultural rights pursuant to Recommendation 1201 of 1993, which would enable individuals to petition judicial bodies and ultimately the court.[269] In the meantime, Recommendation 1201 is not completely redundant as the Assembly has never abrogated Order 484 which instructs the Legal Affairs committee to 'make scrupulously sure when examining requests for accession to the Council of Europe that rights included in this Protocol are respected by the applicant countries'.[270]

---

262 Klebes *supra* n230 at 96.

263 *Supra* n221 Articles 24–6.

264 Wheatley *supra* n229 at 8 describes the monitoring system in more detail and concludes that it is 'clearly inadequate'.

265 It has been noted in Chapter 1 at 19 that Germany (despite ratifying the Framework Convention) has failed to recognise the Roma and Sinti as national minorities as they are not territorially defined.

266 Capotorti *supra* n12 p12 at para. 61.

267 *Ibid.*

268 Roth *supra* n117; Wheatley *supra* n229 at 4; Capotorti *supra* n12, para. 62.

269 See for example Parliamentary Assembly Recommendation 1557 (2002) on 'the legal situation of Roma in Europe' and Parliamentary Assembly Recommendation 1255 (1995) on 'the protection of the rights of national minorities'.

270 As noted by Klebes *supra* n230 at 97.

The work of the Advisory Committee

The Advisory Committee established under Article 26 issues a report every 5 years on the implementation of the Convention in each of the ratifying states. These reports are public and are followed up by a Resolution from the Committee of Ministers of the Council of Europe. While the committee can be criticised for the delay in publishing reports and for its lack of teeth, the reports reveal interesting issues specific to the state parties and also some very obvious common issues which suggest a more general pattern of prejudice. In no case is this more apparent than with the Committee's findings pertaining to the Roma. In countries with very different social, economic and political compositions, the adverse situation of the Roma remains a constant.

The Committee of Ministers resolution on the German report identified the over-reliance on special remedial schools for Roma children and required 'substantial efforts ... ensure the participation of this minority particularly in cultural, social and economic life'.[271] The opinion on the Czech report expressed 'deep concern that many Roma in the Czech Republic face considerable socio-economic difficulties in comparison to both the majority and other minorities, in particular in the fields of education, employment and housing'.[272] While the report commended the Czech Government's efforts to develop integration strategies, they noted that the attitudes of local government officials were often 'discriminatory, intolerant and hostile'. The events in Usti Nad Labem illustrated the inability of central Government to tackle such in-built prejudice.[273]

In the case of Italy, the Committee of Ministers observed 'real problems' concerning the Roma in the fields of housing, certain discriminatory practices and socio-economic inequalities and political affairs.[274] Similarly, the Polish report concluded that 'despite efforts by the government, there remain problems in the implementation of the Framework Convention as concerns Roma'.[275] In Slovakia, the government have developed a 'Strategy for the solutions of the problems of the Roma National Minority'. However, the Committee's opinion highlighted the same problems that have been noted elsewhere; namely educational segregation, absence of minority language provisions and the lack of participation in public

---

271   C/E   Committee   of   Ministers   Resolution   ResCMN(2003)3   on Implementation of the Framework Convention for the Protection of National Minorities by Germany.

272   Advisory Committee on the Framework Convention for the Protection of National Minorities Opinion on the the Czech Republic, adopted on 6 April 2001 ACFC/INF/OP/1 (2002) 002 para. 29.

273   Where local councillors authorised construction of a wall to separate Roma from the rest of the town.

274   C/E   Committee   of   Ministers   Resolution   Res   CMN   (2002)10   on Implementation of the Framework Convention for the Protection of National Minorities by Italy.

275   C/E Committee of Ministers Resolution on the implementation of the Framework Convention for the Protection of National Minorities by Poland (2004) Adopted on 30 September 2004 at the 898th meeting of Ministers' Deputies.

life.[276] The opinion also noted that despite the existence of the national strategy, initiatives were seldom supported by local officials and the commitment varied between Government ministries. The Committee's opinion on Spain, where Roma are not formally recognised as a national minority, expressed similar concerns, particularly highlighting social exclusion and marginalisation common to the Spanish Rom.[277] Again, while there are government initiatives aimed at improving this situation, practice on the ground does not reflect these policies. The Advisory Committee's report on the UK highlighted similar issues with a particular emphasis on the lack of stopping places for Gypsy and travellers effectively undermining the travelling lifestyle.[278] The Irish report stressed the need to improve the situation of the traveller community who experience high levels of unemployment and an experience of health 'that falls far short of that enjoyed by the general population'[279] notwithstanding several national initiatives to address these very issues.[280] No other minority is mentioned as frequently as a cause for concern in the Committee's reports suggesting that a transnational policy may be more effective.

The Parliamentary Assembly has formulated several recommendations relating to the operation of the FCNM and have been critical of the slow rate of progress.[281] They have also recommended greater monitoring powers for the advisory committee so that it can adopt a more pro-active, investigatory role.[282]

Cultural autonomy in the Council of Europe

Since Recommendation 1201, the Parliamentary Assembly have maintained interest in cultural autonomy and recently adopted Recommendation 1609 advocating a convention on minority self-government which has received some, albeit limited, limited approval from the Committee of Ministers.[283]

The Committee of Local and Regional Authorities in Europe (CLRAE) have also been active in this respect. Recommendation 43 on *Territorial* Autonomy and national

---

276 Advisory Committee on the Framework Convention for the Protection of National Minorities, Opinion on Slovakia ACFC/INF/OP/1 (2001).

277 Advisory Committee on the Framework Convention for the Protection of National Minorities, Opinion on Spain ACFC/INF/OP/1(2004) 004.

278 Advisory Committee on the Framework Convention for the Protection of National Minorities, Opinion on the United Kingdom ACFC/INF/OP/I (2002)006.

279 Advisory Committee on the Framework Convention for the Protection of National Minorities, Opinion on Ireland ACFC/INF/OP/I (2004)003.

280 Moore, C 'Group rights for nomadic minorities: Ireland's traveller community' (2004) *IJHR* Vol 8. No 2 pp 175–197.

281 Recommendation 1285 on the Rights of National Minorities (1996) http://assembly. coe.int/Docuemnts/AdoptedText/ta95/EREC1231.htm.

282 Recommendation 1623 (2003) on the Rights of National Minorities available at: http://assembly.coe.int/Documents/adoptedText/ta03/EREC1623.htm.

283 Recommendation 1609 Positive Experiences of autonomous regions as a source of inspiration for conflict resolution in Europe (2003) available as http://assembly.coe.int/ Docuemnts/AdoptedText/ta03?EREC1609.htm.

Minorities[284] relied on the principle of subsidiarity to recommend greater autonomy for territorially defined collectivities. The Committee of Ministers acknowledged the importance of subsidiarity for greater minority participation, but declined to accept the recommendation and any advancement of territorial autonomy.[285]

Specific recommendations concerning the Roma

The Council of Europe has long been concerned with the situation of Roma and other travellers in Europe, in recent years this concern has been voiced in several recommendations which plainly regard the 'Gypsies' or Roma as a minority group.[286]

Over 20 years have passed since the Committee of Ministers resolution 'on the social situation of nomads in Europe'.[287] The recommendations contained in that document were concerned with discrimination against travelling people generally, many of them being Roma. Suggested measures included legislation to safeguard the cultural heritage and identity of nomads; provision of camping and housing; education, health and social security. A further resolution was adopted in 1983 on the position of stateless nomads which again emphasises an individualistic angle by focusing on non-discrimination and allowing freedom of movement so long as there is no incompatibility with territorial integrity.[288]

The Parliamentary Assembly has also been active in this field. A recommendation of 1969 'on the situation of gypsies [sic] and other travellers in Europe,' had pinpointed the main areas of concern: discrimination, the construction of caravan sites, health, education and social security.[289] By 1993 it was apparent that the situation of the Roma and other travellers was not improving significantly and the Parliamentary Assembly noted that their numbers had increased dramatically, particularly with the addition of former Communist states, and 'as Gypsies are one of the very few non-territorial minorities in Europe, they need special protection'.[290] In their general observations, the Assembly noted:

---

284   Recommendation 43 on Territorial Autonomy and national minorities (1998) http://www.coe.int/minorities.

285   Malloy *supra* n233 at 245.

286   The Council of Europe have in the past tended to favour the label 'Gypsy' over Roma (see for example the report from the European Committee on migration *The Situation of Gypsies (Roma and Sinti) in Europe* (1995) CDMG (95) 11) this may be attributable to the west European origins of the Council and increasingly the label. Roma is appearing in documents, reflecting an increased awareness of the unpopularity of the term Gypsy amongst many Rom.

287   Council of Ministers Resolution (75) 13–22 May 1975.

288   Committee of Ministers Recommendation No R (83) 1 on Stateless nomads and nomads of undetermined nationality.

289   Consultative Assembly Recommendation 563 (1969) on the situation of gypsies and other travellers in Europe.

290   Parliamentary Assembly Recommendation 1203 (1993) on Gypsies in Europe (note the capitalisation of Gypsy when contrasted with the 1969 version), para. 9.

Intolerance of Gypsies by others has existed throughout the ages. Outbursts of racial or social hatred however occur more and more regularly and the strained relations between communities have contributed to the deplorable situation in which the majority of Gypsies live today.[291]

The measures recommended were divided into: education; culture (including music and language); information (including a proposal to establish a European information centre on the situation and culture of Gypsies);[292] equal rights, where it was stated that the provision of minority protocols or conventions should apply equally to non-territorial minorities;[293] everyday life; and general measures aimed at improving information through research on the situation of the Gypsies including the appointment of a mediator for Gypsies.[294]

The same year, the CLRAE issued a resolution specifically on the situation of Gypsies in Europe. It was noted that the afore-mentioned texts had been 'followed up with little concrete action'.[295] Indeed, the proposal for a mediator for Gypsies, which could have enabled greater monitoring and cooperation to address common problems, never materialised. Nevertheless, the European Committee on Migration did issue a follow-up report to recommendation 1203 and a Specialist Group on Roma/ Gypsies was established to advise member states on Roma/Gypsy issues. According to Xanthaki, this group has been instrumental in the developments of key policy initiatives as well as providing training and support for the police and judiciary.[296] It has been engaged in fact-finding missions and has drafted recommendations to the Committee on Migration which feeds into the Committee of Ministers. Additionally, there have been a number of other specific recommendations by the Committee of Ministers on education (2000)[297] and employment (2001).[298] The most recent recommendation concerns the housing conditions of Roma and travellers in Europe.[299] 'Housing' is defined to include the right to reside in caravans and to adopt nomadic lifestyles. States are required to improve a whole range of services and support for travellers occupying sites. Unlawful evictions are prohibited and, when lawful evictions occur, states are obliged to offer alternative accommodation.

These are undoubtedly positive developments but such statements of intent are seldom evidenced by positive results. As the work of the Advisory Committee

---

291 *Ibid.* at para. 5.

292 *Ibid.* at para. 11(x).

293 *Ibid.* at para. 11(xiii).

294 *Ibid.* at para. 11(xxii).

295 Standing Conference of Local and Regional Authorities of Europe 28th session Resolution 249 (1993) on Gypsies in Europe: The Role and Responsibility of Local and Regional Authorities.

296 Xanthaki, A 'Protection of a specific minority: The case of Roma/Gypsies' in Thornberry *supra* n243

297 Recommendation R (2000) 4 on education of Roma/Gypsy children in Europe.

298 Recommendation (2001) 17 on improving the economic and employment situation of Roma/Gypsies in Europe.

299 Recommendation Rec (2005) 4 on improving the housing conditions of Roma and Travellers in Europe.

on the Framework Convention demonstrates, little has changed in the situation of Gypsies and Roma over the past decade.[300] In 2002, a new Parliamentary Assembly Recommendation on 'the legal situation of the Roma in Europe' implicitly recognised the failings of such statements of intent. Again, the need for a mediator or ombudsman was emphasised as was the need for an additional 'minorities protocol' to the ECHR.

The European Union has also shown increasing interest in the plight of the Roma as the Union moves from a strictly economic agenda towards a political agenda encompassing human rights and fundamental freedoms. The Directorate of Employment and Social Affairs report *The Situation of Roma in an Enlarged European Union* reinforces much of the work from the Council of Europe. The report observes: The treatment of Roma is today among the most pressing political, social and human rights issues facing Europe'.[301] Yet the report searches for solutions within the individual rights paradigm, including the ratification of Protocol 12 to the European Convention and the Race Equality Directive discussed in Chapter 3. Member States are requested to take account of Roma/Gypsies in their social inclusion strategies which are submitted periodically to the European Commission for review. However, few of the social inclusion plans that were submitted for 2003–05 make any specific reference to Roma policies.

Aware of the limitations of the individual, non-discrimination approach, the report concludes that there is a clear need for a specific Roma Integration Directive. This directive would complement the new Race Directive 2000/43 (discussed in Chapter 3) and could make states accountable for discriminatory and segregationist policies.[302] Such a directive would require states to take action to improve the economic, social and political disadvantage of Roma. It would enable states to share expertise and identify and develop successful programmes, particularly in areas such as education and housing. However, two years on and it is apparent that there is no political will to draft such a directive. Most states remain unwilling to tackle one of Europe's most pressing 'political, social and human rights' problems. As a result of the failures of these international commitments, Pogany concludes 'For the mass of impoverished Roma, notions of minority rights are irrelevant'.[303]

The inadequacy of minority rights protection for the Roma

Despite the clear prevalence of the individualist human rights approach in international minority rights documents, there is some evidence to suggest that collective rights are necessary and have indeed been recognised as such by some international institutions.

---

300   Hofmann, Rainer 'Introduction' in Weller *supra* n222 at 23.

301   European Commission (2004) *The Situation of Roma in an Enlarged European Union*, p10, para. 14.

302   Xanthaki, A discusses the possible content of the directive in 'Hope dies last: an EU Directive on Roma Integration' (2005) *EPL* Vol 11, 4, 515–526.

303   Pogany, I 'Refashioning rights in Central and Eastern Europe: some implications for the regions Roma' (2004) *EPL* Vol 10, 1 85–106.

The right of 'peoples' to self-determination is clearly a collective right in that it can only be claimed by a people and not by an individual. Its' position in Article 1 of the two United Nations Covenants suggests that it is a fundamental prerequisite to the realisation of individual human rights.

The emphasis on 'persons belonging to minorities' rather than the groups per se and the absence of a collective right of petition to the Human Rights Commission fail to protect adequately the human rights of those members. The adoption of the UN Declaration on the Rights of Minorities in 1992 and the Council of Europe's Framework Convention do not substantially alter this deficiency.

Although the number of ratifications to the Framework Convention is encouraging, there remain substantial problems when the convention is applied to Roma in virtually all states. The OSCE's High Commissioner for National Minorities has spoken of the need for cooperation with the C/E to be extended to identify common 'thematic issues'.[304] The most obvious thematic issue could be said to be the discrimination experienced by the Roma yet real action in this area remains piecemeal and insufficient. It is arguable that, as the Parliamentary Assembly suggest, without an additional protocol to the European Convention on Human Rights providing a right of petition, many of these issues will remain unresolved.

The decision of the European Court of Human Rights in the Buckley case, discussed in Chapter 3, exhibits the need for such a minority protocol. The majority of the Court felt that Mrs Buckley's private and home life had been adversely affected contrary to Article 8 of the European Convention, when she was not allowed to reside in her caravan on the land which she owned. However, the interference was deemed to be proportionate and 'necessary in the interests of a democratic society'. The rights of one individual were simply balanced against the interests of the majority without significant regard to her status as a member of the Gypsy minority.[305] If the Framework Convention provisions had been incorporated into the European Convention, the Court would arguably have felt obliged to devote greater attention to her needs as a member of a minority group.

The watering down process from the political commitments in the OSCE to the Framework Convention further suggests that any translation into an Optional Protocol will result in an even weaker, more nebulous approach. The failure of some major Council of Europe states to ratify either the Framework Convention or the Convention on Regional and Minority Languages leaves little room for enthusiasm about the potential of these documents to provide effective protection for the minority rights of the Roma. It cannot be denied that there is more awareness about the situation of Roma in Europe and there have been some incremental improvements. However, as Xanthaki is compelled to admit: 'Unfortunately, the existing reality for many Roma/Gypsies is a sad reminder that there is still a lot to be achieved'.[306]

---

304   OSCE Contribution by Rolf Ekeus, High Commissioner for National Minorities, The Hague 19 April 2005 HCNM. GAL/2/05, Agenda item 2.

305   O'Nions, H 'The First in a series of Gypsy-Cases to challenge UK Legislation' (1996) 5 *Web JCLI*.

306   Xanthaki *supra* n296 at 189.

It is unlikely, given the present emphasis on persons belonging to minorities rather than group rights, that the situation of the Roma will be significantly improved. As Alfredsson argues in the context of the Framework Convention:

> If group rights are not forthcoming, discriminatory patterns are likely to persist and the achievement of equal rights by minorities becomes less likely. It is therefore unfortunate that the FC relies solely on individual rights and omits group rights.[307]

---

307 Alfredsson *supra* n251 at 294 Recommendation 1623 (2003) on the Rights of National Minorities available at: http://assembly.coe.int/Documents/adoptedText/ta03/EREC1623.htm.

Chapter 7

Extending Collective Rights:
The Roma Nation, Self-Determination
and Minority Autonomy

Introduction

The Council of Europe's Framework Convention and the UN Declaration on the Rights of People Belonging to National, Ethnic or Religious Minorities have been criticised for doing too little too late to help solve the discrimination and under-representation faced by many ethnic minorities. It has become apparent that existing minority rights standards are insufficient to protect the rights of members of groups that do not seek assimilation with the dominant culture. International lawyer, Hurst Hannum, contends:

> Few [ethnic groups] demand independence, but most seek a greater degree of group autonomy than would be allowed under traditional standards of minority rights.[1]

In this chapter I will examine options for extending minority participation and group focused efforts in order to reduce discrimination and ensure de facto equality.

High-profile members of the Roma community have debated the concept of a Roma nation and the drafting of a European Roma Charter recognising their unique situation as a non-territorial minority. The use of the concept of self-determination and more specifically, the scope of 'internal' self-determination will be examined in the light of this approach, along with alternative methods which could be used to extend autonomy and protect the identity of minorities.

This analysis will focus on the Hungarian Law on National and Ethnic Minorities, described as 'an effort to implement a new theory of human rights based upon collective rights'.[2] This pioneering statute aimed to guarantee a level of political participation and funding for specific minority groups including the Roma. The potential for the extension of this approach elsewhere in Europe will be discussed.

---

1   Hannum, H 'The Limits of Sovereignty and Majority Rule: Minorities, Indigenous Peoples and the Rights to Autonomy' in Lutz, Hannum, Burke (eds) (1989) *New Directions in Human Rights* Univ. of Pennsylvania Press, Philadelphia at 3.

2   'Hungary and a new Paradigm for the Protection of Ethnic Minorities in Central and Eastern Europe' (1995) Note in *Columbia Journal of Transnational Law* Vol. 3, 3 pp 673–705 at 675.

The international human right of self-determination

Group rights as a prerequisite to the realisation of human rights

The definition and application of the right of self-determination is fraught with difficulties, raising more questions than it answers. Brownlie notes however that the right has a 'core of reasonable certainty' which:

> Consists in the right of a community which has a distinct character to have this character reflected in the institutions of government under which it lives.[3]

As a legal principle it has gradually evolved into a legal right – the exercise of which may lead to consequences ranging from limited self-government to revolution and ultimately, in extreme cases, secession. In his study on the *Right to Self-determination*, Aureliu Cristescu noted:

> Today it is generally recognised that the concept of self-determination entails international legal rights and obligations and that a right of self-determination definitely exists.[4]

The imprecision of the scope and application of the right has limited but not prevented its use in international practice, particularly in the decolonialisation process and most recently in the former Yugoslavia.

It is clearly a group right.[5] Its place in the opening Article of the two UN Covenants recognises that there is little advantage to be gained in recognising individual and freedoms if the community which individuals inhabit is not free.[6] The Human Rights Committee have stressed the link between self-determination and the realisation of individual human rights:

> The right of self-determination is of particular importance because its realisation is an essential condition for the effective guarantee and observance of individual human rights and for the promotion and strengthening of those rights. It is for this reason that States set forth

---

3   Brownlie, I 'The Rights of Peoples in Modern International Law' in Crawford, J (ed.) *The Rights of Peoples* (1988) Clarendon, Oxford at 5.

4   Cristescu, A *The Right to Self-determination. Historical and Current Development on the Basis of United Nations Instruments.* E/CN.4/Sub.2/404/Revelation 1 para. 95.

5   White, Robin notes 'The right of self-determination goes one step further than individual human rights in that it grants to a group those rights necessary for the preservation of a group identity. These rights involve positive obligations on states such as the duty to respect the cultural heritage of peoples, which may involve, for example, ensuring the availability of education in a particular language, or respecting the observance of particular religious customs' in 'Self-determination: Time for a Re-assessment?' in (1981) *Neth Int 'l L Rev* Vol.28, 2 pp 147–170 at 168.

6   Cassese, A 'The Helsinki Declaration and Self-determination' in Buergenthal, T (ed.) (1977) *Human Rights, International Law and the Helsinki Accord*, Allanheld, Osmun and Co, NJ. Robert McCoquodale notes that the purpose of the right is to enable such communities to transmit their culture and to participate fully in the social, economic and political process – 'Self-determination: Human Rights Approach' in (1994) *ICLQ* 43 at 859.

the right of self-determination in a provision of positive law in both Covenants and placed this provision as *Article 1* apart from and before all the other rights in the two Covenants.[7]

During the debates in the General Assembly's 10th session on the draft Article 1 of the covenants, it was argued by some that as a 'principle' rather than a 'right,' self-determination was inappropriate for inclusion in the covenants.[8] Moreover, the collective nature of the principle was at odds with the emphasis on individual rights. To the contrary it was persuasively argued that as a pre-requisite to the realisation of individual rights, self-determination must be situated at the opening of the international human rights covenants. Article 1(1) ICCPR reads:

> All peoples have the right to self-determination. By virtue of that right they freely determine their political status and freely pursue their economic, social and cultural development.

In 1992, the United Nations General Assembly adopted a resolution reaffirming the right of all peoples to self-determination. The opening paragraph states that the realisation of universal self-determination is a fundamental condition for the effective guarantee and observation of human rights.[9]

The scope and content of the legal right

i) A collective right vesting in 'peoples'
Self-determination is a right vesting in 'peoples' rather than the individuals. Thus, the scope is wider than simple minority rights; embracing the protection and advancement of political organisation and development outside the state.[10] The right can only be claimed by the group; an individual member would have to show that they represented the people in question in order to lobby for self-determination. It represents a departure with traditional individualist language of the covenants and is excluded altogether from the staunchly individualist European Convention on Human Rights.

ii) The link between territory and self-determination
The principle of self-determination is strongly equated with a defined territory. Judge Rosalyn Higgins talks more generally of 'an acceptable political unit'[11] but such a unit would need to be territorially based in order to be administratively efficient. Ofuatey-Kodjoe observes that the main two factors which attach to communities that wish to invoke the right of self-determination are political coherence and subject status.[12] The

---

7   HRC General Comments 12(21) para. 1 (G. A. Official Records Doc. A/39/40 pp 142–143).

8   *Official Records of the General Assembly Tenth Session, Annexes*. Agenda item 28-1, document A/3077, paras 27–77.

9   G. A Res 47/83 *Universal Realisation of the Right of Peoples to Self-determination.*

10   Drost, Pieter N *Human Rights as Legal Rights* (1965) A.W. Sijthoff, Leyden at 199.

11   Higgins, Rosalyn (1963) *The Development of International Law through the Political Organs of the United Nations* Oxford Univ. Press, London at 104.

12   Ofuatey-Kodjoe, W (1977) *The Principle of Self-determination in International Law* Nellen Publishing House, NY at 36.

subject status qualification is of little problem for the Roma who can be commonly interpreted as oppressed or 'subject nationalities'. However, political coherence, along with the requirement that the group generally desire the goal of self-determination, is typically associated with a specific territory.[13]

Anthropologists have taken a different perspective on the importance of the territory to nation consciousness. Barth argues that such identity is bounded by social barriers rather than territorial ones.[14] Similarly, Armstrong claims that the:

> Primary characteristic of ethnic boundaries is attitudinal. In their origins and in their most fundamental effects, ethnic boundary mechanisms exist in the minds of their subjects rather than as lines on a map or norms in a rule book.[15]

This theory holds that the members, as well as the culture, of the ethnic group can change and the sense of belonging to the group is defined by sociological factors such as myth, symbol, and communication, as well as attitudinal factors.[16] The ethnic group, therefore, need not be defined by the territory it inhabits. Cara Feys argues that a new definition of a nation is required to reflect this reality:

> A more useful definition of a nation for the purposes of the contemporary international system is a politicized ethnic group acting with or without attachment to a territory. This definition more adequately captures the goals of a nation without undermining the territorial integrity of existing structures.[17]

Nevertheless, in the present language of international law the concept of territory is still an important aspect.[18] Not only will a group claiming self-determination benefit by showing a territorial basis, but in order to achieve international recognition, the claim of the group must not be incompatible with the territorial basis of the state concerned. The recognition of territorial units claiming self-determination could pose significant problems for the Roma who may find themselves again disenfranchised by the new territorial units.[19] Indeed, Malloy has argued that consociationalism may pose problems for minorities within the territory of co-nations.[20]

---

13   *Supra* n11 158.

14   Barth, Fredrik (1969) *Ethnic Groups and Boundaries*, Waveland Press Inc, Illinois Chapter 1.

15   Armstrong (1982) in Anderton, Benedict (1983) *Imagined Communities: Reflections on the origins and Spread of Nationalism* London: Verso at 78.

16   *Ibid.* at79.

17   Feys, Cara (1998) 'Towards a new Paradigm of the Nation: The case of the Roma' *PATRIN* no pagination.

18   Eide, Asbjorn 'National Sovereignty and International Efforts to Realise Human Rights' in Eide and Blackwell(1992) *Human Rights in Perspective*, Blackwell, Nobel Symposium 74 at 16.

19   This can be seen clearly in the former Yugoslavia, see Edwards, Alice 'New Roma Rights legislation in Bosnia and Herzegovina: positive, neutral of indifferent?' (2005) *IJHR* Vol 9, 4 pp 465–478.

20   Malloy, Tove (2005) *National Minorities in Europe* OUP at 43.

The importance of territorial integrity is seen in the Declaration on the Granting of Independence to Colonial Countries and Peoples (1960), which proclaims:

> Any attempt aimed at the partial or total disruption of the national unity and the territorial integrity of a country is incompatible with the purposes and principles of the Charter of the United Nations.[21]

The Declaration on Friendly Relations is also explicit in its condemnation of action which would impair the principle of the territorial integrity of states.[22]

Thus, the application of self-determination today depends on the willingness of particular states. The principle of territorial integrity effectively eradicates international solutions in all but the most extreme cases such as the former Yugoslavia where widespread human rights violations eventually resulted in reluctant international intervention.

iii) The 'internal' dimension as an endorsement of cultural autonomy

Since the drafting of the UN Charter in 1945[23] and its clarification in the Covenants, the right of self-determination has evolved to include an internal aspect as well as the more traditionally conceived external aspect (which allows for the claims of secession and independence).[24] The difference between the internal and external aspects is explained by Asbjorn Eide:

> [internal self-determination] *can be understood as the right of a people to control significant aspects of its internal matters* (culture, education, property relations, social matters and welfare) *while external matters* (defence against armed attack from third States, international trade relations, diplomatic intercourse) *are left in the hands of a larger political entity*, e.g., *a federal state*.[25]

---

21   Declaration on Principles of International Law Concerning Friendly Relations and Co-operation among states in Accordance with the Charter of the United Nations, Ga. Res 2625 (XXV) 24 October 1970 at para. 6.

22   *Ibid.* states: 'Nothing in the foregoing paragraphs shall be construed as authorising or encouraging any action which would dismember or impair, totally or in part, the territorial integrity or political unity of sovereign and independent States conducting themselves in compliance with the principle of equal rights and self-determination of peoples ...'.

23   The principle (as it was in 1945) of self-determination was not included in the Declaration of 1948, presumably because it was not considered a human right until some years later. The 1960 *Declaration on the Granting of Independence to Colonial countries and Peoples* declared that 'all peoples have the right to self-determination' GA. Res. 1514, 15 UN GAOR, Supp. No 16, UN Doc. A/4684 (1960) Preamble para. 2.

24   President Wilson recognised the need for a link between self-determination and democracy in 1919 at Versailles − Hannum, H (1990) *Autonomy, Sovereignty and Self-determination: The Adjudication of Conflicting Rights* Pennsylvania Press, Philadelphia at 30.

25   Eide *supra* n18 at 16.

Internal self-determination may be applied to peoples living under the territorial jurisdiction of a state and essentially concerns the rights of such peoples to have meaningful participation in the processes of government.[26] Antonio Cassese asserts:

> ... internal self-determination [i]s a truly democratic decision-making process, offering the population of sovereign States a real and genuine choice between various economic and political options.[27]

While the gradual recognition of the internal dimension of self-determination supports pluralism as the 'hallmark' of a democratic society,[28] it can be seen that international law does not expressly provide for collective autonomy[29] and international practice has been cautious in this respect.[30] The word 'people' has become closely equated with the notion of the nation-state and the status of smaller, non-dominant groups is largely a matter for the particular state.

The right of self-determination was not part of the UN Declaration, being included in the Covenant following debates in the General Assembly.[31] During its evolution from political principle to legal right there was concern expressed over its scope[32] and in the Third Committee sessions it was argued that 'the authors of Article 1 were attempting to write a whole chapter of highly complicated international law into a single article'.[33] The problem of minorities who may wish to secede was also raised: 'much suffering had, in the past, been caused by the incitement of discontented minorities in the name of self-determination'.[34]

The proponents of the legal rights approach argued that it was a fundamental 'collective' right on which the whole of the Covenant rested.[35] Clear definitions of 'peoples;' 'nations' and indeed 'self-determination' were considered less necessary due to the difficulty in finding a consensus; a view that was ultimately supported by the Human Rights Commission.[36]

---

26   Hannum *supra* n24 at 30.

27   Cassese, Antonio (1995) *Self-determination of Peoples* Cambridge Univ. Press at 64–5.

28   As suggested by Cassese *ibid.* at 65.

29   Heintze, Hans-Joachim 'Implementation of minority Rights through the Devolution of Powers – The concept of Autonomy Revisited' (2002) *Int. Journal of Minority and Group Rights* Vol 9 pp 325–343 at 329.

30   Hannum *supra* n24 at 49.

31   GAOR, 6th session, Supp. no 20, UN Doc A/2119, 36.

32   *Ibid.* at 20. Some delegates had argued that the controversy surrounding the concept of self-determination should not diminish its importance and advocated a separate international document or declaration E/CN.4/SR.255, p 5 (AUS), p 7 (F).

33   Bossuyt (1987) *Guide to the 'Travaux Preparatoires' of the ICCPR* Martinus-Nijhoff, Dordrecht at 24 A/3077, s32.

34   *Ibid.*

35   *Ibid.* refers to: E/CN.4/SR.254, p 8 (RL); E/CN.4/SR.255, p 6 (PL); E/CN.4/SR.256, p 7 (YU).

36   E/CN.4/SR.254, p 8 (RL); Commission on Human rights, 8th session (1952) A/2929 Chapter IV s8.9 in Bossuyt, *supra* n33 at p32; van Dyke, V (1980) 'The Cultural Rights of Peoples' in *Universal Human Rights* Vol. 2, 2 April–June pp 1–21 at 2 notes that

In looking at the meaning of Article 1 of the Covenants, Cassese considers the position of minorities. It will be recalled that Article 27 of the ICCPR provides that members of minority groups have the right to maintain their identity through the development of religious, linguistic and cultural freedoms.[37] Article 27 does not extend to political, economic or social autonomy. Having asked whether the freedoms in Article 27 should be read cumulatively in conjunction with Article 1 he is compelled to conclude that such a cumulative approach is at odds with the restrictive view of self-determination exhibited by the UN delegates.[38] His analysis concludes that 'these minority groups are not entitled to self-determination'.[39]

The UN Declaration on Friendly Relations (1970)[40] elaborates on the Covenant contents and contains both external and internal dimensions. Although it is suggested that elements of the declaration constitute *jus cogens*,[41] it is deficient in many respects and lacks direction when it comes to the internal dimension. The Declaration centres on political exclusion without reference to more subtle forms of exclusion, notably economic, cultural and social.[42] Furthermore, any option of self-determination is limited by the requirement to promote friendly relations between states. It has already been noted that in some cases self-determination may lead to claims for independence or secession and in such cases there will be ethnic tension between peoples, kin states (where applicable) and host states. This is clearly at odds with the effort to promote friendly relations and this link therefore deprives the right of much of its meaning.[43] Such restrictions on the exercise of the rights led Cassese to conclude in 1977:

> The principles governing internal self-determination are decidedly moderate and cautious and reflect a definite tendency to defend established governments even when this is detrimental to the effective implementation of the rights of peoples.[44]

Twenty years later it became clear to Cassese, having examined UN action or, 'inaction,' on behalf of ethnic groups such as the Kurds and Armenians, that there was a tendency towards a broadening concept of internal self-determination was emerging.[45] The UN

---

the difficulties in defining terms such as nation and people makes it difficult to assess the implications of Article 1, but he argues it should not be dismissed out of hand as it is already a politically significant issue.

37   For a full discussion of Article 27 see above at Chapter 6 at 277.

38   Cassese, *supra* n27 at 61–2.

39   *Ibid.* at 62.

40   Declaration on Principles of International Law Concerning Friendly Relations and Co-operation among States in Accordance with the Charter of the United Nations, G. A. Res. 2625, Annex, 25 UN GAOR Supp. (no 28) UN Doc. A/5217 (1970) at 121.

41   Brownlie *supra* n3 at 599–601.

42   Cassese (1977) *supra* n6 at 91.

43   *Ibid.*

44   *Ibid.* at 93.

45   Cassese 1995 *supra* n27 at103-108.

has typically preferred the language of autonomy[46] yet this has not, as Alfredsson observes, been 'anchored in international instruments'.[47]

The non-legally binding Helsinki Declaration appears favourable by comparison. The right of peoples to internal self-determination includes a permanent right to choose a new representative social or political regime.[48] This provides a framework by which excluded groups, such as the Roma, may be able to argue for increased autonomy and local self-government. Nevertheless, again the restrictions on the extension of this right to minority groups are clearly established and commentators suggest that the OSCE follow-up conferences have downplayed the embracing approach of the Helsinki principle. Cassese speculates on the reasoning for this implicit retraction:

> … it may well open a Pandora's box for many States and because it may complicate rather than solve the issues facing contemporary Europe, it is very likely that the CSCE will focus more attention on minority rights and less on self-determination.[49]

Yet conversely the recognition of internal self-determination as a dynamic concept is emerging as part of the minority rights discourse.[50] The HCNM has advocated internal self-determination measures including self-government and cultural autonomy as a solution to inter-ethnic conflicts.[51] One could argue that territorial integrity and sovereignty is actually enhanced by such a conception. As Kristin Henrard acknowledges, minority rights as presently construed in international law, fail to offer enhanced minority protection as recognition of the group dimension is insufficiently appreciated. Therefore, internal self-determination may step in to achieve the, much needed, additional protection.[52] Alfredsson also considers that in circumstances where minorities are deprived of representation they may have claims

---

46   *Ibid.* in the Tyrol/Alto Adige case concerning the right of German-speakers in an Austrian territory awarded to Italy after the First World War, the Austrian delegate complained to the UN that the rights of full autonomy had not been realised. The rights agreed under an agreement of September 1946 which provided complete 'equality of rights' with the Italian speakers' and for 'the exercise of autonomous legislative and executive regional powers' had not been upheld. However, the Austrian delegate was careful to avoid use of the term 'self-determination' in advocating autonomy for the Boven region; GA res. 1497 (XV) 31 October 1960 and 1661 (XVI) 28 November 1961; Cassese (1995) *supra* n27 at 107.

47   Afredsson, Gudmundur 'Different forms of and claims to the right of self-determination' in Clark, D and Williamson, R (1996) *Self-Determination. International Perspectives* Macmillan pp 58–86 at 72.

48   Cassese (1977) *supra* n6 at 103.

49   Cassese (1995) *supra* n27 at 293.

50   Macklem, Patrick 'Militant democracy, legal pluralism and the paradox of self-determination' (2006) *Int. Journal of Constitutional Law*, 1 July, Vol 4, 3 at 488.

51   Zellner and Lange (1999) *Peace and Stability through Human and minority Rights: Speeches by the OSCE HCNM*, Institute for Peace Research and Security Policy, University of Hamburg at 165–173.

52   Henrard, Kristin (2000) *Devising an Adequate System of Minority Protection* Kluwer Int. Chapter IV at 316–7.

to a range of self-determination options.[53] However he cautions against the abuse of the term self-determination and prefers to legitimise autonomy provisions within other, more specific Covenant rights including Article 25 ICCPR.[54]

iv) Minorities as 'peoples'

In keeping with the theme of importance of territory, the right contained in the United Nations Charter and elaborated in the Covenants is vested in 'peoples' rather than minorities or ethnic communities. In the European system the principle is similarly restricted, The Helsinki Declaration notes that minorities should be excluded from the purview of self-determination.[55]

'Peoples' are not defined in the international instruments and it is submitted[56] that a broad interpretation should be given with self-identification an important factor.[57] The International Commission of Jurists suggested that the following criteria could be used: 1) common history, 2) racial and ethnic ties, 3) cultural and linguistic ties, 4) religious and ideological ties, 5) a common geographical location, 6) common economic base, 7) a sufficient number of people.[58] Whereas, Special Rapportuer Cristescu reasoned that there were three essential elements. Namely, that the term 'people' connotes a social entity possessing a clear identity and its own characteristics; it also implies a relationship with territory; and thirdly, a people should not be confused with an ethnic, linguistic or religious minority.[59]

The vesting of this right in 'peoples' is at odds with the complaints procedure which vests in individual applicants under the Optional Protocol.[60] This leads to a somewhat bizarre scenario in that Article 1, considered so fundamental that it is situated at the opening of the Covenant, cannot be enforced through the individual complaints mechanism. Indeed, the Human Rights Committee has confirmed that it has no jurisdiction in this respect.[61]

The distinction between minorities and peoples is not clearly understood and may be viewed as fallacious. Jane Wright argues that such distinctions are 'more apparent than real' and serve only to support majoritarian systems of government.[62] Indeed, the status of Iraqi Kurds, defined as a minority rather than a people, suggests

---

53   *Supra* n47 at 66.

54   *Ibid.* at 76.

55   Principle VIII Helsinki Declaration, Cassese (1995) *supra* n27 at 289.

56   See McCorquodale *supra* n6 at 867.

57   As reflected in the wording of the ILO Convention concerning Indigenous and Tribal People in Independent Countries 1989 Art. 1(2) (1989) 28 ILM 1382.

58   Secretariat of the International Commission of Jurists the Events in East Pakistan (1972) at 70 quoted in White *supra* n5 at 165.

59   Cristescu *supra* n4 at para. 279.

60   See Chapter 6 at 279.

61   UN, *Report of the Human Rights Committee*, 42 UN GAOR, Supp. (No. 40) UN Doc. A/42/40 (1987) at 106; *Mikmaq Tribal Society v Canada*, GAOR A/39/40 (1981) 134.

62   Wright, Jane 'Minority groups, autonomy and self-determination' (1999) *Oxford* Journal of Legal Studies Dec Vol 19 pp 605–629.

that such assessments will often be politically motivated.[63] As Alfredsson asks, how can a distinction legitimately be made between the people of Monaco or Andorra and the Basque and Breton national minorities?[64]

An enhancement of self-determination: The emerging right to democratic participation

Several writers have suggested that for a meaningful application in the modern state, self-determination must be extended. Ofuatey-Kodjoe argues that if the international community is to achieve justice, peace and security then it must be re-considered to apply to all subjugated people including minorities and tribes, emphasising the logical relationship between human rights and self-determination.[65] McCorquodale, writing some 17 years later, has argued along the same lines that if self-determination is viewed as part of the human rights approach, its meaning can be extended to cover a variety of situations including federations; constitutional guarantees for minorities and consociational democracy.[66] He goes on to conclude that the present focus on peoples and territory is too rigid to be able to be used in the present variety of applications and exercises of this right, especially regarding internal self-determination.[67] Robin White is similarly concerned that traditional notions of self-determination have ignored the problems of non-territorial minorities:

> The United Nations needs to turn its attention to the plight of minorities and to attempt to provide some effective machinery for assuring self-determination and equal rights for such peoples.[68]

The legal doctrine could be extended to reflect the importance, irrespective of territory, of a group's subjugation based on its distinctiveness. Once this is understood self-determination can be extended to colonies, minorities and scattered communities.[69] White concurs with this approach, contending that self determination provides:

> The key to one of the most pressing social needs for international standard setting in the establishment of unequivocal standards for the protection of identified minorities.[70]

In the OSCE process the Paris Charter expressly recognised the link between political pluralism, democracy and human rights. Although noticeably there is no mention of self-determination, the approach taken in the Helsinki principles, discussed above,

---

63   Discussed by Castellino, Joshua (2000) *International Law and Self-Determination* Kluwer Int.
64   Alfredsson, G 'Different forms of and claims to the right to self-determination' in Clark and Williamson *supra* n47 at 41.
65   Ofuatey-Kodjoe *supra* n12 at 188.
66   McCorquodale *supra* n6 at 877.
67   McCorquodale *supra* n6 at 883.
68   White *supra* n5 at 148.
69   Ofuatey-Kodjoe *supra* n12 at 188–9.
70   White *supra* n5 at 170.

clearly associates the concept with political pluralism and representative government. The Charter recognises:

> Democratic government is based on the will of the people, expressed regularly through free and fair elections. Democracy has at its foundation respect for the human person and the rule of law. Democracy is the best safeguard of freedom of expression, tolerance of all groups of society, and equality of opportunity for each person.[71]

Yet it is unclear how far the international community has come in the development of self-determination and the recognition of cultural autonomy. Thomas Franck argues that since the International Civil and Political Covenant, self-determination has developed into a notion of internationally validated political consultation. The principle of exclusion (secession), Franck argues, has moved to one of inclusion, necessitating full participation in the democratic process.[72] In this respect he notes that there is an 'emerging normative requirement of a participatory electoral process'.[73]

The United Nations response to the tragic events in the former Yugoslavia provides an indicator of current and potential interpretations of the concept of self-determination. The Badinter Arbitration Committee recognised the rights of peoples living in a specific territory to self-determination, but only so far as there were already established spheres of autonomy.[74] It remains evident, from the importance the Committee attributed to *uti possidetis*, which aims to respect established territorial boundaries, that boundary changes are not envisaged as part of the right to self-determination.[75] But the response also suggests that the typical focus on external self-determination is giving way to a more purposive approach that recognises the reality of multi-ethnic, heterogeneous states. This approach views self determination and minority rights as entwined.[76] Marc Weller notes that the type of self-determination applied to the Serbs did not constitute an entitlement to independent statehood but represented instead recognition of minority rights and self-government.[77] Internal self-determination must be regarded as preferable to the one-nation, one-state

---

71   30 *ILM*, (1991) at 194.

72   Franck, Thomas 'The emerging right to democratic governance' (1992) *Am Journal of Int. Law* Vol 86 pp 46–91 at 58.

73   *Ibid.* at 63.

74   Weller, Marc 'The international response to the dissolution of the Socialist Federal Republic of Yugoslavia' (1992) *Am Journal of Int. Law* 86 pp 569–607. See also Rady, Martyn 'Minority Rights and Self-determination in Eastern Europe' (1993) *Slavonic and East European Rev* Vol.71, 4 pp 717–728 at 727.

75   Yugoslav Arbitration Commission Opinion No 2 92 *ILR* p168, discussed in Shaw, M (1997) *International Law* Univ. of Cambridge pp 356–360 and Castellino *supra* n63.

76   Pentassuglia, Gaetano 'State sovereignty, minorities and self-determination: a comprehensive legal view' (2002) *Int. Journal of Minority and Group Rights* Vol 9 pp 303–324 at 316.

77   Weller, Mark 'The Rambouillet Conference on Kosovo' *International Affairs* (1999) Vol 75, 2 pp 211–251 at 221.

ideology which privileges one particular ethnicity through external recognition.[78] Nevertheless, this remains a highly sensitive subject as evidenced by the international community's struggle with the status of Kosovo.

Political participation and representation may be the way forward to an enhanced conception of internal self-determination that is capable of embracing minority interests. It certainly mitigates the secessionist concerns of states and accords with the language of international law. The Copenhagen Document of the CSCE noted that national minorities had a right to effective participation in debates concerning the protection and promotion of their identity.[79] However, the Council of Europe's Framework Convention is cautious about advocating greater autonomy for minorities. Article 15 provides a right to full and effective participation in public affairs and in cultural, social and economic life but it does not extend to effective representation or self-governance. In fact, Weller notes that the Advisory Committee's reports suggest that states are becoming more cautious in introducing such measures.[80] While one may struggle to situate full democratic participation within the collective right of self-determination, it could certainly be argued that a failure to provide a participative and representative political system may infringe the right to effective participation.[81] Rather than rely on the 'uncertain penumbra' surrounding the concept of self-determination Jane Wright argues that the language of equality and non-discrimination necessitate measures of cultural autonomy. Indeed, the focus on equality through measures increasing political participation is supported by the comments of the ad hoc Committee on the Protection of National Minorities when drafting Article 15.[82] In this sense, cultural autonomy can be seen as a derivate right or, as Stephen Roach suggests, a second level right.[83] Having provided a comprehensive analysis of Article 15, Weller also observes:

> In relation to general full equality, it is now clear that the overall state structure must not be such as to exclude persons belonging to national minorities from the democratic process.[84]

Developing the deliberative model of justice espoused by Habermas, Wheatley advocates a constitutional arrangement providing minorities with direct participation

---

78   Kovács, Mária M 'Standards of self-determination and standards of minority-rights in the post Communist era: a historical perspective' (2003) *Nations and Nationalism* Vol 9, 3 pp 433–450 at 446–7.

79   Document of the Copenhagen Meeting of the Conference on the Human Dimension of the CSCE 1990 para. 35

80   Weller, Marc (ed.) (2005) *The Rights of Minorities in Europe* OUP at 436–7. The European Commission for democracy through law in its Draft Convention on the Protection of Minorities 1990 had recommended that minorities were represented proportionately in parliament DAJ.SC.DEMOCRACY, Conv. Min 21 May 1990 Draft Article 8 (2).

81   Wright *supra* n62.

82   Ad hoc Committee for the Protection of Minorities 7th Meeting CAHMIN (94) 32.

83   Roach, Stephen *Cultural Autonomy, Minority rights and Globalization* (2005) Ashgate at 27.

84   Weller *supra* n80 at 457.

and representation at all levels of government.[85] Acknowledging that consensus is not always possible he emphasises the importance of recognising and appreciating difference rather than aiming to subsume it into the majority will. There can be no one-size fits all approach but the OSCE's Lund Recommendations offer a variety of mechanisms whereby deliberative democracy may be enabled.

The Lund Recommendations

Adopted by the foundation on Inter-ethnic Relations, a non-governmental organisation working under the auspices of the HCNM, the Lund Recommendations *on the Effective Participation of National Minorities in Public Life* are indicative of a new direction for the debate on minority cultural autonomy and internal self-determination. The recommendations specifically apply to minorities rather than simply 'peoples' and they encompass a range of possible solutions to improve access to participation and representation. It is explicitly recognised that 'effective participation of national minorities in public life is an essential component of a peaceful and democratic society'.[86] The right of an individual to affiliate with a minority is specifically recognised along with the statement that no disadvantage should be suffered as a result of such choice.[87] In terms of national participation, the recommendations specifically endorse adaptations of current voting systems including proportional representation and lower thresholds to 'enhance inclusion of national minorities in governance'.[88] Consultative and advisory bodies are also required to ensure a process of dialogue and these bodies must be adequately funded by the state.[89]

Self-determination and the Roma people

The structure of Romani society, where leadership and authority tends to come from family associations, is at odds with modern political structures and it is often asserted that Roma do not court political organisation:

> The Gypsies have no leaders, no executive committees, no nationalist movement ... I know of no authenticated case of genuine Gypsy allegiance to political or religious causes.[90]

The importance of a conception of a 'genuine' nation to the concept of self-determination has been discussed and this has led some Roma representatives to

---

85   Wheatley, Steven 'Deliberative democracy and minorities' (2003) *European Journal of Int. Law* Vol 1, 4 at 507.

86   Foundation on Inter-ethnic Relations Lund Recommendations on the Effective Participation of National Minorities in Public life September 1999 para. 1.

87   *Ibid.* para. 4.

88   *Ibid.* at para. 9.

89   *Ibid.* at paras 12 and 13.

90   Werner Cohn quoted in Hancock, Ian *The Pariah Syndrome: an Account of Gypsy slavery and Persecution*' (1987) Karoma Publishers, Ann Arbor.

engage in a process of ethnogenesis, focused on delineating a specific Roma nation.[91] Commonalties including cultural and geographical routes are emphasised in order to redefine and reconstruct a new homogenised Romani identity.[92] This has had the positive effect of introducing the language and concepts of human rights into Roma public space. Yet it is reasonable to be wary about such a strategy, especially given the risk of cultural manipulation and dominance from any such elite. Joseph Pestieau explains the pressure on peoples and minorities to fit into the categories established by international human rights standards:

> These peoples and minorities are thus encouraged to use all possible means to establish a right which will be recognised only if they can make themselves sufficiently noticed and feared.[93]

This 'enthogenesis' has been traced back to the formal recognition of the International Romani Union by the United Nations in 1979. The IRU worked to develop the core attributes of a nation – the anthem and flag, with attempts to create a Romani standardised language, receiving encouragement from the Council of Europe.[94] The common history of discrimination and persecution is underpinned by the experience of the Porajmos (Romani holocaust) which forges a link between disparate communities.

The Roma National Congress built on this conception of a Romani nation to lobby for a legally binding 'European Charter on Romani Rights'. The proposal for the Charter encompasses the right to receive protection against racist incitement, discrimination and violence; freedom of movement; freedom of cultural and political organisation; the right to political representation as a national minority; the right of veto in projects concerning the Roma; the right to receive native language instruction and training and the right to run autonomous schools.[95]

While encouraging an illuminating public debate on Romani culture and identity, there are dangers with this approach. Those Roma who do not have the fortune of being able to speak for their people may have their voices silenced again, only this time the control is exerted by their 'representatives' rather than governments and gadje observers. This is not to blame the members of the Romani elite or the gadje 'experts,'[96] the fault lies at the door of the international human rights community

---

91	*Ibid.* at 17.
92	Mirga, A and Gheorghe, N (1997) *The Roma in the twenty-first Century: A policy paper* Project on Ethnic Relations at 6.
93	Pestieau, Jospeh 'Minority Rights' (1991) *Canadian Journal of Law and Jurisprudence* Vol. IV, 2 pp 361–373 at 365 – he cites several examples of this process such as the creation of the Islamic state in India which was provoked by the fear of Hindu nationalism following the creation of a secular Indian state.
94	*Supra* n92 at 18.
95	*Roma National Congress Report on the* Situation *of the Roma in Europe* (1995) RNC, Hamburg at 3.
96	Kawczynski, Rudko 'The Politics of Romani Politics' (1997) *Transitions* Vol.4, 4 no pagination. The controversial article places much of the blame on non-Romani Gypsy 'experts' who often have leading roles in Romani organisations and manipulate the language of human rights to exclude real recognition for the Roma as a genuine minority. It

and the language of individualism it has come to embrace. The traditional language of self-determination and its underlying ideology of one-nation one-State is clearly questionable. James Graff goes so far as to state that 'the ghettoized world envisioned by advocates of that right for each such people is racist in nature'.[97] The individual must be subjected to the will of the whole community if the language of nationalist rhetoric is to be satisfied.[98]

Practical problems with the application of self-determination to the Roma

The Roma are not a 'people' as envisaged in international human rights law. The absence of a specific territory is particularly problematic in terms of both traditional conceptions of self-determination and practical solutions. Writing on the experience of Hungarian Vlach Rom, Michael Stewart observes:

> Lacking even the desire for a shared territory, the basis of a nation, Gypsies constitute a kind of awful historical mistake, a blot on the parsimonious schema of 'one people, one state' with which we try conceptually to order Europe today.[99]

While sharing many experiences, including common geographical origins and the sustained persecution and exclusion, there are substantial barriers in the creation of a Romani nation. As I mentioned in the opening chapter, many of the cultural values of the British Gypsy are very different from that of the East European Roma. Any attempt to strive for a modern 'Romanestan' has a potential to enhance societal alienation and would emphasise a particular identity of the group at the expense of individual rights. It is firmly at odds with the language and approach of international human rights law.

An alternative method of realising self-determination for the Roma could lie in its application to specific territories where the Roma already comprise a majority of the population. However, such a retrogressive approach may not only serve to increase inter-ethnic tensions with the dominant population in the state, but it could also spell disaster for the cultural development of the Roma. For example, those who still pursue a nomadic or partially nomadic lifestyle, would be likely to find their movement restricted to territorially controlled regions or between them. In the latter case, the vast range of Roma sub-groups speaking different language varieties and practising different traditions has been noted earlier. Such groups may be intolerant of other groups, perhaps emphasising and contrasting notions of Romani identity. It is thus possible that travelling Roma will be unwelcome guests in many enclaves and

---

goes without saying that there is no substitute for the involvement of the community itself at all levels of the political process.

97   Graff James. A. 'Human Rights, Peoples, and Self-determination' in Baker, J *Group Rights* (1994) Univ. of Toronto Press pp 186–215 at192.

98   Koskenniemi, Martii 'National Self-Determination' (1994) *ICLQ* Vol.43, April p 241–269 at 250.

99   Stewart, M 'The Puzzle of Roma Persistence: Group Identity Without a Nation' in Acton and Mundy (1996) *Romani Culture and Gypsy Identity* Univ. of Hertfordshire Press at 84.

may find themselves 'encouraged' into settling in order to pursue the other aspects of their lifestyle in comfort. Furthermore, such an approach will result in self-imposed segregation and consequent ghettoisation that has already been witnessed in much of Eastern Europe.

With all these inherent difficulties, it is illuminating to consider the Hungarian political experiment based on internal self-determination in the form of minority self-government.

The Hungarian experiment in minority power-sharing

Historical perspective on the Roma of Hungary

The Roma began to arrive in Hungary in the Middle-Ages. David Crowe has provided an illuminating account of their experiences and portrays the now typical story of an unusually persecuted and victimised minority, the unpopularity of which has helped to unify the dominant Magyar society.[100]

In the eighteenth century, Roma in the Habsburg lands were the subjects of expulsion followed by attempts to assimilate under decree by the Empress Maria Theresa. As well as forcing them to settle and abandon their horses and wagons, she also introduced a decree to change the name Gypsy to 'new Hungarian' (Ujmagyar). Her fourth decree prohibited inter-marriage and the transfer of children to non-Gypsy children at the age of five.[101]

By the close of the nineteenth century the vast majority of Roma were settled. The Romani language was generally used only by nomadic Roma, estimated to comprise about 10% of the Roma population at that time.[102] Nevertheless, the unpopularity of these Roma 'outsiders' enabled the Nazis to deport and exterminate an estimated 32,000 Hungarian Roma in the porajmos with few gadje objections.[103]

Following the Second World War, a brand of Stalinist Communism took hold of Hungary and, as in the Czech Republic, the ethnicity of the Roma was denied. The strong link between the Communist State and nationalism meant that members of minorities were disinclined to identify themselves as such.[104] Over 98% of inhabitants declared themselves as ethnic Hungarian in the 1949 census.[105] The Roma were uncomfortably accommodated within this regime and reports suggest

---

100   Crowe, D (1995) *A History of the Gypsies of Eastern Europe and Russia* St Martins Press NY Chapter 3.

101   Fraser, Angus (1992) *The Gypsies* Blackwell, London at 158–9.

102   Census results of January 1893 reprinted in Fraser *supra* n101 at 212.

103   Huttenbach, H 'The Romani Porajmos: The Nazi Genocide of Europe's Gypsies' in Crowe and Kolsti (eds) (1991) *The Gypsies of Eastern Europe* M. E. Sharpe NY at 31–50; Kenrick and Puxon (eds) (1972) *The Destiny of Europe's Gypsies* passim. For a personal account see Bandy, Alex 'The Forgotten Holocaust' *The Hungary Report* 3.05, 28 July 1997.

104   Rady *supra* n74 at 719.

105   Hoensch, Jorg (1988) *History of Modern Hungary* Longman, London p 161–177; Siklós, László 'The Gypsies' (1970) *New Hungarian Quarterly* Vol. 11, 40 at 151.

that approximately 150,000 emigrated to the West following the Hungarian uprising of 1956.[106]

The new Kádár era brought increased minority awareness[107] as the government began to consider ways of countering the prejudice towards the Rom.[108] However, as Kovats notes, the strategy for curing racism focused on abolishing that which 'provoked' it rather than the challenging Magyar attitudes.[109] Yet many of the Communist programmes illustrate an ignorance of the Romani culture, indeed their status as an ethnic group was not recognised by the Hungarian Socialist Workers party until the 1980s.[110]

Despite the denial of a particular Romani identity, politicians were still able to identify a 'Gypsy problem'.[111] Re-settlement programmes aimed to improve the housing situation of Roma by destroying the most primitive shanty dwellings and providing loans for house construction.[112] The programme was hailed a success by the Government[113] but further studies suggest that as many as 100,000 Roma were still occupying shanty housing in the mid-1980s.[114]

An aggressive educational programme was also adopted to educate a largely illiterate Gypsy population. The programme did dramatically increase school attendance and literacy but, as we have seen in the Czech Republic, these results were achievable largely due to the use of special, remedial education.[115]

As far as employment was concerned, the Roma were concentrated in low-paid, 'harder and dirtier jobs'.[116] Although the employment rate was high, the vast majority or Roma were unskilled and this would have devastating consequences for many families when the Communist regime collapsed.[117]

---

106   Fraser *supra* n101 at 272.

107   Crowe *supra* n100 at 92.

108   *Ibid.* at 93.

109   Kovats, M 'Hungary: politics, difference and equality' in Guy, Will (2001) *Between past and future: the Roma of Central and Eastern Europe* Univ. of Hertfordshire Press pp 333–350 at 338.

110   Stewart *supra* n99 at 85.

111   Human Rights Watch (1995) *Struggling for Ethnic Identity – The Gypsies of Hungary* at 5 HRW, NY.

112   Crowe, D (1991) 'The Roma (Gypsies) in Hungary Through the Kádár Era' *Nationalities Papers* Autumn pp 297–311 at 300–1.

113   Crowe *supra* n100 at 95.

114   Puxon *Roma: Europe's Gypsies* (1987) Minority Rights Group London at 10.

115   Brown, J F (1991) *Surge to Freedom: the end of Communist Rule in Eastern Europe* Duke Univ. Press, Durham NC at 105 – between 1974–5, 25% of children in special schools were of Gypsy origin and 11.7% of all Rom in schools were in schools for the mentally handicapped, both figures were to rise over the next decade. For the present use of special schools see above Chapter 5 at 222.

116   Markos, Edith 'The Fast growing Gypsy minority and its Problems' (1987) *RFE Research* No 5, June pp 13–16 at 14.

117   Markos, Edith (1985) 'Dim prospects for improving the plight of the Gypsies' *RFE Research* No 10 September pp 13–14 notes that a secretary to a government department

Communism bought employment for most adult male Roma and a basic degree of education for many Roma children.[118] Yet, poverty and disadvantage remained, as did the Magyar perception of the Roma as 'outsiders'.[119] Indeed, the collapse of Communism re-ignited ethnic tensions throughout the region and led to renewed marginalisation and exclusion.

Problems facing the Hungarian Roma today

There are no reliable statistics on the number of Roma in Hungary today. One writer dubiously contends that the number of Roma in Hungary after the Second World War (approx 60,000) has altered little today.[120] However, more accurate estimates suggest a figure somewhere between 450,000[121] and 800,000;[122] they certainly constitute Hungary's largest minority group.[123]

Around 30% of Roma now live in urban areas − often in slums and ghettos and a significant number live on separated sites despite a general improvement in the state of housing.[124] Many of the supposed improvements in the social situation of the Roma have back-fired largely because of their cultural insensitivity.[125] Temporary, over-crowded accommodation with inadequate utilities is a common story. Preferential loans offered to families as part of the resettlement programme have had mixed successes. Unemployment has meant that many families have been unable to meet utility bills and loan repayments. The situation in the Kunszentmiklós settlement is not atypical. One hundred and fifty families started to build their own homes with preferential credit in 1989 and 1990. However, privatisation of local factories resulted in their unemployment and inability to repay the loans resulted in increased debts, poverty and potential eviction.[126]

---

dealing with Gypsies revealed that a mere 8% of Roma were skilled workers compared to 30% of non-Roma.

118   Barany, Zoltan (2002) *The East European Gypsies* Cambridge Univ. Press Chapter 4.

119   Kovats *supra* n109.

120   Valki *supra* n130 at 453.

121   Hungarian Gov. Report below n138 at 24 and Liegeois and Gheorghe (1995) *Roma/Gypsies: A European Minority* Minority Rights Group, London at 7.

122   Kechichian, Joseph A 'International: Ethnic, Political Aspirations in Eastern Europe' (1991) *Armenian International Magazine* 28 November.

123   Reisch, Alfred A 'First law on Minorities Drafted' *Report on Eastern Europe* 13 December 1991 pp 14−18 at 15. This article also includes some of the reasons why census figures are so unreliable at pp 14−15.

124   Report No J/3670 of the Government of the Republic of Hungary to the National Assembly on the situation of the national and ethnic minorities living in the Republic of Hungary (1997: Budapest) p 19.

125   Hockenos, Paul 'Xenophobia and Racism unbound in the land of the Magyars' (1993) *New Politics* Winter pp 69−81 at 153.

126   *Magyar Hírlap* 22 December 1997.

Educational segregation has now been prohibited by new legislation but de facto segregation remains widespread.[127] It is no coincidence that the infant mortality rate among Roma is twice the national average as research has suggested that infant mortality is inversely proportional to the level of education.[128] The Roma have a life expectancy between 10 and 15 years less than that of the average Hungarian. Education has again been identified as a key factor as have living conditions and poverty.[129] Addictive illnesses, including drug addiction and alcoholism are also widespread. Rather than been seeing as a symptom of this malaise, the comparatively high level of Roma criminality (Roma are considered to be responsible for approximately 30% of all crimes) is often cited as a reason for maintaining exclusion and discrimination.[130]

It has been noted that Roma unemployment is a comparatively recent problem. Despite the common perception that Roma are traditionally unwilling to engage in work, until the mid-80s when the present economic crisis began to take hold, there was no substantial difference in the employment rate of the two communities.[131] Today however, unemployment is much higher than the national average, in some settlement areas as much as 90–100%.[132] The average income of a Romany family is from two-thirds to three-quarters of the Hungarian minimum living standard.[133]

This disparity can be attributed in part to the lack of skilled Roma workers and discrimination in the workplace.[134] However, the main factor has been the difficult transition to a market economy which left many unskilled workers, disproportionately Roma, unable to find alternative employment. In a survey of 171 adults carried out by one minority self-government, only 13 had regular work while 42% had no form of income at all.[135]

---

127 While 90% of Hungarian children continue education beyond eighth grade, only 4.5% of Roma children do so. According to Karcagi, K *Minorities/Hungary: Hungarian Gypsy Struggle Starts in School*, Interpress Service English News 11 January 1996. See Chapter 5 at 223 for details on education in Hungary.

128 *Népszava*, 'Infant Mortality rate Twice Higher among Roma' 19 November 1997.

129 Puporka, Lajos and Zsolt, Zádori (1998) *The Health Status of Roma in Hungary* Roma Press Centre, Budapest

130 Valki, Laszlo 'Minority Protection in Hungary – Hungarian Minorities Abroad' in Dinstein and Tabory (1992) *The Protection of Minorities and Human Rights* Martinus-Nijhoff, Dordrecht at 457.

131 Statistics in letter concerning statements by the Prime Minister written by the Roma Press Centre, Budapest and distributed to Romnet members in 1998. Prime Minister, Gyula Horn noted that the problems of the Hungarian Roma would be solved if 'only they entered employment' in *Népszava*, 17 January 1998; Wagner, Francis 'The Gypsy in Post-war Hungary' (1987) *Hungarian Studies Review* Vol. 14, 2 pp 33–43 at 38 (NB this article contains some useful statistics but unfortunately makes some unpleasant generalisations).

132 The national average is estimated at 11%.

133 *MTI* 'MTI views Hungarian support program for Gypsies' Budapest 30 December 1997.

134 *Supra* n132 at 27.

135 Kovats, Martin 'Gypsy self-governments in post-Socialist Hungary' in Bridger, S and Pine, F (eds) (1997) *Surviving Post-Socialism – Local Strategies and Regional responses in Eastern Europe and the Former Soviet Union*, Routledge, London pp 124–147.

Post-war Hungary has not typically been associated with racism and ethnic hatred. It appears however, that anti-Roma sentiment, common in the past, intensified with the arrival of democracy.[136] Paul Hockenos notes that in the past resentment towards the Roma was not considered to deserve the ugly title of racism.[137] Today, discrimination and violence persist and are promoted by a cultural crisis over the national identity fuelled by the comparatively high Roma birth rate.[138] In 1998, a Gallup opinion poll revealed that 50% of Hungarians expressed dislike of Gypsies, including 41% of people with an advanced educational qualification.[139]

Immediately after the instillation of the democratically elected Government in 1990, gangs of skinheads attacked Rom ghettos in Egher and Miiskloc. It has been claimed that the vast increase in racist attacks against foreigners in Hungary is inextricably linked to the racial prejudices against the Roma minority. The structures of racist thinking, directed at the Roma, were already in place before the collapse of Communism and the popularity of racism spread quickly.[140]

The problem seems more than transitional in nature. A report presented to the Hungarian parliament by the Minister of Justice and the Secretary of State on Minorities in 1997 noted that the number and gravity of ethnic conflicts was increasing and anticipated a general growth of such conflicts in the future. The report concluded that the Hungarian legal system was unable to deal with these conflicts.[141] These problems are compounded by serious problems of discrimination within the police force including several documented incidents of police violence.[142] The European Court of Human Rights recently found a violation of Article 3 in one such case where a Roma man had sustained injuries after being questioned by the police for a petty offence.[143] The investigating authorities had failed to provide an alternative explanation for Mr Balogh's injuries, requiring him to prove that the police were responsible.

Discriminatory attitudes are exhibited at the highest levels of Hungarian society with former Prime Minister Gyula Horn publicly commenting on the unwillingness of the Roma to engage in work and to help themselves.[144] As in the Czech Republic, the judicial system has failed to recognise the racial motivation behind criminal

---

136   Valki *supra* n130 at 456.

137   Hockenos *supra* n125 at 69.

138   Crowe *supra* n100 notes that between 1984 and 1987 Hungary's population dropped from 10.7 to 10.6 million, while Rom birth rates were doubling every 20–30 years at 98.

139   'Hungarians admit their hatred of other races' *The Budapest Sun*, 15 January 1998.

140   Acc to sociologist Ottila Solt in Hockenos (1992) *Freedom to Hate* Routledge NY at 150.

141   *Népszava*, 10 January 1997.

142   Roma Press Centre 'Police and the Roma – Conference' 26 June 1997; Human Rights Watch (2002) *World Report. Hungary* HRW, New York.

143   *Balogh* vs. *Hungary* 2004 App 47040/99.

144   Roma Press Centre 'New National Gypsy organisation founded' 16 January 1998.

attacks.[145] Reports suggest that the integration of the Roma lags far behind that of the other groups and is far from complete.[146]

Background to minority protection in Hungary[147]

In 1979, the Hungarian Roma were granted ethnic group status rather than the status of nationality.[148] The refusal to grant nationality status was apparently based on the fact that some 75% of Roma spoke Hungarian.[149] The consequence of the designation was to deprive the Roma of full cultural development supported by the Government. The aim of financial aid and the other paternalist efforts of the Communists was undoubtedly one of cultural assimilation.[150]

Martin Kovats observes that the assimilation policy of the Communist era has been replaced by a policy of 'dialogue'.[151] This policy of dialogue has concentrated primarily on cultural and political rights, while the poverty experienced by the majority of the Hungarian Roma continues unabated. The need for Roma cultural development and political participation was apparent by 1989 when the gradual transformation of the Hungarian political system saw the rise of several new Roma organisations lobbying for improved rights in the workplace and improved housing policies.[152] In the 1990 elections, the second largest political party, Association of Free Democrats (AFD) supported four Gypsy candidates, and two were elected to the new legislature.[153] Today however, there are no Roma politicians in the national legislature (although there are two Hungarian Roma in the European Parliament).

Article 68 of the Hungarian Constitution of 1990 provides that minorities shall be afforded collective participation in public life; the right to establish local and national self-governments; the fostering of their own culture; the use of their mother tongue and the right to use their names in their own language.

In 1990, the Office for National and Ethnic Minorities was established to replace the Council of Nationalities to carry out state tasks associated with these minorities.[154] The tasks of the office include preparation and elaboration of government policy, co-ordination of government tasks, maintaining contacts and promoting the exchange of opinion between the government and the various minorities. They also examine

---

145   *Népszava*, 28 February 1997. They have been numerous similar incidents reported; see *Magyar Hírlap*, 7 December 1995 and 10 January 1996 for two further examples.

146   *Supra* n124 at 11.

147   ERRC Press Release 11 March 1997.

148   Council of Ministers' Resolution No 1, 019/1979.

149   According to the newspaper *Magyar Hirlap* quoted in Crowe *supra* n100 at 99.

150   Markos, Edith (1987) 'The fast-growing Gypsy Minority and its problems' *RFE* Research 15 June 1987 pp 13–16 at 14.

151   Kovats, Martin '*The Good, the Bad and the Ugly*: Three Faces of "Dialogue" – the Development of Roma Politics in Hungary' (1997) *Contemporary Politics* Vol. 3 No 1 passim.

152   Crowe notes that many of the organisations were beset with infighting and family rivalry making their success limited *supra* n100 at 102.

153   *Ibid.*

154   Gov. Resolution no. 34/1990 (VIII.30).

public attitudes on minorities, which includes the operation of a documentation service holding information on the different minorities and minority policy.[155] The office encompasses a Department of Roma/Gypsy issues as well as departments representing other minorities including Germans and Romanians.

The Act on the Rights of National and Ethnic Minorities

In 1993, the Act on the Rights of National and Ethnic Minorities of 7 July was introduced, providing that the 13 designated minority groups in Hungary shall have the right to personal autonomy and the right to establish self-governments. The Act is a clear indication of the value of autonomy and recognition of collective rights. Speaking at a conference in early 1990, the then Director of the Secretariat for National and Ethnic Minorities with the Council of Ministers and Hungarian Vice-Minister, captured the essence of a new era based firmly on recognition of both individual and collective rights:

> Autonomy is not the precursor of separatism – there are many who fear the very notion of autonomy … to put it a different way, autonomy guarantees that national minorities will be able to preserve their own identity and feel at home within existing frontiers.[156]

The preamble of the statute is promising in its clear statement as to the value of minority communities to Hungarian society:

> The mother tongue, the intellectual and material culture, the historical traditions of the national and ethnic minorities who are Hungarian citizens and live in Hungary, and other characteristic qualities which support their minority status are considered aspects of their identity as individuals and as a community.

> All these are special values, the preservation, cultivation and augmentation of which is not only a basic right of the national and ethnic minorities, but also in the interest of the Hungarian nation, and ultimately in that of the community of governments and nations.

Furthermore, the preamble goes on to stress the importance of cultural autonomy for the realisation of the human rights:

> In consideration of the fact that self-governments form the basis of democratic systems, the establishment of minority self-governments, their operation and the resulting cultural autonomy is regarded by the National Assembly as one of the fundamental preconditions of the special enforcement of the rights of minorities.[157]

---

155 Res. 34/1990 (VIII.30).

156 Csabada Tabajdi, repirnted in Liégeois *A Programme of case studies concerning the inclusion of minorities as factors of cultural policy and action* 'Roma policy: Gypsy national self-government and local self-governments' CDCC, C/E 1996 DECS/SE/ DHRM (96) 23 at 11.

157 Act on the Rights of Ethnic and National Minorities (1993) No. LXXVIII.

Undeterred by the absence of an internationally accepted definition of 'minority,' Article 1(2) provides several criteria for the recognition of a minority for the purposes of the statute. Along with the standard criteria such as numerical inferiority and a desire on the part of the minority to preserve their ethnic distinctions, there are additional requirements that the minority must have been resident in Hungary for at least one century; and that members of the minority must be Hungarian citizens[158] (immigrants, the homeless and foreign citizens are additionally expressly excluded in Article 2).

Article 3(2) recognises the ethnic identity of individuals and their communities as a fundamental human right. Unequivocal support for collective rights is also provided in Article 15 which states that 'The preservation, fostering, strengthening and passing on of their minority identity is the unalienable collective right of minorities.'[159] Any policy aiming at assimilation is expressly prohibited by the statute[160] and there is a positive obligation placed on the Government to promote equality of opportunity in the political and cultural sphere.[161]

The most innovative measure of all however, is found in Article 5(1) which provides 'the constitutional right to establish local and national self-governments'. Such a provision translates the rhetoric of group rights into a practical possibility. The right to establish minority self-government is reinforced by the right, vesting in members of minorities, to learn of their history, culture and traditions and to communicate in their mother tongue.[162]

The drafting process recognised that effective minority representation needed more than local implementation and thus the statute provides that minorities have the right to be represented in the Hungarian National Assembly.[163] In 1994, the Hungarian Supreme Court ruled that parliament had been violating this constitutional principle by failing to provide for minority representation in the national legislature.[164] This provision has still not been implemented despite being planned for the 2002 elections.[165] Nevertheless, the Act on the Rights of National and Ethnic Minorities constitutes a unique, pioneering step forward in the protection of the rights of

---

158   *Ibid.* at Article 1(2).

159   *Ibid.* at Article 15.

160   *Ibid.* Article 4(1).

161   *Ibid.* Article 9.

162   *Ibid.* Article 13, strengthened by the provision in Article 16 which gives minorities the right to cultivate and develop their culture and traditions, and Article 18(4) which guarantees the rights of minorities to hold celebrations and events which help to preserve and maintain their culture and traditions.

163   *Ibid.* Article 20(1).

164   Romania has a constitutional provision which guarantees a right to one parliamentary representative for persons belonging to national minorities if they have been unable to secure sufficient votes.

165   *MTI*, Budapest 'Parliamentary Representation of Minorities – New Proposal' 27 January 1998. The proposal was made by MP Mihaly Bihari of the Hungarian Socialist Party. In 2004 proposals were introduced to prevent ethnic Hungarians from standing as candidates in minority self-government elections, however the proposals were defeated after opposition from the Alliance of Young Democrats (FIDESZ).

minorities and their members. It is thus interesting to compare these commitments to the main initiatives in the regional minority rights provisions.

The Hungarian legislation in the European human rights context

The standards established in the United Nations Declaration on the Rights of Persons belonging to National or Ethnic Minorities provide little in the way of positive obligations on states.[166] Original proposals to include a right to autonomy and/or a second level right to cultural autonomy were rejected by delegates. Article 2 includes a right to participate in decisions involving the minority, there is nothing concerned with regional or national representation in the way envisaged in the Hungarian law.[167]

The Helsinki Final Act contains a short, simple provision dealing with collective rights to culture and identity stating:

> The participating states, recognizing the contribution that national minorities or regional cultures can make to co-operation among them in the various fields of education, intend, when such minorities or cultures exist within their territory, to facilitate this contribution, taking into account the legitimate interests of their members.[168]

The follow-up conference document of 1986 required 'legislative, administrative and judicial measures be adopted' to ensure the protection of fundamental human rights to members of national minorities.[169] However, it was the Copenhagen document on the Human Dimension part IV which specifically focused and expanded international commitments to the protection of minorities.[170] A recommendation signed by five states was put to the Conference that 'minorities should be given the right to an appropriate form self-government on the territory in which they live'.[171] More recently, the 'Lund Recommendations on Effective Participation in Public Life' can be viewed as part of the OSCE's mandate to promote security and peace in Europe.[172] They explicitly recognise the beneficial nature of self-government in fields including education, culture, local planning, health and housing.

In the field of education, the Copenhagen document provides that persons belonging to national minorities shall have the right to freely use their mother tongue

---

166   G.A. Res 47/135, annex, 47 UN GAOR Supp (No 49). At 210, UN Doc. A/47/49 (1993).

167   *Supra* n127 Article 2(3).

168   Helsinki Final Act 1975 Co-operation in Humanitarian and Other Fields, section 4(e).

169   Reprinted in (1989) 28 *ILM* 527.

170   Document of the Copenhagen meeting of the Conference on the Human Dimension of the CSCE, June 29th 1990 reprinted in (1990) *HRLJ* 232.

171   Maresca, John. A 'The people have a right to choose' *International Herald Tribune* 21 June 1989, cited in Mastny, Vojtech (1992) *The Heslinki Process and the Reintegration of Europe 1986–1991, Analysis and Documentation*, London p187.

172   Packer, John (2000) 'The origin and nature of the Lund Recommendations on Effective Participation of National Minorities in Public Life' *Helsinki Monitor* 11 p 31.

in private as well as public; and to establish and maintain educational institutions.[173] The state has a duty to 'endeavour to ensure' adequate opportunities for instruction in the mother tongue.[174] Similarly, the Council of Europe's FCNM does not recognise group rights for minorities.[175] Article 5 places a positive obligation on states in the fields of education and culture but refers explicitly to 'persons belonging to national minorities' rather than minorities per se.

As far as the Hungarian statute is concerned, the rights are more specific and the state's responsibilities are clearly spelled out.[176] Article 43 supports the teaching of mother tongue languages even in areas where there is no municipal minority government. Furthermore, it is provided that where the parents of eight or more students so request, it becomes *compulsory* to run a minority class or group.[177] The state takes on the responsibility of funding such an initiative and the policy of training native teachers to provide education in the mother tongue or 'bilingually'.[178]

Rights of group autonomy and self-government compared

The Copenhagen Document implicitly recognises that majoritarian democracy may be insufficient to protect the interests of minority groups. Furthermore, a collectivist approach is adopted whereby 'appropriate local or autonomous administrations are envisaged' as one of the means to enable minorities to develop their ethnic religious or linguistic identity.[179] This view is also apparent in the Parliamentary Assembly's *Recommendation on an Additional Protocol to the European Convention on the Rights of Minorities*.[180] Article 11 of the draft protocol includes a right of national minorities to representation through local/autonomous authorities. However, as already mentioned, the FCNM does not go so far and clearly avoids recognising group rights.[181]

The Hungarian Law on National and Ethnic Minorities with its recognition of the need for a collective dimension to human rights protection thus compares favourably to regional human rights standards. The Hungarian experiment has been watched closely by other states with a significant number of minority groups. If successful in reducing ethnic tension and promoting internal stability, the collective rights

---

173 Document of the Copenhagen Meting of the CSCE of 29 June 1990 Part IV paras 32.1 and 32.2.

174 *Ibid.* Part IV para. 34.

175 Discussed in Chapter 6 at 299.

176 The Slovenian constitution recognises collective rights in relation to education also. Article 64 guarantees minorities the right to plan their own educational curricula and the right to be represented at a local level: Blaustein Albert, Flanz Gisbert (eds) (1990) *Constitutions of the World*, Slovenia Dobbs Ferry NY.

177 Article 43(4).

178 Article 46(2).

179 *Supra* n124 at para. 35.

180 C/E Recommendation 1201 (1993).

181 See discussion in Chapter 6 at 299.

approach may well be introduced elsewhere.[182] To assess success of the project a closer examination of the practice of minority self-government must be considered.

Minority self-government in practice

Although not originally included within the auspices of the legislation, Gypsies or Roma are now included as one of the 13 recognised minorities for the purpose of the statute.[183] The Gypsy languages of Romani and Beash are also recognised by the 1993 statute.[184]

Following the local elections of 19 November 1995 there were 792 functioning local minority governments. This number demonstrated that members of minorities welcomed the chance at greater participation but also that there was an unexpected level of support from the majority population. Nevertheless, there is still a great deal of voter apathy to be overcome. The Central Registration and Election Office reported that only 40,000 of 3.5 million eligible voters cast their ballots.[185] Evidence collated from around Eastern Europe by Barany suggests that most Roma do not vote and are unlikely to support a Romani candidate.[186] This in part reflects the awkward relationship that many Roma have with their identity in a climate of misrecognition and exclusion.

The self-governments receive a transfer of assets or subsidies from the state budget. By 1995 477 Roma self-governments had been elected, challenging the perception that Roma have no interest in political organisation.[187] The local elections of 1998, resulted in 2,779 seats going to representatives of the Roma community, including two mayors.[188] Notwithstanding the criticisms that have been levied at the self-government system, it has enabled thousands of Roma to engage directly in the political process. This achievement alone is something to be praised and encouraged.

---

182 Although Roe notes that there is some suspicion that the law was only introduced to show states with Hungarian minorities a blue-print of how the Hungarian minority should be treated, 'Progressive Inaction Towards Minorities' *Transition* (1997) Vol. 4 no 4 no pagination. Prime Minister Antall's speech of 1990 bears out this suspicion: 'the main aim of our minority policy is to gain assertion for human rights, and within this, the rights of minorities, both outside and inside our borders. With regard to the fact that one-third of Margyardom lives outside our borders, the Hungarian state has a particular responsibility to supp. ort everywhere the preservation of the Magyar nation as a cultural and ethnic community' *Premier Jozsef Antall presents Government programme*, BBC Summary of World Broadcasts, Eastern Europe section EE/0773/c1/1, 25 May 1990. See also Reisch *supra* n90 at 16.

183 Article 2.

184 Article 42.

185 *OMRI Daily Digest* 'Low Turn-out at Hungary's Minority elections' 21 November 1995.

186 Barany *supra* n118 at 237.

187 *Supra* n179 at 59. This is by far the largest number of minority self-governments (the nearest figure being the 162 German self-governments and the 57 Croat self-governments).

188 'Most Minority seats go to Gypsies and Germans' Posted to Romnet 21 October 1998; Gusztáv Koszltolányi (2000) 'All roads lead to Roma' *Central European Review* Vol 2, No 35 16 October.

In an unprecedented development, the head of the Roma national self-government, Flórián Farkas was invited to speak about the plight of the Hungarian Roma before a meeting of the European Parliament. The following elections in 2002 led to the establishment of more than 1,000 Roma minority self-governments, amongst them 998 settlements with Roma self-governments including four mayors.

The local minority self-governments are empowered to run institutions within their authority, especially in the fields of education; media; promotion of traditions; adult education and socio-cultural animation.[189] They work with the local government on a predominately consultative basis but they also have a power of veto in relation to decisions on a range of issues including education, language and culture affecting the minority population. Furthermore, they are able to run businesses, establish scholarships and collect project proposals.[190] Administrative tasks, such as budgeting and developing an appropriate organisational structure inevitably demand a high standard of education and a variety of business skills; as such they present some particular challenges for the Roma. In addition to local self-governments there is a national self-government for each minority which works with the Office for National and Ethnic Minorities and advises the government on minority affairs.

In 1995, a Co-ordination Council for Gypsy Affairs was established 'to manage the problems of the Gypsy minority, to promote the social integration and to co-ordinate the policy national agencies'.[191] The Council was charged with developing a package of long- and medium-term measures to promote these objectives.[192] The same year a Public Foundation was established with the express aim of facilitating measures to decrease 'the imbalance of the Gypsy minority'.[193] The Foundation receives a limited sum of $1.1 million per year to help deal with the most serious problems affecting the Roma. Projects include buying land for farmers, loan-guarantees for Gypsy businesses and educational scholarships.[194] In 1999, the CCGA was abolished and replaced by the Inter-Ministerial Committee for Gypsy Affairs which is supervised by the Minister of Justice and the Office of National and Ethnic Minorities and is charged with implementing the medium-range policies. These policies are described in detail by Zoltan Barany and include initiatives in the fields of education, health and housing.[195]

Roma representation in national government

Participation in public life is essential to the development of minority identity and mutual understanding between minority and majority.[196] It is essential to a broad,

---

189   Article 27(3).

190   Article 27(4).

191   Gov. resolution 1120/1995 (XII.7.) *On the Establishment of the Co-ordination Council of Gypsy Affairs*, para.1.

192   *Supra* n179 at para. 2

193   Gov. resolution 1121/1995 (XII.7.) *On the establishment of the Public Foundation for the Gypsy Minorities in Hungary*.

194   Karcagi *supra* n127.

195   Barany *supra* n118 at 326–330.

196   Heintze, *supra* n29 at 326.

purposive conception of self-determination applying to the whole of the people within the state rather than simply the majority.[197]

While representation in local government is an important step in the realisation of human rights, such representation is also guaranteed at the national level.[198] Such representation is vital if the prejudices of the public and many politicians are to be redressed, especially given the increasingly populist appeal of some far-right extremist political groups. In the 1990 election campaign the President of the Hungarian Democratic Forum, Istvan Csurka, became noted for his inflammatory, racist language. In one such article he referred to the Roma:

> We must end the unhealthy practice of blaming the skinheads for all that is bad among the youth, while leniently acknowledging other sicknesses, crimes and cultural crimes. We can no longer recoil from the fact that there are also genetic reasons behind degeneration. We must acknowledge that disadvantaged groups and strata of society have been with us for too long, groups where the severity of natural selection has not worked.[199]

The need for the Hungarian Government to implement its constitutional commitment to national minority representation has been raised the Advisory Committee on the FCNM, yet the commitment remains unfulfilled.[200] In a number of other opinions, the Committee has suggested that states consider methods to improve participation of minorities including reducing the number of votes required to gain seats in the legislature.[201] The one Roma MP left in the Hungarian parliament lost his seat in the 1998 elections, where fascists polled 5% of the popular vote. One of the biggest problems facing Roma representation at this level is the nature of the Hungarian Roma community itself. Infighting and cultural differences have meant that the two largest Romani organisations – *Phralipe* and the *Lungo Drom* were unable to agree to form a coalition party.[202] Organisation of Romani politics is still a very new experience and difficult lessons are inevitable.[203]

---

197   Pentassuglia *supra* n76 at 316; de, A 'Peaceful group accommodation as an alternative to secession in sovereign states' in Clark and Wiliamson *supra* n47 pp 87–110 at 94.

198   Article 68(3) *supra* n157.

199   Magyar Forum 20 August 1992.

200   Concluding comments of the Advisory Committee on the FCNM Opinion on Hungary, adopted on 22 September 2000.

201   Ad Com *Opinion on Switzerland* ACFC/INF/OP/1 (2003) 007 paras 76 and Ad Com Opinion on Germany ACFC/INF/OP/1 (2002) 008 para. 66.

202   The plight of the Roma parliament is discussed by Kovats *supra* n151.

203   Barany, Zoltan (1995) 'Grim Realities in Eastern Europe' *Transmission* 29 March pp 3–8 at 6. Ericka Schlager noted in 1994 that 700 out of some 1600 Romani settlements have established Romani Unions. She reported the comments made by some representatives that the minorities law had disrupted Roma political organisation by playing organisations off against each other, Comments to Romnet after a visit to Hungary 12–17 July 1998 as staff member of the Commission on Security and Cooperation in Europe (unpublished).

Implementing the self-government system

There have been some notable difficulties with the self-government system. Some can be attributed to teething problems, whereas other criticisms are more serious and require structural changes.

One of the teething problems for the Roma has been the lack of political experience of their elected representatives. The Office for National and Ethnic Minorities has engaged with this problem by introducing a series of regional courses providing legal and administrative information to enable minority members to participate effectively.

There is also a deeper criticism aimed at the policy of self-government, namely that it may increase irredentist tendencies. However, the Hungarian statute emphasises a strong link between self-government, political participation and the full realisation of human rights. Furthermore, far from promoting secessionism, the Hungarian Government considers that it may actually increase the civic responsibility of minority members:

> It is our opinion that the involvement of the minorities in the public life of local communities will lead to the development of an increased sense of responsibility on the part of the minorities. It will also exert a positive influence on their consciousness of identity and civil standing.[204]

Perhaps the biggest threat to the system's success lies in the concern that with the extension of the local self-government scheme, the responsibility of the national government towards minorities will reduce. The minorities may find that they are criticised and blamed for failing to make dramatic changes in the situation of their people. The Hungarian Government's own report recognises that the expectations placed on Roma self-governments are 'too great' to be achievable at present:

> The Gypsy minority self-governments find themselves in a special situation. Whereas the self-governments of the national minorities are active mainly in the fields of education, culture and preserving traditions, the Gypsy governments have additional tasks which relate to social, health and employment questions.[205]

Lack of funding is a major problem with the system at present.[206] The minority self-governments depend on extra support from their local councils and are encouraged to apply for grants when available. Research by Martin Kovats found that every self-government received the same level of funding, irrespective of size and particular problems:

---

204 *Supra* n124 at 14.

205 *Ibid.* at 28.

206 For comments and views on lack of funding and other obstacles see 'Self-government in Hungary: The Romani/Gypsy Experience and prospects for the future' Project on Ethnic Relations Conference 9–11 May 1997, Budapest; see also the comments of Schlager *supra* n203.

> The amount was far too small to allow self-governments to exercise their rights and fails even to cover the annual administration costs of these bodies and honouraria for representatives.[207]

In the town of ózd, where there is total unemployment in some villages, there have been improvements in the fields of health care and funds have also been directed at education and training. However, the president of the minority government reports that many of his staff work without pay in order to reduce the high administrative costs.[208] Alison Lys concludes: 'In theory the Act is wonderful, but in practice it produces an instant ghetto system'.[209]

Related to this criticism, is the concern that resources ploughed into the minority self-governments and their elected representatives will be diverted from minority organisations and projects which do not have the full support of the representatives. Barany refers to the dominance of *Lungo Drom* in the national self-government which distorts Roma representation by failing to reflect the diversity of Gypsy organisations and Romani society.[210] Article 30(2) of the Act on the Rights of National and Ethnic Minorities allows such organisations, institutions and associations to submit applications for state funding on issues such as culture, education and science, in the same way as local minority self-governments. Nevertheless, it may be presumed that extent of funding given to the self-governments will often operate to curtail funding for other minority-based projects which do not have the backing of the self-government.

Kovats argues that the Hungarian 'dialogue' policy operates to keep the Roma subordinate in society.[211] The emphasis on cultural and political rights does not help to address the main problems facing the Roma, namely education and unemployment. Furthermore, the minority representatives themselves have a vested interest in maintaining a reasonable amount of support for the environment in which they were elected:

> Many of the 2,000 plus Roma activists receive some or most of their income from their public duties, making it in their interests to protect and develop the system and their position within it.[212]

This can be clearly seen in respect of the right of minority self-governments to veto some local decisions. In many cases, it would appear that the veto is not used and it is difficult for representatives to compel the local authorities to consider their views.[213]

An atmosphere of compromise and co-operation has been established in which Roma representatives are unlikely to create much discomfort for a government

---

207   Kovats *supra* n135 at 131.
208   Roe *supra* n182 no pagination.
209   *Ibid.*
210   *Supra* n118 at327.
211   Kovats *supra* n151.
212   *Ibid.* at 68.
213   Kovats *supra* n135.

determined to play a part in the new integrated Europe.[214] Kai Schafft also notes that the Act's provisions have been inconsistently enforced with regard to the Roma and that there is a perception held by many Roma representatives that their role in local politics is minimal.[215]

Harmonisation of the law in other areas

If Kovats' analysis is accepted, the picture is pessimistic. Yet there is some room for optimism. A minority actively involved in planning their own future is an improvement on times gone by. The policy of dialogue may not be entirely negative in encouraging compromise and shared responsibility. Indeed, there have been some encouraging signs that the Government is addressing the economic and social demands of an increasingly vocal minority.

In 1996, an amendment to the criminal code was introduced to enable prosecutions against people who commit racially motivated criminal acts.[216] The previous law had made it possible for a conviction for an offence committed against a national, ethnic, racial or religious group.[217] However, this provision had received criticism following the 'great skin-head trial' of 1992 when the chief prosecutor had been unsuccessful in proving that racial motive in violence perpetrated by 48 skinhead youths. The Court of Capital had reduced the charges to hooliganism, breach of the peace and slander.[218] On 21 April 1998 paragraph 174/B of the Criminal Code was successfully used in the Heves County Court to sentence a 19-year-old man who attacked a student believing him to be of Jewish origin. The legal counsel from the National and Ethnic Minorities Legal Defense Bureau told the Roma Press Centre:

> It is essential that finally there is a valid verdict in Hungary based in paragraph 174/B of the criminal Code, as racial hatred is on the rise, and therefore it is important that in similar cases courts rule in the same manner.[219]

In 1997, the Parliamentary Commissioner of National Minorities and the Commissioner of Data Protection criticised the police and media for publicising the ethnicity of perpetrators of crime, as a contravention of the rights to free choice and declaration of identity. They found:

> The publication of ethnic affiliation in crime news, warrants and police announcements can be instrumental in strengthening prejudices, and it may implicitly suggest that there is a connexion [sic] between belonging to an ethnic group and criminal activities.[220]

---

214   This is demonstrated in part by the success of *Lungo Drom* over radicals from the *Phralipe* organisation.

215   Schafft, Kai (1999) 'Local minority self-governance and Hungary's Roma' *Hungarian Quarterly* Vol XL No 155 Autumn.

216   ACT XVII of 1996.

217   s156 penal Code.

218   Beszelo 5.12.92 quoted in Human Rights Watch (1993) *supra* n111 at 21.

219   Roma Press Centre 'Valid verdict for the felony of violence against the member of a racial group,' May 1998.

220   *Népszava*, 5 February 1997.

Such a move follows criticism of the practice by the Head of the Hungarian police forces, Sándor Pintér, whose letter to police departments in November 1996 appears to have received little attention at the time.

A new Hungarian law on child protection has also come into force. At present, many Roma children are taken into care as a result of evictions and other social reasons. In some areas the number of Roma in such care reaches 60–70%. The introduction of the new legislation aimed to prevent children being taken into care solely for social reasons.[221] However, in 2006 the Committee on the Rights of the Child continued to exhibit concern about the situation of Romani children including their disproportionate representation in state child care and in juvenile justice institutions.[222]

After the establishment of the Co-ordination Council for Gypsy Affairs and the Public Foundation for Gypsy Minorities in 1995, a series of medium and long-term measures were devised in an attempt to improve the living standards of the Roma in Hungary.

An action programme was established in 1995 in the fields of education, employment, housing and non-discrimination. The strategy noted the urgency of the situation in concluding: 'a package of medium measures must be prepared to improve the living conditions of the Gypsy minority'.[223] The programme introduced in resolution 1093/1997 specifically focused on the Roma and consisted of a variety of measures and feasibility studies for the next two years.[224] In the field of education, pre-school programmes for Gypsy children were advocated and policies to increase involvement in secondary education were demanded. One such policy was the extension of the boarding school scheme which enables gifted children and those under-achieving to receive a more concerted, thorough schooling. The Ministry is aware of the need to increase the number of Romani scholars. At a conference for Gypsy social work students and their teachers in July 1997, the Minister of Culture and Education, Bálint Magyar, spoke of the intention to introduce a special curriculum about Gypsies in higher education that would be compulsory for those becoming teachers.[225] As far as training and employment are concerned, the resolution notes that methods to enhance Gypsy employment and training need to be assessed. One specific initiative has established microregional projects providing land for the

---

221 *Magyar Hírlap* 'Romani children in State Care in Hungary' 31 October 1997.

222 Committee on the Rights of the Child 41st session *Concluding Observations: Hungary* CRC/C/HUN/C0/ 2–27 January 2006.

223 Gov. Resolution No. 1125/1995 (XII.12) *on the most urgent issues of the Gypsy minorities*, para. 3.

224 Resolution 1093/1997 (VII.29) *on a package of medium-term measures intended to improve the living standards of the Gypsies*. See also Roma press centre 'Increasing normative support for Romani students' November 21st 1997; MTI News *Support for Minority Education – Press briefing* 4 March 1998.

225 Roma press Centre 'Bálint Magyar: the government regards the training of Roma intellectuals a prime task' 2 July1997.

socially disadvantaged in smaller regions.[226] The central employment and training project established in 1997 to improve the labour market conditions for long term unemployed Gypsies will be continued in an attempt to reduce the unemployment of a greater number.[227] Furthermore, positive action is expressly endorsed as a method of giving job opportunities to the socially disadvantaged.[228]

In the housing sphere an implementation schedule was directed in order to resolve once and for all the extremely poor standards of housing of many Romani families living in colonies and settlements. The programme noted that the needs of the community itself must be fully taken into account.

As new members of the European Union, Hungary had to comply with the Race Equality Directive 2000/43 EC.[229] This encompasses the prohibition of direct and indirect discrimination, victimisation and harassment as well as effective enforcement and monitoring.[230] After initial concern about the lack of effective enforcement in the discrimination field and the absence of compliant definitions of indirect discrimination, victimisation and harassment and Act was introduced on Equal Treatment and the Promotion of Equal opportunities.[231] The Act establishes a new agency for examining complaints of discrimination, the Equal Opportunity Authority.[232] In one of the first cases under the Act, the Szabolcs-Szatmár-Bereg County Court awarded damages to a group of Roma that had been refused entry to a discotheque in Nagyhalasz. The court held that the key principles of equal treatment and human dignity had been violated when the proprietors had only denied entry to those suspected of being Roma.[233]

Discriminatory attitudes in the police force have been officially recognised and police training has been updated to include information about the Roma minority so the service is 'humane and free from discrimination'. The police have been criticised for attributing blame collectively and for failing to protect the Roma and other

---

226   As of 1996, the 'Social Land Programme' enabled 124 Roma communities to use vacant land to produce food for themselves: Kovats *supra* n151 at 58.

227   *Supra* n224 at para. 2.1.2.

228   *Ibid.* at para. 2.1.3.

229   Discussed in Chapter 3 at 132.

230   Kádár, A and Farkas, L 'Country Report Hungary' May 2003 in *Report on Measures to Combat Discrimination in the 13 Candidate Countries VT/2002/45* MEDE European Consultancy and Migration Policy Group.

231   Act CXXV of 2003. For problems with the previous Hungarian legal position see Farkas, Lilla 'Will the groom adopt the Bride's Unwanted child? The Race Equality Directive, Hungary and its Roma' 2003 in *Roma Rights Notebook*, ERRC.

232   See Homicsko, Oliver Arpad 'Equal treatment and the promotion of equal opportunities in Hungary'. Available at: www.comptrasec.u-bordeaux4.fr/static/ SEMINAIRES/ HOMICSKO1.pdf.

233   ERRC 'Hungarian Discotheque fined for unequal treatment' 21 June 2005 Litigation, ERRC Budapest.

minorities against racist attacks and violence.[234] The attitudes of the police service are now being subject to more effective monitoring.[235]

A sub-committee of the Human Rights, Minorities and Religious Affairs Committee specifically concentrating on Roma Affairs was formed in June 1997. It was charged with reviewing the work of public organisations and foundations as well as the different Roma councils. The profile of this body has now been raised and it has been renamed the Council of Roma Affairs which is chaired by the Prime Minister and consists of 21 experts including many senior figures in Roma politics. Several ministerial posts have been established within various government departments to provide advice on Roma issues. There have been various plans established aimed at improving the situation of the Roma, notably in employment and education. In a departure with the past, many of these initiatives have resulted from Roma consultation at the highest policy levels.[236]

Self-determination or autonomy: Hungarian self-government and the language of international human rights law

It has been noted that the Hungarian law goes beyond the minority rights standards laid down in the FCNM and the focus on greater political participation fits more easily into a broader conception of self-determination. We now need to consider whether this approach could be regarded as the future direction for self-determination.

At the Eighth Session of the Commission on Human Rights it was suggested that a concrete definition should be applied to the right of self-determination.[237] It should enumerate the right 'to create an independent State' and the right 'to secession or union with another people or nation'. Such a formulation was rejected in preference for the abstract wording of the Covenants; concern having been expressed that such an approach would limit the scope of the right. In reality however, self-determination is very much limited as a right, not just by the accompanying provisos of territorial integrity and its application to 'peoples' only, but also because of its limited interpretation by states; it is still strongly linked with secession and demands for independence. The existence of a 'democratic' electoral system is often considered to provide sufficient representation for all members of the state and therefore the demand for self-determination is considered redundant.

---

234   Human Rights Watch (1993) *supra* n111 at 31. The Martin Luther King Association (1991) documented 90 skinhead attacks between January 1991 and April 1992. Police were on the scene in less than 12 occasions: in three they refused to intervene; in one the victim was arrested; in at least one case the victim was assaulted and in two further cases, they refused to register the complaint.

235   *Supra* n224 at para. 5.3.

236   See the report of the Human Rights Committee *Concluding Observations of the Human Rights Committee – Additional information: Hungary.* 29 March 2003 CCPR/CO/74/HUN/Add. 1 (Follow-up response by State-party).

237   *Official Records of the Economic and Social Council, fourteenth session supplement No.4* (E/2,256) para. 34.

However, some states are recognising that the international human rights standards are not only minimal standards that need further elaboration, but that there are some situations that challenge the present 'individual' focus of those instruments and demand a new approach in the scope and content of these standards. As Alfredsson argues, self-control by the minority over its own affairs may be the most effective means of protecting minority dignity and identity.[238]

Self-determination is the only expressly group-centred right in these instruments and such a development could come in the extension of the concept of internal self-determination. Hurst Hannum and Thomas Franck agree that the internal aspect has become the most important conception of the right to self-determination in modern times.[239] Yet Hannum is unable to agree that a right to democratic governance is now emerging as an international norm.[240] Cultural autonomy is certainly viewed as part of the right to international self-determination and this may include participation in the democratic process,[241] but there is also a reluctance to apply self-determination to internal minorities. In fact, extending the reach of the right to minorities may be counter-productive in that, as self-determination is applied to more groups, the totality of measures included is likely to be watered down to avoid any possible demands for independence from smaller minority groups.

The language of autonomy

In dealing with internal self-determination, the language of autonomy is often preferred. One of the reasons for this may be the vagueness of the term which is clearly indicated by its absence from major international human rights documents. If there is no specifically defined human right to autonomy, states are probably happier to consider demands for autonomy without fear of international criticism. Wheatley notes that there is no international right to minority autonomy in international law outside of that recognise to peoples under the guise of self-determination.[242] To have any real meaning, autonomy must have individual and collective dimensions. Personal autonomy is very significant in the liberal tradition – as demonstrated by the value attached to free choice and expression. The collective dimension of autonomy is less well developed; presumably as it may appear at odds with the individualistic emphasis of human rights law. A flexible approach is required, not simply linked to self-government but also including political and cultural representation, to ensure that democracy does not simply equate to majoritarianism. Such political representation and engagement may be essential to the realisation of other rights but remains largely outside the sphere of international minority rights provisions.

---

238 Alfredsson, G 'Minority rights and a new world order' in Gomien, D (ed) (1993) *Broadening the Frontiers of Human Rights: Essays in Honour of Asbjorn Eide* OUP, New York pp 55–77.

239 Franck, Thomas (1995) *Fairness in International Law and Institutions* OUP at 84.

240 Hannum, H 'Self determination in the post-colonial era' in Clark and Williamson *supra* n47 at 25.

241 Roach *supra* n83 at 34.

242 Wheatley *supra* n85.

The content of autonomy according to Hannum covers basic issues such as language; social services; education; access to the civil services; land and natural resources as well as representative local government structures.[243] Taking the example of education which is already included under Article 27 of the ICCPR, Hannum emphasises that under that provision the state is given no positive obligation to assist minority education structures,[244] thus the state can promote one education system for all pupils irrespective of cultural differences. However, in situations where autonomy is sought there is likely to be a consensus as to the best method of schooling for that community. Thus, with financial support, the communication promoted by autonomy regimes would appear more likely to yield positive results. Hannum's study of various autonomy arrangements notes the use of partial autonomy:

> ... there are several entities that have been granted 'autonomy' not as a response to desires for political self-government, but rather as a means of guaranteeing to certain social or ethnic groups a degree of independence from governmental interferences in matters of particular concern to these groups, e.g., cultural autonomy or religious freedom.[245]

Autonomy and ethnicity: dangerous bed-fellows?

Heintze argues that modern society should seek to promote democratic society rather than pure democracy.[246] The latter may promote the interests of the majority without due respect to alternative, minority interests. Whereas a democratic society will encompass participation from all sections of society and this may, depending on the particular situation, necessitate cultural autonomy and self-government this support for autonomy engenders a contentious recognition, that difference and ethnicity should be encouraged and promoted rather than ignored. Further that simple equality and non-discrimination strategies cannot redress the problems faced by many minorities. This view is compatible with a purposive conception of self-determination which is afforded to 'peoples,' defined as everyone within a given territory rather than as a majoritarian, national community.[247] According to Alain Pellet, this was the approach of the Badinter Arbitration Commission when they denied claims of Croatian Serbs to secede and instead recognised them as a national minority.[248]

The opposing view holds that effective representation and participation are issues for human rights law rather than minority rights. As such the emphasis must be on equality of opportunity for all rather than on difference. Roach observes the paradox inherent in liberal multicultural theory whereby the consequences of special

---

243 Hannum *supra* n26 at 458.

244 *Ibid.* at 461.

245 Hannum, H (1980) 'The concept of Autonomy in International Law' *AJIL* 858–889 at 883.

246 Heintze *supra* n29 at 333–4.

247 Pentassuglia *supra* n76 at 316 argues that this notion is emerging in international legal discourse.

248 Pellet, Alain (1992) 'A second breath for the self-determination of peoples' *European Journal of International Law* Vol 3 (1) 178–185.

representational rights for minorities, namely the conflict with individual rights of members of other minorities and majority populations, are seldom addressed.[249] The argument espoused by Martin Kovats, who has researched the Hungarian system at length, is that emphasis on self-government and autonomy may make things worse for members of minority groups. He argues that the promotion of ethnic difference and cultural identity is cheaper than the 'prohibitive' costs of improving people's living standards.[250] A process of further alienation is predicted whereby the majority can marginalise the minority's problems without taking direct responsibility for them. Consequently, Kovats is strongly opposed to the artificial creation of a Roma nation or homeland. The international lawyer, Thomas Franck, has also expressed concern at the recent growth of 'post-modern neo-tribalism' which has led to separatism and a 'neo-apartheid agenda'.[251] He perceives this as a real threat to individual human rights although he does recognise that sub-state groups may need greater representation at an international level.[252]

These arguments have some strength; there are obvious problems of finding Roma representatives who can truly represent the myriad of European Roma. Further, the codification of the true-Roma identity has echoes of the romanticism observed by Judith Okely and has potential to undermine individual human rights of those who do not fit this image.[253] Alienated from the dominant identity a sizeable number may also be alienated from a 'new-Roma' identity, unless the latter is interpreted to be so inclusive as to deprive it of much meaning. Kovats argues that Roma nationalism 'represents the politicisation of the Romantic racial myth of the "Gypsy people"'.[254] For this reason, he argues that the European Roma Parliament is an essentially negative development.

The European Roma Parliament established in 1992 by the leaders of 22 organisations from 10 countries, has certainly not lived up to the expectations placed upon it. Indeed, Barany notes that some five years later Florin Cioabă attempted to form his own European Roma Parliament apparently unaware of the existing incarnation.[255] However, in my view such a development should not be seen as entirely negative. The Roma are Europe's biggest minority but as they lack a homeland they have been largely excluded from the European agenda. Their status has been passive, as recipients of European money and initiatives rather than as drivers of these initiatives. A supranational Roma body would not necessarily be totally representative of the Romani diaspora anymore than representatives of European member states will represent the desire and wishes of all their people.

---

249   Roach *supra* n83 at 39–40.

250   Kovats, M 'The politics of Roma identity: between nationalism and destitution' 20 July 2003 www.opendemocracy.net; and *supra* n340. 109 at 340.

251   Franck *supra* n239 at 144.

252   Franck, T (1995) *The Empowered Self: Law and Society in the Age of Individualism* at 30–35. An illuminating analysis of Franck's views are presented by Tierney, Stephen 'The search for a new normativity: Franck, T (2002), 'Post-modern neo-tribalism and the law of self-determination' *European Journal of Int. Law* Vol 13 at 941.

253   Okely, J (1983) *The Traveller-Gypsies* Cambridge Univ. Press.

254   Kovats *supra* n250 at 4.

255   Barany *supra* n118 at 261–2.

My view is that autonomy is not an alternative to individual human rights – rather it is a means of securing human rights and participation in public life which might otherwise be unavailable. It may even be a transitional need that, if it succeeds in its stated objective, will be the victim of its own success. Kovats' point that the state should not emphasise ethnicity and difference is also subject to Kymlickas' benign neglect argument in that it fails to recognise the way that majorities have their own cultural agenda – this is often couched in terms of civic rather than ethnic identity but in many cases the latter underpins the former.[256] Musgrave echoes the views of many other human rights theorists in arguing that it is both unrealistic and naive to anticipate that ethnic groups can survive and protect their identity through a discourse that represents the dominant state view. In his view, minority autonomy represents the only alternative to demands for secession:

> Ideally we want equality and non-discrimination to work at securing rights for all but the reality is evidently very different and the promotion of individual human rights of equality and non-discrimination ideal is not (and can not) be value neutral.[257]

Conclusion: Improving participation through cultural autonomy

It is clear that the Roma fall outside the traditionally conceived interpretations of self-determination. While some writers have suggested an expansion of the concept to include under-represented minorities there remains a long way to go before collective rights become part of accepted human rights discourse. A focus on the individual and collective dimensions of autonomy may provide a way forward without igniting fears of secession and the pressures of presenting a homogeneous Romani identity which relies on out-dated concepts of the 'true-Romany' and the pure nation.

Only a greater involvement in the political process is likely to have any effect on mobilising ethnic identity at the grass roots level. Debates about the Romani flag and a Charter enumerating Romani rights are inherently beneficial in that they stimulate public discussion and awareness. But this debate demands flexibility – reflecting the different experiences of a geographically diverse population as well as commonalties. The autonomy of the individual must not be sacrificed to the 'good' of the community. If the community itself is to survive the modernisation inherent in the democratic process it must encourage rather than stifle such debate.

Development of the collective aspects of autonomy alongside the present emphasis on individual autonomy could facilitate personal growth in the context of the community. Local self-government, participation in public debate and national government constitute important measures through which members of minorities may be able to develop and enjoy their identity in a secure environment. They are also crucial in educating the public at large as to the traditions, customs and values of

---

256   Consider for example the endorsement of the official state language and public holidays which often coincide with religious tradition.

257   Musgrave, Thomas D (1997) *Self determination and National Minorities* OUP at 104–5; see also Wheatley *supra* n85.

the minority as it interacts with the dominant political forces. Hungary's experiment is described as being significant on two levels:

> First, it reinforced the shared desire to improve minority rights and to establish and refine mechanisms to protect individual self-expression, cultural identity, and minority rights. Second, it underscored the fact that the efforts to develop and enhance these mechanisms are not necessarily inherently antagonistic to the larger goals of the societies in which the minorities live.[258]

Hungarian developments will be watched with interest by all those advocating greater recognition of group identity. The granting of Roma minority status and the emergence of a new wave of Roma politicians should at least serve to keep the complex issues facing the Roma in Hungary on the political agenda. Perhaps it can be said that:

> the greatest issue, though, is the mutual fear and distrust that clouds relations between Hungary's Gypsies and non-Gypsies, a problem that lies beyond the scope of any legislative solution.[259]

As Kovats has argued, cultural rights are nothing without economic and social stability.[260] Recognising minority rights and cultural autonomy cannot replace economic and social policies but it can add to their success. Additionally, it can improve the individual's sense of self, community and security. Poverty in all its forms is the greatest obstacle to the realisation of equality.[261] Discrimination and violence are nourished in environments of deprivation and poverty. It is argued that Romani participation in the governing forces of the state can serve to recognise and over-come these barriers to equality. However, the success of such policies depends to a large extent on the importance attributed to addressing pervasive economic and social disadvantage. Minority self-government, as Schafft recognises, is part of a package of measures that can ensure improved participation for minorities but it cannot be the primary solution to problems affecting the Roma.[262]

---

258   Livia Plaks, Executive Director PER *supra* n206.

259   Crowe *supra* n100 at 106.

260   Kovats *supra* n151 at 69.

261   See also Kovats *supra* n135 especially the views of the representatives of Kakucs, Myíregyháza and Csepel.

262   Schafft *supra* n215.

Chapter 8

Conclusion: A Complimentary Approach to Human Rights for Minorities

Introduction

Jurgen Habermas has argued that in order for law to achieve legitimacy in a democratic state it must safeguard the autonomy of all citizens to an equal degree.[1] The way that the legal system provides for members of minorities is a good indicator of this legitimacy. Factors such as economic and social marginalisation, political disengagement and discrimination undermine autonomy and legitimacy. In this respect, as Václav Havel observed, the treatment of the Roma, as such a uniquely misunderstood and unpopular minority, has become a measure of democratic legitimacy.

The application of equality and non-discrimination is only one part of the human rights contribution to a democratic society. There are strong arguments that when considered in isolation, they may actually encourage the marginalisation of minorities by promoting one vision of civic identity, forged through ethnicity and nationalism. Thus, a debate has emerged over the best way of protecting minorities interests including a specific perspective advocating the extension of individual human rights to particular groups.

Problems with individualism

Individual rights have often proved inaccessible for Roma people. Segregated education policies, based on culturally inappropriate testing criteria, which target intellectually disadvantaged students for special treatment, have been routinely used to discriminate against Roma pupils.[2] According to the European Court of Human Rights this policy is perfectly compatible with the international human rights standards laid down in the ECHR. It does not discriminate for a proscribed reason and it aims to offer special assistance to those that cannot cope with the demands of regular schooling. Yet this supposedly value-neutral, benevolent policy has resulted in the gross over-representation of Roma pupils in special education and remedial classes which in turn increases the likelihood of unemployment and welfare reliance. Constrained by the language of individualism characterising the Convention, the

---

1   Habermas, J (1994) 'Struggles for Recognition' in Gutmann (ed.) *Multiculturalism* Princeton Univ. Press, NJ.

2   See Chapter 5 at 208.

European Court was unable to address the pattern of entrenched discrimination and inequality lying at the root of this practice.[3]

An education policy based specifically on the needs of individuals in a climate of formal equality fails to consider the importance of cultural identity in formulating and developing personality. There has typically been no opportunity for Roma children to learn in their mother tongue (if applicable) or learn anything of their own culture and how it relates to the dominant culture. Where curricula have addressed these issues the Roma culture has been reduced to a primitive, romantic world which is unrecognisable to the Roma pupil.[4]

An approach based on pluralism supports intercultural teaching and challenges this deficiency by enabling cultural understanding and exchange to take place within the classroom. Such an approach recognises and respects difference without undermining individual human rights.

The fallacy of the neutral legal order

Liberal neutrality has been exposed as a myth in that it cannot remain indifferent to competing claims of the good life. The interests of the majority are always reflected in state policy and where this is framed as a civic identity it is typically based on an underlying ethnicity or nationalism. The liberal vision of universal human rights for all is not value-free as Dworkin suggests.[5] It promotes a particular vision of autonomy as the greatest good and is significantly cooler concerning attitudes that prioritise group identity. Van Dyke argues that blindness to group difference promotes the inaccurate assumption that societies are homogeneous and this in turn can mask serious inequalities.[6]

Liberalism has traditionally divorced the individual from her culture in the pursuit of autonomy and freedom. This is particularly apparent in the work of John Rawls where the veil of ignorance operates to strip people of ties such as culture, class and religion.[7] Rawls's basic system of civil liberties corresponds to the development of human rights standards in the Western tradition yet they lack relevance for people unable to conceive of themselves in such abstract terms. Certainly, non-Western academics have offered criticism of individual-centred human rights[8] and it has been conceded by some liberal writers, that the language of individual rights is at odds

---

3   *DH and Others v Czech Republic* App 57325/00 Judgement of 7 February 2006.

4   Derrington, Chris and Kendall, Sally (2004) *Gypsy Traveller Students in Secondary Schools* Trentham Books, Stoke-on-Trent at 99.

5   Dworkin, R (1978) 'Liberalism' in Hampshire, in Stuart *Public and Private Morality* Cambridge Univ. Press *passim*.

6   Van Dyke (1995a) 'Ethnic Communities in Political Theory' in Kymlicka (ed) *The Rights of Minority Cultures* OUP, Oxford at 48.

7   Rawls, John (1973) *A Theory of Justice* OUP, Oxford.

8   See for example Legesse, Asmaron 'Human Rights in African Political Culture' in Thompson (ed.) (1980) The *Moral Interpretation of Human Rights: A World Survey* University Press of America, Washington DC at 124.

with the culture of many communities.[9] Although, as Kovats has cautioned, one should seek to avoid presenting the Roma as a homogenised culture, the importance attached to the group, including family, does appear as a common factor in Roma communities.[10] Liégeois writes:

> The individual is that which his belonging to a group makes him. He is neither known nor recognised as an individual, but by the situation within the group, which determines his identity both for himself – his self-designation – and for others.[11]

Despite the argument that liberalism allows many versions of the good life to be pursued, those with an entirely different conception may be labelled as undeveloped and primitive. Habermas notes that ethnic conflict is fuelled in the liberal legal order which, far from being ethically neutral, is permeated by ethical values.[12]

This underlying dilemma must be recognised before an adequate critique of the prevailing human rights standards can be understood. The two tenets of international human rights standards: non-discrimination and equality, are ambiguous terms.[13] The notion of non-discrimination itself implies that every person is treated equally with the same standards of justice. Yet when we treat each person equally it soon becomes apparent that *de facto* inequality may be unaffected and even promoted. As a result, international human rights documents have recognised that affirmative action measures do not constitute discrimination for the purposes of international law. The *ICERD* provides that in some cases:

> … special and concrete measures to ensure the adequate development and protection of certain racial groups or individuals belonging to them, for the purposes of guaranteeing them the full and equal enjoyment of human rights and fundamental freedoms.[14]

Such measures are construed to be of temporary duration with the aim of eliminating the effects of past discrimination. As a result, they are not incompatible with an overall strategy of assimilation. There is no intention to promote difference and cultural identity can be gradually undermined through the general policy of equality and undifferentiated citizenship.

Will Kymlicka has criticised the liberal state's policy of 'benign neglect' arguing that it is unrealistic to presume that the government, which represents the dominant cultural group in most societies, can be neutral to the needs of non-dominant cultural groups.[15]

---

9   Donnelly, J 'Human rights, Individual rights and Collective rights' in Berting (1990) *Human rights in a Pluralist World: Individuals and Collectivities* Roosevelt Study Centre, Meckler The Netherlands at 39–62 with comments on Aboriginal communities at 52–3.

10   Kovats, M 'The emergence of European Roma policy' in Guy, W. (2001) *Between Past and Future. The Roma of Central and Eastern Europe* Univ. of Hertfordshire Press at 93–116.

11   Liégeois, J P (1994) *Roma, Gypsies, Travellers* C/E at 63.

12   Habermas *supra* n1 at 125–6.

13   See Chapter 3 p 98.

14   Article 2(2) *ibid.*

15   Kymlicka *supra* n6 at 127.

This is evident from the recognition of particular religious holidays, the adoption of one state language and in national education policies. From this analysis it is apparent that group rights and collective rights are already recognised, albeit implicitly, in international human rights law. The dominant cultural group offers a certain amount of protection to its members while maintaining its own boundaries through bureaucracy and the legal system. The identity of the dominant group is secured. It thus appears simplistic to argue that collective rights are anomalous in international law and it can be coherently argued that the extension of collective rights to minority groups is essential to the notion of equal treatment. It is surely discriminatory to protect the dominant interests and fail to provide a similar protection for the non-dominant interests. This would indeed fall fowl of Habermas's legitimacy test.[16]

The right of recognition

Common to the work of Habermas and the collectivist thinkers is a belief in the value of cultural identity and recognition. If the culture of a group is not recognised as worthy of equal respect, the individual herself will be insecure in her identity.[17]

The present individualist bias of human rights instruments does not give sufficient weight to the importance of cultural identity. The denial of Roma ethnicity fuels misrecognition. It enabled the Caravan Sites Act to be replaced by the Criminal Justice and Public Order Act without any regard to the rights of travelling gipsies [*sic*] who were to be defined economically rather than culturally. It also plays into the hands of racists who are able to deny any cultural roots:

> [How about] a demonstration of synchronised scrounging by Czech and Slovakian gipsies dressed in their traditional costume of Adidas shell suits.[18]

Misrecognition can lead members of minorities to seek to distance themselves from their culture. This can be seen in census data where the majority of Czech Roma declined to identify themselves as such.[19] Yet at the same time such cultural distancing is not achievable as the dominant group forges its own identity in part through the classification of others as different. As a result, the label will remain and will become increasingly negative if it is stripped from its cultural dimension and re-interpreted as a socio-economic condition. This can be viewed in the context of education where there is a perception amongst educators that Roma children do not wish to learn. The importance of education within the family is undermined and cultural attitudes to mainstream education are seen as weaknesses and deficiencies

---

16 See above at 375.

17 Taylor, C (1994) 'The Politics of Recognition' in Gutmann (ed.) *Multiculturalism* Princeton Univ. Press, NJ, *passim*.

18 *The Daily Mail* 23 October 1997 quoted in Bancroft, (2005) Angus *Roma and Gypsy-travellers in Europe* Ashgate at p 48.

19 Radio Prague 'Ever less citizens consider themselves members of a Roma community' 5 July 2001 found that only 11,716 Roma identified themselves as such in the 2001 Czech Census (less than 5% of the actual Romani population). Discussed in Chapter 1 p 2.

to be corrected. This approach has failed miserably with very few Roma children completing secondary school across Europe.

Framing collective rights in International law

While it has been argued that collective rights are not entirely alien to the language of international human rights, it would be a gross over-statement to contend that they are accepted as desirable. International law prioritises the rights of states and individuals; the limited recognition afforded to peoples pales into insignificance when juxtaposed with the state's territorial integrity.

International law does not provide a positive right for minorities to enjoy their identity. Article 27 of the *ICCPR* provides that members of minorities 'shall not be denied the right' to enjoy culture and practice their religion. The reticence to include a positive right to enjoy ones culture is explained by Nowak as:

> The fear marking the entire historical background of *Article 27* that effective, collective protection of minorities might threaten national unity in some States.[20]

Since 1966 there has been a definite but gradual realisation that a liberal democracy demands more than this negative formulation. Individual identity is framed by a 'struggle for recognition' which depends on dialogue, both positive and negative, with others.[21] It is inappropriate to view individuals as anomic units removed from their social and cultural framework.[22]

International law has not kept up with current political thinking in this respect. The approach of the Council of Europe Framework Convention on the Rights of persons Belonging to National Minorities expands on the formulation in Article 27 but makes little significant alteration to its negative construction.[23] The United Nations Declaration on the Rights of Minorities is similarly limited in scope.[24] There is no support in either document for a legally recognised collective right nor, it is submitted, is their likely to be in the foreseeable future. The Hungarian experiment in minority self-government, while endorsed in international human rights instruments such as the Framework Convention, is something of an anomaly.[25] Consent-based as it is, the international political arena is unlikely to see the biggest collective powers devolving limited powers to smaller collective entities.

---

20   Nowak, Manfred C. C. P. R. Commentary 1993 N. P Engel, Kehl at 495.

21   The phrase is borrowed from Habermas and receives support in the writings of Taylor *supra* n1 *passim*.

22   For criticisms of the individualist theory see Chapter 2 *passim*.

23   See Chapter 6 p264.

24   UN Res. 47/135 of 18 December 1992.

25   Other examples of collective rights do exist. For example the Belgium system of power sharing between Dutch and French speakers and the autonomy of the Aaland Islands within Swedish sovereignty.

An enhanced conception of self-determination: 'Active citizenship'

If collective rights are not immediately realisable in the present construction of international human rights law, is there any way in which the Roma and members of other minorities can become full citizens of the society in which they live?

At a national level an enhanced conception of self-determination may prove fruitful. The right to self-determination, a group right, is already recognised as the cornerstone of the two international covenants. A degree of cultural autonomy in addition to the full recognition of individual rights can facilitate this process.

Habermas articulates a notion of active citizenship based on two levels of integration: 'The ethical integration of groups within their own collective identities must be uncoupled from the abstract political integration that includes all citizens equally'.[26] Political integration forges loyalty to a common political culture, the legitimacy of which is partially derived from its mutual respect and neutrality for subcultures and their particularist conceptions of the good life. He notes the radical criticism of liberalism that it represents one particular vision of the good life, however he contends that as long as liberalism does not seek to privilege that particular vision at the expense of others, it remains legitimate. The right to equal respect endowed in each subculture may be interpreted in a variety of ways; it may demand affirmative action or self-administration. In the political, public sphere, the citizens are encouraged to actively articulate their private interests in the spirit of democracy. The aim of this division is to protect autonomy: both public and private. Habermas' theory is applied to the unequal status of women:

> The individual rights that are supposed to guarantee women the autonomy to shape their private lives cannot even be appropriately formulated unless those affected articulate and justify in public discussion what is relevant to equal or unequal treatment in typical cases. Safeguarding the private autonomy of citizens with equal rights must go hand in hand with activating their autonomy as citizens of the nation.[27]

Thus, a legitimate democracy must be concerned to avoid the privileging of a particular set of values, and instead attempt to provide a system based on equal respect for all people and the life context that shape their identity. This notion of full or active citizenship is supported by Paul Close in *Citizenship, Europe and Change*:

> Citizens are those people who have acquired full citizenship rights -the full range of legal rights necessary for full membership of (or full inclusion within) society. But such rights in themselves are insufficient for real citizenship. Citizens are divided between those who are able to realise citizenship rights and those who are unable; between those who really enjoy and experience full inclusion, participation and membership and those who do nor. Between those who have sufficient enabling resources to allow them to be included as full

---

26   Habermas *supra* n1 at 133–134.

27   *Ibid.* at 116.

members of society and those who have insufficient, between those who enjoy the power to be real citizens and those who do not.[28]

In Chapter 4, the denial of citizenship rights in the Czech Republic was discussed. It was observed that even when the Roma satisfied the onerous citizenship criteria, there were clear efforts to maintain the division between the true citizen and the Romani 'outsider'.[29] The extent of violent attacks on Roma, public hostility expressed through opinion polls, and the comparative social and economic deprivation to which they are exposed, suggest that the Roma are excluded from 'active citizenship' in the Czech Republic and indeed across much of Europe.

The public dialogue that is so significant in Habermas' analysis of full citizenship is resisted in the Czech Republic. The efforts to encourage Roma representation in public debate have been illusory. Indeed, they may have been aimed more at satisfying the Copenhagen accession criteria rather than creating a real active citizenry.[30] When considered in this way only the Hungarian Government has made any noticeable efforts to engage the Roma in public dialogue and promote the notion of active citizenship.

Practical applications of minority-based rights

Increasingly, the interests of minorities are coming to be perceived as essential in maintaining peace and security in Europe. The principal role of the High Commissioner on National Minorities in the OSCE is to act as an early warning mechanism in times of impending conflict.[31] The crisis in the Balkan states suggests that the repression of minority identity is a major trigger in societal divisions. Rather than encouraging secession, the recognition of minorities may be essential to achieve peace and security. The Council of Europe and the Organisation on Security and Co-operation in Europe have been anxious to put the question of minority rights on the international agenda. The Parliamentary Assembly of the Council of Europe has been particularly active in this respect and has paid increased attention to the subject of territorial and cultural autonomy.[32]

Individual human rights cannot be dismissed out of hand. The aftermath of two World Wars when individual rights were systematically destroyed by the oppressive policies of particular groups led the United Nations to emphatically reject rights afforded to particular groups, emphasising instead the universality of individual human rights.[33] Group rights pose particular challenges for a liberal human rights regime including the politicisation of ethnicity; the artificial maintenance of group

---

28   Close, Paul (1994) *Citizenship, Europe and Change* Macmillan, London at 52.

29   See Chapter 4 *passim*.

30   O'Nions, H (1999) 'Bonafide or Bogus?' 3 *Web JCLI*.

31   See Chapter 6 at 297.

32   See Chapter 6 at 307.

33   See Chapter 6 *passim*.

boundaries; the potential problem of illiberal practices; and the difficulty of finding suitable minority representatives.

John Packer and Jack Donnelly have argued that, given these problems, the adequate realisation of individual rights is the key to the protection of group interests.[34] This appears to be a sound argument if the group is in a dominant position in society and is able to articulate its demands, *i.e.*, if freedom of expression is not hampered by deeper, entrenched inequalities. It could be argued that a person who chooses not to articulate their demands does not require or deserve to have them protected. This was the attitude of the Czech Minister who argued that as the Roma have not asked for minority language teaching, they have no need for it.[35] Such a simple explanation cannot be regarded as legitimate. The Roma have typically been cast in the role of passive recipients rather than active participants and are unfamiliar with active engagement in political debate.

It is for these reasons that minority rights should be seen as complementary, rather than opposed, to individual rights. In case of conflict, the latter should prevail thus enabling people who are dissatisfied with aspects of their culture to question it and to seek alternatives. Cultural identity should be seen as flexible and transformative rather than static and fixed.[36] It is submitted that questioning of and active engagement with ones cultural values can only take place if the minority is protected rather than simply tolerated in the constitutional framework.

The argument that group rights are not justiciable deserves some attention in the light of the Hungarian experiment in power-sharing. Analysis of the legislation indicates that group-based rights can be justiciable if applied in a flexible, contextualised manner. The Hungarian Act on the Rights of National and Ethnic Minorities is described as 'an effort to implement a new theory of human rights based upon collective rights'.[37] It recognises a right of groups to representation through self-government and involvement in the national political process[38] but does not extend as far as McGarry and O'Leary have advocated by providing a constitutional minority veto and a coalition government.[39]

The statutory criteria for self-government are based on reality rather than arbitrary supposedly objective characteristics. The Act does not extend to recent immigrant

---

34　Donnelly *supra* n9; Packer 'On the Definition of Minorities' pp 23–65 in Packer and Myntti *The Protection of Ethnic and Linguistic Minorities in Europe* (1993) Abo Akademie Univ., Finland.

35　This comment from the Czech Governments report to the ICERD was criticised by the Committee: ICERD *Summary Record of the 1255th Meeting: Czech Republic 30 March 1998* CERD/C/SR.1255.

36　Packer, John 'On the definition of minorities' in Packer and Myntti *The Protection of Ethnic and Linguistic Minorities in Europe* (1993) Abo Akademie Univ., Finland pp 23–65.

37　'Hungary and a New Paradigm for the Protection of Ethnic Minorities in Central and Eastern Europe' (1995) Note in *Columbia Journal of Transnational Law* Vol. 3, 3 pp 673–705 at 675.

38　See Chapter 7 at 348.

39　McGarry and O'Leary (1993) *The Politics of Ethnic Conflict* Routledge London p 35–6.

populations who have migrated by choice (it is necessary for the group to establish that they have been present in Hungary for at least one century). Any member of the community may stand in the local elections but they tend to depend on the support of one of the major Romani organisations.

Minority self-governments are a recent development and the evaluative response has not been uncritical. However, this criticism centres on the dynamics of the relationship with central government, primarily in terms of funding and support.[40] The criticism does not generally target the existence of the self-governments themselves, although Kovats is concerned that they may become scapegoats for inadequately resourced government initiatives.[41] It does seem clear that the voices of the Roma community are being heard in Hungary. If nothing else, the political engagement of an estimated 2,000 Romani activists must be a positive development making it difficult for those voices to be ignored. In the past, attempts at assimilating or excluding the Roma from society have been facilitated by their absence from public political space.

The Roma as a transnational minority

A gradual political awakening amongst Europe's Roma is occurring and the 'Roma issue' is now firmly on the European agenda. My view is that a dual approach offers the best chance of tackling this entrenched disadvantage: recognising special group rights where needed in addition to the principles of equality and non-discrimination. There can be no one-size fits all approach to the problem but the conception of the Roma as a unique, transnational minority may assist in this process.

A rise in the number of non-governmental organisations, particularly those with an active Roma participation, demonstrates that a public space for the Roma is beginning to emerge.[42] There is a recognition that effective participation should draw on common roots and transnational perspectives beyond national citizenship, narrow group affiliation, or country of residence.

The leader of the European Roma Forum, Rudko Kawczynski, rejects the assertion that Romani organisations cannot be united arguing that they have been dominated by so-called gadje experts and this has led to political disengagement.[43] He is a key figure in the process of political activism and ethnogenesis which seeks to build and forge a sense of Romani transnational identity.[44] The Forum's membership

---

40   For comments and views on lack of funding and other obstacles see 'Self-government in Hungary: The Romani/Gypsy Experience and Prospects for the Future' Project on Ethnic Relations Conference 9–11th May 1997, Budapest.

41   Kovats, M 'Hungary, politics, difference and equality' in Guy *supra* n10 at 333–350.

42   Trehan, Nidhi analyses this development and is critical of the 'ethno-business' which has often left Roma grassroots activists out in the cold. 'In the name of the Roma' in Guy, Will *supra* n10 pp 134–149.

43   Nicolae, Valeriu 'The Decade of Roma Inclusion – Between Hopes, Glitches and Failures' August 2005 www.eumap.org.

44   Kawczynski, Rudko (1997) 'The Politics of Romani Politics' *Transitions* Vol 4, (4).

of the Council of Europe suggests that this approach is also being supported by the European political structures.[45]

One part of the solution is thus presented as transnational. The problems faced by Roma are similar across Europe; they stem from discrimination, marginalisation and non-recognition. In the past there was little political will to address these problems. Increasingly however, the need to afford all ethnic minorities equal respect is evolving as a logical development of self-determination.

The post-modern neo-tribal world has enabled its own ethnic essentialism in the guise of civic identity which has maintained a boundary dictating who is to be included and who is to be excluded.[46] Angus Bancroft argues that EU citizenship may provide an opportunity for transnational minorities to assert their rights given that European recognition will not depend solely on national identity.[47] The new enlarged and refocused EU may open up a political space for the Roma to articulate their politics.[48] Stephen Roach has argued that a stronger, more representative European parliament could redress the democratic deficit of the EU and may evolve to become the impetus for transnational minority representation as part of a new European constitutionalism.[49] New forms of political representation could provide a constitutional status and security for minorities which is compatible with an evolving conception of self-determination.[50] Such an approach recognises deficiencies in the present system and enables identity issues to be articulated without threatening the stability of the state. Indeed, for Roach a European recognition of transnational minorities coupled with greater cultural autonomy at state level may actually strengthen ties between national governments and the EU while protecting minority cultural identity.[51]

The advantages of constructing a multi-layered European citizenship are numerous. The national civic vision which has denied active participation to the Roma in the Czech Republic will be supplemented and may eventually be supplanted by a European conception which is broadly construed to address the needs of all Europeans including minorities. The European Parliament considered this approach in their 1991 *Resolution on Union Citizenship*[52] which makes reference to the importance of non-discrimination alongside diversity and the rights of citizens

---

45   Speech by the Deputy Secretary General of the Council of Europe, conference 'Roma in an Expanding Europe' Budapest 30 June 2003. http://www.coe.int/t/e/SG/SGA/documents/speeches/2003/ZC_2003_%20300603_Budapest.asp.

46   Bancroft *supra* n18 at 171.

47   *Ibid.* at 157.

48   Laitin, David D 'National identities in the European state' in Keating and McGarry (eds) (2001) *Minority Nationalism and The Changing International Order* OUP at 110.

49   Roach, Steven *Cultural Autonomy, Minority rights and Globalization* (2005) Ashgate at 71.

50   *Ibid.* at 54–5 and 61.

51   *Ibid.* at 66–67.

52   14 June 1991 *Official Journal of the European Communities* C 183/473 of 15 July 1991 at 18, A3/0139/91.

to develop 'their potential within their habitual surroundings'.[53] The European Council's Luxembourg Declaration also emphasised the importance of respecting cultural identity and the rights of members of minorities.[54]

The EU Constitution moves on from the reference to non-discrimination exhibited in the Treaty of Nice to list respect for persons belonging to minorities as a core value in Article I-2.[55] Here the Network of Independent Experts on Fundamental Rights will have a key role to play. The Network has already requested a broad interpretation of Article 21 of the Charter on Fundamental Rights to include minority protection, which may encompass positive action.[56] In addition, the Network has recognised the specific difficulties faced by the Roma and has recently called for a Roma Integration Directive which it regards as 'the most important contribution which the European Community could make to the protection of minorities'. This Directive would encompass a dual approach predicated on non-discrimination and equality but also respect and protection for particular minority needs.[57] Indeed, the report concludes that the Race Equality Directive is inadequate and that an exception to the general non-discrimination approach is required in order to preserve essential elements of Roma identity.[58] Thematic Comment No 3 on the Rights of Minorities in the European Union again advances the need for a specific directive:

It should provide that effective accommodations will be made to ensure the Roma/Gypsies will be able to maintain their traditional lifestyle, when they have chosen the nomadic or semi-nomadic mode of life, without being forced into sedentarisation. It should take account the need to effectuate the desegregation of the Romani/Gypsy communities, where this is required, especially in employment, housing and education. It should address the question of the inaccessibility of certain social and economic rights due to the administrative situation of Roma/Gypsies to whom administrative documents are denied or who are considered stateless.[59]

The role of the Committee of Regions under the new Constitution will be strengthened through an enhanced conception of subsidiarity which may enable particular national minorities to petition the ECJ as members of the Committee.[60] Transnational Roma politics could benefit from Articles 1–47 which invites citizens of not less than

53   *Ibid.* para. M. Discussed in Malloy, Tove (2005) National Minority Rights in Europe OUP at 259.

54   Conclusions of the European Council 28–9 June 1991 Annex V *EC* Bulletin 6-1991.

55   *Treaty Establishing a Constitution for Europe* 2004.

56   *Report on the Situation of Fundamental Rights in the EU in 2002* January 2004 CFR-CDF.

57   Chapter 6 at 317.

58   Network of Independent experts on fundamental rights *Report on the Situation of Fundamental Rights in the European Union for 2003* 26 May 2004 CFR-CDF.

59   EU Network of Independent Experts on Fundamental Rights (CFR-CDF) *Thematic Comment No 3 on the Protection of Minorities in the European Union* 25 April 2005 ThemmComm2005.en.

60   *Treaty Establishing a* Constitution of Europe Article 1-11(3) and Article 111-365(3).

one million people from across Europe to submit proposals on issues related to the implementation of the Constitution to the Commission. This clearly constitutes recognition that nationally defined representation may not address the concerns of large European minorities.

The Lund recommendations provide a starting point for a fresh debate on cultural autonomy so that every minority has a voice and can participate in national and transnational politics. This is not necessarily the antithesis of globalisation as it may appear. Rather it brings greater opportunity for representation and participation for individuals. It also reduced demands of secession and encourages wider European cooperation. Article 151 of the EC Treaty as amended by Maastricht also refers to cultural diversity but, as Malloy, argues it is fraught with ambiguity and certainly does not constitute a demand for minority protection.[61]

Developments in the E.U may provide the transnational recognition that Roma politics requires. De Witte argues that the plurinational, multicultural identity of the European Community is significant in the protection of minorities and the weakening of national borders.[62] Malloy also notes that the Union is moving towards a multi-layered constitutionalism which may eventually enable the 'full emancipation of all co-nations through the discursive rights to co-decision'.[63]

While transnational recognition is an important development it must be clear that such a status does not depend on a false homogenisation of Roma culture. Kawszynski's strategy in this respect is unclear but it seems likely, based on his previous work with the Roma National Congress, that it will encompass a degree of redefinition and homogenisation of Roma identity. Not unrelated is the risk posed by certain activists who may hijack the notion in order to further their own political cause. Yet this is politics in action – the Roma are comparatively new to political organisation and as such they cannot be expected to be familiar with all the procedural safeguards of democratic institutions.

In addition to the Forum, the 'Decade for Roma inclusion' has been established to consider a European strategy to address social exclusion for the Roma. Unlike the Forum, the Decade is largely the initiative of eight Central and East European governments in addition to The World Bank, the Open Society institute and a number of prominent Roma representatives. It is to be hoped that the two trans-European Roma organisations will develop a relationship of mutual cooperation, although early signs have not been encouraging in this respect.[64]

---

61   Malloy *supra* n53 at 262.

62   De Witte, Bruno 'Politics versus Law in the EU's approach to ethnic minorities' in Zielonka, January (ed) (2002) *Europe Unbound. Enlarging and reshaping the boundaries of the European Union* Routledge at 153–55.

63   Malloy *supra* n53 at 281–2.

64   Nicolae, Valeriu 'The decade of Roma inclusion – between hopes, glitches and failures' August 2005, eumap.org.

Redressing the past failures of human rights for minorities

Professor István Pogány has recently criticised the application of minority rights to the Roma:

> The rhetoric of minority rights has failed to arrest the erosion of what were already grossly unsatisfactory living conditions for Roma in the CEE states or assure them equal access to public services. Nor have minority rights instruments reversed the escalation of anti-Roma sentiment and violence that has been a feature of the CEE region since the ousting of Communist administrations.[65]

Pogány argues that Roma identity has been eroded and that most Roma are concerned about poverty and rather than the loss of cultural identity. He observes that the rise in importance of minority rights coincided with the withdrawal of financial support and social and economic rights such as employment and housing.[66] Yash Ghai expresses a similar point in relation to conflicts labelled as 'ethnic'. Where the focus changes from an analysis of underlying socio-economic problems to the accommodation of competing ethnic claims – thus simplifying the issue and simultaneously rendering its solution more complex.[67]

Even if we accept that the previous Communist regime was an age of economic opportunity and prosperity it is evident that discrimination towards the Roma was prevalent. Hostility may have been kept under control by restrictions on free expression but this cannot be seen as a climate of toleration enabling every citizen to achieve their full potential and enjoy their identity. Why else would the collapse of this system of control see such an immediate rise in racist violence across the CEE region?

Pogány characterises the educational disadvantage of the Roma as primarily a matter of poverty, which could be solved by material support, encouragement and incentives.[68] While not denying the significance of poverty I cannot accept that this can be the solution in the absence of a recognition of an intercultural teaching approach which expressly recognises the cultural perspectives of minorities and majorities in a climate of tolerance. The testimonies of Roma pupils and parents from both the CEE states and Western Europe suggest that discrimination and culturally insensitive, homogenised curricula are key factors in Romani absenteeism.[69] In the UK the Department for Education and Skills has identified the threat of constant

---

65   Pogány, István (2006) 'Minority rights and the Roma of Central and Eastern Europe' *HumRLR* Vol 6, 1 p 1 at 3.

66   *Ibid.* at 12.

67   Ghai, Yash (2001) Autonomy *and Ethnicity. Negotiating competing claims in multi-ethnic states* University Press at 5.

68   Pogány *supra* n65 at 21.

69   Chapter 5 at 216; OFSTED (2003) *Provision of Support for Traveller Pupils* OFSTED; Crawley, Heaven (2004) *Moving Forward: the provision of accommodation of travellers and Gypsies* IPPR at 33.

eviction as the biggest obstacle to traveller education.[70] This represents a failure by local authorities to fully consider the travelling lifestyle of many British Gypsies and to adopt specific, supportive educational strategies.

The complexity of Roma exclusion requires a multi-faceted solution drawing on both individual rights and the recognition of minority identity to enable the individual, secure in her identity, to participate as an active citizen in society. An exclusive emphasis on individual or group rights cannot be the way forward.

In his forthcoming work Professor Bill Bowring argues that substantive human rights cannot simply be based on methodological individualism yet he also seeks to avoid the antagonism of the communitarian *versus* individualist debate. Building on the work of Habermas and Salter,[71] Bowring advocates a discursive approach incorporating a dialectic of identity and recognition.[72]

Paradoxically, it is the new multi-layered constitutionalism offered by European citizenship which may facilitate the procedural possibility for this debate. Malloy argues that where the Council of Europe has struggled to protect minority identity:

> The EU is working its way towards a self-constituting society fostering a unity of consciousness based on a plurality of identities, a state of mind which may also include the enactment and enforcement of a new social philosophy through a new multi-layered legal system.[73]

As the Lund Recommendations recognise, participation and dialogue are essential to notions of active citizenship both at a national and European level and they require mechanisms to ensure minority representation.[74]

At a national level cultural autonomy may provide a solution to the problem of representation for minorities through a broad construction of self-determination. Such a conception is compatible with the objective of ensuring legitimacy in a democratic society which respects the interests of all individuals and groups rather than simply the majority.[75] Although a right to cultural autonomy is essentially a group right it can be seen to supplement individual rights and indeed to strengthen them providing it is viewed as part of a package of measures.

---

70   DFES *Aiming High: Raising the achievement of Gypsy and Traveller Pupils-Good Practice Guide* 2003 DFES.

71   Salter, Michael (1997) 'Habermas' New Contribution to Legal Scholarship' *Journal of Law and Society* 285.

72   Bowring, Bill *The degradation of the international legal order: the rehabilitation of law and the possibility of politics* July 2006 Routledge.

73   Malloy *supra* n53 at 314.

74   Heintze, Hans-Joachim (2002) 'Implementation of minority rights through the devolution of powers-the concept of autonomy reconsidered' *Int. Journal of Minority and Group Rights* Vol 9 pp 325–343 at 326; *Lund Recommendations on the Effective Participation in Public Life* discussed by Packer, John 'The origin and nature of the Lund Recommendations on Effective Participation of National Minorities in Public Life' *Helsinki Monitor* 11 (2000) p31.

75   Heintze *ibid.* at 333.

A complementary approach

A negative assessment of minority rights is emerging from some of those most concerned with the interests of the Roma. The OSCE and Council of Europe's approach epitomised by Josephine Verspaget's 1995 report have been criticised for their essentialism which has over-emphasised cultural factors at the expense of socio-economic factors.[76] Martin Kovats argues that European institutions have failed to appreciate that the role of European policy must be to overcome the financial obstacles to effective policies within national policies.[77] According to Pogány:

> Minority rights ... are simply not designed for tackling issues of chronic poverty, economic
> – marginalisation and cultural alienation.[78]

While I accept the importance of economic disadvantage and the need to direct resources appropriately I do not see this as incompatible or antagonistic to the recognition of minority rights. Human rights demand a complementary approach so that some minorities are not simply excluded from the political and social space. Individual rights may require a group dimension to be effective. Group-based rights can enable groups to articulate their history and values in a climate of tolerance and security, enabling respect for diversity. Nowhere is this more apparent than in the classroom, where intolerance can either be challenged or fuelled. A democratic society must represent the interests of a mosaic of cultures in a pluralist-integrationist framework. This can only be achieved through a complementary approach to human rights which emphasises the importance of cultural identity and autonomy in addition to the prevention of discrimination and promotion of equality.

---

76   Kovats in Guy, Will at 103; *HCNM Report on the Situation of Roma and Sinti in the OSCE Area*, Office of the High Commissioner on National Minorities, March 2000 and J, Verspaget, *The Situation of Gypsies* (Roma and Sinti) *in* Europe (Report adopted by the CDMG (Council of Europe) 5 May 1995.

77   *Ibid.* at 110.

78   Pogány *supra* n65 at 19.

Bibliography

ACERT (eds) (1993), *The Education of Gypsy and Traveller Children* (Hatfield: University of Hertfordshire Press).

ACERT (Advisory Council for the Education of Roma and Travellers) (1993–94), *Annual Report 1995* (Harlow: ACERT). [PubMed 12321719,8456179,8416141]

ACERT (1994–95), *Annual Report 1996* (Harlow: ACERT).

ACERT (1995), *Education for All: Working for Equal Rights* (Harlow: ACERT).

ACERT (1995), '8 out of 10 Teenagers Out of School', *Press Release*, February.

Acton, T. (1974), *Gypsy Politics and Social Change* (London: Routledge and Keegan Paul).

Acton, T. (1978), 'Gypsy Education at the Cross-Roads', *British Journal of Special Education*, **12**(1), 6–8.

Acton, T. (1994), 'Moral Panics, Modernisation, Globalisation and the Gypsies', *Sociology Review*, **4**, 24–28.

Acton, T. (1996), *Gypsy Politics and Traveller Identity* (Hatfield: University of Hertfordshire Press).

Acton, T. and Davies, G. (1979), 'Educational Policy and Language Use Among English Romanies and Irish Travellers in England and Wales', *International Journal of the Sociology of Language*, **19**, 91–110.

Acton, T. and Gheorghe, N. (1995), 'Dealing with Multiculturality: Minority, Ethnic, National and Human Rights', *ODIHR Bulletin (Office for Democratic Institutions and Human Rights, OSCE)*, **3**(2), 29.

Acton, T. and Kenrick, D. (1991), 'From Summer Voluntary Schemes to European Community Bureaucracy', *European Journal of Intercultural Studies*, **1**(3), 47–62.

Acton, T. and Mundy, G. (1996), *Romani Culture and Gypsy Identity* (Hatfield: University of Hertfordshire Press).

Adams, B., Okely, J., Morgan, D. and Smith, D. (1975), *Gypsies and Government Policy in England* (London: Heinemann).

Addis, A. (1991–92), 'Individualism, Communitarianism and the Rights of Ethnic Minorities', *Notre Dame Law Review*, **67**, 615–676.

AFP News (1998), *January 16th* (Budapest: AFP).

Agence France Press (1998), 'Europe's Roma Demand Recognition as a Minority', *November 19th*.

Agh, A. (1994), 'Citizenship and Civil Society in Central Europe' in *The Conditions of Citizenship*. Van Steenbergen, B. (ed.) (London: Sage), 108–125.

Akehurst, M.A. (1987), *Modern Introduction to International Law* (London: Harper Collins).

Åkermark, A.S. (1996), *Justifications for Minority Protection in International Law* (The Hague: Kluwer).

Albrecht, H.J. (1995), 'Ethnic Minorities, Culture Conflicts and Crime', *Crime Law and Social Change*, 24, 19–36. [DOI: 10.1007/BF01297655]

Alcock, A. (1977), 'A New Look at the Protection of Minorities and the Principle of Human Rights', *Community Development*, **12**(2), 85–95.

Alcock, A. (1979), 'The Development of Governmental Attitudes to Cultural Minorities in Western Industrialized States', in *The Future of Cultural Minorities*. Alcock, A., Taylor, B. and Welton, J. (eds) (London: Macmillan), 102–119.

Alcock, A., Taylor, B. and Welton, J. (eds) (1979), *The Future of Cultural Minorities* (London: Macmillan).

Alderman, G. (ed.) (1993), *Governments, Ethnic Groups and Political Representation* (Dartmouth: New York University Press).

Aleinikoff, T.A. and Klusmeyer, D. (eds) (2001), *Citizenship Today: Global Perspectives and Practices* (Washington, DC: Carngeie Endowment for International Peace).

Alfredsson, G. (2000), 'A Frame and Incomplete Painting: Comparison of the Framework Convention for the Protection of National Minorities with International Standards and Monitoring Procedures', *International Journal on Minority and Group Rights*, **7**, 291–304. [DOI: 10.1163/15718110020908061]

Alfredsson, G. and Zayas, D. (1993), 'Minority Rights: Protection by the United Nations', *HRLJ*, **14**(1–02), 1–8.

Alston, P. (ed.) (1992), *The United Nations and Human Rights* (Oxford: Clarendon).

Altheer, D. (1993), 'Roma Suffer as Eastern Europe Explodes', *Roma*, **38–39**(Jan–Jul), 1–4.

Altheer, D. (1993), 'Travelling Hopelessly: Who Are Britain's Gypsies', *Roma*, **38–39**(Jan–Jul), 68–71.

Anaya, S.J. (1991), 'The Capacity of International Law to Advance Ethnic or Nationality Claims', *HRQ*, **13**, 403–41. Reprinted in *The Rights of Minority Cultures*. Kymlicka, W. (ed.) (1995) (Oxford: Oxford University Press), 321–330.

Anderton, B. (1983), *Imagined Communities: Reflections on the Origins and Spread of Nationalism* (London: Verto).

Anghie, A. (1992), 'Human Rights and Cultural Identity: New Hope for Ethnic Peace?', *Harvard International Law Journal*, **33**(spring), 341–352.

Ansell-Pearson, K. (1994), *An Introduction to Nietzsche As Political Thinker* (Cambridge: Cambridge University Press).

Apel, K.-O. (1997), 'Plurality of the Good? The Problem of Affirmative Tolerance in a Multicultural Society from an Ethical Point of View', *Ratio Juris*, **10**(2), 199–212. [DOI: 10.1111/1467-9337.00055]

Apps, E. (1985), 'Minority Language Education Rights', *University of Toronto Faculty of Law Review*, **43**, 45–71.

Associated Press (1977), 'Gypsies Seek Good Life in Canada', *August 13th*.

Auer, S. (2006), 'After 1989, Who Are the Czechs?', *Nationalism and Ethnic Politics*, **12**, 411–430. [DOI: 10.1080/13537110600882627]

Aukerman, M.J. (1995), 'Discrimination in Germany: A Call for Minority Rights', *NQHR*, **3**(3), 237–257.

Avineri, S. and De-Shalit, A. (eds) (1992), *Communitarianism and Individualism*, (Oxford: Oxford University Press).

Badurikova, Z.R. (2005), *Education Initiative Annual Research and Evaluation Report Slovakia* (Open Society Institute). http://www.osi.hu/esp/rei/.

Baehr, P. (1990), 'Human Rights and Peoples Rights', in *Human Rights in a Pluralist World: Individuals and Collectivities*. Berting, J. (ed.) (Meckler: Roosevelt Study Centre), 99–107.

Bagley, T.H. (1950), *General Principles and Problems in the Protection of Minorities* (Geneva: Imprimeries Populaires).

Baka, A.B. (1993), 'The ECHR and Protection of Minorities under International Law', *Connecticut Journal of International Law*, **8**(8), 227–242.

Baker, J. (1994), *Group Rights* (Toronto: University of Toronto Press).

Bancroft, A. (2005), *Roma and Gypsy-Travellers in Europe* (Aldershot: Ashgate).

Bandy, A. (1997), 'The Forgotten Holocaust', *The Hungary Report*, July 28th.

Banks, J.A. (1981), *Multiethnic Education: Theory and Practice* (Boston, MA: Allyn & Bacon).

Bárány, Z. (1992), 'Democratic Changes Bring Mixed Blessings for Gypsies', *Radio Free Europe Research Report*, **1**(20), 40–47.

Bárány, Z. (1995), 'Grim Realities in Eastern Europe', *Transmission 29th March*, 3–8.

Bárány, Z. (2002), *The East European Gypsies* (Cambridge: Cambridge University Press).

Barbalet, J.M. (1988), *Citizenship Rights, Struggle and Class Equality* (Milton Keynes: Open University Press).

Barnard, C. and Hepple, B. (2000), 'Substantive Equality', *Cambridge Law Journal*, **59**(November), 573–574.

Barnett, H. (1994), 'A Privileged Position? Gypsies and Planning', *Conveyancer*, 454–464.

Barnett, H. (1995), 'The End of the Road for Gypsies', *The Anglo American Law Review*, **24**(2), 133–167.

Baron, S.W. (1985), *Ethnic Minority Rights: Some Older and Newer Trends* (Oxford: Oxford Centre for Postgraduate Hebrew Studies).

Barry, B. (2001), *Culture and Equality. An Egalitarian Critique of Multiculturalism* (Cambridge: Polity).

Barry, N. (1986), *On Classical Liberalism and Libertarianism* (London: Macmillan).

Barth, F. (1969), *Ethnic Groups and Boundaries* (Chicago: Waveland Press Inc.).

Batchelor, C.A. (1995), 'Stateless Persons: Some Gaps in International Protection', *International Journal of Refugee Law*, **7**(2), 232–259. [DOI: 10.1093/ijrl%2F7.2.232]

BBC (1990), *Premier Jozsef Antall Presents Government Programme*, BBC Summary of World Broadcasts, Eastern Europe Section EE/0773/c1/1, May 25th.

Beale, A. and Geary, R. (1994), 'Gypsies, Judges and the State: A Review of the CSA 1968', *The Cambrian Law Review*, **25**, 89–101.

Beale, A. and Geary, R. (1994), 'Abolition of an Unenforced Duty', *NLJ*, **145**(January, 6679), 47–61.

Beck, S. (1989), 'The Origins of Gypsy Slavery in Romania', *Dialectical Anthropology*, **14**, 53–61.

Beck, S. (1984), 'Ethnicity, Class and Public Policy: Tiganii/Gypsies in Socialist Romania', *5th Congress of South East European Studies* (Columbus: Slavica).

Beddard, R. (1993), *Human Rights and Europe* (Cambridge: Grotius).

Beiner, R. (1995), *Theorizing Citizenship* (New York: University of New York Press).

Bell, D. (1993), *Communitarianism and Its Critics* (Oxford: Clarendon Press).

Bellamy, R. (1999), *Liberalism and Pluralism: Towards a Politics of Compromise* (London: Routledge).

Bellamy, R. (1998), 'Justice in the Community', in *Social Justice – from Hume to Waltzer*. Boucher, D. and Kelly, P. (eds) (London: Routledge), 157–180.

Berlin, I. (1984), 'Two Concepts of Liberty', in *Liberalism and Its Critics*. Sandel, M. (ed.) (Oxford: Blackwell), 15–36.

Berman, S. (1994), 'Gypsies: A National Group or a Social Group', *Refugee Survey Quarterly*, **13**(4), 51–61.

Berting, J. (1990), *Human Rights in a Pluralist World: Individuals and Collectivities* (Meckler: Roosevelt Study Centre).

Bilder, R.B. (1992), 'Can Minority Treaties Work?', in *The Protection of Minorities and Human Rights*. Dinstein, Y. and Tabory, M. (eds) (Dordrecht: Martinus Nijhoff), 59–82.

Binns, D. (1990), 'History and Growth of Traveller Education', *British Journal of Educational Studies*, **38**(3), 251–258.

Biro, A. (1996), 'The Prince, the Merchant, the Citizen ... and the Romany', *ODIHR Bulletin*, **4**(2), 21–22.

Blackburn, R. (1993), *The Rights of Citizenship* (London: Mansell).

Blaustein, A. and Flanz, G. (1971), *Constitutions of the World 1971* (New York: Dobbs Ferry).

Bogdanor, V. (1997), 'Forms of Autonomy and the Protection of Minorities', *Daedalus: Proceedings of the American Academy of Arts and Sciences*, **126**(2), 47.

Bossuyt, M.J. (1987), *Guide to the 'Travaux Preparatoires' of the ICCPR* (Dordrecht: Martinus-Nijhoff).

Boucher, D. and Kelly, P. (eds) (1998), *Social Justice – from Hume to Waltzer* (London: Routledge).

Boucková, P. (2005), *Czech Republic Executive Summary March 2005*, (Brussels: European Commission). europa.eu.org.

Bowring, B. (forthcoming), *Degradation of the International Legal Order: The Rehabilitation of Law and the Possibility of Politics* (London: Routledge).

Bradney, A. (1993), *Religion, Rights and Laws* (Leicester: Leicester University Press).

Bradney, A.G.D. (1987), 'Separate Schools, Ethnic Minorities and the Law', *New Community*, **XIII**(3), 412–420.

Braham, M. (1984), *The Untouchables: A Survey of the Roma People of Central and Eastern Europe* (New York: UNHCR).

Brearley, M. (1996), *The Roma/Gypsies of Europe: A Persecuted People* (London: Institute for Jewish Policy Research).

Breitenmoser, S. and Richter, D. (1991), 'Proposal for an Additional Protocol to the European Convention on Human Rights Concerning the Protection of Minorities in the Participating States of the CSCE', *HRLJ*, **12**(6–7), 262–273.

Brett, R. (1996), 'Human Rights and the OSCE', *HRQ*, **18**, 668.

Bridger, S. and Pine, F. (eds) (1997), *Surviving Post-Socialism: Local Strategies and Regional Responses in Eastern Europe and the Former Soviet Union* (London: Routledge).

Britton, R. (1984), 'The Education of Travellers as a Contemporary Issue in Multicultural Education', *Multicultural Teaching*, **2**(3), 9–12.

Brolmann, C., Lefeber, R. and Zieck, M. (eds) (1993), *Peoples and Minorities in International Law* (Amsterdam; International Law Conference).

Brown, J.F. (1991), *Surge to Freedom: The End of Communist Rule in Eastern Europe* (Durham NC: Duke University Press).

Brownlie, I. (1965), 'The Relations of Nationality in Public International Law', *BYIL*, 284.

Brownlie, I. (1988), 'The Rights of Peoples in Modern International Law', in *The Rights of Peoples*. Crawford, J.E.S. (ed.) (Oxford: Clarendon), 1–16.

Brownlie, I. (1998), *Principles of Public International Law* (Oxford: Clarendon).

Budapest Sun (1998), 'Hungarians Admit their Hatred of Other Races', *15th January*.

Bruegel, A. (1971), 'A Neglected Field: The Protection of Minorities', *Revue de Droits de l'Homme*.

Buergenthal, T. (ed.) (1977), *Human Rights, International Law and the Helsinki Accord* (Totowa, NJ: Allanheld, Osmun and Co.).

Buis, H. (1990), 'With the Letter "Z" on the Back', *O'Drom*, **April**, 258–260.

Bukovská, B. (2002), 'Difference and Indifference: Bringing Czech Roma Ghettoes to Europe's Court', *Eumap.org*. http://www.eumap.org/journal/features/2002/may02/czechromaghettoes.

Bulgarian Helsinki Committee (2001), *Social-Educational Boarding Schools and Reform Schools* (Sofia: Bulgarian Helsinki Committee).

Bulgarian Helsinki Committee (2002), *The Special Schools in Bulgaria* (Sofia: Bulgarian Helsinki Committee).

Bunyan, T. (1993), *Statewatching the New Europe* (London: Statewatch).

Burgers, J.H. (1990), 'The Function of Human Rights as Collective and Individual Rights', in *Human Rights in a Pluralist World: Individuals and Collectivities*. Berting, J. (ed.) (Meckler: Roosevelt Study Centre), 63–74.

Butler, J. (1983), *Gypsies and the Personal Social Services* (Leicester: University of Leicester).

Butler, J., Elphick, R. and Welsh, D. (eds) (1987), *Democratic Liberalism in South Africa* (Connecticut: Wesleyan University Press).

C/E Directorate of Human Rights (1985), *Human Rights of Aliens in Europe* (Strasbourg: C/E).

Caffrey, S. and Mundy, G. (1996), 'Informal Systems of Justice: the Formation of Law within Gypsy Communities', *Romani Studies and Work with Travellers Conference*, July 1996 (London: University of Greenwich).

Cahn, C. (1997), 'An Ordinary Pogrom', *Transitions*, **4**(4, September), no pagination.

Cahn, C. (2004), 'Racial Preference, Racial Exclusion: Administrative Efforts to Enforce the Separation of Roma and Non-Roma in Europe through Migration Controls', *European Journal of Migration and Law*, **5**, 479–490. [DOI: 10.1163/157181603322849361]

Cahn, C., Chirico, D., McDonald, C., Mohácsi, V., Peric, T. and Székely, A. (1998), 'Roma in the Educational Systems of Central and Eastern Europe', *ERRC Report* (Budapest: European Roma Rights Centre).

Campbell, T. (1992), *Housing Gypsies* (Cardiff: Cardiff Law School).

Campbell, T. (1988), *Justice* (London: Macmillan).

Caney, S. (1992), 'Liberalism and Communitarianism: A Misconceived Debate', *Political Studies*, **40**, 273–289.

Cannon, J. (1989), *Travellers: An Introduction* (London: Interchange Books).

Capotorti, F. (1992), 'Are Minorities Entitled to Collective International Rights?', in *The Protection of Minorities and Human Rights*. Dinstein, Y. and Tabory, M. (eds) (Dordrecht: Martinus Nijhoff), 505–512.

Capotorti, F. (1979), *Study on the Rights of Persons Belonging to Ethnic, Religious and Linguistic Minorities*, UN Doc E/CN 4/Sub, 2/384 Revelation 1 (New York: UN).

Carens, J.H. (1995), 'Aliens and Citizens: The Case for Open Borders', in *The Rights of Minority Cultures*. Kymlicka, W. (ed.) (Oxford: Oxford University Press), 331–349.

Carolina News Agency (1998), 'Young Woman Dies after Racially Motivated Attack', *20th February*.

Carolina News Agency (1998), 'Romany Family Granted Asylum in Great Britain', *6th March*.

Cassese, A. (1977), 'The Helsinki Declaration and Self-Determination', in *Human Rights, International Law and the Helsinki Accord*. Buergenthal, T. (ed.) (Totowa, NJ: Allanheld, Osmun and Co), 83–110.

Cassese, A. (1979), *UN Law/Fundamental Rights: Two Topics in International Law* (Groningen, the Netherlands: Sijthoff and Noordhoff).

Cassese, A. (1986), *International Law in a Divided World* (Oxford: Clarendon Press).

Cassese, A. (1981), 'The Self-Determination of Peoples', in *The International Bill of Rights: The Covenant on Civil and Political Rights*. Henkin, L. (ed.) (New York: Columbia University Press), 92–427.

Cassese, A. (1995), *Self-Determination of Peoples* (Cambridge: Cambridge University Press).

Castellino, J. (2000), *International Law and Self-Determination* (The Hague: Kluwer).

Central Advisory Council for Education (1967), *Children and Their Primary Schools* (London: HMSO).

Central Europe Online (1997), 'Interview with Milan Pospisil', *November 6th*.

Central Europe Online (1997), 'Czech Official Says Government is Doing its Part to Help Roma', *October 10th*.

Centre for Cooperation with the Economies in Transition (1996), 'Regional Problems and Policies in the Czech Republic and Slovak Republic', *CCET Update*, **June** (OECD Internet).

Centre for Reproductive Rights and Poradňa pre občianske a ludské práva, with Zoon, I. (2003), *Body and Soul: Forced Sterilisation and Other Assaults on Roma Reproductive Freedom in Slovakia* (New York: Centre for Reproductive Rights), 119.

Chan, J.M.M. (1991), 'The Right to Nationality as a Human Right', *HRLJ*, **12**(1–2), 1–15.

Chaplin, J. (1993), 'How much Cultural and Religious Pluralism can Liberalism Tolerate?', in *Liberalism, Multiculturalism and Toleration*. Horton, J. (ed.) (London: Macmillan), 32–49.

Charlemagne, J. (1984), 'Bridging the Culture Gap', *Unesco Courier*, **October**, 11–14.

Childrens' Rights Development Unit (1993), *Children's Rights to an Adequate Standard of Living*, **Aug**, 20–22.

Cingranelli, D.L. (ed.) (1988), *Human Rights Theory and Measurement* (London: Macmillan).

Clark, C. (1998), 'Counting Backwards: The Roma "Numbers Game" in Central and Eastern Europe', *Radical Statistics*, **69**, 35–46.

Clark, D. and Williamson, R. (eds) (1996), *Self-Determination: International Perspectives* (London: Macmillan).

Claude, I. (1955), *National Minorities: An International Problem* (Cambridge MA: Harvard University Press).

Clements, L. (1992), 'Gypsy Bashing', *LA*, **November**, 10.

Clements, L. (1992), 'Traveller Update', *LA*, **January**, 14.

Clements, L. and Morris, R. (2002), *At What Cost? the Economics of Gypsy and Traveller Encampments* (Bristol: Policy Press).

Clements, L., Thomas, P. and Thomas, R. (1996), 'The Rights of Minorities – A Romany Perspective', *ODIHR Bulletin*, **4**(4), 3–10.

Close, P. (1995), *Citizenship, Europe and Change* (London: Macmillan).

Commission for Race Equality (2004), *Gypsy and Traveller: A Strategy for the CRE, 2004–2007* (London: CRE).

Connor, W. (1994), *Ethnonationalism: The Quest for Understanding* (Princeton, NJ: Princeton University Press).

Conway, L. (1996), *Report on the Status of Romani Education in the Czech Republic* (Prague: HOST).

Cozma, T., Cucos, C. and Momanu, M. (2000), 'The Education of Roma Children in Romania: Description, Difficulties, Solutions', *Intercultural Education*, **11**(3), 281–288.

Cotonnec, A. (1983), 'Groupe scolaire de Clayes-sous-bois', *Journee D'etudes Sur La Scolarisation des Enfants Tsiganes* (Caen: Ministere De l'education Nationale).

Cottaar, A.M., Lucassen, L. and Willems, W. (1992), 'Justice or Injustice?. A Survey of Government Policy Towards Gypsy and Caravan Dwellers in W Europe in the Nineteenth and Twentieth Centuries', *Immigrants and Minorities*, **2**(1), 42–66.

Cottaar, A. and Willems, W. (1992), 'The Image of Holland: Caravan Dwellers and Other Minorities in Dutch Society', *Immigrants and Minorities*, **11**(1), 67–80.

Council of Europe (2005), *Mechanisms for the Implementation of Minority Rights* (Strasbourg: Council of Europe).

Council of Europe (2005), *Framework Convention for the Protection of National Minorities: Collected Texts* (Strasbourg: Council of Europe).

Cranston, M. (1979), 'What Are Human Rights?', in *The Human Rights Reader*. Lacquer, W. and Rubin, B. (eds) (Philadelphia: Temple University Press), 17–25.

Crawford, J.E.S. (ed.) (1988), *The Rights of Peoples* (Oxford: Clarendon).

Crawley, H. (2004), *Moving Forward: The Provision of Accommodation for Travellers and Gypsies* (London: IPPR).

Cristescu, A. (1981), *The Right to Self Determination*, N E/CN, 4/Sub.2/404/Rev.1 (New York: UN).

Crowder, G. (2001), *Liberalism and Pluralism* (London: Continuum).

Crowe, A. (1996), 'The Czech Roma. Foreigners in their Own Land', *European Update Online*, **4**(2).

Crowe, D. (1991), 'The Roma (Gypsies) in Hungary through the Kadar Era', *Nationalities Papers*, **Autumn**, 297–310.

Crowe, D. (1991), 'The Gypsies in Hungary', in *The Gypsies of Eastern Europe*. Crowe, D. and Kolsti, J. (New York: M.E. Sharpe), 117–132.

Crowe, D. (1995), *A History of the Gypsies of Eastern Europe and Russia* (New York: St Martins Press).

Crowe, D. and Kolsti, J. (1991), *The Gypsies of Eastern Europe* (New York: M.E. Sharpe).

Csapo, M. (1982), 'Concerns Related to the Education of Romany Students in Hungary, Austria and Finland', *Comparative Education*, **18**(2), 205–219.

Csáky, P. (2001), 'Experiences from Cooperating with the OSCE HCNM: The Case of the Slovak Republic', *Journal of Minority and Group Rights*, **8**, 21–22.

Csillei, B. (1998), '"Roma Opportunity": The Alternative Vocational Foundation School of Szolnok', Unpublished Paper, Szolnok, Hungary.

CTK News Agency (1997, 'EC Points to Romany Human Rights in the Czech Republic', *17th July*.

CTK News Agency (1998), 'Czech Cabinet Drafting Legislation to Solve Romanies Problems', *16th January*.

Cullen, H. (1993), 'Education Rights or Minority Rights?', *Int'l J L & Fam*, **7**(2), 144–177.

Cullen, H. (1994), 'Concluding Comments', in *Self Determination: Cases of Crisis*. Kritsiotis, D. (ed.) (Hull: University of Hull Law School), 114–120.

Cuthbertson, I.M. (1992), *Redefining the CSCER: Challenges and Opportunities in the New Europe* (Hong Kong: Institute for East West Studies).

Czech Helsinki Committee (1996), *Report on the State of Human Rights in the Czech Republic in 1995* (Prague: Helsinki Committee).

Daly, M. (ed.) (1994), *Communitarianism: A New Public Ethics* (Belmont, CA: Wadsworth).

Danbakli, M. (1994), *On Gypsies: Texts Issued by International Institutions* (Toulouse: Centre de Recherches Tsiganes, CRDP).

Davies, E. (1987), *Gypsies and Housing – the Results of a Survey* (London: D/E).

De Zayas, A. (1993), 'International Judicial Protection of Peoples and Minorities', in *Peoples and Minorities in International Law.* Brolmann, C., Lefeber, R. and Zieck, M. (eds) (Amsterdam: International Law Conference), 253–287.

Degenaar, J. (1987), 'Nationalism, Liberalism and Pluralism', in *Democratic Liberalism in South Africa.* Butler, J., Elphick, R. and Welsh, D. (eds) (Connecticut: Wesleyan University Press), 236–249.

Delaney, C.F. (1994), *The Liberalism-Communitarianism Debate* (Lanham, MD: Rowman and Littlefield).

Demaine, J. and Entwistle, H. (1996), *Beyond Communitarianism, Citizenship, Politics and Education* (London: Macmillan).

Dembour, M.B. (2006), *Who Believes in Human Rights?, Reflections on the European Convention* (Cambridge: Cambridge University Press).

Department for Education and Employment (1999), *Tackling Truancy Together: A Strategy Document* (London: DfEE).

Department for Education and Skills (2003), *Aiming High: Raising the Achievement of Minority Ethnic Pupils* (London: DfES).

Department for Education and Skills (1985), *Education for All: The Report of the Committee of Inquiry into the Education of Children from Ethnic Minority Groups (The Swann Report)* (London: DfES).

Department of Environment (1992–95), *Count of Gypsy Caravans*, Bi-annual (London: DoE).

Derrington, C. and Kendall, S.G. (2004), *Traveller Students in Secondary Schools* (Stoke-on-Trent: Trentham Books).

De Schutter, O. and Verstichel, A. (2005), *The Role of the Union in Integrating the Roma: Present and Possible Future* (Bozen, Italy: EURAC).

Dickinson, I.S. (1994), 'Collective Trespass: The CJPOA (1994) Part V', *JLS Scotland*, **40**(2), 63–66.

Dimitras, P.E. (2004), *Recognition of Minorities in Europe: Protecting Rights and Dignity*, Minority Rights Group International Briefing (London: Minority Rights Group).

Dimitrijevic, V. (1992), 'Political Pluralism in the Aftermath of the Eastern European Upheavals', in *The Strength of Diversity: Human Rights and Pluralist Democracy.* Rosas, A. and Helgesen, J. (eds) (Dordrecht: Martinus-Nijhoff), 5–25.

Dinstein, Y. (1993), 'The Degree of Self-Rule of Minorities in Unitarian and Federal States', in *Peoples and Minorities in International Law.* Brolmann, C., Lefeber, R. and Zieck, M. (eds) (Amsterdam: International Law Conference), 221–235.

Dinstein, Y. (1976), 'Collective Human Rights of Peoples and Minorities', *ICLQ*, 102.

Dinstein, Y. and Tabory, M. (1992), *The Protection of Minorities and Human Rights* (Dordrecht: Martinus-Nijhoff).

Donnelly, J. (1984), 'Cultural Relativism and Universal Human Rights', *HRQ*, **6**, 400–419. [DOI: 10.2307/762182]

Donnelly, J. (1985), *The Concept of Human Rights* (London: Routledge).

Donnelly, J. (1990), 'Human Rights, Individual Rights and Collective Rights', in *Human Rights in a Pluralist World: Individuals and Collectivities.* Berting, J. (ed.) (Meckler: Roosevelt Study Centre), 39–62.

Donnelly, J. (1993), 'Third Generation Rights', in *Peoples and Minorities in International Law.* Brolmann, C., Lefeber, R. and Zieck, M. (eds) (Amsterdam: International Law Conference), 119–150.

Donner, R. (1994), *The Regulation of Nationality in International Law* (Irvington-on-Hudson, NY: Transnational).

Drost, P.N. (1965), *Human Rights as Legal Rights* (Leyden: A.W. Sijthoff).

Druker, J. (1997), 'Present but Unaccounted For', *Transitions*, **4**(4, September), no pagination.

Drzemczewski, A. (1984), *The Right to Respect for Private and Family Life, Home and Correspondence: Human Rights Files No 7* (Strasbourg: C/E).

Dunbar, R. (2000), 'Implications of the European Charter for Regional or Minority Languages for British Linguistic Minorities', *E Law Rev*, **25**, SUPP (Human Rights).

Dworkin, R. (1977), *Taking Rights Seriously* (London: Duckworth).

Dworkin, R. (1978), 'Liberalism', in *Public and Private Morality*. Hampshire, S. (ed.) (Cambridge: Cambridge University Press), 113–143.

Dworkin, R. (1985), *A Matter of Principle* (Oxford: Clarendon).

Dworkin, R. (1984), 'Liberalism', in *Liberalism and Its Critics*. Sandel, M. (ed.) (Oxford: Blackwell), 60–79.

Economist (1991), 'True Tormented Pan-Europeans/Sad Gypsies', *26th October*.

Economist (1993), 'His Struggle/Slovak Prime Minister Under Fire over Gypsy Comments', *18th September*.

Edginton, B. (1994), 'The Czech Citizenship Law: Still Causing Problems for Roma', *International Helsinki Federation for Human Rights Newsletter*, **4**, 9.

Edginton, B. (1992–93), 'To Kill a Romany', *Race and Class*, **35**(3), 80–83.

Edwards, A. (2005), 'New Roma Rights Legislation in Bosnia and Herzegovina: Positive, Neutral of Indifferent?', *IJHR*, **9**(4), 465–478. [DOI: 10.1080/136429 80500349881]

Edwards, J. (1996), 'Affirmative Action Social Policy Analysis', Paper delivered at *Minority Rights in the 'New' Europe Conference*, University of London, November.

Ehnes, H. (1994), 'Protection of Minorities in Europe', *Reformed World*, **44**(4), 169–174.

Eide, A. (1993), *Protection of Minorities: Possible Ways and Means of Facilitating the Peaceful and Constructive Solution of Problems Involving Minorities*, UN Doc E/CN4/Sub2/1993/34 (New York: UN).

Eide, A. (1993), *New Approaches to Minority Protection* (London: Minority Rights Group).

Eide, A. (1990), 'The Universal Declaration in Space and Time', in *Human Rights in a Pluralist World: Individuals and Collectivities*. Berting, J. (ed.) (Meckler: Roosevelt Study Centre), 15–32.

Eide, A. and Hagtvet, B. (1992), *Human Rights in Perspective* (Oxford: Blackwell).

Eide, A., Alfredsson, G., Melander, G., Rehof, L. and Rosas, A. (eds) (1992), *The UDHR: A Commentary* (Oslo: Scandinavian University Press).

Emerson, M. (1996), 'Minority Rights Group', *CPRSI Newsletter* (Contact Point for Roma and Sinti Issues, Warsaw), **2**(3), 4–7.

Erdos, A. (1987), 'Minority Rights', *The New Hungarian Quarterly*, **28**(106), 131–135.

Ermacora, F. (1983), *The Protection of Minorities Before the United Nations: Collected Courses of the Hague Academy of International Law* (Dordrecht: Martinus-Nijhoff).

Espiell, H.G. (1979), 'Self-determination and Jus Cogens', in *UN Law/Fundamental Rights: Two Topics in International Law.* Cassese, A. (ed.) (Groningen, the Netherlands: Sijthoff and Noordhoff), 167–174.

Estebanez, M. M.A. (1996), 'The OSCE Implementation Meeting on Human Dimension Issues 1995', *Helsinki Monitor*, **7**(1), no pagination.

Etxeberria, F. (2002), 'Education and Roma Children in the Basque Region of Spain', *Intercultural Education*, **13**(3), 291–304.

Etzioni, A. (1995), *The Spirit of Community* (London: Fontana).

European Monitoring Centre on Racism and Xenophobia (2006), *Roma and Travellers in Public Education: An Overview of the Situation on the EU Member States* (Vienna: EUMC).

European Roma Rights Centre (1995), 'Police in Slovakia Use Electric Cattle Prods during Raid on Romani Community', *ERRC Press Release*.

European Roma Rights Centre (1996), *Divide and Deport: Roma and Sinti in Austria* (Budapest: ERRC).

European Roma Rights Centre (1996), *Sudden Rage at Dawn, Violence Against Roma in Romania* (Budapest: ERRC).

European Roma Rights Centre (1996), 'Open Letter to the Austrian Ministry of the Interior', *ERRC Press Release*, **May 15th**.

European Roma Rights Centre (1996), 'Romani Raped by Police Officers in Ukraine Newsbrief', *ERRC Press Release*.

European Roma Rights Centre (1997), *Time of the Skinheads: Denial and Exclusion of Roma in Slovakia* (Budapest: ERRC).

European Roma Rights Centre (1997), 'Statement of the ERRC on acceptance into NATO of Czech republic, Hungary and Poland', *ERRC Press Release*.

European Roma Rights Centre (1997), 'Police Brutality in Hungary', *ERRC Press Release*, **March 21st**.

European Roma Rights Centre (1997), 'Letter to the Prime Minister of Greece Concerning Events in the Roma Community in Ano Liosa', *ERRC Press Release*, **May 23rd**.

European Roma Rights Centre (1997), 'Letter to the Czech General Prosecutor', *ERRC Press Release*, **June 13th**.

European Roma Rights Centre (1998), 'The Submission Against the Principal of the Ferenc Pethe Primary School, Tiszavavari, Hungary', *Roma Rights Newsletter*, **Spring**.

European Roma Rights Centre (1998), 'On the Concluding Observations Concerning the Czech Republic of the UN Committee on the Elimination of Racial Discrimination', *ERRC Press Release*, **March**.

European Roma Rights Centre (2000), *Campland: Racial Segregation of Roma in Italy* (Budapest: ERRC).

European Roma Rights Centre (2000), 'Personal Documents and Threats to the Exercise of Fundamental Rights among Roma in the Former Yugoslavia', *ERRC Workshop*, Igalo, Montenegro, 6–8th September.

European Roma Rights Centre (2001), *State of Impunity* (Budapest: ERRC).

European Roma Rights Centre (2003), 'Croatian Romani Children Sue at European Court of Human Rights over Racial Segregation in Schools', *ERRC Press Release* (Budapest: ERRC).

European Roma Rights Centre (2003), 'Legitimacy, Statistics and Research Methodology – Who is Romani in Hungary Today and What are We (not) Allowed to Know about Roma', *ERRC Notebook*.

European Roma Rights Centre (2004), 'Human Rights Protection Is Unavailable to Those Most in Need of It', *ERRC Notebook*, **2nd November**.

European Roma Rights Centre (2005), *Always Somewhere Else: Anti-Gypsyism in France* (Budapest: ERRC).

European Roma Rights Centre (2005), 'Hungarian Discotheque Fined for Unequal Treatment', *ERRC Litigation*, **21st June**.

European Roma Rights Centre (2006), 'UN Committee on the Rights of the Child Concerned about the Situation of Romani Children in Hungary', *ERRC Snapshot* (Budapest: ERRC).

Evans, S. (1996), 'Separate but Superior?', *Hungary Report Archive*, **2**(5), 22 July.

Falk, R. (1979), 'The Algiers Declaration of the Rights of Peoples and the Struggle for Human Rights' in *UN Law/Fundamental Rights: Two Topics in International Law.* Cassese, A. (ed.) (Groningen, the Netherlands: Sijthoff and Noordhoff), 225–236.

Fanon, F. (1961), *Les Damnés de la Terre* (Paris: Maspero).

Farkas, I. (1982), 'Transformation of our Fellow Gypsy Citizens', *Pravda, Bratislava*, **23rd September**, 5.

Farkas, L. (2004), 'Education, Education and More Education', *EUMap*, Open Society Institute. www.eumap.org/journal/features/2004/minority_education/edmore/.

Farkas, L. (2003), 'Will the Groom Adopt the Bride's Unwanted Child? The Race Equality Directive, Hungary and its Roma', *Roma Rights Notebook* (Budapest: ERRC).

Fawcett, J. (1979), *The Creation of States in International Law* (Oxford: Clarendon).

Fawcett, J. (1979), *International Protection of Minorities* (London: MRG).

Fawcett, J. (1984), 'Intervention to Protect Minorities', in *Minorities: A Question of Human Rights?* Whitaker, B. (ed.) (Oxford: Pergamon Press), 69–77.

Fawn, R. (2001), 'Czech Attitudes towards the Roma: "Expecting More of Havel's Country"?', *Europe-Asia Studies*, **53**(8), 1193–1219.

Feldman, D. (1997), 'The Developing Scope of Article 8 of the European Convention on Human Rights', *EHRLR*, **3**, 265–274.

Feldman, D. (1993), *Civil Liberties and Human Rights* (Oxford: Clarendon Press).

Fernandez-Albor, G. (1994), 'Question 94/C 102/47', *Official Journal of the European Communities: Information and Notices*, **37**(102), 21.

Field, S. (1995), 'The End of the Road', *Sol.J*, **139**(31), 786–787.

Financial Times (1997), 'Austria Police Arrest Suspect', **6th October**.

Fisher, B. (1996), 'The Bosnian War: Religion, History and the Gypsies', *Whittier Law Review*, **17**(Spring), 467–475.

Fisher, S. (1994), 'Czech-Slovak Relations Two Years after the Elections', *RFE/RL Research Report*, **3**(27, 8th July), 9−17.

Fisher, M. (1997), 'Now Czech TV Sending Gypsies to UK', *Toronto Sun*, **26th October**.

Fishman, J. (1989), *Language and Ethnicity in Minority Sociolinguistic Perspective* (Clevedon: Multilingual Matters Ltd).

Fitzmaurice, D. (1993), 'Liberal Neutrality, Traditional Minorities and Education', in *Liberalism, Multiculturalism and Toleration*. Horton, J. (ed.) (London: Macmillan Publishing).

Fleming, J.E. (2003−2004), 'Securing Deliberative Democracy', *Fordham Law Review*, **72**, 1435−1475. [PubMed 15828129,14968794,12523370]

FOCUS Agency (1994), *Current Problems in Slovakia* (Bratislava: FOCUS).

Foley, D. (2004), 'Ogbu's Theory of Academic Disengagement: Its Evolution and its Critics', *Intercultural Education*, **15**(4), 385−397.

Foncesca, I. (1995), *Bury Me Standing: The Gypsies and Their Journey* (New York: Alfred A. Knopf).

Forced Migration Project (1998), 'Expert Examines Roma Rights in Hungary', *ALERT*, **II**(48), 4 December, no pagination.

Forrester, B. (1985), *The Travellers Handbook* (London: Interchange Books).

Foster, C. (ed.) (1980), *Nations Without a State* (New York: Praeger).

Foster, K.M. (2004), 'Coming to Terms: A Discussion of John Ogbus' Cultural-Ecological Theory of Minority Academic Achievement', *Intercultural Education*, **15**(4), 369−384. [DOI: 10.1080/1467598042000313403]

Franck, T. (1992), 'The Emerging Right to Democratic Governance', *The American Journal of International Law*, **86**, 46−91. [DOI: 10.2307/2203138]

Franck, T. (1995), *Fairness in International Law and Institutions* (Oxford: Oxford University Press).

Franck, T.M. (1996), 'Clan and Superclan: Loyalty, Identity and Community in Law and Practice', *The American Journal of International Law*, **90**, 359−383. [DOI: 10.2307/2204063]

Franck, T.M. (2000), *The Empowered Self: Law and Society in the Age of Individualism* (Oxford: Oxford University Press).

Fraser, A. (1996), *The Gypsies*, 2nd ed. (London: Blackwell).

Frazer, E. (1999), *The Problems of Communitarian Politics* (Oxford: Oxford University Press).

Frazer, E. and Lacey, E. (1993), *The Politics of Community: A Feminist Critique of the Liberal-Communitarian* (New York: Harvester Wheatsheaf).

Fredman, S. (2001), 'Equality: A New Generation?', *International Law Review*, **30**, 2.

Fredman, S. (2002), 'Why the UK Government Should Sign and Ratify Protocol 12', *Equal Opportunities Review*, **21**, 23.

Fredman, S. and Alston, P. (eds) (2001), *Discrimination and Human Rights: The Case of Racism* (Oxford: Oxford University Press).

Freeden, M. (1991), *Rights* (Milton Keynes: Open University Press).

Freeman, M.A. (1988), 'Racism, Rights and the Quest for Equality of Opportunity: A Critical Legal Essay', *Har CR-CL Law Review*, **23**, 295−335.

Freeman, M.A. (1994), 'The Philosophical Foundations of Human Rights', *HRQ*, **16**, 491–514. [DOI: 10.2307/762434]

Freestone, D. (1990), 'The UN Convention on the Rights of the Child', in *Children and the Law*. Freestone, D. (ed.) (Hull: Hull University Press), 288–323.

Freestone, D. (1990), *Children and the Law* (Hull: Hull University Press).

Fresco, M.F. and van Tongeren, P. (1991), *Perspectives on Minorities: Philosophical Reflections on Identity and the Rights of Cultural Minorities* (Le Tilburg: Tilburg University Press).

Friedman, M. (1964), *Capitalism and Freedom* (Chicago: University of Chicago Press).

Friedman, M. (1992), 'Feminism and Modern Friendship: Dislocating the Community', in *Communitarianism and Individualism*. Avineri, S. and De-Shalit, A. (eds) (Oxford: Oxford University Press), 101–119.

Gaay Fortman, B., de (1990), 'The Dialectics of Western Law in a Non Western World', in *Human Rights in a Pluralist World: Individuals and Collectivities*. Berting, J. (ed.) (Meckler: Roosevelt Study Centre), 237–250.

Gál, K. (1999), 'Bilateral Agreements in Central and Eastern Europe: A New Inter-State Framework for Minority Protection?', *ECMI Working Paper*, 4 May (European Centre for Minority Issues).

Galenkamp, M. (1991), 'Collective Rights: Much Ado about Nothing', *NQHR*, **9**(3), 291–307.

Galjus, O. (1997), 'A Media Guided by our Own Hand', *Transitions*, **4**(4, September), no pagination.

Galston, W. (2002), *A Liberal Pluralism* (Cambridge: Cambridge University Press).

Galvin, R. (1994), 'Moral Pluralism, Disintegration and Liberalism', in *The Liberalism-Communitarianism Debate*. Delaney, C.F. (ed.) (Maryland: Rowman and Littlefield), 39–56.

Garvey, J. (1991), 'Introduction: The Rights of Groups', *Kentucky Law Journal*, **2**(80), 862–867.

Gauthier, D. (1992), 'The Liberal Individual', in *Communitarianism and Individualism*. Avinieri, S. and De-Shalit, A. (eds) (Oxford: Oxford University Press), 151–164.

Geary, R. and O'Shea, C. (1995), 'Defining the Traveller: From Legal Theory to Practical Action', *JSWFL*, **17**(2), 167–178.

George, D. (1993), 'The Right to National Self-Determination', *History of European Ideas*, **16**(4), 507–514. [DOI: 10.1016/0191-6599%2893%2990182-P]

Gerganov, E., Varbanova, S. and Kyuchukov, H. (2005), 'School Adaptation of Roma Children', *Intercultural Education*, **16**(5), 495–511.

Geroe, M. and Gump, T. (1995), 'Hungary and a New Paradigm for the Protection of Ethnic Minorities in Central and Eastern Europe', *Columbia Journal of Transnational Law*, **32**(3), 673–705.

Ghai, Y. (ed.) (2000), *Autonomy and Ethnicity: Negotiating Competing Claims in Multi-Ethnic States* (Cambridge: Cambridge University Press).

Ghanea, N. and Xanthaki, A. (eds) (2005), *Minorities, Peoples and Self-Determination* (Dordrecht: Martinus-Nijhoff).

Gheorghe, N. (1991), 'Roma – Gypsy Ethnicity in Eastern Europe', *Social Research*, **58**(4), 829–844.

Gheorghe, N. and Acton, T. (1995), 'Dealing with Multiculturality: Minority Ethnic, National and Human Rights', *ODIHR Bulletin*, **3**(2), 28–40.

Gheorghe, N. and Hancock, I. (1991), *Report of the International Romani Union on the Current Situation of Roma Throughout the World* (Manchaca, Texas: International World Romani Union).

Gibney, M. (1992), 'Foreign Policy: Ideological and Human Rights Factors', *Journal of Political History*, **4**(1), 36–53.

Gil-Robles, A., Commissioner for Human Rights (2006), 'On the Human Rights Situation of the Roma, Sinti and Travellers in Europe', *C/E Comm. DH* (Strasbourg: C/E), 15 February.

Gilberg, T. (1974), 'Ethnic Minorities in Romania under Socialism', *East European Quarterly*, **7**(4), 435–458.

Gilbert, G. (1996), 'The Council of Europe and Minority Rights', *HRQ*, **18**, 160–189.

Gilbert, G. (1996), 'Minority Rights under the Council of Europe', *Conference Minority Rights in the 'New' Europe*, University of London, November.

Gilbert, G. (2002), 'The Burgeoning Minority Rights Jurisprudence of the European Court of Human Rights', *HRQ*, **24**, 736–780.

Gillborn, D. (1990), *Race Ethnicity and Education* (London: Unwin-Hyman).

Glazer, N. (1975), *Affirmative Discrimination: Ethnic Inequality and Public Policy* (New York: Basic Books).

Glazer, N. (1977), 'Cultural Pluralism: the Social Aspect', in *Pluralism in a Democratic Society.* Tumin, M. and Plotch, W. (eds) (New York: Praeger), 3–24.

Glazer, N. (1978), 'Individual Rights Against Group Rights', in *Human Rights.* Kamenka, E. and Tay, E. (eds) (London: Edward Arnold), 87–103.

Globe and Mail, Canada (1997), 'Hungarian Gypsies Court Victory Hailed', **27th August**.

Globe and Mail, Canada (1997), 'Visiting Czechs Need Visas', **8th October**.

Globe and Mail, Canada (1997), 'Special to the Globe and Mail', **19th August**.

Glover, A. (1995), 'The Human Dimension of the OSCE: From Standard Setting to Implementation', *Helsinki Monitor*, **3**, no pagination.

Gmelch, S.B. (1986), 'Groups that Don't Want in: Gypsies and Other Artisan, Trader and Entertainer Minorities', *Annual Review of Anthropology*, 307–330.

Goldston, J. (1997), 'Claiming Civil Rights for Roma', *Christian Science Monitor*, 3rd September, no pagination.

Gomien, D. (ed.) (1993), *Broadening the Frontiers of Human Rights: Essays in Honour of Asbjorn Eide* (New York: Oxford University Press).

Gordon, M.M. (1978), *Human Nature, Class and Ethnicity* (Oxford: Oxford University Press).

Gostin, L. (1988), *Civil Liberties in Conflict* (London: Routledge).

Gotleib, A. (ed.) (1970), *Human Rights, Federalism and Minorities* (Toronto: Canadian Institute of International Affairs).

Gould, M. (1990), 'Children's Education and the European Court of Justice', in *Children and the Law.* Freestone, D. (ed.) (Hull: Hull University Press), 172.

Grande, F. (1984), '"Flamenco": A Taste of Blood in the Mouth', *UNESCO Courier*, **October**, 29–31.

Gray, J. (1986), *Liberalism* (Buckingham: Open University Press).

Gray, J. (1995), *Berlin* (New York: Harper Collins).

Gray, J. (1998), 'Where Pluralists and Liberals Part Company', *International Journal of Philosophical Studies*, **6**, 17–36.

Gray, J. (2000), *Two Faces of Liberalism* (Cambridge: Polity Press).

Green, L. (1995), 'Internal Minorities and their Rights', in *The Rights of Minority Cultures*. Kymlicka, W. (ed.) (Oxford: Oxford University Press), 257–272.

Green, L.C. (1970), 'Protection of Minorities in the League of Nations and the United Nations', in *Human Rights, Federalism and Minorities*. Gotlieb, A. (ed.) (Toronto: Canadian Institute of International Affairs), 180–210.

Greiper, E.H. (1985), 'Stateless Persons and Their Lack of Access to Judicial Forums', *Brooklyn Journal of International Law*, **XI**(2), 439–457.

Groarke, P. (2002), *Dividing the State: Legitimacy, Secession and the Doctrine of Oppression* (Aldershot: Ashgate).

Gronfors, M. (1981), 'Police Perceptions of Social Problems and Clients: The Case of the Gypsies in Finland', *Int'l J Soc L*, **9**, 345–359.

Grotrian, A. (1994), 'Article 6 of the ECHR – the Right to *a* Fair Trial', *C/E HR Files* No 13 (Strasbourg: C/E).

Groves, R. (1996), 'Changing the Face of Policing in Bulgaria', *CPRSI Newsletter*, **2**(2), 1–3.

Grumet, J. (ed.) (1985), *Papers from 4th and 5th Annual Meetings of the Gypsy Lore Society Annual Conference* (Maryland: Gypsy Lore Society).

Guardian Newspaper (1998), 'Czech Gypsies fear Ghetto Wall', **20th June**, 16.

Guardian Newspaper (1998), 'Straw's Travellers Gaffe "Misconstrued"', **20th August**, 5.

Guibernau, M. and Rex, J. (eds) (1997), *The Ethnicity Reader* (Cambridge: Polity).

Gundara, J.S. (1993), 'Multiculturalism and the British Nation-State', in *Liberalism, Multiculturalism and Toleration*. Horton, J. (ed.), (London: Macmillan Publishing).

Gurr, T.R. and Scarritt, J.R. (1989), 'Minorities at Risk: A Global Survey', *HRQ*, **11**, 375.

Gutmann, A. (1992), 'Communitarian Critics of Liberalism', *Communitarianism and Individualism*. Averini, S. and De-Shalit, A. (eds) (Oxford: Oxford University Press), 120–136.

Gutmann, A. (1993), 'The Challenge of Multiculturalism in Political Ethics', *Philosophy and Public Affairs*, **22**(3), 171–206.

Gutmann, A. (ed.) (1994), *Multiculturalism* (Princeton, NJ: Princeton University Press).

Guy, W. (ed.) (2001), *Between Past and Future. The Roma of Central and Eastern Europe* (Hatfield: University of Hertfordshire).

Guy, W. (1975), 'Ways of Looking at Rom', in *Gypsies, Tinkers and Other Travellers*. Rehfisch, F. (ed.) (London: Academic Press).

Gyarfasova, O. (1995), 'Slovakia after the Split: Dilemmas of the New Citizenship', in *Citizenship East and West*. Liebich, A., Warner, D. and Dragovic, G. (eds) (London: Keegan, Paul), 165–184.

Gypsy Council for Education Welfare and Civil Rights (1994), *The First Romani Congress of the EU*, Seville, 18th–21st May. GCEWCR, Essex.

Habermas, J. (1984), *The Theory of Communicative Action* (London: Heinemann).

Habermas, J. (1992), 'Citizenship and National Identity: Some Reflections on the Future of Europe', *Praxis International*, **12**(1), 1–19.

Habermas, J. (1994), 'Struggles for Recognition in the Democratic Constitutional State', in *Multiculturalism*. Gutmann, A. (ed.) (Princeton, NJ: Princeton University Press), 107–148.

Hailbronner, K. (1990), 'The Legal Status of Population Groups in a Multi-National State under Public International Law', in *The Protection of Minorities and Human Rights*. Dinstein, Y. and Tabory, M. (eds) (Dordrecht: Martinus Nijhoff), 117–144.

Halvorsen, K. (1990), 'Notes on the Realization of the Human Right to Education', *HRQ*, **12**, 341–364.

Hampshire, S. (1978), *Public and Private Morality* (Cambridge: Cambridge University Press).

Hancock, I. (1987), *The Pariah Syndrome* (Ann Arbor: Karoma).

Hancock, I. (1991), 'The East European Roots of Romani Nationalism', in *The Gypsies of Eastern Europe*. Crowe, D. and Kolsti, J. (New York: M.E Sharpe), 133–150.

Hancock, I. (1992), 'The Roots of Inequity: Romani Cultural Rights in their Historical and Social Context', *Immigrants and Minorities*, **II**(1), 3–20.

Hancock, I. (1993), 'Anti Gypsism in the New Europe', *Roma*, **38**(9), 5–29.

Hancock, I. (1997), 'The Struggle for the Control of Identity', *Transitions*, **4**(4, September), no pagination.

Hannum, H. (1991), 'Contemporary Developments In the International Protection of the Rights Of Minorities', *The Notre Dame Law Review*, **66**, 1431–1448.

Hannum, H. (1990), *Autonomy, Sovereignty and Self-Determination: The Adjudication of Conflicting Rights* (Philadelphia: University of Pennsylvania Press).

Hannum, H. and Lillich, R. (1980), 'The Concept of Autonomy in International Law', *American Journal of International Law*, **74**, 858–889.

Harris , D.J., O'Boyle, M. and Warbrick, C. (1995), *Law of the ECHR* (London: Butterworths).

Hartney, M. (1995), 'Some Confusions Concerning Collective Rights', in *The Rights of Minority Cultures*. Kymlicka, W. (ed.) (Oxford: Oxford University Press), 202–227.

Hatley-Broad, B. (2004), 'Problems and Good Practice in Post-Compulsory Educational Provision for Travellers: The Wakefield Kushti Project', *Intercultural Education*, **15**(3), 267–281.

Hastrup, K. (ed.) (2001), *Legal Cultures and Human Rights: The Challenge of Diversity* (The Hague: Kluwer).

Hawes, D. (1995), 'Gypsies, Deprivation and the Law', *Legal Action*, **May**, 8.

Hawes, D. (1995), 'Natural Born Travellers', *Housing*, **March**, 34–36.

Hawes, D. and Perez, B. (1995), *The Gypsy and the State* (Bristol: School of Advanced Urban Studies, University of Bristol).

Hayek, F.A. (1984), 'Equality, Value and Merit', in *Liberalism and Its Critics*. Sandel, M. (ed.) (Oxford: Blackwell), 80–99.

Hegedus, A.T. (1998), 'The Tasks Concerning Gypsy Children's Socialisation at School', *Social Cohesion,* Szolnok.

Heinrich, H.G. (1986), *Hungary, Politics, Economics and Society* (London: Frances Pinter Publications).

Heintze, H.J. (2000), 'Minority Issues in Western Europe and the OSCE High Commissioner on National Minorities', *International Journal on Minority and Group Rights,* **7**, 381–392.

Heintze, H.J. (2002), 'Implementation of Minority Rights through Devolution of Powers – the Concept of Autonomy Reconsidered', *International Journal on Minority and Group Rights,* **9**, 325–343.

Heinz, W.S. (1988), *Indigenous Populations, Ethnic Minorities and Human Rights* (Berlin: Quorum Verlag).

Held, D. and Pollitt, C. (1986), *New Forms of Democracy* (London: Sage).

Held, J. (1993), *Democracy and Right Wing Politics in Eastern Europe in the 1990s, e European Monographs* (New York: Columbia University Press).

Helgesen, J. (1992), 'Protecting Minorities in the CSCE Process', in *The Strength of Diversity: Human Rights and Pluralist Democracy.* Rosas, A. and Helgesen, J. (eds) (Dordrecht: Martinus-Nijhoff), 159–186.

Helleiner, J. (1995), 'Gypsies, Celts and Tinkers: Colonial Antecedents of Anti-Traveller Racism in Ireland', *Ethnic and Racial Studies,* **18**, 3.

Helton, A.C. (1997), 'Should the West Open its Doors to the East's Roma?', *Transitions,* **4**(4, September), no pagination.

Henkin, L. (1979), *The Rights of Man Today* (London: Stevens and Son).

Henkin, L. (1981), *The International Bill of Rights: Yhe Covenant on Civil and Political Rights* (New York: Columbia University Press).

Henrard, K. (2000), *Devising an Adequate System of Minority Protection* (The Hague: Kluwer).

Henrard, K. (2000), 'Education and Multiculturalism: The Contribution of Minority Rights?', *International Journal on Minority and Group Rights,* **7**, 393–410.

Henrard, K. (2004), 'Charting the Gradual Emergence of a more Robust Level of Minority Protection: Minority Specific Instruments and the European Union', *NQHR,* **22**(4), 559–584.

Herder, J.G. (1969), *JG Herder on Social and Political Culture* (Cambridge: Cambridge University Press).

Herman, D. (1993), 'Beyond the Rights Debate', *Social and Legal Studies,* **2**, 25–43.

Hersch, J. (1986), 'Human Rights in Western Thought: Conflicting Dimensions', in *Philosophical Foundations of Human Rights.* UNESCO (ed.) (Paris: UNESCO), 131–148. [PubMed 3715660,3698699,3726380,3949642]

Higgins, R. (1963), *The Development of International Law Through the Political Organs of the UN* (Oxford: Oxford University Press).

Higgins, R. (1993), *Problems and Process: International Law and How We Use It* (Oxford: Clarendon).

Higgins, R. (1995), 'Minority Rights: Discrepancies and Divergence's between the International Covenant and the Council of Europe System', in *The Dynamics of the Protection of Human Rights in Europe.* Lawson, R. and de Blois, M. (eds) (Dordrecht: Martinus-Nijhoff), 195–209.

HMI (1983), *The Education of Travellers' Children* (London: DES).

Hockenos, P. (1993), 'Xenophobia and Racism Unbound in the Land of the Magyars', *New Politics*, **4**(2), 69–81.

Hockenos, P. (1993), *Free to Hate* (New York: Routledge).

Hoensch, J. (1988), *A History of Modern Hungary* (London: Longman).

Holme, T. (1994), *The Importance of Self-Esteem* (TMH Teacher Training Manuals).

Holme, T. (1994), *Enhancing Self-Concept* (TMH Teacher Training Manuals).

Homicsko, O.A. (undated), *Equal Treatment and the Promotion of Equal Opportunities in Hungary*.www.comptrasec.u-bordeaux4.fr/static/SEMINAIRES/HOMICSKO1.pdf.

Horak, S.M. (1985), *Eastern European National Minorities: A Handbook* (Colorado: Libraries Unlimited).

Horn, G. (1989), 'Protection of Minority Rights and the International Community', *The New Hungarian Quarterly*, **30**(114), 9–14.

Horowitz, D.L. (1985), *Ethnic Groups in Conflict* (Berkeley: University of California Press).

Horton, J. (ed.) (1993), *Liberalism, Multiculturalism and Toleration* (London: Macmillan Publishing).

Hovens, P. (1990), 'High Expectations in the Low Countries: Gypsy Policy in the Netherlands 1978-1990', Unpublished Paper at the 12th Annual Conference of Gypsy Lore Society, Wagner College, US.

Hubschmanova, M. (1993), '3 yrs of Democracy in Czechoslovakia and the Roma', *Roma*, **38**(9), 30–49.

Hudson, M. (1952), *Report on Nationality Including Statelessness*, International Law Commission 4th Session UN Doc A/CN, 4/50 21.2.52.

Hudson, R. and Réno, F. (eds) (2000), *Politics of Identity. Migrants and Minorities in Multicultural States* (London: Palgrave).

Human Rights Project, Bulgaria (2003), 'The Government worked out its action plan for the Roma Minority bit it raises number of questions', **Oct 16th** (Sofia: Human Rights Project).

Human Rights Project, Bulgaria (2004), 'Roma public Officials in Bulgaria criticize the policy of the Government in open letter to the Prime Minister', **May 21st** (Sofia: Human Rights Project).

Human Rights Watch (1991), *Destroying Ethnic Identity: The Persecution of Gypsies in Romania* (New York: Human Rights Watch).

Human Rights Watch (1991), *Destroying Ethnic Identity: The Gypsies of Bulgaria* (New York: Human Rights Watch).

Human Rights Watch (1992), Struggling for Ethnic Identity: Czechoslovakia's Endangered Gypsies (New York: Human Rights Watch).

Human Rights Watch (1994), 'Lynch Law: Violence Against Roma in Romania', *Human Rights Watch Report*, **6**, 17.

Human Rights Watch (1996), 'Roma in the Czech RepublicForeigners in their Own Land', *Human Rights Watch Report*, **8**, 11.

Human Rights Watch (2002), *World Reporthungary* (New York: Human Rights Watch).

Hungarian Helsinki Committee and the Roma Press Centre (2002), 'Regarding the Joint 14th, 15th,16th and 17th Periodic report of Hungary Under Article 9 of the International Convention on the Elimination of All Forms of Racial Discrimination' (Budapest: Hungarian Helsinki Committee).

Huttenbach, H. (1991), 'The Romani Porajmos', in The Gypsies of Eastern Europe. Crowe, D. and Kolsti, J. (eds) (New York: M.E. Sharpe), 31–50.

Igarashi, K. (2005), 'Support Programmes for Roma Children: Do the Help or Promote Exclusion?', *Intercultural Education*, **16**(5, December), 443–452.

Independent (1997), 'Gypsies Invade Dover, Hoping for a Handout', **20th October**, 1.

Interface (1995), 'Programme', **19**, 3–5.

Interface (1995), 'Theme', **17**, 5–10.

Interface (1995), 'Training Provided by ATERPS', **17**, 11–12.

Interface (1995), 'Information File', **15**, 16.

Interface (1995), 'Information File', **15**, 14.

Interface (1995), 'Information File', **16**, 16.

International Helsinki Federation for Human Rights (1996 and 1997), *Annual Report* (Vienna: IHF).

Ivatts, A. (1996), 'The Education of Travelling Children', *CPRSI Newsletter*, **2**(3), 2–3.

Jackson-Preece, J. (1998), *National Minorities and the European-Nation States System* (Oxford: OUP).

Jackson-Preece, J. (2005), *Minority Rights: Between Diversity and Community* (Cambridge: Polity).

Jacobs, F.G. (1975), *The ECHR*, (Oxford: Oxford University Press).

Jacobs, F.G. and White, R. (1996), *The ECHR* 2nd ed. (Oxford: Clarendon).

Jahoda, M. (1984), 'The Roots of Prejudice', in *Minorities A Question of Human Rights?* Whitaker, B. (ed.) (Oxford: Pergamon Press), 43.

Janis, M., Kay, R., Bradley, A. (1995), *European Human Rights Law: Text and Materials* (Oxford: Clarendon).

Jansen, M. (1993), 'Sinti and Roma: An Ethnic Minority in Germany', in *The Protection of Ethnic and Linguistic Minorities in Europe*. Packer, J. and Myntti, K. (eds) (Turku: Abo Akademie University), 167.

Jeffcoate, R. (1984), *Ethnic Minorities and Education* (London: Harper & Row).

Jenkings, R. (1997), *Rethinking Ethnicity* (London: Sage).

Jiri, D. and Palatova, H. (1998), 'Results from Research on the Use of Psychological Tests in Pedagogical Psychological Advice Centres', *Vychovne Poradenstvi*, **16**(August).

Johnson, C. and Willers, M. (2004), *Gypsy and Traveller Law* (London: LAG).

Johnson, G. (1988), 'Human Rights in Divergent Conceptual Settings: How Do Ideas Influence Policy Choices?', in *Human Rights Theory and Measurement* Cingranelli, D.L. (ed.) (London: Macmillan), 41–59.

Johnston, D. (1995), 'Native Rights', in *The Rights of Minority Cultures*. Kymlicka, W. (ed.) (Oxford: Oxford University Press), 179–201.

Joly, D. (1990), *Refugees in Europe* (London: Minority Rights Group).

Jones, G. (1980), 'The UN and the Domestic Jurisdiction of States: Interpretations and Applications of the Non-Intervention Principle', *International Affairs*, **56**(4), 685–686.

Jones, P. (1999), 'Human Rights, Group Rights and Peoples' Rights', *HRQ*, **21**, 80–107.

Jones, T. (2003), 'The Race Directive: Redefining Protection from Discrimination in the EU', *EHRLR*, **5**, 515–526.

Jones, T.H. (1995), 'The Devaluation of Human Rights under the ECHR', *Public Law 1995*, 430–450.

Juviler, P. (1993), 'Are Collective Rights Anti-Human?', *NQHR*, **3**, 267–282.

Kadar, A. and Farkas, L. (2003), 'Country Report Hungary', in *Report on Measures to Combat Discrimination in the 13 Candidate Countries VT/2002/45* MEDE European Consultancy and Migration Policy Group report for the European Commission.

Kadar, A.L., Farkas, L. and Pardavi, M. (2001), 'Legal Analysis of National and EU Anti-Discrimination Legislation: A Comparison of the EU Racial Equality Directive and Protocol 12 with Anti-Discrimination Legislation in Hungary', *ERRC* (Budapest: Interights and the Migration Policy Group).

Kalvoda, J. (1991), 'The Gypsies of Czechoslovakia', in *The Gypsies of Eastern Europe*. Crowe, D. and Kolsti, J. (eds) (New York: M.E. Sharpe), 93–116.

Kamenka, E. and Tay, E. (eds) (1978), *Human Rights* (London: Edward Arnold).

Kanstroom, D. (1993), 'Wer sind wir Wieder? Laws of Asylum, Immigration and Citizenship in the Struggle for the Soul of the New Germany', *Yale Law Journal of International Law*, **18**(Winter), 155–211.

Karcagi, K. (1996), 'Minorities/Hungary: Hungarian Gypsy Struggle Starts in School', *Interpress Service English News*, **11 January**.

Kardos, G. (1992), 'The Market, Human Rights and Pluralism', in *The Strength of Diversity. Human Rights and Pluralist Democracy*. Rosas, A. and Helgesen, J. (eds) (Dordrecht: Martinus-Nijhoff), 127.

Kardos, G. (1995), 'Human Rights: A Matter of Individual or Collective Concern?', in *Human Rights in Eastern Europe*. Pogány, I. (ed.) (Aldershot: Edward Elgar), 169–183.

Kartashkin, V. (1982), 'Economic, Social and Cultural Rights', in *The International Dimensions of Human Rights*. Vasak, K. (ed.) (Paris: UNESCO), 111–134.

Kateb, G. (1994), 'Notes on Pluralism', *Social Research*, **61**(3), 512–537.

Katz, S. (2005), 'Emerging from the Cocoon of Romani Pride: The First Graduates of the Gandhi Secondary School in Hungary', *Intercultural Education*, **16**(3, August), 247–261. [DOI: 10.1080/14675980500212004]

Kawczynski, R. (1997), 'The Politics of Romani Politics', *Transitions*, **4**(4, September), no pagination.

Keating, M. (1988), *State and Regional Nationalism* (Brighton: Harvester Wheatsheaf).

Keating, M. and McGarry, J. (eds) (2001), *Minority Nationalism and the Changing International Order* (Oxford: OUP).

Kechichian, J.A. (1991), 'International: Ethnic, Political Aspirations in Eastern Europe', *Armenian International Magazine*, November 28th.

Kedzia, Z., Leuprecht, P. and Nowak, M. (eds) (1991), 'Perspectives of an All-European System of Human Rights Protection', *AEHRYB*, **1**, 269–278.

Keller, P. (1996), 'Justice and Ethnicity', *MLR*, **59**(Nov), 903–917.

Kenrick, D. (1991), 'The Gypsies of Bulgaria Before and After November 10th 1989', Unpublished Paper at 13th Annual Meeting of Gypsy Lore Society, Leicester, UK.

Kenrick, D. (1994), *Gypsies: From India to the Mediterranean* (Toulouse: Interface Collection Gypsy Research Centre).

Kenrick, D. (2004), *Gypsies: From the Ganges to the Thames* (Hatfield: University of Hertfordshire Press).

Kenrick, D. and Clark, C. (1995), *Moving On* (Hatfield: University of Hertfordshire Press).

Kenrick, D. and Puxon, G. (1972), *The Destiny of Europe's Gypsies* (Brighton: Sussex University Press).

Kertzer, D. and Arel, D. (2002), *Census and Identity: The Politics of Race, Ethnicity and Language in National Censuses* (Cambridge: Cambridge University Press).

Kessler, J. (1996), 'The Cultural Survival of Ethnic Minorities', *Midstream: Jewish Monthly Review*, **42**(8), 16–19.

Khazanov, A.M. (1984), *Nomads and the Outside World* (Cambridge: Cambridge University Press).

Killian, L. (1981), *Affirmative Action and Positive Discrimination: A Comparison of the US and India*, Occasional paper No 3 (London: University of London, Centre for Multicultural Education).

Kiss, A. (1986), 'The Right to Self-Determination', *HRLJ*, **7**(2–4), 165–175.

Kitwood, T. and Borrill, C. (1980), 'The Significance of Schooling for an Ethnic Minority', *Oxford Review of Education*, **6**, 241–253.

Klebes, H. (1993), 'Draft Protocol on Minority Rights to the ECHR', *HRLJ*, **14**, 140–144.

Klebes, H. (1995), 'The Council of Europe's Framework Convention for the Protection of National Minorities', *HRLJ*, **16**(1–3), 92–115.

Klein, G. and Reban, M. (1981), *The Politics of Ethnicity in Eastern Europe* (Boulder, NY: East European Monographs).

Klinke, A., Renn, O. and Lehners, J.-P. (1997), *Ethnic Conflicts and Civil Society* (Aldershot: Ashgate).

Knop, K. (2002), *Diversity and Self-Determination in International Law* (Cambridge: Cambridge University Press).

Kocze, A. (1996), 'The Roma of Central and Eastern Europe: Legal Remedies or Invisibility?', *CPRSI Newsletter*, **2**(5), 8–9.

Kohn, M., *The Race Gallery* (London: Vintage).

Kommers, D.P. and Loescher, G.D. (1979), *Human Rights and American Foreign Policy* (Paris: University of Notre Dame Press).

Koskenniemi, M. (1994), 'National Self-Determination', *ICLQ*, **43**, 241–269.

Kostelanick, D.J. (1989), 'The Gypsies of Czechoslovakia. Political and Ideological Considerations in the Development of Policy', *Studies in Comparative Communism*, **XXII**(4, Winter), 307–321.

Kosztolányi, G. (2000), 'All Roads Lead to Roma', *Central Europe Review Online*, **2**, 35.

Kosztolányi, G. (2000), 'All Roads Lead to Roma (Part 2)', *Central Europe Review Online*, **2**(35), no pagination.

Koudelka, J. (1975), *Gypsies* (London: Aperture).

Kovács, M. (2003), 'Standards of Self-Determination and Standards of Minority Rights in the Post-Communist Era', *Nations and Nationalism*, **9**(3), 433–450.

Kovats, M. (1997), 'Gypsy Self-Governments in Post-Socialist Hungary', in *Surviving Post-Socialism: Local Strategies and Regional Responses in Eastern Europe and the Former Soviet Union*. Bridger, S. and Pine, F. (eds) (London: Routledge), 124–147.

Kovats, M. (2002), *The European Roma Question*, Royal Institute of International Affairs Briefing Paper, 31st March.

Kovats, M. (2002/2003), 'Roma Politics and Policy in Hungary 1999-2003', *European Yearbook of Minority Issues*, **2**, 73–93.

Kovats, M. (2003), 'The Politics of Roma Identity: Between Nationalism and Destitution', *Open Democracy*, 30th July. www.openDemocracy.net.

Kovats, M. (1997), 'The Good, the Bad and the Ugly: Three Faces of "Dialogue" – the Development of Roma Politics in Hungary', *Contemporary Politics*, **3**(1), 55–57.

Krejci, J. and Velimsky, V. (1981), *Ethnic and Political Nations in Europe* (London: Croom-Helm).

Kritsiotis, D. (ed.) (1994), *Self Determination: Cases of Crisis* (Hull: University of Hull Law School).

Kubánová, M. (2005), 'The Missing Link: Monitoring and Evaluation of Roma-Related Policies in Slovakia', *Journal of the Open Society Institute*, EUMap.org.

Kukathas, C. (1993), *Multicultural Citizens: The Philosophy and Politics of Identity* (St Leonards: Centre for Independent Studies).

Kukathas, C. (1995), 'Are There Any Cultural Rights?', in *The Rights of Minority Cultures*. Kymlicka, W. (ed.) (Oxford: Oxford University Press).

Kusy, M. (1996), 'Minorities and Regionalization in Slovakia: Regionalisation as a Solution for the Hungarian Minority Issue in Slovakia', *Helsinki Monitor*, **7**(1), no pagination.

Kymlicka, W. (1989), *Liberalism, Community and Culture* (Oxford: OUP).

Kymlicka, W. (1991), 'Liberalism and the Politicization of Ethnicity', *The Canadian Journal of Law and Jurisprudence*, **IV**(2), 239–256, reprinted in *Group Rights*. Stapleton, J. (ed.) (1995) (Bristol: Thoemmes Press).

Kymlicka, W. (1992), 'Liberal Individualism and Liberal Neutrality', in *Communitarianism and Individualism*. Avineri, S. and De Shalit, A. (eds) (Oxford: Oxford University Press), 165–185.

Kymlicka, W. (1994), 'Individual and Community Rights', in *Group Rights*. Baker, J. (ed.) (Toronto: University of Toronto Press), 17–33.

Kymlicka, W. (1995), *Multicultural Citizenship: A Liberal Theory of Minority Rights* (Oxford: Oxford University Press).

Kymlicka, W. (1995a), *The Rights of Minority Cultures* (Oxford: Oxford University Press).

Kymlicka, W. (2001), *Politics in the Vernacular* (Oxford: OUP).

Kymlicka, W. and Norman, W. (2000), *Citizenship in Diverse Societies* (Oxford: Oxford University Press).

Kymlicka, W. and Opalski, M. (eds) (2001), *Can Liberal Pluralism Be Exported?* (Oxford: Oxford University Press).

Kyuchukov, H. (2000), 'Transformative Education for Roma (Gypsy) Children: An Insider's View', *Intercultural Education*, **11**(3), 273–280.

Lacquer, W. and Rubin, B. (1979), *The Human Rights Reader* (Philadelphia: Temple University Press).

Laitin, D. (1995), 'Marginality: A Microperspective', *Rationality and Society*, **7**(1), 31–57.

Lauterpacht, H. (1968), *International Law and Human Rights* (North Have, CT: Aaron Books).

Lauwagie, B,N. (1979), 'Ethnic Boundaries in Modern States: *Romano Lavo-lil* Revisited', *AJS*, **85**(2), 310–337.

Lawson, R. (1995), 'Confusion and Conflict?, Diverging Interpretations of the ECHR in Strasbourg and Luxembourg', in *The Dynamics of the Protection of Human Rights in Europe*. Lawson, R. and de Blois, M. (eds) (Dordrecht: M. Nijhoff), 219–252.

Lawson, R. and de Blois, M. (eds) (1995), *The Dynamics of the Protection of Human Rights in Europe* (Dordrecht: M. Nijhoff).

Lawson, R., Livingston, K. and Mistrik, E. (2003), 'Teacher Training and Multiculturalism in a transitional Society: The Case of the Slovak Republic', *Intercultural Education*, 14(4, December), 409–421.

Lee, K.W. (1997), 'Man whose Tale Prompted Scores of Gypsies to Follow him to Dover has no Regrets', *The Times*, **23 October**.

Lee, K.W. and Warren W.G. (1991), 'Alternative Education: Lessons from Gypsy Thought and Practice', *British Journal of Educational Studies*, **39**(3), 311–324.

Lefeber, R., Fitzmaurice, M. and Vierdag, E.W. (1991), *The Changing Political Structure of Europe* (Dordrecht: M. Nijhoff).

Legomsky, S.H. (1994), 'Why Citizenship?', *Virginia Journal of International Law*, **1994**, 279–300.

Leicester Herald and Post (1991), 'BNP Denies Dirty Tricks', **15th April**, 1.

Lemarchand, R. (1993), 'The Siren Song of Self-Determination', *The UNESCO Courier*, **46**, 29–33.

Lerner, N. (1991), *Group Rights and Discrimination in International Law* (Dordrecht: M. Nijhoff).

Lerner, N. (1993), 'The Evolution of Minority Rights in International Law', in *Peoples and Minorities in International Law*, Amsterdam International Law Conference Brolmann, C., Lefeber, R. and Zieck, M. (eds), 77–101.

Lester, A. and Pannick, D. (eds) (1999), *Human Rights Law and Practice* (London: Reed Elsevier).

Levey, G.B. (1997), 'Equality, Autonomy and Cultural Rights', *Political Theory*, **25**(2), 215–248.

Levy, O. (ed.) (1991), *The Complete Works of Frederich Nietzsche* (London: T.A. Foulis).

Liberty (1994), *Defend Diversity Defend Dissent: What's Wrong with the CJPOA* (London: Liberty).

Liebich, A., Warner, D. and Dragovic, J. (1995), *Citizenship East and West* (London: Keegan, Paul).

Liégeois, J.P. (1986), *Gypsies: An Illustrated History* (London: Al Saqi).

Liégeois, J.P. (1987), *School Provision for Gypsy and Traveller Children: A Synthesis Report* (Luxembourg: Commission of the EC).

Liégeois, J.P. (1988), *School Provision for Ethnic Minorities: The Gypsy Paradigm* (Hatfield: University of Hertfordshire Press).

Liégeois, J.P. (1989), *Report of the European Teachers Seminar Benidorm June.*

Liégeois, J.P. (1990), *European Teachers Seminar*, France December 1990.

Liégeois, J.P. (1991), *Gypsies and Travellers: Community Work in Europe* (Brussels: Inter-University Institute on Social Welfare).

Liégeois, J.P. (1992), *School Provision for Gypsy and Traveller Children: Distance Learning and Pedagogical Follow-Up* (Paris: CDCC).

Liégeois, J.P. (1992), *Towards Intercultural Education – Training Teachers of Gypsy Pupils* (Paris: CDCC).

Liégeois, J.P. (1994), *Roma, Gypsies, Travellers* (Strasbourg: C/E Publications).

Liégeois, J.P. (1996), *Roma Policy: Gypsy National Self-Governments and Local Self-Government*, CDCC, C/E A Programme of Case Studies concerning the Inclusion of Minorities as Factors of Cultural Policy and Action DECS/SE/ DHRM (96) 23.

Lijphart, A. (1977), *Democracy in Plural Societies: A Comparative Exploration* (New Haven, Conn.: Yale University Press).

Lijphart, A. (1995), 'Self-determination Versus Pre-Determination of Ethnic Minorities in Power-Sharing Systems', in The Rights of Minority Cultures Kymlicka, W. (ed.) (Oxford: Oxford University Press), 278–287.

Lillich, R. (1984), 'Civil Rights', in *Human Rights in International Law, 2 Vols.* Meron, T. (ed.) (New York: Oxford University Press), 115–170.

Lloyd, G., Stead, J., Jordan, E. and Norris, C. (1999), 'Teachers and Gypsy-Travellers', *Scottish Educational Review*, **31**, 48–65.

Livingstone, S. (1997), 'Article 14 and the Prevention of Discrimination in the European Convention on Human Rights', *EHRLR*, **1**, 25–34.

Lockwood, W.G. (1986), 'E European Gypsies in Western Europe: The Social and Cultural Adaptation of the Xoraxane', *Nomadic Peoples*, **21**(2), 63–70.

Loescher, G. (ed.) (1992), *Refugees and the Asylum Dilemma in the West* (Pennsylvania: State University Press).

Lorette, L.H. (1990), *Communitarianism: A Prospectus for Revolution* (Texas: Communitarian Press).

Lowe, R. and Shaw, W. (1994), *Travellers: Voices of the New Age Nomads* (London: Fourth Estate).

Luard, E. (ed.) (1967), *The International Protection of Human Rights* (London: Thames & Hudson).

Lucassen, L. (1991), 'The Power of Definition: Stigmatization, Minoritisation and Ethnicity Illustrated by the History of the Gypsies of the Netherlands', *Netherlands' Journal of Social Sciences*, **27**(2), 80–91.

Luciak, M. (2006), 'Minority Schooling and Intercultural Education: A Comparison of Recent Developments in the Old and New EU Member States', *Intercultural Education*, **17**, 73–80.

Lukes, S. (1993), 'Five Fables About Human Rights', in *On Human Rights: The Oxford Amnesty Lectures.* Shute, S. and Hurley, S. (eds) (New York: Basic Books/ Harper Collins), 19–40.

Lutz, E.L., Hannum, H., Burke, K. (1989), *New Directions in Human Rights* (Philadelphia: University of Pennsylvania Press).

Lyons, G. and Mayall, J. (eds) (2003), *International Human Rights in the Twenty-First Century* (Maryland: Rowman and Littlefield).

Lyotard, J.-F. (1993), 'The Other's Rights', in *On Human Rights: The Oxford Amnesty Lectures.* Shute, S. and Hurley, S. (eds) (New York: Basic Books/Harper Collins), 135–148.

McCagg, W. (1991), 'Gypsy Policy in Socialist Hungary and Czechoslovakia 1945–89', *Nationalities Papers*, **19**(3), 313–336.

Macartney, C.A. (1967), 'League of Nations' Protection of Minority Rights', in *The International Protection of Human Rights.* Luard, E. (ed.) (London: Thames & Hudson), 22–38.

McDonald, C. (2004), 'The Education of Roma Children: Inroads to Good Practice, the REI Example', *EUMAP* (www.eumap.org).

MacDonald, I. (1989), 'Group Rights', *Philosophical Papers*, **XVIII**(2), 117–136.

Macedo, S. (1990), *Liberal Virtues: Citizenship, Virtue and Community in Liberal Constitutionalism* (Oxford: Oxford University Press).

McGarry, J. and O'Leary, B. (1993), *The Politics of Ethnic Conflict* (London: Routledge).

McGoldrick, D. (1990), 'Human Rights Developments in the Helsinki Process', *ICLQ*, **39**, 923–940.

McIntosh, M., MacIver, M., Abele, D. and Nolle, D. (1995), 'Minority Rights and Majority Rule: Ethnic Tolerance in Romania and Bulgaria', *Social Forces*, **73**(3), 939–967.

MacIntyre, A. (1984), 'The Virtues, the Unity of a Human Life, and the Concept of a Tradition', in *Liberalism and Its Critics.* Sandel, M. (ed.) (Oxford: Blackwell), 125–149.

MacIntyre, A. (1992), 'Justice As Virtue: Changing Conceptions', in *Communitarianism and Individualism.* Avineri, S. and De-Shalit, A. (eds) (Oxford: Oxford University Press), 51–64.

MacIver, R.M. (1911), 'Society and State', *The Philosophical Review*, **XX**, 41.

Mack, R.W. and Duster, T.S. (1964), *Patterns of Minority Relations* (New York: Anti Defamation League of B'nai B'rith).

McKean, W.A. (1970), 'The Meaning of Discrimination in International and Municipal Law', *BYIL*, **1970**(44), 177–192.

McKean, W.A. (1983), *Equality and Discrimination Under International Law* (Oxford: Clarendon Press).

McLean, M. (1980), 'Cultural Autonomy and the Education of Ethnic Minority Groups', *BJEd Studies*, **28**(1), 7–12.

Macklem, P. (2006), 'Militant Democracy, Legal Pluralism and the Paradox of Self-Determination', *Int Journal of Constitutional Law*, **4**(3), 488.

McVeigh, R. (1991), 'The Specificity of Irish Racism', *Race and Class*, **33**(4), 31.

Magyar Hírlap (1995), December 7th (Budapest).

Magyar Hírlap (1996), January 10th (Budapest).

Magyar Hírlap (1997), 'Romani children in State Care in Hungary', 31 October (Budapest).

Magyar Narancs (1997), 'Graduation in Separate Ways', June 19th (Hungary).

Maitland, F.W. (1934), *Natural Law and the Theory of Society, 1500–1800* (Cambridge: Cambridge University Press).

Maksoud, C. (1994), 'Autonomy and Minorities: the Status of the Kurds and Palestinians', *Loyola of los Angeles Int and Comparative Law*, **16 February**, 291–298.

Maliverni, G. (1991), 'The Draft Convention for the Protection of Minorities: The Proposal of the European Commission for Democracy through the William Law', *HRLJ*, **12**(6–7), 265–269.

Malloy, T. (2005), *National Minority Rights in Europe* (Oxford: Oxford University Press).

Mann, A.B. (1994), *The Romanies in Slovakia, Local History and Minorities Training Course* (Slovakia: Council of Europe), DECS/SE/BS/Sem (94) Misc 6.

Maresca, J.A. (1989), 'The People Have a Right to Choose', *International Herald Tribune*, **21st June**.

Margalit, A. and Raz, J. (1995), 'National Self-Determination', in *The Rights of Minority Cultures*. Kymlicka, W. (ed.) (Oxford: Oxford University Press), 79–92.

Marias, E. (1994), *European Citizenship* (Maastricht: European Institute of Public Administration).

Marie, J.B. (1995), 'International Instruments Relating to Human Rights Classification and Status as of 1.1.95', *HRLJ*, 75.

Markos, E. (1985), 'Dim Prospects for Improving the Plight of the Gypsies', *RFE Research*, **10**, 13–14.

Markos, E. (1987), 'The Fast Growing Gypsy Minority and its Problems', *RFE Research*, **5**, 13–16.

Markovic, M. (1986), 'Differing Conceptions of Human Rights in Europe: Towards a Resolution', *UNESCO Courier*, 113–130.

Marquand, C. (1994), 'Human Rights Protection and Minorities', *Public Law*, **Autumn**, 359–366.

Marshall, T.H. (1964), *Class, Citizenship and Social Development* (New York: Doubleday).

Marshall, T.H. and Bottomore, T. (1992), *Citizenship and Social Class* (London: Pluto Press).

Marushiakova, E. and Popov, V. (1993), 'Roma in Bulgaria – History and Present Day', *Roma*, **38**(9), 50–67.

Massey, D.S., Arango, J., Hugo, G., Kouaouci, A., Pellegrino, A. and Taylor, J.E. (1997), 'Migration Theory and Ethnic Mobilisation and Globalisation', in *The Ethnicity Reader*. Guibernau, M. and Rex, J. (eds) (Cambridge: Polity), 257–269.

Mastny, V. (1992), *The Helsinki Process and the Reintegration of Europe 1986–1991, Analysis and Documentation* (New York: New York University Press).

Matscher, F. and Liddy, J. (1993), 'Report on the Legislation in the Czech Republic', *HRLJ*, **14**(11–12), 442.

May, L., Friedman, M. and Clark, A.G. (eds) (1996), *Mind and Morals: Essays on Cognitive Science and Ethics* (Cambridge, Mass.: MIT Press).

May, S., Modood, T. and Squires, J. (eds) (2004), *Ethnicity, Nationalism and Minority Rights* (Cambridge: Cambridge University Press).

Mayall, D. (1988), *Gypsy Travellers in Nineteenth Century Society* (Cambridge: Cambridge University Press).

Mayall, D. (1992), 'The Making of British Gypsy Identity', *Immigrants and Minorities*, **II**(1), 21–41.

Mayall, D. (1995), *English Gypsies and State Policies* (Hatfield: University of Hertfordshire Press).

Means, G.P. (1974), 'Human Rights and the Rights of Ethnic Groups – a Commentary', *International Studies Notes*, **17**.

Meijknecht, A. (2004), *Minority Protection: Standards and Reality: Implementation of Council of Europe Standards in Slovakia, Romania and Bulgaria* (The Hague: RMC Asser Press).

Meron, T. (ed.) (1984), *Human Rights in International Law* (New York: Oxford University Press).

Meron, T. (1986), *Human Rights Law Making in the United Nations* (Oxford: Clarendon).

Metcalfe, E. (1996), 'Illiberal Citizenship? A Critique of Will Kymlicka's *Liberal Theory of Minority Rights*', *Queens Law Journal*, **22**, 167–207.

Miall, H. (ed.) (1994), *Minority Rights in Europe. The Scope for a Transnational Regime* (London: Pinter).

Michalska, A. (1990), 'The Socialist Conception of Human Rights: The Polish Perspective', in *Human Rights in a Pluralist World: Individuals and Collectivities*. Berting, J. (ed.) (Meckler: Roosevelt Study Centre), 155–165.

Mijs, J. (1990), 'Cursed Is the Country from which the Gypsies Flee: The Invisible Gypsies of Poland', *O'Drom*, **April**, 237–243.

Mill, J.S. (1958), *Considerations on Representative Government* (New York; Liberal Arts Press).

Millward, S.M.T. (1986), 'Travellers and the Law', *The Cambrian Law Review*, **17**, 76–93.

Milton, S. (1990), 'The Context of the Holocaust', *German Studies Review*, **XIII**(2), 269–284.

Minogue, K. (1979), 'The History of the Idea of Human Rights', in *The Human Rights Reader*. Lacquer, W. and Rubin, B. (eds) (Philadelphia: Temple University Press), 3–17.

Minority Rights Group (ed.) (1986), *Co-Existence in Some Plural European Societies* (London: Minority Rights Group).

Minority Rights Group (ed.) (1991), *Minorities and Autonomy in Western Europe* (London: Minority Rights Group).

Minority Rights Group (ed.) (1993), *Minorities in Central and Eastern Europe* (London: Minority Rights Group).

Minority Rights Group (ed.) (1994), *Education Rights and Minorities* (London: Minority Rights Group).

Mirga, A. (1993), 'The Effects of the State Assimilation Policy on Polish Gypsies', *Journal of the Gypsy Lore Society*, **3**(2 August). 69–76.

Mirga, A. and Gheorghe, N. (1997), *The Roma in the Twenty-First Century: A Policy Paper* (Princeton, NJ: PER).

Moody, T. (1992), 'Some Comparisons between Liberalism and Eccentric Communitarianism', in *Communitarianism, Liberalism and Social Responsibility*. Peden, C. and Hudson, Y. (eds) Studies in Social and Political Theory Vol. 14 (Lewiston: The Edwin Mellen Press), 187–198.

Moon, G. (2003), 'Complying with its International human Rights Obligations: The United Kingdom and Article 26 of the ICCPR', *EHRLR*, **3**, 283–307.

Moon, J.D. (1993), *Constructing Community* (Princeton, NJ: Princeton University Press).

Moore, C. (2004), 'Group Rights for Nomadic Minorities: Ireland's Traveller Community', *IJHR*, **8**(2), 175–197.

Morelli, M. (1992), 'Education as A Right', in *Communitarianism, Liberalism and Social Responsibility*. Peden, C. and Hudson, Y. (eds) Studies in Social and Political Theory Vol. 14 (Lewiston: The Edwin Mellen Press), 139–150.

Morrill, K. (1996/97), 'Implementation of OSCE Commitments in the Human Dimension Report of Working Group One, Review Meeting, Vienna 4–28th November', *ODIHR Bulletin*, **5**(1), 11.

Morsink, J. (1999), 'Cultural Genocide, The Universal Declaration and Minority Rights', *HRQ*, **21**, 1009–1060.

MTI News (1997), 'MTI Views Hungarian support Program for Gypsies', **30 December** (Budapest).

MTI News (1998), 'Parliamentary Representation of Minorities – New Proposal', **27 January** (Budapest).

MTI News (1998), 'Support for Minority Education', Press Briefing March 4th (Budapest).

Mullerson, R. (1993), 'Minorities in Eastern Europe and the Former USSR: Problems, Tendencies and Protection', *MLR*, **56**(6), 793–811.

Mulhall, S. and Swift, A. (1996), Liberals and Communitarians (Oxford: Blackwell).

Murdie, A. (1995), 'Trespassers Will Be Prosecuted', *NLJ,* **145**(6687) 389–390.

Musschenga, A.W., Voorzanger, B. and Soeteman A. (eds) (1992), *Morality, Worldview and Law* (Maastricht, the Kingdom of the Netherlands: Van Gorcum).

Nartowski, A.S. (1974), 'The UNESCO System of Protection of the Right to Education', *Polish YB Int*, **6**, 289–309.

National Gypsy Council (1981), *Report on Discrimination* (Oldham: NGC).

National Gypsy Council (1992), *Response to Government Consultation Paper on Reform of the Caravan Sites Act 1968* (Oldham: NGC).

Nietzsche, F. (1968), *Twilight of the Idols* (Middlesex: Penguin).

Nemeth, S. (2005), *Roma Education Initiative Annual Research and Evaluation Report Hungary* (Open Society Institute). http://www.osi.hu/esp/rei/.

Népszabadság Newspaper (1996), **2 February**.

Népszava Newspaper (1997), **10 January**.

Népszava Newspaper (1997), **5 February**.

Népszava Newspaper (1997), **28 February**.

Népszava Newspaper (1997), **19 November**.

Népszava Newspaper (1998), **17 January**.

Newman, F. and Vasak, K. (1982), 'Civil and Political Rights' in *The International Dimensions of Human Rights Vol. 2*. Vasak, K. (ed.) (Paris: UNESCO).

Newman, F. and Weissbrodt, D. (eds) (1990), *International Human Rights* (Cincinnati: Anderson Publishing Company).

New York Times (1991), 'Catalan is Spoken Here (Do you Hear Madrid)', **19 April**, A9.

New York Times (1993), 'Havel Calls Gypsies "Litmus test"', **10 December**, A11.

Newton, L. (1973), 'Reverse Discrimination as Unjustified', *Ethics*, **83**, 308–312.

Nickel, J. (1987), 'Making Sense of Human Rights: Philosophical Reflections on the Universal Declaration of Human Rights', in *International Human Rights*. Newman, F. and Weissbrodt, D. (eds) (Cincinnati: Anderson Publishing Company), 74–79.

Nickel, J. (1994), 'The Value of Cultural Belonging: Expanding Kymlicka's Theory', *Dialogue*, **33**, 636–642.

Niessen, J. (2003), 'Making the Law Work: The Enforcement and Implementation of Anti-Discrimination Legislation', *European Journal of Migration and Law*, **5**, 249–257.

Nieuwsma, G. (1999), 'A Depressing Decade: Czech-Roma Relations after the Velvet Revolution', *Central Europe Online*, **1**, 18.

Niner, P. (2003), *Local Authority Gypsy/Traveller Sites in England* (London: Office of the Deputy Prime Minister/University of Birmingham).

Niner, P. (2004), 'Accommodating Nomadism? An Examination of Housing Options for Gypsies and Travellers in England', *Housing Studies*, **19**(2), 141–159.

Niner, P. (2004), *Counting Gypsies and Travellers: A Review of the Gypsy Caravan Count System* (London: Office of the Deputy Prime Minister).

Noorani, A.G. (1992), 'Minority Rights and Human Rights', *Economic and Political Weekly*, **15 August**.

Noorderhaven, N.G. and Halman, L. (2003), 'Does Intercultural Education Lead to more Cultural Homogeneity and Tolerance?', *Intercultural Education*, 14(1), 67–76.

Note (1995), 'Hungary and a New Paradigm for the Protection of Ethnic Minorities in Central and Eastern Europe', *Columbia Journal of Transnational Law*, **3**(3), 673–705.

Novak, M. (1997), 'Cultural Pluralism for Individuals: a Social Vision', in *Pluralism in a Democratic Society*. Tumin, M. and Plotch, W. (eds), (New York: Praeger), 25–57.

Nowak, M. (1991), 'The Right to Education: It's Meaning, Significance and Limitations', *NQHR*, **4**, 418–425.

Nowak, M. (1993), 'The Evolution of Minority Rights in International Law – Comments', in *Peoples and Minorities in International Law* Brolmann, C., Lefeber, R. and Zieck, M. (eds) (Amsterdam: Amsterdam International Law Conference), 103–118.

Nowak, M. (1993), *CCPR Commentary* (Kehl: N.P. Engel).

Nozick, R. (1992), 'Distributive Justice', in *Communitarianism and Individualism.* Avineri, S. and De-Shalit, A. (eds) (Oxford: Oxford University Press), 137–150.

Oakeshott, M. (1994), 'The Tower of Babel', in *Communitarianism: A New Public Ethics.* Daly, M. (ed.) (Belmont, CA: Wadsworth), 243–254.

O'Donnell, K. (1995), 'Protection of Family Life: Positive Approaches and the ECHR', *JSWFL*, **17**(3), 261–279.

OECD (1983), *The Education of Minority Groups* (Aldershot: Gower).

OECD (1995), 'Gypsy Populations and their Movements within Central and Eastern Europe and towards some OECD Countries', *Working Papers*, **3**, 9.

Oestreich, J.E. (1999), 'Liberal Theory and Minority Group Rights', *HRQ*, **21**, 108–132.

Ofner, P. (1990), 'Sterilisation in Practice in Czechoslovakia', *O'Drom*, **April**, 263–269.

OFSTED (1996), *The Education of Travelling Children HMR/12/96/NS* (London: HMSO).

OFSTED (1999), *Raising the Attainment of Minority Ethnic Pupils* (London: HMSO).

OFSTED (2003), *Provision and Support for Traveller Pupils* (London: HMSO).

Ofuatey-Kodjoe, W. (1977), *The Principle of Self-Determination in International Law* (New York: Nellen Publishing House).

Ogbu, J. (1992), 'Adaptation to Minority Status and School Experience', *Theory into Practice*, **31**(4), 287–295.

O'Hanlon, C. and Homes, P. (2004), *Education of Gypsy and Traveller Children: Towards Inclusion and Educational Achievement* (Stoke On Trent: Trentham Books and OFSTED).

Okely, J. (1983), *The Traveller-Gypsies* (Cambridge: Cambridge University Press).

Okin, S.M. (1989), 'Whose Traditions?, Which Understandings?', in *Communitarianism: A New Public Ethics.* Daly, M. (ed.) (Belmont, CA: Wadsworth), 126–136.

Oldenquist, A. (1986), 'Group Egoism', in *Communitarianism: A New Public Ethics.* Daly, M. (ed.) (Belmont, CA: Wadsworth), 255–267.

O'Nions, H. (1995), The Marginalisation of Gypsies, *Web JCLI*, 3.

O'Nions, H. (1996), 'The First in a Series of "Gypsy Cases" to Challenge UK Legislation', *Web JCLI*, 5.

O'Nions, H. (1997), 'Czech Citizenship Restrictions and the Roma', Paper delivered at Roma Studies Day, University of London.

O'Nions, H. (1999), 'Bonafide of Bogus?', *Web JCLI*, 3.

Open Media Research Institute (1992), 'Repatriation of Romanian Gypsies from Germany', *Daily Digest*, **11 March**.

Open Media Research Institute (1995), 'Low Turn-out at Hungary's Minority Elections', *Daily Digest*, **21 November**.

Open Society Institute (2006), *Roma Inclusion: Lessons Learned from OSI's Roma Programming* (New York: OSI).

Open Society Institute (2002), *Accession Progress Report on Romania* (New York: OSI).

Open Society Institute (2001), *Monitoring the EU Accession Process: Minority Protection* (New York: OSI).

Open Society Institute (2001), *Monitoring the EU Accession Process: Minority Protection in Slovakia* (New York: OSI).

Open Society Institute (2001), *EU Accession Monitoring Program: Minority Protection in the Czech Republic* (New York: OSI).

Ottay, E. (1991), 'Crime Rate Rising Sharply', in *Report on Eastern Europe*, Radio Free Europe, 32–55.

Packer, J. (1996), 'Keynote address', Minority Rights in the New Europe Conference November, University of London.

Packer, J. (2000), 'The Origin and Nature of the Lund Recommendations on Effective Participation of National Minorities in Public Life', *Helsinki Monitor*, **11**, 31.

Packer, J. and Myntti, K. (eds) (1993), *The Protection of Ethnic and Linguistic Minorities in Europe* (Turku, Finland: Abo Akademie University.

Palermo, F. and Woelk, J. (2003/2004), 'From Minority Protection to a Law of Diversity? Reflections on the Evolution of Minority Rights', *European Yearbook of Minority Issues*, **3**, 5–13.

Palley, C. (1978), *Constitutional Law and Minorities* (London: MRG).

Palley, C. (1995), 'The Role of Law in Relation to Minority Groups', in *The Future of Cultural* Minorities. Alcock, A., Taylor, B. and Welton, J. (eds) (London: Macmillan).

Palous, M. (1995), 'Questions of Czech Citizenship', in *Citizenship East and West*. Liebich, A., Warner, D. and Dragovic, J. (eds) (London: Keegan, Paul), 141–164.

Panikaar, R. (1982), 'Is the Notion of Human Rights a Western Concept?', *Diogenes*, **120**, 75–102.

Papp, T. (1999), *Who Is In, Who Is Out? Citizenship, Nationhood, Democracy and European Integration in the Czech Republic and Slovakia*, EUI Working Paper RSC No 99/13 (Florence: European University Institute).

Parekh, B. (1990), 'The Rushdie Affair: Research Agenda for Political Philosophy', *Political Studies*, **38**, 659–709.

Partsch, K.J. (1982), 'Fundamental Principles of Human Rights: Self-determination, Equality and Non-Discrimination', in *The International Dimensions of Human Rights Vol. 2*. Vasak, K. (ed.) (Paris: UNESCO), 61–86.

Partsch, K.J. (1986), 'Recent Developments in the Field of Peoples Rights', *HRLJ*, 177–182.

Paul, E.F., Miller, F.D. and Paul, J. (eds) (1996), *The Communitarian Challenge to Liberalism* (Cambridge: Cambridge University Press).

Peden, C. and Hudson, Y. (eds) (1992), *Communitarianism, Liberalism and Social Responsibility: Studies in Social and Political Theory Vol. 14* (Lewiston: The Edwin Mellen Press).

Pehe, J. (1990), 'Racial Violence Increasing', *RFE/RL Research*, **1**(20), 14–18.

Pehe, J. (1993), 'Law on Romanies Causes Uproar in the Czech Republic', *RFE/RL Research*, **2**(7), 18–22.

Pehe, J. (1998), 'Attitude to Foreigners Must Change', *Prague Post*, **24 June**.

Pejic, J. (1997), Minority Rights in International Law, *HRQ*, 666–695.

Pellet, A. (1992), 'A Second Breath for the Self-determination of Peoples', *European Journal of International Law*, **3**(1), 178–185.

Pentassuglia, G. (2001), 'The EU and the Protection of Minorities: The Case of Eastern Europe', *EJIL*, **12**, 13–38.

Pentassuglia, G. (2002), 'State Sovereignty, Minorities and Self Determination: A Comprehensive Legal View', *International Journal on Minority and Group Rights*, **9**, 303–324.

Pentassuglia, G. (2003), 'Minority Issues as a Challenge in the European Court of Human Rights: A Comparison with the Case Law of the United Nations Human Rights Committee', *German Yearbook of International Law*, **46**, 401–451.

Pestieau, J. (1991), 'Minority Rights: Caught Between Individual Rights and People's Rights', *The Canadian Journal of Law and Jurisprudence*, **IV**(2 July), 361–373.

Phillips, A. (1995), 'Democracy and Difference', in *The Rights of Minority Cultures*. Kymlicka, W. (ed.) (Oxford: Oxford University Press), 288–299.

Plant, R. (1994), *Land Rights and Minorities* (London: MRG).

Pleşe, B. (2003), 'The Strasbourg Court Finally Redresses Racial Discrimination', *Roma Rights Legal Defence* (Budapest: European Roma Rights Centre).

Pogány, I. (ed.) (1995), *Human Rights in Eastern Europe* (Aldershot: Edward Elgar).

Pogány, I. (1996), 'Minority Rights in Central and Eastern Europe: Old Dilemmas, New Solutions'. Unpublished Conference Paper.

Pogány, I. (1996), 'Bilateralism vs Regionalism in the Resolution of Minority Problems', Minority Rights in the 'New' Europe Conference, November, University of London.

Pogány, I. (2004), 'Refashioning Rights in Central and Eastern Europe: Some Implications for the Regions Roma', *EPL*, **10**(1), 85–106.

Pogány, I. (2006), 'Minority Rights and the Roma of Central and Eastern Europe', *HumRLR*, **6**, 1–22.

Poleshchuk, V. (2001), *Multiculturalism, Minority Education and Language Policy* (Flensburg, Germany: European Centre for Minority Issues).

Pomerance, M. (1982), *Self-Determination in Law and Practice* (The Hague: Kluwer).

Poole, R. (1999), *Nation and Identity* (London: Routledge).

Poulter, S. (1987), 'Ethnic Minority Customs, English Law and Human Rights', *ICLQ*, **36**(3), 589.

Poulter, S. (1992), 'Gypsy Sites: An Unacceptable Volte-face', *Runnymede Bulletin*, **260**, 10–12.

Poulter, S. (1997), *Ethnicity, Law and Human Rights* (Oxford: Oxford University Press).

Poulter, S. (1997), 'Gypsies: The Pursuit of a Nomadic Lifestyle', in *Ethnicity, Law and Human Rights*. Poulter, S. (ed.) (Oxford: Oxford University Press), 147–194.

Poulter, S. (1997), 'The Rights of Ethnic, Religions and Linguistic Minorities', *EHRLR*, **3**, 254–264.

Powell, C. (1994), 'Time for Another Immoral Panic? The Case of the Czechoslovak Gypsies', *Int'l J Soc L*, **22**, 105–121.

Powell, C. (1996), 'Razor Blades Amidst the Velvet?, Changes and Continuities in the Gypsy Experiences of the Czech and Slovak Lands', in *Gypsy Politics and Traveller Identity*. Acton, T. (ed.) (Hatfield: University of Hertfordshire Press), 90–99.

Pravda (1992), 'Transform our Fellow Gypsy Citizens', **23 September** (Bratislava), 5.

Project on Ethnic Relations (1992), *The Romanies in Central and Eastern Europe: Illusions and Reality* (Princeton, NJ: PER).

Project on Ethnic Relations (1994), *Countering Anti-Roma Violence in Eastern Europe: The Snagov Conference and Related. Efforts* (Princeton, NJ: PER).

Project on Ethnic Relations (1996), *The Media and the Roma in Contemporary Europe: Facts and Fictions* (Princeton, NJ: PER).

Project on Ethnic Relations (1997), *Self-Government in Hungary: The Romani/ Gypsy Experience and Prospects for the Future* (Princeton, NJ: PER).

Project on Ethnic Relations (1999), *The Roma in Hungary: Government Policies, Minority Expectations and the International Community* (Budapest: Project on Ethnic Relations).

Project on Ethnic Relations (2000), *Parliamentary Representation of Minorities in Hungary: Legal and Political Issues* (Budapest: Project on Ethnic Relations).

Preece, J.J. (1997), 'Minority Rights in Europe: From Westphalia to Helsinki', *Review of International Studies*, **23**, 75–92.

Presov Vecernik News (1995), **23 August** (Slovakia).

Public Interest Law Initiative (2005), *Separate and Unequal* (Budapest: PILI).

Public Interest Law Initiative (2005), *Press Release: Appeal Victory for Roma in Miskolc, Hungary* (Budapest: PILI).

Puporka, L. and Zsolt, Z. (1998), *The Health Status of Roma in Hungary* (Budapest: Roma Press Centre).

Puxon, G. (1987), *Roma: Europe's Gypsies* (London: Minority Rights Group).

Radio Free Europe (1997), 'Czech Premier Meets with Roma', *Newsline*, 15 August.

Radio Free Europe (1998), 'Czech Senate Revokes Anti-Romany Law', *Newsline*, 5 March.

Radio Prague News (1998), 'Romanies Invited to Join Police Force', 7 March.

Radio Prague News (1998), 'Romanies Come Home', 15 June.

Rady, M. (1993), 'Minority Rights and Self-Determination in Contemporary Eastern Europe', *Slavonic and East European Review*, **71**(4), 717–728.

Raes, K. (1992), 'The Ethics of Community and the Ethics of Rawlsian Justice – A Misunderstood Relationship', in *Morality, Worldview and Law*. Musschenga, A.W., Voorzanger, B. and Soeteman, A. (eds) (Maastricht: Van Gorcum), 191–203.

Raic, D. (2002), *Statehood and the Law of Self-Determination* (The Hague: Kluwer).

Räikkä, J. (ed.) (1996), *Do We Need Minority Rights?* (The Hague: Kluwer).

Ramaga, P.V. (1992), 'Relativity of the Minority Concept', *HRQ*, **14**, 104–119.

Ramaga, P.V. (1992), 'The Bases of Minority Identity', *HRQ*, **14**, 409–428.

Ramaga, P.V. (1993), 'The Group Concept in Minority Protection', *HRQ*, **15**, 575–588.

Ramcharam, B.G. (1979), *Thirty Years after the Universal Declaration* (The Hague: Martinus-Nijhoff).

Ramcharam, B.G. (1981), 'Equality and Non-Discrimination', in *The International Bill of Rights: The Covenant on Civil and Political Rights*. Henkin, L. (ed.) (New York: Columbia University Press), 246–269.

Ramcharam, B.G. (1989), *Concept and Present Status of the International Protection of Human Rights: 40 Years after the Universal Declaration* (Dordrecht: M. Nijhoff).

Ramcharam, B.G. (1993), 'Fact-Finding into the Problems of Minorities', in *Peoples and Minorities in International Law*. Brolmann, C., Lefeber, R. and Zieck, M. (eds) (Amsterdam: Amsterdam International Law Conference), 239–251.

Rao, A. (ed.) (1987), *The Other Nomads* (Cologne: Bohlau).

Rawls, J. (1973), *A Theory of Justice* (Oxford: OUP).

Rawls, J. (1993), 'The Law of Peoples', in *On Human Rights the Oxford Amnesty Lectures*. Shute, S. and Hurley, S. (eds) (New York: Basic Books/Harper Collins), 41–82.

Rawls, J. (1984), 'The Right and the Good Contrasted', in *Liberalism and Its Critics*. Sandel, M. (ed.) (Oxford: Blackwell), 37–59.

Rehfisch, F. (ed.) (1975), *Gypsies, Tinkers and Other Travellers* (London: Academic Press).

Reierson, K. and Weissbrodt, D. (1992), 'The 43rd Session of the UN Subcommission on Prevention of Discrimination and the Protection of Minorities: The Sub-Commission under Scrutiny', *HRQ*, **14**, 232–277.

Reiman, J. (1992), 'Liberalism and its Critics', in *Communitarianism, Liberalism and Social Responsibility*. Peden, C. and Hudson, Y. (eds) Studies in Social and Political Theory Vol. 14 (Lewiston: The Edwin Mellen Press), 217–236 and in *The Liberalism-Communitarianism Debate*. Delaney, C.F. (ed.) (Maryland: Rowman and Littlefield), 19–37 (1994).

Reinders, H. (1992), 'Ethical Universalism and Human Rights', in *Morality, Worldview and Law*. Musschenga, A.W., Voorzanger, B. and Soeteman, A. (eds) (Maastricht: Van Gorcum), 83–98.

Reisch, A. (1991), 'First Law on Minorities Drafted', *Report on Eastern Europe 13.12.91*, 14–18.

Reiss, C. (1975), *Education of Travelling Children* (London: Macmillan).

Reuters News Agency (1998), 'Report Shows Romany Segregation in Hungarian Schools', 5 February.

Reuters News Agency (1998), 'Bulgaria to Promote Integration of its Gypsies', 7 April.

Revenga, A., Ringold, D. and Tracy, W. (1998), *Poverty and Ethnicity. A Cross-Country Study of Roma Poverty in Central Europe*, World Bank Technical Paper No 531 (Washington, D.C.: World Bank).

Rex, J. (1997), 'The Nature of Ethnicity on the Project of Migration', in *The Ethnicity Reader*. Guibernau, M. and Rex, J. (eds) (Cambridge: Polity), 269–282.

Rhodes, M. (1995), 'National Identity and Minority Rights in the Constitutions of the Czech and Slovak Republic', *East European Quarterly*, **29**(3), 347–369.

Rhys Morris, D. (1995), 'The Education of Gypsy and Traveller Children in the European Community', Unpublished MA thesis, Leicester University School of Education, Leicester.

Riedlsperger, M. (1994), 'Europe of the Regions: New Hope for Ethnic Minorities?', *History of European Ideas*, **19**(4/5), 655–661.

Rigaux, F. (1979), 'The Algiers Declaration of the Rights of Peoples', in *UN Law/Fundamental Rights: Two Topics in International Law*. Cassese, A. (ed.) (Groningen, the Netherlands: Sijthoff and Noordhoff), 211–224.

Rigo Sureda, A. (1973), *The Evolution of the Right to Self-Determination* (Leiden: A.W. Sijthoff).

Ringold, D. (2000), *Roma and the Transition in Central and Eastern Europe: Trends and Challenges* (Washington, D.C.: World Bank).

Roach, S. (2005), *Cultural Autonomy, Minority Rights and Globalization* (Aldershot: Ashgate).

Robertson, A.H. and Merrills, J.G. (1994), *Human Rights in Europe* (Manchester: Manchester University Press).

Rockefeller, S. (1994), 'Comment', in *Multiculturalism*. Gutmann, A. (ed.) (Princeton, NJ: Princeton University Press), 87–98.

Rodley, N.S. (1995), 'Conceptual Problems in the Protection of Minorities: International Legal Developments', *HRQ*, **17**, 48–71.

Roe, S. (1997), 'Progressive Inaction in Hungary 1997', *Transitions*, **4**(4), no pagination.

Roma Education Initiative (2001), *Research on Selected Roma Education Programmes in Central and Eastern Europe, Final Report* (Budapest: Open Society Institute).

Roma National Congress (1995), *Report on the Situation of the Roma in Europe* (Hamburg: RNC).

Roma Participation Project (1998), 'About the RRP', *Reporter* (Budapest: Open Society Institute).

Roma Press Centre (1996), 'The Roma Are Not Stupider than Others', February.

Roma Press Centre (1997), 'Police and the Roma – Conference' 26 June.

Roma Press Centre (1997), 'Bálint Magyar: The Government Regards the Training of Roma Intellectuals a Prime Task', 2 July.

Roma Press Centre (1998), 'New National Gypsy Organisation Founded', 16 January.

Roma Press Centre (1998), 'News Release', February (Budapest: Sajtokozpont).

Roma Press Centre (1998), 'Local Government in Zámoly Refuses to Help Roma', 29 April.

Roma Press Centre (1998), 'Ethnic Conflict or Damaging', 16 March.

Roma Press Centre (1998), 'Valid Verdict for the Felony of Violence Against the Member of a Racial Group', May.

Rooker, M. (2004), *The International Supervision of Protection of Romany People in Europe* (Nijmegen: University of Nijmegen).

Rooker, M. (2004), 'Romany People and the International Agenda', *European Journal of Migration and Law*, **5**, 491–495.

Rooker, M. (1997), 'Monitoring Human Rights: The Importance of the Universal Level for Roma and Sinti', *CPRSI Newsletter*, **3**(1), 3–8.

Rooker, M. (1995), 'Stateless and Marginal', Unpublished Conference Paper.

Rooker, M. (1993), 'Gypsies in the Netherlands: Problems, Policies and Prospects', Netherlands Delegation to CSCE Seminar.

Rorty, R. (1993), 'Human Rights, Rationality, and Sentimentality', in *On Human Rights the Oxford Amnesty Lectures*. Shute, S. and Hurley, S. (eds) (New York: Basic Books/Harper Collins), 111–134.

Rosas, A. and Helgesen, J. (1992), *The Strength of Diversity: Human Rights and Pluralist Democracy* (Dordrecht: Martinus-Nijhoff).

Rose, R. (1995), 'Sinti and Roma as National Minorities in the Countries of Europe', *OSCE ODIHR Bulletin*, **3**(2), 41–46.

Rosenblum, N.L. (1994), 'Romantic Communitarianism: Blithedale Romance versus the Custom Mouse', in *The Liberalism-Communitarianism Debate*. Delaney, C.F. (ed.) (Maryland: Rowman and Littlefield), 57–90.

Rosenne, S. (1990), 'The Protection of Minorities and Human Rights', in *The Protection of Minorities and Human Rights*. Dinstein, Y. and Tabory, M. (eds) (Dordrecht: Martinus Nijhoff), 513–518.

Roth, S. (1990), 'Towards a Minority Convention: Its Need and Content', *Israel YBHR*, **20**, 93–126.

Roth, S. (1991), 'Comments on the CSCE Meeting of Experts of National Minorities and its Concluding Document', *HRLJ*, **12**(8–9), 330–331.

Russinov, R. (1996), 'Roma Crime – Emblematic of Ethnic Stereotyping?', *Human Rights and Civil Society*, **2**(3), 1–2.

Sacerdoti, G. (1993), 'New Developments in Group Consciousness and International Protection of the Rights of Minorities', *Israel YBHR*, **13**, 116–146.

Saladin, C. (1991), 'Self-determination, Minority Rights and Constitutional Accommodation: The Example of the Czech and Slovak Federal Republic', *Michigan Journal of International Law*, **13**(Fall), 127–217. [PubMed 1894637,9 967451,1864236,1793266]

Salo, M.T. (1990), *100 Years of Gypsy Studies* (Cheverly, Maryland: Gypsy Lore Society).

Salter, M. (1997), 'Habermas' New Contribution to Legal Scholarship', *Journal of Law and Society*, **24**(2), 285–305.

Samuels, A. (1992), 'Gypsies: Some Observations Prompted by the Governments Proposals to Curb Illegal Camping', *LGR*, **26.9.92**.

Samuels, A. (1992), 'Gypsy Law', *LGR*, **20.4.92**.

Samuels, A. (1992), 'Gypsy Law', *Journal of Planning and Environment Law*, **August**, 719–725.

Sandel, M. (1996), *Democracy's Discontent* (Cambridge, MA: Belknap Press).

Sandel, M. (1992), 'The Procedural Republic and the Unencumbered Self', in *Communitarianism and Individualism*. Avineri, S. and De-Shalit, A. (eds) (Oxford: Oxford University Press), 12–28.

Sandel, M. (1984), *Liberalism and Its Critics* (Oxford: Blackwell).

Sandel, M. (1984), 'Justice and the Good', in *Liberalism and Its Critics*. Sandel, M. (ed.) (Oxford: Blackwell), 159–177.

Save the Children (2001), *Denied a Future: The Right to Education of Roma, Gypsy and Traveller Children* (London: Save the Children).

Scarman, L.G., Lord (1984), 'Minority Rights in Plural Society', in *Minorities: A Question of Human Rights?* Whitaker, B. (ed.) (Oxford: Pergamon Press), 79–82.

Schafft, K. (1999), 'Local Minority Self-Governance and Hungary's Roma', *Hungarian Quarterly*, **XL**, 155.

Schifter, R. (1991), 'Address Delivered before the International Conference on Ethnic Conflict Resolution under Rule of Law', *HRLJ*, **12**(8–9), 327–330.

Schlager, E. (1996), 'UNHCR Report Says Czech Citizenship Law Violates International Law; Council of Europe Experts Say Czechs Violate Rule of Law', *CSCE Digest*, **June**, 5–6.

Segesvary, V. (1995), 'Group Rights: The Definition of Group Rights in Contemporary Legal Debate Based on Socio-Cultural Analysis', *Int Journal of Group Rights*, **3**, 89–107.

Sepúlveda, M. (2003), *The Nature of the Obligations Under the International Covenant on Economic, Social and Cultural Rights* (Antwerp: Intersentia).

Seymour, D. (1993), 'The Extension of the ECHR to Central and Eastern Europe: Prospects and Risks', *Connecticut Journal of International Law*, **8**, 243–261.

Shaw, M. (1991), 'The Definition of Minorities in International Law', *Israel YBHR*, **20**, 13–43.

Shaw, M. (ed.) (1997), *International Law 4th Edition* (Cambridge: Cambridge University Press).

Shestack, J. (1984), 'The Jurisprudence of Human Rights', in *Human Rights in International Law, 2 Vols*. Meron, T. (ed.) (New York: Oxford University Press), 69–114.

Shute, S. and Hurley, S. (eds), *On Human Rights: The Oxford Amnesty Lectures* (New York: Basic Books/Harper Collins).

Sibley, D. (1981), *Outsiders in Urban Society* (London: Blackwell).

Sieghart, P. (1983), *The International Law of Human Rights* (Oxford: Clarendon).

Sieghart, P. (1986), *The Lawful Rights of Mankind* (Oxford: Oxford University Press).

Sieghart, P., Blackburn, R. and Taylor, J. (eds) (1991), *Human Rights for the 1990's* (London: Mansell).

Sigler, J. (1983), *Minority Rights: A Comparative Analysis* (Westport: Greenwood).

Siklos, L. (1970), 'The Gypsies', *The New Hungarian Quarterly*, **11**(40), 151.

Siklova, J. and Miklusakova, M. (1998), 'Law as an Instrument of Discrimination Denying Citizenship to the Czech Roma', *East European Constitutional Review*, **7**, 2.

Simon, T.W. (1994), 'The Theoretical Marginalization of the Disadvantaged: A Liberal/Communitarian Failing', in *The Liberalism-Communitarianism Debate*. Delaney, C.F. (ed.) (Maryland: Rowman and Littlefield), 103–135.

Simonov, S. (1990), 'The Gypsies: A Re-Emerging Minority', *Report on Eastern Europe*, **21**, 12–16.

Singh, R. (2004), 'Equality: the Neglected Virtue', *EHRLR*, **2**, 141–157.

Skubarty, Z. (2000), *As If Peoples Mattered* (The Hague: Kluwer).

Skutnabb-Kangas, T. (1990), *Language, Literacy and Minorities* (London: MRG).

Smart, C. (1989), *Feminism and the Power of Law* (London: Routledge).

Smith, A.T.H. (1995), 'The Public Order Elements of the CJPOA', *Crimlr*, **January**, 19–27.

Smith, M. (1975), *Gypsies: Where Now?* (London: Fabian Society).

Smith, D. and Blanc, M. (1996), 'Citizenship Nationality and Ethnic Minorities in 3 European Nations', *International Journal of Urban and Regional Research*, **20**, 1.

Smith, T. (1997), 'Recognising Difference: The Romani "Gypsy" Child Socialisation and Education Progress', *British Journal of Sociology of Education*, **18**(2), 243–257.

Sohn, L.B. (1981), 'The Rights of Minorities', in *The International Bill of Rights: The Covenant on Civil and Political Rights*. Henkin, L. (ed.) (New York: Columbia University Press), 270–289.

Soifer, A. (1990), 'On Being Overly Discrete and Insular: Involuntary Groups and the Anglo-American Judicial Tradition', in *The Protection of Minorities and Human Rights*. Dinstein, Y. and Tabory, M. (eds) (Dordrecht: Martinus Nijhoff), 233–276.

Somers, M. (1994), 'Rights, Relationality and Membership: Rethinking the Making and Meaning of Citizenship', *Law and Social Inquiry*, **19**(Winter), 63–112.

Spencer, S. (2005), 'Gypsies and Travellers: Britain's Forgotten Minority', *EHRLR*, **4**, 335–343.

Stapleton, J. (ed.) (1995), *Group Rights* (Bristol: Thoemmes Press).

Starkie, W. (1953), *In Sara's Tents* (London: John Murray).

Stavenhagen, R. (1992), 'Universal Human Rights and the Cultures of Indigenous Peoples and other Ethnic Groups: The Critical Frontier of the 1990's', in *Human Rights in Perspective*. Eide, A. and Hagtvet, B. (eds) (Oxford: Blackwell), 135–151.

Stavenhagen, R. (1990), 'The Right to Cultural Identity', in *Human Rights in a Pluralist World: Individuals and Collectivities*. Berting, J. (ed.) (Meckler: Roosevelt Study Centre), 255–258.

Stavenhagen, R. (1990), *The Ethnic Question. Conflicts, Development and Human Rights* (Tokyo: UN University Press).

Stearns, D. (1991), 'Rendered Stateless: The Extraordinary Apprehension of Foreign Nationals and the Policy of Exclusion', *Wisconsin International Law Journal*, **10**(Fall), 78–149.

Steketee, F. (2001), 'The Framework Convention: A Piece of Art or a Tool for Action?', *International Journal on Minority and Group Rights*, **8**, 1–15.

Stein, E. (1997), *Czecho/Slovakia* (Ann Arbor: University of Michigan Press).

Steiner, H. and Alston, P. (1996), *International Human Rights in Context* (Oxford: Clarendon Press).

Steinerte, E., 'Self-Determination Strategies for Minorities within the Framework of the Organisation for Security and Cooperation in Europe, Part 2', *Human Rights and UK Practice*, **5**(4), 13.

Sterba, J.P. (1994), 'Liberalism and a Non-Question Begging Conception of the Good', in *The Liberalism-Communitarianism Debate*. Delaney, C.F. (ed.) (Maryland: Rowman and Littlefield), 227–244.

Stevens, D. (2004), 'The Migration of the Romanian Roma to the UK: A Contextual Study', *European Journal of Migration and the Law*, **5**, 439–461.

Stewart, M. (1996), 'The Puzzle of Roma Persistence: Group Identity Without a Nation', in *Romani Culture and Gypsy Identity*. Acton, T. and Mundy, G. (eds) (Hatfield: University of Hertfordshire Press), 82–96.

Subedi, S. (1994), 'The Right to Self-Determination and the Tibetan People', in *Self Determination: Cases of Crisis*. Kritsiotis, D. (ed.) (Hull: University of Hull Law School), 1–16.

Sullivan, W.M. (1982), 'A Renewal of Civic Philosophy', in *Communitarianism: A New Public Ethics*. Daly, M. (ed.) (Belmont, CA: Wadsworth), 190–202.

Sun (1999), 'Straw Lashes Thieving Gypsies', **19 August**, 2.

Sutherland, A. (1975), *Gypsies: The Hidden Americans* (Illinois: Waveland Press).

Surdu, L. and Surdu, M. (2006), *Broadening the Agenda: The Status of Romani Women in Romania* (New York: OSI).

Sutherland, M., Comparative Perspectives on the Education of Cultural Minorities, in *The Future of Cultural Minorities*. Alcock, A., Taylor, B. and Welton, J. (eds) (London: Macmillan), 44–62.

Svennson, F. (1979), 'Liberal Democracy and Group Rights: The Legacy of Individualism and its Impact on American Indian Tribes', *Political Studies*, **27**, 421–439.

Sway, M. (1981), 'Simmel's Concept of the Stranger and the Gypsies', *The Social Science Journal*, **18**(1), 41–50.

Symonides, J. (1991), Collective Rights of Minorities in Europe, in *The Changing Political Structure of Europe*. Lefeber, R., Fitzmaurice, M. and Vierdag, E.W. (eds) (Dordrecht: M. Nijhoff), 109–125.

Szabo, I. (1974), *Cultural Rights* (Leiden: A.W. Sitjhoff).

Szabo, I. (1982), 'Historical Foundations of Human Rights', in *The International Dimensions of Human Rights Vol. 2*. Vasak, K. (ed.) (Paris: UNESCO), 11–34.

Tabory, M. (1992), 'Minority Rights in the CSCE Context', in *The Protection of Minorities and Human Rights*. Dinstein, Y. and Tabory, M. (eds) (Dordrecht: Martinus Nijhoff), 187–212.

Tanaka, J. (2005), 'Economic Development Perspectives of Roma – Looking Critically at Reality and the Social Impact of Development Measures', *eumap. org*.

Tanja, J. (1990), 'More than a Million Gypsies in Romania', *O'Drom*, **April**, 244–246.

Tanja, J. (1990), 'To Change a Gypsy into a Bulgarian', *O'Drom*, 31–32.

Tamir, Y. (1993), *Liberal Nationalism* (Princeton, NJ: Princeton University Press).

Taylor, C. (1986), 'Human Rights: The Legal Culture', *UNESCO Courier*, 49–57.

Taylor, C. (1992), *Multiculturalism and 'The Politics of Recognition'* (Princeton, NJ: Princeton University Press).

Taylor, C. (1992), 'Atomism', in *Communitarianism and Individualism*. Avineri, S. and De-Shalit, A. (eds) (Oxford: Oxford University Press), 29–50.

Taylor, C. (1994), 'The Politics of Recognition', in *Multiculturalism*. Gutmann, A. (ed.) (Princeton, NJ: Princeton University Press), 25–73.

Taylor, C. (1994), 'The Modern Identity', in *Communitarianism: A New Public Ethics*. Daly, M. (ed.) (Belmont, CA: Wadsworth), 55–71.

Taylor, C. (1995), *Philosophical Arguments* (Cambridge, MA: Harvard University Press).

TAZ News Agency (1994), 'Pècs Is Home to First All Romany High School', **14 November**, 11.

Telegraph (1997), 'UK "Dover Nightmare"', **20 October**, 2.

Thio, L.-A. (2003), 'Developing a "Peace and Security" Approach towards Minorities' Problems', *Int Comparative Law Quarterly*, **51**(1), 115.

Thompson, K.W. (1980), *The Moral Imperatives of Human Rights: A World Survey* (Washington, D.C.: University Press of America).

Thornberry, P. (1987), *Minorities and Human Rights Law* (London: MRG).

Thornberry, P. (1991), *International Law and the Rights of Minorities* (Oxford: Oxford University Press).

Thornberry, P. (1994), 'International and European Standards on Minority Rights', in *Minority Rights in Europe: The Scope for a Transnational Regime*. Miall, H. (ed.) (London: Pinter), 14–21.

Thornberry, P. (ed.) (2004), *Minority Rights in Europe* (Strabourg: Council of Europe Publishing).

Thornton, P. (1987), *Public Order Law* (London: Blackstone).

Tierney, S. (2002), 'The Search for a Neo Normativity: Thomas Franck, Post-Modern Neo-Tribalism and the Law of Self-Determination', *EJIL*, **13**, 941.

Toggenburg, G. (ed.) (2004), *Minority Protection and the Enlarged European Union: The Way Forward* (Budapest: LGI Books).

Tomasevic, N.B., Djuric, R. and Zamurovic, R.U.D. (1989), *Gypsies of the World* (London: Flint River).

Tomasi, J. (1995), 'Kymlicka, Liberalism and Respect for Cultural Minorities', *Ethics*, **105**(April), 580–603.

Tomka, M. (1984), 'The Gypsy Craftsmen of Europe', *UNESCO Courier,* **October**, 15–17.

Tomlinson, S. and Craft, M. (1995), *Ethnic Relations and Schooling: Policy and Practice in the 1990's* (London: Athlone Press).

Tomuschat, C. (1992), 'Democratic Pluralism and the Right to Political Opposition', in *The Strength of Diversity: Human Rights and Pluralist Democracy*. Rosas, A. and Helgesen, J. (eds) (Dordrecht: Martinus-Nijhoff), 39.

Tomuschat, C. (2003), *Human Rights. Between Idealism and Realism* (Oxford: Oxford University Press).

Tong, D. (1991), 'Gypsies: A Selected Bibliography', *Nationalities Papers*, **19**(3), 413–427.

Tong, D. (1995), *Gypsies: A Multidisciplinary Annotated Bibliography* (New York: Garland).

Toronto Star (1997), 'Gypsy Accuses "Arrogant" Canada', **24 August**, A2.

Trakman, L.E. (1992), 'Group Rights: A Canadian Perspective', *NY University Journal of International Law and Politics*, **24**, 1579–1650.

Trifunovska, S. (ed.) (1999), *Minorities in Europe: Croatia, Estonia and Slovakia* (The Hague: TMC Asser).

Triggs, G. (1988), 'The Rights of "Peoples" and Individual Rights: Conflict or Harmony?', in *The Rights of Peoples*. Crawford, J.E.S. (ed.) (Oxford: Clarendon), 141–157.

Tritt, R. (1992), *Struggling for Ethnic Identity: Czechslovakia's Endangered Gypsies* (New York: Human Rights Watch).

Troxel, L. (1992), 'Bulgarian Gypsies: Numerically Strong, Politically Weak', *RFE/RL Research Report*, 1, 58–61.

Tumin, M. and Plotch, W. (1977), *Pluralism in a Democratic Society* 1977 (New York: Praeger).

Turgeon, L. (1990), 'Discrimination Against and Affirmative Action for Gypsies in Eastern Europe', in The Political Economy of Ethnic Discrimination and Affirmative Action: *A* Comparative Perspective. Wyzan, M.L. (ed.) (New York: Praeger), 155–165.

Turk, D. (1991), 'Minorities, Self-Determination and Other Crucial Issues of Human Rights in Europe', in 'Perspectives of an All-European System of Human Rights Protection'. Kedzia, Z., Leuprecht, P. and Nowak, M. (eds), *AEHRYB*, 1, 279–290.

TV Nova (1997), 'Prague Gypsies Go to Heaven', 5 August.

Twomey, P.M. (1994), 'European Citizenship and Human Rights: Actual Situation and Future Perspectives', in *European Citizenship*. Marias, E. (ed.) (Maastricht: European Institute of Public Administration).

Uibopuu, H.-J. (1991), 'Comments', in *The Changing Political Structure of Europe*. Lefeber, R., Fitzmaurice, M. and Vierdag, E.W. (eds) (Dordrecht: M. Nijhoff), 127–130.

Ulc, O. (1988), 'Gypsies in Czechoslovakia: A Case of Unfinished Integration', *East European Politics and Societies*, 2(2), 306–332.

Ulc, O. (1991), 'Integration of the Gypsies in Czechoslovakia', *Ethnic Groups*, 9, 107–117.

Ulc, O. (1995), 'The Plight of the Gypsies', *Freedom Review*, 26(3), 27.

UN Development Program (2002), *Avoiding the Dependency Trap* (Bratislava: UNDP).

UNESCO (ed.) (1986), *Philosophical Foundations of Human Rights* (Paris: UNESCO).

US State Department (2002), *Czech Republic: Country Reports on Human Rights Practices, 2001*, 4 March (Washington, D.C.: US State Department).

Vallen, T. (1991), 'Ethnic Minorities and Ethnic Minority Languages in Dutch Primary Schools: Problems and Challenges', *Language and Education*, 5(2), 113–123.

Van Boven, T. (2003), 'The Committee on the Elimination of Racial Discrimination: Trends and Developments', in *Roma Rights Notebook*, ERRC (ed.), no pagination.

Van Boven, T. (1982), 'Distinguishing Criteria of Human Rights', in *The International Dimensions of Human Rights Vol. 2*. Vasak, K. (ed.) (Paris: UNESCO), 43–59.

Van Boven, T. (1979), 'UN and Human Rights: A Critical Appraisal', in *UN Law/Fundamental Rights: Two Topics in International Law.* Cassese, A. (ed.) (Groningen, the Netherlands: Sijthoff and Noordhoff), 119–136.

Van Dyke, V. (1973), 'Equality and Discrimination in Education: A Comparative International Analysis', *International Studies Quarterly*, **17**(4), 375–404.

Van Dyke, V. (1975), 'Justice As Fairness for Groups?', *The American Political Science Review*, **69**, 607–614.

Van Dyke, V. (1980), 'The Cultural Rights of Peoples', *Universal Human Rights*, **2**(2), 1–21.

Van Dyke, V. (1985), *Human Rights, Ethnicity and Discrimination* (Westport: Greenwood).

Van Dyke, V. (1995), 'Ethnic Communities in Political Theory', in in *The Rights of Minority Cultures.* Kymlicka, W. (ed.) (Oxford: Oxford University Press), 30–56.

Van Gunsteren, H. (1994), 'Four Conditions of Citizenship', in *The Conditions of Citizenship.* Van Steenbergen, B. (ed.) (London: Sage), 36–48.

Van Krieken, P. (1994), 'Disintegration and Statelessness', *NQHR*, **12**(1), 23–33.

Van Steenbergen, B. (ed.), *The Conditions of Citizenship* (London: Sage).

Vander-Wal, K. (1990), 'Collective Human Rights: A Western View', in *Human Rights in a Pluralist World: Individuals and Collectivities.* Berting, J. (ed.) (Meckler: Roosevelt Study Centre), 83–98.

Vasak, K. (ed.) (1982), *The International Dimensions of Human Rights Vol. 2* (Paris: UNESCO).

Verma, G.K. and Pumfrey, P.D. (1993), *Cultural Diversity and the Curriculum* (London: Falmer Press).

Vermeersch, P. (2004), 'Minority Policy in Central Europe: Exploring the Impact of the EU's Enlargement Strategy', *Global Review of Ethnopolitics*, **3**(2), 3–19.

Vesey-Fitzgerald, B. (1973), *Gypsies of Britain* (Newton Abbot: David & Charles).

Vierdag, E.W. (ed.) (1973), *The Concept of Discrimination in International Law* (The Hague: Nijhoff).

Waddington, L. (2004), 'European Developments – Taking stock and Looking Forward: The Commission and Green Paper on Equality and Non-Discrimination in an Enlarged European Union', *Industrial Law Journal*, **33**, 367.

Wagner, F. (1987), 'The Gypsy in Post War Hungary', *Hungarian Studies Review*, **14**(2), 33–43.

Waldron, J. (1995), 'The Cosmopolitan Alternative', in *The Rights of Minority Cultures.* Kymlicka, W. (ed.) (Oxford: Oxford University Press), 93–119.

Waldron, J. (ed.) (1993), *Liberal Rights Collected Papers 1981–1991* (Cambridge: Cambridge University Press).

Wallace, R. (1999), *Companion to the European Convention on Human Rights* (London: Trenton).

Wallbridge, J. (1972), *The Shadow on the Cheese: Some Light on Gypsy Education* (London: Gypsy Education Council).

Walzer, M. (1982), *The Politics of Ethnicity* (Cambridge, MA: Harvard University Press).

Walzer, M. (1983), *Spheres of Justice: A Defence of Pluralism and Equality* (Oxford: Martin Robertson).

Walzer, M. (1983), 'Complex Equality', in *Communitarianism: A New Public Ethics.* Daly, M. (ed.) (Belmont, CA: Wadsworth), 101–110.

Walzer, M. (1992), 'Membership', in *Communitarianism and Individualism.* Avineri, S. and De-Shalit, A. (eds) (Oxford: Oxford University Press), 65–84.

Walzer, M. (1994), 'Comment', in *Multiculturalism.* Gutmann, A. (ed.) (Princeton, NJ: Princeton University Press), 99–103.

Walzer, M. (1995), 'Pluralism: A Political Perspective', in *The Rights of Minority Cultures.* Kymlicka, W. (ed.) (Oxford: Oxford University Press), 139–154.

Walzer, M. (1997), 'The Politics of Difference: Statehood and Toleration in a Multicultural World', *Ratio Juris*, **10**(2), 165–176.

Wang, K. (1986), 'The Present Situation of the Spanish Gitano's', Paper from the 6th Annual meeting of the Gypsy Lore Society, North American Chapter, New York.

Warbrick, C. (1992), 'Recognition of States', *ICLQ*, **41**, 473.

Warrington, C. and Peck, S. (2005), *Gypsy and Traveller Communities: Accommodation, Education, Health, Skills and Employment – An East of England Perspective* (Histon: East of England Development Agency).

Waterson, M. (1976), 'The Traveller Child', *English in Education*, **10**(2), 1–10.

Webber, F. (1995), *Crimes of Arrival: Immigrants and Asylum Seekers in the New Europe* (London: Statewatch).

Weber, R. (1995), 'Minority Rights: Too Often Wronged', *Human Rights and Civil Society*, **2**(1), 1–3.

Weinstein, B. (1983), *The Civic Tongue: Political Consequences of Language Choices* (New York: Longman).

Weinstein, B. (1990), *Language Policy and Political Development* (Norwood, NJ: Ablex Publishing House).

Weis, P. (1979), *Nationality and Statelessness in International Law* (The Hague: Sijthoff and Noordhoff).

Welhengama, G. (1992), 'Is there any Room for Minorities in the Much Promised "New World Order"?', *The Liverpool Law Review*, **14**(2), 135–158.

Weller, M. (1992), 'The International Response to the Dissolution of the Socialist Federal Republic of Yugoslavia', *The American Journal of International Law*, **86**, 569–607.

Weller, M. (1999), 'The Rambouillet Conference on Kosovo', *International Affairs*, **75**(2), 211–251.

Weller, M. (ed.) (2005), *The Rights of Minorities in Europe* (Oxford: OUP).

West Midlands Consortium, *Education Service for Travelling Children Information Pack* (Wolverhampton: WMESTC).

Weyrauch, W. and Bell, M. (1993), 'Autonomous Law Making: The Case of the Gypsies', *The Yale Law Journal*, **November**, 212–299.

Wheatley, S. (1996), 'The Council of Europe's Framework Convention on National Minorities', *5 Web JCLI*, no pagination..

Wheatley, S. (2003), 'Deliberative Democracy and Minorities', *EJIL*, **14**, 507.

Whitaker, B. (ed.) (1984), *Minorities: A Question of Human Rights?* (Oxford: Pergamon Press).

White, R.C.A. (1981), 'Self Determination: Time for A Re-Assessment?', *NILR*, **28**(2), 147–170.

Widder, N. (1995), *Liberalism, Communitarianism and Otherness*, Essex Papers in Politics and Government (Colchester: University of Essex).

Wieruszewski, R. (1992), 'Human Rights and Constitutional Debates in Central and Eastern Europe', in *The Strength of Diversity: Human Rights and Pluralist Democracy*. Rosas, A. and Helgesen, J. (eds) (Dordrecht: Martinus-Nijhoff), 187–206.

Willems, W. and Lucassen, L.W. (1992), 'Silent War: Foreign Gypsies and Dutch Government Policy 1969–89', *Immigrants and Minorities*, **II**(1), 81–101.

Williams, M.S. (1994), 'Group Inequality and the Public Culture of Justice', in *Group Rights*. Baker, J. (ed.) (Toronto: University of Toronto Press), 36–64.

Williams, P. (1984), *Special Education in Minority Communities* (Milton Keynes: Open University Press).

Wintemute, R. (2004), 'Filling the Article 14 "Gap": Government Ratification and Judicial Control of Protocol No 12 ECHR: Part 2', *EHRLR*, **5**, 484–499.

Wintemute, R. (2004), '"Within the Ambit" How Big is the "Gap" in Article 14 ECHR: Part 1', *EHRLR*, **4**, 366–382.

Wirsing, R. (1981), *Protection of Ethnic Minorities: Comparative Perspectives* (New York: Pergamon).

Wolf, S. (1994), 'Comment', in *Multiculturalism*. Gutmann, A. (ed.) (Princeton, NJ: Princeton University Press), 75–85.

Wolfrum, R. (1985), 'The Legal Status of Sinti and Roma in Europe: A Case Study Concerning the Shortcomings of the Protection of Minorities', *Israel YBHR*, **33**, 75–90.

Wolfrum, R. (1991), 'The Legal Status of Minorities in South-Eastern Europe', in *The Changing Political Structure of Europe*. Lefeber, R., Fitzmaurice, M. and Vierdag, E.W. (eds) (Dordrecht: M. Nijhoff), 131–148.

Wolfrum, R. (1993), 'The Emergence of "New Minorities" as a Result of Migration', in *Peoples and Minorities in International Law*. Brolmann, C., Lefeber, R. and Zieck, M. (eds) (Amsterdam: Amsterdam International Law Conference), 153–166.

Wolin, S. (1986), 'Contract and Birthright', *Political Theory*, **14**(2), 179–193.

World Bank and Soros Foundation (2003), Roma In an Expanding Europe: Challenges for the Future Conference, Budapest, 30 June–31 July.

Worrall, D. (1979), *Gypsy Education: A Study of Provision in England and Wales* (Walsall: Walsall Council for Community Relations).

Wright, J. (1999), 'Minority Groups, Autonomy and Self-Determination', *Oxford Journal of Legal Studies*, **16**, 605. [DOI: 10.1093/ojls%2F19.4.605]

Wyzan, M.L. (1990), *The Political Economy of Ethnic Discrimination and Affirmative Action: a Comparative Perspective* (New York: Praeger).

Xanthaki, A. (2004), 'Protection of a Specific Minority: The Case of Roma/Gypsies', in *Minority Rights in Europe*. Thornberry, P. (ed.) (Strasbourg: Council of Europe Publishing), 169–194.

Xanthaki, A. (2005), 'Hope Dies Last: An EU Directive on Roma Integration', *European Public Law*, **11**(4), 515–526.

Xinhua News (2005), 'Gypsies' Situation in Romania', **5 October** (Bucharest).

Young, C. (1993), *The Rising Tide of Cultural Pluralism* (Wisconsin: University of Wisconsin Press).

Young, I.M. (1990), *Justice and the Politics of Difference* (Princeton, NJ: Princeton University Press).

Young, I.M. (1995), 'Together in Difference', in *The Rights of Minority Cultures.* Kymlicka, W. (ed.) (Oxford: Oxford University Press), 155–176.

Young, J.A. (1994), 'Is Slovakia Ready for the Potential Influx Of Roma Denied, Czech Citizenship?', *Promoting Human Rights and Civil Society in Central and Eastern Europe*, **4**, 2–3.

Young, J.A. (1994–95), 'Rule of Law in Eastern Europe? The Story of Mr P', *Promoting Human Rights and Civil Society in Central and Eastern Europe*, **5/6**, 2–3.

Zamfir, C. and Zamfir, E. (1993), *The Gypsies: Between Ignoring and Worrying* (Bucharest: Alternative Publishing House).

Zang, T. and Whitman, L. (1991), *Destroying Ethnic Identity – The Gypsies Of Bulgaria* (New York: Human Rights Watch).

Zec, P. (1980), 'Multicultural Relativism: What Kind of Education is Possible?', *Journal of Philosophy of Education*, **14**(1), 77–86. [DOI: 10.1111/j.1467-9752.1980.tb00542.x]

Zellner, H. and Lange, O.L. (1999), *Peace and Stability Through Human and Minority Rights: Speeches by the OSCE HCNM* (Hamburg: Institute for Peace Research and Security Policy, University of Hamburg).

Zielonka, J. (ed.) (2002), *Europe Unbound: Enlarging and Reshaping the Boundaries of the European Union* (London: Routledge).

Zoon, I. (1994), *Report on the Czech Citizenship Law* (Prague: Tolerance Foundation).

Zoon, I. (1994), 'Legal Deficiencies of the Czech Citizenship Law', *Promoting Human Rights and Civil Society in Central and Eastern Europe*, **4**, 11.

Zoon, I. (1994), *A Need for Change: Analysis of 99 Individual Cases* (Prague: Tolerance Foundation).

Zoon, I. (2001), *On the Margins: Roma and Public Services in Romania, Bulgaria and Macedonia* (Budapest: Open Society Institute).

Zoon, I. and Siroka, L. (1995), *The Non-Czech Czechs* (Prague: Tolerance Foundation).

Zubak, K. and Lagryn, A., 'Roma Are Tired of Being Studied', *Roma Participation Program Reporter* (Budapest: Open Society Institute).

Index